THE
HISTORIAN AND
CHARACTER

DOM DAVID KNOWLES

THE
HISTORIAN AND CHARACTER
AND OTHER ESSAYS

BY

DOM DAVID KNOWLES

Collected and presented to him
by his friends, pupils and colleagues on
the occasion of his retirement as
Regius Professor of Modern History
in the University of
Cambridge

CAMBRIDGE
AT THE UNIVERSITY PRESS
1963

86349

PUBLISHED BY
THE SYNDICS OF THE CAMBRIDGE UNIVERSITY PRESS
Bentley House, 200 Euston Road, London, N.W. 1
American Branch: 32 East 57th Street, New York 22, N.Y.
West African Office: P.O. Box 33, Ibadan, Nigeria

©

CAMBRIDGE UNIVERSITY PRESS
1963

Bx
941
K6

Printed in Great Britain at the University Press, Cambridge
(Brooke Crutchley, University Printer)

TO DAVID KNOWLES

This book was yours before we gave it to you. Yet we offer it to you as a token of the admiration, gratitude and affection of your friends, colleagues and pupils.

PHILIP ABRAMS
G. W. O. ADDLESHAW
MILTON V. ANASTOS
JAMES W. ANDERSON
N. G. ANNAN
E. ANSELL
MARGARET ARCHER
AILEEN ARMSTRONG
C. A. J. ARMSTRONG
T. S. ASHTON
HON. MRS M. E. ASTON
JANET M. BACKHOUSE
J. J. BAGLEY
P. G. BALES
E. W. M. BALFOUR-MELVILLE
BALLIOL COLLEGE LIBRARY,
   OXFORD
FRANK BARLOW
A. J. L. BARNES
PATRICIA M. BARNES
GEOFFREY W. S. BARROW
ALBERT C. BAUGH
STEPHEN B. BAXTER
D. E. D. BEALES
J. C. BECKETT
BEDFORD COLLEGE LIBRARY,
   LONDON
H. H. BELLOT
H. S. BENNETT
HUGH F. BENNETT

JOSEPHINE W. BENNETT
JOHN F. BENTON
JAMES P. BERG
S. T. BINDOFF
T. A. M. BISHOP
P. HUNTER BLAIR
E. O. BLAKE
MRS R. W. BLISS
MORTON W. BLOOMFIELD
T. S. R. BOASE
DIANE K. BOLTON
GERALD BONNER
GERALD BORDMAN
M. A. BORRIE
BOSTON ATHENAEUM
MURIEL BOWDEN
LEONARD BOYLE
BRENDAN BRANLEY
BRASENOSE COLLEGE, OXFORD
PETER H. BRIEGER
UNIVERSITY OF BRISTOL
   LIBRARY
THE BRITISH SCHOOL AT
   ROME
WILLIAM BROCK
WALLACE BROCKWAY
D. W. BROGAN
CHRISTOPHER AND ROSALIND
   BROOKE
MRS Z. N. BROOKE

GEORGE A. BROOKS
F. BROOMFIELD
ALFRED L. BROWN
C. K. FRANCIS BROWN
ELIZABETH R. BROWN
R. ALLEN BROWN
ANDREW BROWNING
D. J. BUISSERET
DONALD A. BULLOUGH
P. G. BURBIDGE
J. C. BURKILL
MILES BURKITT
R. V. H. BURNE
J. P. T. BURY
G. H. S. BUSHNELL
E. E. BUTCHER
SIR JAMES BUTLER
H. BUTTERFIELD
DANIEL A. CALLUS
HELEN CAM
J. CAMPBELL
CANTERBURY CATHEDRAL
   LIBRARY
KIERAN J. CARROLL
MRS A. C. CARTER
ELEANORA CARUS-WILSON
THE CATHOLIC UNIVERSITY OF
   AMERICA
FRED A. CAZEL, JR.
W. O. CHADWICK
M. E. CHAMBERLAIN
WILLIAM A. CHANEY
PIERRE CHAPLAIS
MARISTAN CHAPMAN
S. G. CHECKLAND
C. R. AND MARY CHENEY
M. T. CHERNIAVSKY
CHETHAM'S LIBRARY, MAN-
   CHESTER
MARJORIE CHIBNALL
S. B. CHRIMES

CHRIST CHURCH LIBRARY,
   OXFORD
MRS P. A. CLAPP
J. G. D. CLARK
SIR CHARLES CLAY
PAUL M. CLOGAN
HELEN CLOVER
J. COCHLIN
THE CODRINGTON LIBRARY,
   OXFORD
BERTRAM COLGRAVE
MRS FREDERICK COLLINS
H. M. COLVIN
C. R. B. COMBELLACK
KENNETH JOHN CONANT
GILES CONSTABLE
T. CORBISHLEY
CORPUS CHRISTI COLLEGE
   LIBRARY, OXFORD
C. H. COSTER
H. M. COUTTS-TROTTER
H. E. J. COWDREY
L. W. COWIE
MAURICE COWLING
J. S. COX
R. J. CRAMP
C. W. CRAWLEY
JOHN CREASEY
HALLARD THOMAS CROFT
VALERIE CROMWELL
SUMNER McK. CROSBY
JOSEPH R. CRUMP
GERARD CULKIN
MARCUS CUNLIFFE
MGR THOMAS W. CUNNINGHAM
G. P. CUTTINO
R. R. DARLINGTON
R. W. DAVID
JAMES CONWAY DAVIES
R. R. DAVIES
CHARLES T. DAVIS

SUBSCRIBERS

R. H. C. DAVIS
RUTH J. DEAN
MARGARET DEANESLY
ALBERT B. DEARDEN
LAWRENCE A. DESMOND
EDWIN BREZETTE DEWINDT
J. C. DICKINSON
J. G. DICKINSON
S. J. P. VAN DIJK
R. B. DOBSON
C. H. DODD
BARBARA DODWELL
C. R. DODWELL
RICHARD DONEY
DAVID DOUGLAS
D. L. DOUIE
THE ABBOT OF DOWNSIDE
P. H. G. DOYLE
F. R. H. DU BOULAY
CHARLES DUGGAN
DUMBARTON OAKS RESEARCH
    LIBRARY
ANNIE I. DUNLOP
P. J. DUNNING
C. F. ECCLESHARE
EDINBURGH CORPORATION
    PUBLIC LIBRARIES
EDINBURGH UNIVERSITY
    LIBRARY
MRS GEORGE DEFOREST
    EDWARDS
SIR GORONWY EDWARDS
KATHLEEN EDWARDS
KEITH J. EGAN
J. H. ELLIOTT
G. R. ELTON
CATHERINE CRARY ELWOOD
RAYMOND S. EMBREE
EMMANUEL COLLEGE LIBRARY,
    BOSTON, MASS.
EMORY UNIVERSITY LIBRARY

JOAN EVANS
S. J. A. EVANS
CHARLOTTE D'EVELYN
H. O. EVENNETT
EXETER COLLEGE LIBRARY,
    OXFORD
J. E. FAGG
H. H. FARMER
HUGH FARMER
LUCIA N. FERRERO
H. P. R. FINBERG
JOHN F. FINNERTY
D. J. V. FISHER
ERIC G. M. FLETCHER
J. FLITCROFT
ANTHONY H. FORBES
GEORGE H. FORSYTH
WAYNE FOSTER
ROBERT WORTH FRANK, JR.
CONSTANCE M. FRASER
M. D. FRASER
ALBERT B. FRIEDMAN
LEWIS GALANTIÈRE
V. H. GALBRAITH
F. L. GANSHOF
MILTON McC. GATCH, JR.
MYRON P. GILMORE
GIRTON COLLEGE LIBRARY,
    CAMBRIDGE
JOHN GODFREY
GONVILLE AND CAIUS COLLEGE
    LIBRARY, CAMBRIDGE
G. P. GOOCH
A. GOODWIN
R. M. GOODWIN
A. H. GORDON
H. GOTOFF
ROSE GRAHAM
EDGAR B. GRAVES
R. W. GREAVES
RICHARD LEIGHTON GREENE

S. L. GREENSLADE
WILLIAM GREENWAY
PHILIP GRIERSON
W. JARDINE GRISBROOKE
PAUL GROSJEAN
W. K. C. GUTHRIE
A. GWYNN
B. HACKETT
I. M. HACKING
N. HADCOCK
G. D. G. HALL
B. L. HALLWARD
BERNARD HAMILTON
BOROUGH OF HAMPSTEAD
  PUBLIC LIBRARIES
C. J. HAMSON
G. J. HAND
A. J. HANNA
ALAN HARDING
C. J. R. HART
B. F. HARVEY
DENYS HAY
RHŶS W. HAYS
MONA E. HAYWARD
PETER HEATH
J. H. HEXTER
HEYTHROP COLLEGE LIBRARY
A. B. HIBBERT
ROGER HIGHFIELD
BENNETT D. HILL
SIR FRANCIS HILL
ROSALIND M. T. HILL
R. W. K. HINTON
RICHARD L. HOFFMAN
C. J. HOLDSWORTH
HOLLINS COLLEGE LIBRARY
G. A. HOLMES
J. C. HOLT
R. T. HOLTBY
ROBERT S. HOYT
EDWARD HUGHES

KATHLEEN HUGHES
R. A. HUMPHREYS
R. F. HUNNISETT
JOAN HUSSEY
L. V. JACKS
E. F. JACOB
A. M. JAFFÉ
MRS CARTER JEFFERIS
JESUIT NOVITIATE LIBRARY,
  SHERIDAN, OREGON
JESUS COLLEGE LIBRARY,
  CAMBRIDGE
JESUS COLLEGE LIBRARY,
  OXFORD
JAMES J. JOHN
H. C. JOHNSON
JAMES R. JOHNSON
MGR PETER LEO JOHNSON
WILLIAM M. JOHNSTON
A. H. M. JONES
FRED A. JORDAN
A. V. JUDGES
ALFRED L. KELLOGG
E. W. KEMP
J. C. KENDREW
E. J. KENNEY
UNIVERSITY OF KENTUCKY
  LIBRARIES
J. P. KENYON
NEIL R. KER
PEARL KIBRE
LAURENCE KILLIAN
KING'S COLLEGE LIBRARY,
  CAMBRIDGE
KING'S COLLEGE LIBRARY,
  DURHAM
MAURICE R. KINGSFORD
R. J. L. KINGSFORD
G. S. R. KITSON CLARK
C. H. KNOWLES
ELIZABETH KORNERUP

BARNET KOTTLER
H. P. KRAUS
STEPHAN KUTTNER
LADY MARGARET HALL
LIBRARY, OXFORD
M. D. LAMBERT
JOAN LANCASTER
J. R. LANDER
C. H. LAWRENCE
J. S. LAWTON
JANE ACOMB LEAKE
LORD LECONFIELD
SIR FRANK LEE
H. R. LEECH
UNIVERSITY OF LEEDS LIBRARY
G. LEFF
M. DOMINICA LEGGE
LOUIS J. LEKAI
THOMAS B. LEMANN
JOHN LE PATOUREL
HOWARD H. LEWIS
LINCOLN COLLEGE LIBRARY,
OXFORD
FRANCES RANDALL LIPP
LESTER K. LITTLE
LIVERPOOL UNIVERSITY
LIBRARY
F. D. LOGAN
UNIVERSITY OF LONDON
UNION
F. JOÜON DES LONGRAIS
ROGER LOVATT
E. A. LOWE
EDITH CLARK LOWRY
H. R. LOYN
ROY LUBBOCK
EMIL LUCKI
RICHARD LUMAN
D. E. LUSCOMBE
THOMAS F. McALLISTER
OLIVER MACDONAGH

A. H. McDONALD
K. B. McFARLANE
LESLIE J. MACFARLANE
PATRICK McGRATH
MILTON McGREEVY
MAY McKISACK
M. MACLAGAN
MARY MARTIN McLAUGHLIN
K. A. MACMAHON
PATRICIA McNULTY
TERRENCE A. McVEIGH
KATHLEEN MAJOR
KEMP MALONE
UNIVERSITY OF MANCHESTER
LIBRARY
P. N. S. MANSERGH
W. S. MANSFIELD
SISTER MARGARET GERTRUDE
JOSEPH M. F. MARIQUE
GUSTAV K. MARKGRAF
R. A. MARKUS
A. H. R. MARTINDALE
ALEXANDRA MASON
J. F. A. MASON
UNIVERSITY OF MASSACHU-
SETTS LIBRARY
ARCHBISHOP DAVID MATHEW
H. M. R. E. MAYR-HARTING
ANTHONY CLARKE MEISEL
MERTON COLLEGE LIBRARY,
OXFORD
ROGER C. METTAM
ROBERT T. MEYER
FRITZ MEZGER
CHARLES R. D. MILLER
EDWARD MILLER
S. J. MILLER
MILLS MEMORIAL LIBRARY,
McMASTER UNIVERSITY
CHARLES MITCHELL
T. W. MOODY

MRS JOHN STEPHEN MORAN
ADRIAN MOREY
D. A. L. MORGAN
IRVONWY MORGAN
MINNIE CATE MORRELL
C. MORRIS
H. P. MORRISON
VACLAV MUDROCH
E. L. C. MULLINS
A. R. MYERS
SIR ROGER MYNORS
J. N. L. MYRES
NEW COLLEGE LIBRARY,
  OXFORD
COLLEGE OF NEW ROCHELLE
  LIBRARY
NEW YORK UNIVERSITY
  LIBRARIES
D. H. NEWSOME
JOHN A. NEWTON
JOHN F. NICHOLS
W. C. NIXON
EDWARD ROBERT NORMAN
UNIVERSITY OF NOTRE DAME
  LIBRARY
MEDIAEVAL INSTITUTE,
  UNIVERSITY OF NOTRE DAME
UNIVERSITY OF NOTTINGHAM
  LIBRARY
GEOFFREY F. NUTTALL
HEIKO A. OBERMAN
D. OBOLENSKY
MOTHER MARY O'CALLAGHAN
MAURICE R. O'CONNELL
H. S. OFFLER
J. D. A. OGILVY
GLENN WARREN OLSEN
LESLIE E. ORGEL
ORIEL COLLEGE LIBRARY,
  OXFORD
RONALD E. OSBORN

MARY J. DONOVAN O'SULLIVAN
A. J. OTWAY-RUTHVEN
A. E. B. AND MRS OWEN
J. H. OWEN
NANCY H. OWEN
WILLIAM J. PAFF
W. A. PANTIN
BRUCE R. PARKER
T. M. PARKER
SIR DAVID HUGHES PARRY
ROBERT B. PATTERSON
BERNARD M. PEEBLES
EDMUND D. PELLEGRINO
PEMBROKE COLLEGE LIBRARY,
  OXFORD
ROBERT PETERS
JOSEPH L. PIECHOCKI
THEODORE F. T. PLUCKNETT
J. H. PLUMB
D. R. POCOCK
H. C. PORTER
UNIVERSITY OF PORTLAND
  LIBRARY
M. M. POSTAN
G. R. POTTER
C. L. G. PRATT
ROBERT A. PRATT
THE PRIORY, PORTSMOUTH,
  RHODE ISLAND
R. B. PUGH
PURDUE UNIVERSITY LIBRARIES
H. J. PYBUS
EDWIN A. QUAIN
D. B. QUINN
F. J. E. RABY
C. A. RALEGH RADFORD
READING UNIVERSITY LIBRARY
W. B. REDDAWAY
ALBERT G. REDPATH
M. E. REEVES
GRAYDON W. REGENOS

SUBSCRIBERS

H. S. REINMUTH, JR.
PETER RIESENBERG
THE LORD BISHOP OF RIPON
MICHAEL J. ROACH
J. A. ROBSON
R. ROBSON
MARY E. ROGERS
MIRIAM THERESA ROONEY
MARGARET ROPER
ROSARY COLLEGE CLASSICS
  DEPARTMENT
M. C. ROSENFIELD
LESSING J. ROSENWALD
J. S. ROSKELL
S. W. ROSKILL
JAMES BRUCE ROSS
ROYAL HOLLOWAY COLLEGE
  LIBRARY, LONDON
SIR STEVEN RUNCIMAN
J. JOSEPH RYAN
WILLIAM F. RYAN
THE JOHN RYLANDS LIBRARY
MORRIS H. SAFFRON
CARLETON M. SAGE
QUAESTOR AND FACTOR,
  UNIVERSITY OF ST ANDREWS
UNIVERSITY OF ST ANDREWS
  LIBRARY
ST ANSELM'S ABBEY
ST EDMUND HALL LIBRARY,
  OXFORD
ST HILDA'S COLLEGE LIBRARY,
  OXFORD
ST HUGH'S COLLEGE LIBRARY,
  OXFORD
ST JOHN'S UNIVERSITY LIBRARY
J. K. S. ST JOSEPH
G. SALT
JOHN SALTMARSH
JANE E. SAYERS
G. O. SAYLES

G. V. SCAMMELL
PAUL SCHAEFFER
RAYMOND H. SCHMANDT
R. J. SCHOECK
A. N. E. D. SCHOFIELD
JACK SCHULMAN
C. M. E. SEAMAN
IHOR ŠEVČENKO
WILLIAM SHARPE
RICHARD SKAER
QUENTIN R. D. SKINNER
C. F. SLADE
M. D. SLATTER
R. C. SMAIL
BERYL SMALLEY
S. S. SMALLEY
BERNARD S. SMITH
E. A. SMITH
CHARLES SMYTH
LAWRENCE S. SNELL
JANET SONDHEIMER
SOUTHAMPTON UNIVERSITY,
  DEPARTMENT OF HISTORY
R. W. SOUTHERN
FRANCIS W. STEER
S. H. STEINBERG
SIR FRANK AND LADY STENTON
JOHN STEPHAN
SAMUEL STERN
ZEPH STEWART
JOHN O. H. STIGALL
WHITNEY S. STODDARD
E. L. G. AND MRS STONES
RAYMOND STROMBERG
JAMES JOHNSON SWEENEY
MRS NORMAN SYKES
SYRACUSE UNIVERSITY LIBRARY
WINIFRED ANNIE TAFFS
C. H. TALBOT
A. J. TAYLOR
ERICH A. O'D. TAYLOR

xi

J. C. TAYLOR
CRAIG R. THOMPSON
W. D. J. CARGILL THOMPSON
DAVID THOMSON
GLADYS SCOTT THOMSON
J. A. F. THOMSON
CHARLES GREENWOOD THORNE, JR.
SYLVIA L. THRUPP
BRIAN TIERNEY
ARTHUR V. R. TILTON
CHARLES L. TIPTON
REGINALD F. TREHARNE
H. R. TREVOR-ROPER
WILLIAM R. TRIMBLE
TRINITY COLLEGE LIBRARY, GLASGOW
JAMES S. TUCKER, JR.
B. L. ULLMAN
WALTER ULLMANN
HULING E. USSERY
FRANCIS LEE UTLEY
VAN PELT LIBRARY, UNIVERSITY OF PENNSYLVANIA
JOAN VARLEY
A. R. VIDLER
W. B. VINCE
J. R. VINCENT
JOAN WAKE
D. P. WALEY
DAVID WALKER
J. EWING WALKER
J. M. WALLACE-HADRILL
LUITPOLD WALLACH
WARD LIBRARY, PETERHOUSE, CAMBRIDGE

B. H. WARMINGTON
AELRED WATKIN
DONALD E. R. WATT
JOHN A. WATT
B. C. WEBER
BRUCE WEBSTER
JAMES A. WEISHEIPL
E. WELBOURNE
DOROTHY BRUCE WESKE
WESTFIELD COLLEGE LIBRARY, LONDON
F. P. WHITE
JULIAN EUGENE WHITE, JR.
LYNN WHITE, JR.
DOROTHY WHITELOCK
MARTIN WIGHT
M. J. WILKS
RUDOLPH WILLARD
BISHOP A. P. T. WILLIAMS
DR WILLIAMS'S LIBRARY, LONDON
GLANMOR WILLIAMS
SCHAFER WILLIAMS
A. E. WILSON
E. M. WILSON
B. P. WOLFFE
CHARLES T. WOOD
KATHLEEN L. WOOD-LEGH
FRANCIS WORMALD
WORTH PRIORY LIBRARY
C. E. WRIGHT
CONSTANCE S. WRIGHT
E. A. WRIGLEY
JOYCE YOUINGS
JOHN A. YUNCK
GEORGE ZARNECKI

CONTENTS

EDITORS' NOTE

The Historian and Character provides the theme of this collection: almost all the studies which follow illustrate the author's concern with human problems and personality. They also illustrate his concern with medieval monasticism, medieval thought, and monastic historians of the modern world. They are designed within this frame to show both the author's original scholarship and his appeal to a wide public. Each article is labelled with the year of its first publication, and no attempt has been made to bring them systematically up to date. But the opportunity has been taken to correct minor errors, to make the references more or less uniform, to note cross-references within the volume, and occasionally to refer to an important book or article that has appeared since these articles were written. Such additions are given in square brackets. Each article, furthermore, is complete; nothing has been omitted except the bibliography of Abbot Cuthbert Butler which originally appeared with no. 12. No. 9, 'The Monastic Buildings of England', is here printed for the first time.

Many friends of Dom David Knowles have helped in the preparation of this volume. The revision of the articles and the preparation of the book for the press have been undertaken by Professor Christopher Brooke and Professor Giles Constable. The *curriculum vitae* has been written by Mr W. A. Pantin, who also assisted in the selection of articles and in many other ways. The editors would also like to acknowledge the kindness of many others who have given help and advice, and the ready consent for the reprinting of the articles and other extracts from Dom David Knowles's writings granted by the following: the Editor of *Studies*, for no. 2; the *Historical Journal* (formerly *Cambridge Historical Journal*), for no. 5; the *Journal of Ecclesiastical History*, for no. 10; the Council of the Friends of Dr Williams's Library, for no. 4; the Council of the British Academy, for nos. 6 and 7; Miss Veronica Ruffer and Mr

A. J. Taylor, for no. 8; the Athlone Press, for no. 11; the Right Reverend the Abbot of Downside Abbey and the Editor of the *Downside Review*, for no. 12; Messrs Longmans, Green and Co. Ltd and Messrs Sheed and Ward Ltd for the passages quoted on pp. xviii–xix, xxi; and the Syndics of the Cambridge University Press, who granted permission for the reprinting of no. 1 and of the passage quoted on p. xxviii, and have undertaken the publication of the book as a whole. Above all, the editors are indebted to the author himself for providing the material for this volume, for his consent to its publication, and for his help in its preparation. Authors sometimes claim that they are entirely responsible only for the errors in their books. In this book it is the editors who can make this claim without fear of contradiction.

CURRICULUM VITAE[1]

Michael Clive (in religion, Dom David) Knowles was born on
29 September 1896 at Eastfield, Studley, Warwickshire, being the
only son of the late H. H. Knowles and Carrie Knowles. His
father's family came from landowning stock in west Worcestershire
near Bromsgrove, but the family fortunes had collapsed, and his
grandfather made his own way in the world and became a leading
timber merchant in Birmingham. His son, David's father, H. H.
Knowles, went into partnership with a school friend, John Morgan,
who had an old-established family business in the needle- and pin-
making industry at Studley, and lived in the manor house there. At
that time, Redditch and Studley were the great centres for the
making of steel needles and pins, and later, when gramophones
began, the firm made all the H.M.V. needles. In due course
H. H. Knowles married the sister of his friend and partner. Their
only child, David, was born in Studley, and a few years later the
family moved into the manor house, an old house going back to the
last years of the seventeenth century, which thus became David's
childhood home. David's parents were converts to Catholicism, and
he was baptized by the local parish priest, a Benedictine monk of
Douai Abbey; Studley was one of a group of parishes on the borders
of Warwickshire and Worcestershire, which had been connected
with the Throckmorton family (of Coughton) and were served by
Benedictines from Douai. Although David's father was a successful
man of business, he was by tastes and interests a countryman. He
also had a strong interest in art and architecture, and together he
and his son visited most of the medieval English cathedrals; this
early introduction to one aspect of the Middle Ages served no doubt
as a preparation for interests that David was to develop later.
David's father lived until 1944; his help in making possible the

---

[1] An asterisk by a reference to an article by Dom David Knowles indicates that it is
reprinted in this volume.

preparation of *The Monastic Order in England* is acknowledged in the preface of that book.

David Knowles was at school at West House School at Edgbaston from 1906 to 1910, and at Downside from 1910 to 1914; among his exact contemporaries and friends there were Richard Stokes and Ivone Kirkpatrick. He was a classic at school and for some years later, and did not turn over to history until 1929. In October 1914 he entered the noviciate at Downside. He made his simple profession in October 1915 and his solemn profession on 18 October 1918, and was ordained priest on 9 July 1922. He was thus at Downside just in time to overlap with the last years of the great scholar, Edmund Bishop, and it is worth quoting his own description of his meeting with Bishop, taken from the foreword which he contributed to Nigel Abercrombie's biography of Bishop.[1]

I well remember the only conversation of any length that I had with him, in August 1916, the last summer of his life, when I was nineteen and still technically 'in the noviciate' at Downside. He sent for me, ostensibly at least, because he had noticed that I had moved too rapidly about the sanctuary at some ceremony. He wished to tell me that all appearances of haste ruined the dignity of the occasion. He then went on to ask what I was reading in the summer vacation. I happened to be finishing Boswell's *Life of Johnson* for the first time, and he told me that as a child he had known an old lady, who, when a girl, had 'knocked at Mrs Thrale's [must it not have been then Mrs Piozzi's?] door'. I mentioned Macaulay, and he told me to read Trevelyan's Life. I had recently been through *In Memoriam*; he said that many years ago he had analysed the sequence of thought throughout the poem; 'and then', he said, 'I came across a book [no doubt that of A. C. Bradley] in which the author had done the same thing, and we differed all the way through'. As he talked, one great name after another came up. He had seen Swinburne only once 'in a hansom cab—but there was no mistaking him. He made English musical, and you can't ask more than one thing of a man.' Matthew Arnold was blamed for beginning the downward curve (which I remember to have thought a strange one) that led through Walter Pater to Oscar Wilde. Kipling's name occurred, and he surprised me with the warmth of his admiration for the 1897 'Recessional'; *John Inglesant*, another old love

[1] N. Abercrombie, *The Life and Work of Edmund Bishop* (London, 1959), pp. xiv–xv.

of his, was commended to me—I fear, in vain, though the historical novel that won unbounded admiration from Lord Acton and Edmund Bishop was no ordinary book.

It is significant that the conversation turned on English literature; half a century before, Bishop had served a kind of apprenticeship as amanuensis to Thomas Carlyle, and David Knowles was to combine an abiding interest in literature with a growing study of monastic history.

When David Knowles entered Downside, first as a schoolboy, then as a monk, the community was governed by Cuthbert Butler, who was Abbot from 1906 to 1922. It would be difficult to over-estimate the influence which Abbot Butler had on David Knowles and on the community which he joined. As a younger man, Cuthbert Butler had lived through a crucial period, from about 1878 to 1899, in the development of the English Benedictine Congregation and of Downside; briefly, this period saw the change-over from a highly centralized congregation of the post-Tridentine type to the re-establishment of the full autonomy of the individual monasteries and of a full monastic discipline and observance.[1] In this return to traditional Benedictine polity, finally carried through after a prolonged struggle, Cuthbert Butler had taken an active part, aided by Edmund Bishop; and as Abbot of Downside he was able to consolidate the position thus won, and to foster the liturgical and intellectual life of his community. It is always interesting to see how the preoccupations and problems of the day affect the particular lines along which men study history; and we can see very clearly how the struggle for monastic autonomy inspired Cuthbert Butler and Edmund Bishop in their study and interpretation of monastic history.

All this is worth bearing in mind, for it has an important bearing on the development of Father David's interests and work. Every monk is likely to be interested in monastic history, but this was doubly so for a monk coming to live under Abbot Butler, within a few years of a great constitutional development; it was something like

[1] See below, pp. 265 ff.; cf. also Abbot Butler's *Benedictine Monachism* (2nd ed., London, 1924) for his views about the principles of Benedictine life and government.

the influence of parliamentary reform on English constitutional historians of the nineteenth century. From the first, Father David was interested in monastic history; Abbot Butler encouraged this, and suggested that he should work on Cluny, the monolithic monastic empire that has always interested students of Benedictine polity. Father David read Sackur's great work on Cluny, but was not attracted, and he turned instead to English monastic history, a choice which we must all feel was a very happy one. Father David's first readings in monastic history can be seen reflected in the first item in his bibliography, the article which appeared in *The Downside Review* in July 1919, between his solemn profession and his going up to Cambridge; this deals with Mabillon's preface to the third volume of the *Annales Ordinis Sancti Benedicti*, in which he defends the necessity of monastic studies—an echo of his famous controversy with de Rancé. Mabillon was the best possible approach to monastic history, and this was a subject to which Father David was to return with so much affection just forty years later in his papers on the Maurists and on Mabillon*. Father David's attention was soon directed to other topics and other disciplines—the classics, philosophy, theology, English literature and modern history. Those subjects may seem a far cry from the intensive study of monastic history to which he was later to return, but, in the long run, the wide range of interests was to have an important effect on his historical writing. I think that Father David would have had much less understanding and skill in the writing of monastic history, if he had been a monastic historian and nothing more.

There was another way in which Abbot Butler and Edmund Bishop were to influence many generations of Downside monks, including Father David, namely by the part they played in creating the link between Downside and Cambridge. Indeed, an Oxford man may be tempted to think that but for Edmund Bishop's antipathy to Brightman, Father David might be adorning another history school. Cuthbert Butler had been the first head of Benet House, the Downside house of studies at Cambridge, and he had formed close friendships with Cambridge scholars like Armitage Robinson. It was in accordance with this tradition that Father David was sent to Benet House from 1919 to 1922. Here, like other members of Benet House, he became a member of Christ's College; he read for the classical tripos, obtaining a first in Part I (1921) and a first in Part II, with distinction in philosophy (1922), and winning on the way the Skeat Prize in English literature in 1920. Immediately after leaving Cambridge, he was sent for the best part of a year (October 1922 to summer 1923) to study theology at the college of Sant'Anselmo in Rome. The creation of this international, inter-congregational Benedictine house of studies, like the office of Abbot-Primate, had been part of a policy of centralization which, in theory, might seem to cut across the monastic autonomy that men like Abbot Butler had prized so much, but in fact Father David found Sant'Anselmo congenial and edifying, as he has himself described.

At the international theological college of Sant'Anselmo in Rome young monks from all over the world meet and form an always changing community. A monastic family in the full sense it can never be, for the individual members look with true Benedictine affection to the family of their profession, but the family likeness is unmistakable. If it may be permitted to give what is only a personal impression, I would say that at Sant' Anselmo there existed a far greater similarity of outlook—a common *Weltanschauung*—in religious things between the different nationalities (and this, when I saw it, was only three years after the Treaty of Versailles, and when many of the monks had fought and suffered on opposite sides) than would have existed between any other nationalities and their fellow-countrymen at the other Roman colleges.[1]

It is an interesting fact, and a sobering one for the professional historian, that Father David, who was to become one of our leading historians, received practically all his technical, academic training, both at Cambridge and in Rome, in disciplines other than history; for although the classical tripos included ancient history, it was in philosophy that he had specialized in Part II. Nor had he been 'processed' by passing through any system of organized post-graduate research.

After his return from Rome, Father David was occupied in

[1] D. Knowles, *The Benedictines* (London, 1929), pp. 64-5.

teaching in the school at Downside from 1923 to 1928. It was during this period that he visited F. F. Urquhart's chalet in the French Alps on several occasions, and to this period belong a variety of articles and two books, on the American Civil War and on the English mystics. The second book needs no explanation; it was a topic to which he would return repeatedly. The book on the American Civil War, the preface of which is dated July 1925, owed much to the encouragement of Urquhart. To those who know Father David as the historian of medieval English monasticism, it may seem surprising that his first published book should have been on such a subject. This was no pot-boiler, nor was it the conscientiously executed chore of a schoolmaster; on the contrary it represents a quite personal enthusiasm which goes back to his childhood; as he puts it in the preface: 'I can scarcely remember a time when the American Civil War did not charm me with a fascination for which I can give no adequate reason even to myself.' And it is interesting to see already in this book, on such a different theme, some of the traits, such as the analysis of character, which were to mark his work on monastic history.[1]

The next five years were a period of great activity, both monastic and literary: Father David was teaching theology at Downside from 1928; he was temporarily Novice Master in 1928, and Junior Master from 1929 to 1933; and he was editor of *The Downside Review* at the same time. It was at this time too that he began working systematically through the sources on English monastic history, in preparation for the work which was to come out ten years later as *The Monastic Order in England*. It was in the summer of 1929 that he started work on this, by borrowing Domesday Book and Fowler's edition of the Rites of Durham from the Bishop library at Downside; and I remember that when I was visiting Downside in the summer of 1931, he showed me the collection of fiches that he had already accumulated. And as he went along he put out, as it were, a series of interim reports in the 'Essays in Monastic History' which he published in *The Downside Review* between 1930 and 1934.

[1] See the passage about the characters of Robert E. Lee and Lincoln, in 'The Historian and Character' (1955): below, p. 11.

In 1933 Father David moved to Ealing Priory, and he spent the years that followed in working intensively on *The Monastic Order in England*. This was already with the Cambridge University Press at the outbreak of war—the preface is dated 25 March 1939—and it came out in the summer of 1940; there was something very heartening in getting such a book in the summer of Dunkirk and the Battle of Britain. During most of the war years Father David was living in London, working now on the continuation of his history of English monasticism, *The Religious Orders in England*, the first instalment of which came out in 1948, the second in 1955, and the third in 1959. There are a number of articles and books which may be regarded as by-products of the work done on *The Monastic Order* and *The Religious Orders*, particular points that arose and were developed into a definitive treatment. In addition to the 'Essays in Monastic History' already referred to, one may mention the articles on St William of York (1936)*, on the Canterbury election of 1205–6 (1938), on the humanism of the twelfth century—in his best vein (1941)*, on Archbishop Pecham (1942), on Uthred of Boldon (1951)*; the extremely useful list of religious houses of medieval England (1940), recast in collaboration with Neville Hadcock in 1953, and supplemented by *Monastic Sites from the Air*, in collaboration with J. K. S. St Joseph—a happy application of 'visual aids' to monastic history (1952). The same awareness of the growing usefulness of archaeology is shown in his collaboration with W. F. Grimes on the London Charterhouse (1954), where the scene of the most heroic chapter in English monastic history had been laid bare by war damage. The character sketches of Gilbert Foliot and Henry of Blois, which were a notable feature of *The Monastic Order*, found a natural extension in the character study of Archbishop Thomas Becket (1949)* and of his episcopal colleagues (1951).

For many years before 1940, Father David was already well known to specialists as an authority on monastic history, especially from his 'Essays in Monastic History' in *The Downside Review*. With the publication of *The Monastic Order* in 1940, it became clear to a wider public that here was a medieval historian of the first rank, and it is not surprising that he found recognition at his old University. In 1944 he was made a Fellow of Peterhouse, Cambridge, and in 1945 a University Lecturer, and he took his share of the *pondus diei et aestus* of college teaching in the post-war years. On the death of his close friend Z. N. Brooke in 1946, Father David was elected to succeed him as Professor of Medieval History (1947), and in 1954 he was appointed to succeed J. R. M. Butler as Regius Professor of Modern History, a signal recognition both of his own scholarship and of the importance of those aspects of history which he has made his own.

He has served as chairman of the History Faculty at Cambridge, and has influenced historical studies in Cambridge in a number of ways: in the historical tripos, for instance, by helping to introduce as a subject the intellectual history of Western Europe 1000–1350, and special subjects on St Francis and on St Bernard; by supervising post-graduate research; and by reviving the series of monographs published under the title of 'Cambridge Studies in Medieval Life and Thought'. He has naturally had activities and recognition in other quarters as well as Cambridge. He was Ford's Lecturer in English history at Oxford in 1949, Raleigh Lecturer (British Academy) in 1949, and Creighton Lecturer in the University of London in 1956, and he was given the honorary degree of Doctor of Letters at Oxford in 1952, at Bristol in 1956 and at Leicester in 1962. He has been a Fellow of the British Academy since 1947 and has served as a Vice-President and as a member of its Council. He was President of the Royal Historical Society from 1956 to 1960; he is a Fellow of the Society of Antiquaries, and has served on the Council of the Canterbury and York Society.

If one was asked to sum up the impression made upon one by Father David's personality, one might say that it is a combination of quietness and strength, and it is a combination which commands instinctive respect. It would be difficult to imagine anyone further removed from the combative, self-assertive, self-important personalities that are sometimes to be found in the academic jungle, or from the dons

> Who shout and bang and roar and bawl
> The Absolute across the hall.

At the same time, no one who has met him could fail to see at once that his quietness is not due to timidity or to lack of conviction or of toughness. As a lecturer and a speaker, the impression is the same: there is a quiet, deliberate, vibrant tone which is very characteristic and never fails to get his personality across; there are the flashes of wit and humour, all the more effective from their impassive delivery; and, from time to time, the deep and firm statement of faith.

I have already referred to the wide range of Father David's articles and books; but there is in fact an underlying unity in them, particularly in the way in which they tie up with certain strands that appear in his work on English monastic history. Among his earliest articles is one which vividly describes visits to places in Italy such as Subiaco, Monte Cassino, Montevergine, in 1923, and another describes a visit to Greece (1930–31). This strong feeling for places is something that has never left Father David; it can be seen continually coming out in *The Monastic Order* and *The Religious Orders*, not only in the 'conducted tour' of monastic England which he introduces from time to time, but in numerous other ways: the picture of Prior Henry of Eastry travelling round Kent, seeing the pastures 'with the eyes of Shallow, not with those of Perdita'; Wyclif's feeling, yet lack of feeling, for Oxford—'rue, not snapdragon, clung to the walls of Balliol';[1] the humanist monk, Robert Joseph, in the vale of Evesham, where the very place-names are 'sweet symphonies' to those familiar with the district; Prior More among the 'rewards and fairies', on his manors buried in Worcestershire; the great east window of Gloucester, with the dawn stealing upon the end of a long Office—*lux intrat, albescit polus, Christus venit*; or the moving description of Durham, with 'the sound of bells at midnight, "in the lanthorne called the new worke", clear in the magical silence of midsummer or borne fitfully across the Wear in winter storms'. One is reminded of Sir Maurice Powicke's passages about Rievaulx and Great Coxwold.

[1] This is an echo of the passage in Newman's *Apologia*, at the end of chapter IV: 'Trinity had never been unkind to me. There used to be much snapdragon growing on the walls opposite my freshman's rooms there, and I had for years taken it as the emblem of my own perpetual residence even unto death in my University.'

Another recurring topic is mystical theology and the spiritual life: not only in the two books on the English mystics, the earlier more biographical, the later more theoretical in its treatment, but also in the articles on St Teresa, *The Cloud of Unknowing*, St Thomas, Father Baker, and in the edition of the spiritual biography of an English Benedictine abbess of the early seventeenth century, Lady Lucy Knatchbull. And all through the four volumes of *The Monastic Order* and *The Religious Orders*, participation in and contribution to the spiritual life is the underlying test, applied to all men, all movements and all periods; it is the existence of this unfailing, rigorous standard which gives a unique character to these volumes. All will agree with him in admiring the best and in censuring the worst; some may feel that Father David is sometimes a little hard on the mediocre, the smoking flax. But if he is severe, this, I think, like his interest in character study, is because Father David cares deeply for the people and the things he is writing about. This is an attractive trait, and one not universal among scholars.

Another group of topics, closely interrelated, are literary criticism, the analysis of character, and biography. The essays on the Greek witness to the immortality of the soul and on the thought and art of Thomas Hardy deal with the ideas underlying great literature. 'Animus and Anima' takes Henri Bremond's *Prière et Poésie* as its starting point. 'Honest Iago', one of Father David's most interesting literary essays, is an analysis of Iago's character and how Shakespeare reveals it: it is very characteristic both of his love of Shakespeare and of his interest in the portrayal of character; the same searchlight is turned on a character in *Othello* that is turned on many a personality revealed in a monastic chronicle or a twelfth-century letter-writer. It is not accidental that Father David has always had this interest in literature and literary craftsmanship; it is reflected in the quality of his writing and in his unfailing supply of apt allusions; as when, for instance, he demonstrates the strong personal feeling which twelfth-century humanists like Ailred or Héloïse had for the men of antiquity, and clinches this by quoting: 'Then 'twas the Roman, now 'tis I.'

Perhaps most central of all is Father David's interest in biography and the study of personality. It is significant that his inaugural lecture as Regius Professor was on 'The Historian and Character'*; and we can literally read between the lines of the title on the original wrapper: *Quid est homo quod memor es eius? Minuisti eum paulo minus ab angelis.* His biographical studies range from an appreciation of a great and very 'modern' headmaster like Sanderson of Oundle, or of an early seventeenth-century abbess, or from a page on Urquhart's religious life contributed to Cyril Bailey's memoir, to judicious estimates of such very different men as Gasquet* and Macaulay. There are the character sketches scattered throughout *The Monastic Order* and *The Religious Orders.* There is the long essay on the life and work of Abbot Butler*, written with a characteristic combination of sympathy and candour, which seems to me one of Father David's most important pieces of writing; and there is the equally characteristic memoir of a young friend, R. A. L. Smith, a pupil of Eileen Power and a medievalist of great promise, who died at a tragically early age. And while the four papers on great historical enterprises—the Bollandists, the Maurists, the German *Monumenta* and the Rolls Series—are from one point of view a study in historical method, from another point of view they are essays in collective biography.

I have left to the last the four volumes of *The Monastic Order in England* and *The Religious Orders in England,* which have occupied thirty years of his life, and must be regarded as his chief contribution to historical literature. This is not the place to make a detailed review. It is perhaps enough to say that he has produced what students of history and indeed all educated Englishmen have been waiting for, for a hundred years and more: a definitive history of the religious life in England from the tenth to the seventeenth century, written with complete understanding, sympathy and objectivity. This has of course been a controversial subject, not least at Cambridge, and it may be said that Father David, like Mabillon in his dealings with Papebroch and de Rancé, has in effect closed a controversy simply by making a great positive contribution. Father David shows himself equally concerned with personalities and with institutions, and makes the one illuminate the other. Perhaps his greatest *tour de force* is that he has produced a beautifully constructed and written narrative which is at the same time a mine of detailed information that can be constantly used, *experto crede*, as a work of reference. It makes the hackneyed dilemma, whether history is an art or a science, look meaningless. Like Maitland, he has the happy knack of being able to explain the most abstruse or technical matters in lucid and simple language. And if we want to know what is the meaning of this massive survey to the man who wrote it, we cannot do better than quote the closing paragraph of his final volume:[1]

At the end of this long review of monastic history, with its splendours and its miseries, and with its rhythm of recurring rise and fall, a monk cannot but ask what message for himself and for his brethren the long story may carry. It is the old and simple one; only in fidelity to the Rule can a monk or a monastery find security. A Rule, given by a founder with an acknowledged fullness of spiritual wisdom, approved by the Church and tested by the experience of saints, is a safe path, and it is for the religious the only safe path. It comes to him not as a rigid, mechanical code of works, but as a sure guide to one who seeks God, and who seeks that he may indeed find. If he truly seeks and truly loves, the way will not be hard, but if he would love and find the unseen God he must pass beyond things seen and walk in faith and hope, leaving all human ways and means and trusting the Father to whom all things are possible. When once a religious house or a religious order ceases to direct its sons to the abandonment of all that is not God, and ceases to show them the rigours of the narrow way that leads to the imitation of Christ in His Love, it sinks to the level of a purely human institution, and whatever its works may be, they are the works of time and not of eternity. The true monk, in whatever century he is found, looks not to the changing ways around him or to his own mean condition, but to the unchanging everlasting God, and his trust is in the everlasting arms that hold him. Christ's words are true: He who doth not renounce all that he possesseth cannot be my disciple. His promise also is true: He that followeth me walketh not in darkness, but shall have the light of life.[2]

W.A.P.

[1] *The Religious Orders in England*, vol. III, p. 468.
[2] Since this *Curriculum Vitae* was written, Father David has given an account of how he approached historical studies, in *History*, vol. XLVII (1962), pp. 229–31.

LIST OF ABBREVIATIONS

CHJ   *The Cambridge Historical Journal*

DACL *Dictionnaire d'archéologie chrétienne et de liturgie*

DR   *The Downside Review*

DubR *The Dublin Review*

EHR   *The English Historical Review*

JEH   *The Journal of Ecclesiastical History*

L & P *Letters and papers, foreign and domestic, of the reign of Henry VIII*, ed. J. S. Brewer, J. Gairdner, and R. H. Brodie. 23 vols. (Public Record Office Texts and Calendars, 1862–1932.)

PBA   *Proceedings of the British Academy*

PL   *Patrologiae cursus completus, series Latina*, ed. J. P. Migne

RS   The Rolls Series

TRHS *Transactions of the Royal Historical Society*

1

THE HISTORIAN AND CHARACTER[1]

There is a tradition, though not an unbroken one, that the inaugural lecture of the Regius Professor of Modern History should be concerned with the nature or demands of historical writing as such, rather than with any particular historical topic. Difficult as it may be to follow this tradition, and those who established it, the attempt shall be made, and this lecture has been given the title 'The Historian and Character'.

It is a commonplace among historians today to lament, perhaps not very sincerely, that history, which till comparatively recently was primarily the history of the state or the Church, has now proliferated in every direction into constitutional, social, economic, administrative, cultural, imperial and what not, so that the being who is sometimes quaintly known as the 'straight' historian, or even as the 'pure' historian, is a great rarity. One of the many consequences of this is that academic historians are notably less concerned with men and women, their personalities and their characters, than they were a century ago. If Charles Kingsley's saying, that 'History is the history of men and women, and of nothing else', seemed paradoxical in his own day, it would seem scandalous now. Even when the historian treats of individuals, he does so with a greater diffidence than before. The individual appears so small in the universe of events; he is so straitly bound by heredity, by ignorance, and by circumstance; the alternatives before him are so limited, the space for manœuvre so small; the predicament (if I may borrow what is almost a signature word) is so urgent. And, finally, our generation is less convinced of its standards and laws than were those of Macaulay and Stubbs. Some historians, like some philosophers,

---

[1] [Inaugural Lecture as Regius Professor of Modern History, delivered at Cambridge, 17 November 1954. (Cambridge, 1955.)]

have ceased, when it comes to pronouncements in print, to be certain about ethical values; they fear that a moral judgement may be no more absolute than—may indeed be the same as—an expression of taste or emotion. The robust phrases of an earlier age jar upon the ear.

Are we, then, to think that character is to be the province of the biographer rather than of the historian? We may surely say that in so far as a man's life is spent in private station—a George Herbert, a Samuel Johnson, a John Sterling, to take familiar examples—the historian has no concern with it. Even when a man's work has a vast influence, but he himself remains outside the stream of what is called public life—a Rousseau or a Marx—the historian may wish to absolve himself from care, though more questionably, for men do not gather grapes from thorns, and if the historian has to describe the fruit, he should know the tree; certainly, the personality of John Wesley was more significant for England than that of the elder Pitt. But when it is a matter of actors who move and mingle in the forefront of the stage, whatever stage it be, and whatever actors are summoned to tread it, then their characters are within the province of the historian.

Moreover, the tasks of biographer and historian are different. Biography, the poet tells us, 'is about chaps'; but if it be, it takes them one at a time, whereas the historian's regard sweeps wider and deeper over a field of folk. For the biographer, his subject is the centre of his world, and he is concerned with presentation rather than with assessment, illustrating every facet of character with a careless bounty that a historian cannot afford. The greatest biographers are those who have been linked in relationship with their subjects, or at least have been their constant companions—a Tacitus, a Joinville, a Roper, a Boswell, a Lockhart, a Trevelyan—and their achievement is to create in the reader the illusion that he also knows the hero, has shared with Scott the exhilaration of splashing from stone to stone across the Tweed in the midst of an improvised dialogue, or has left Macaulay talking in front of the breakfast-room fire at Bowood, and has returned after a day's shooting to find him talking still—the same Macaulay who would play tigers with a little girl behind the sofa.[1] The more a biographer can conceal himself or, better still, become an actor in his subject's life, the better. Roper when he misunderstands More's word in the barge or bridles at his forebodings, Boswell smothering his antipathy to cats while he watches Hodge scrambling up Johnson's waistcoat ('Why yes, Sir, but I have had cats whom I liked better than Hodge')—these achieve what a historian cannot hope to rival. A biography which is not by an associate, or at least by a contemporary, belongs properly to another literary family. Pollard's trilogy of Tudor lives, Professor Neale's *Queen Elizabeth*, are in fact studies in Tudor history. Only when a man of the past has put almost his whole self into words, as Cicero did, or Erasmus, can we come near to seeing him as a biographer must see him.

The historian, working in a wider field, must use more economy and weigh his instances. He must know what he is looking for and what he can hope to do. But before all, he must be sincere: he must not write nonsense or present a character such as never was on sea or land. And here I would wish to read two pieces from two eminent historians of the last century, that may serve as texts or warnings to bear in mind as we proceed. The first is from Motley's final verdict on Philip II of Spain:

There have been few men known to history who have been able to accomplish by their own exertions so vast an amount of evil as the king who had just died. If Philip possessed a single virtue it has eluded the conscientious research of the writer of these pages. If there are vices—as possibly there are—from which he was exempt, it is because it is not permitted by human nature to attain perfection even in evil....The horrible monotony of his career stupefies the mind until it is ready to accept the principle of evil as the fundamental law of the world.... He endured the martyrdom of his last illness with the heroism of a saint, and died in the certainty of immortal bliss as the reward of his life of evil.[2]

---

[1] Actually, in the incident recorded by Trevelyan, the house-party sat in 'a silent circle' around the speakers, Austin and Macaulay, till dinner time, 'with a short break for lunch' (*Life of Macaulay*, ed. 1876, vol. I, ch. II, p. 83). I owe the reference, which I had forgotten, to Dr G. M. Trevelyan.

[2] J. L. Motley, *History of the United Netherlands* (ed. 1867), vol. III, ch. XXXV, pp. 534-43.

1-2

The second is from Mommsen's final pronouncement on Julius Caesar:

The secret [of Caesar's character] lies in its perfection.... Caesar was the entire and perfect man.... As the artist can paint everything save only consummate beauty, so the historian, when once in a thousand years he encounters the perfect, can only be silent regarding it.... The secret of nature, whereby in her most finished manifestations normality and individuality are combined, is beyond expression. Nothing is left for us but to deem those fortunate who beheld this perfection.[1]

Having heard this, we may perhaps agree that we must have some principles, at least, in our minds before we attempt to portray a character. Motley was a distinguished man, and Mommsen a historian of the very first rank; we may allow that Catholic Spain of the Counter-Reformation, and Philip II in his own person, are difficult food for Anglo-Saxon minds, while a strong draught of Caesar goes to almost anybody's head, but Motley wrote as a peculiarly righteous and enlightened New Englander, and Mommsen as the German who saw in Caesar all that he longed for of realist action in his own expanding nation. Neither of them can be acquitted of having used words without due care. It is sometimes given as a rule to writers of school essays that they should strike out of the rough copy the passages that give them the most satisfaction in writing; historians would do well to carry the advice in their mind when approaching their best-loved or best-hated character. They should at least refrain from writing nonsense. The term saint is not convertible with the term fanatic. A saint is one whose heroism is a reflection of the fortitude of God. If Philip had a trace of that, he possessed more than a single virtue. Similarly with Mommsen. If Caesar was the perfect and entire man, are licence, ruthlessness and an entire lack of scruple a part of perfection? Mommsen, indeed, by the last words of his that I have quoted, invites wittingly or not a terrible comparison.[2]

Mommsen, in fact, reminds us also that the historian must avoid bestowing upon all the realms of a man's activity the admiration that is only due in one or some. He must distinguish between ethical

---

[1] T. Mommsen, *History of Rome*, Book v, ch. xi (tr. W. P. Dickson, ed. 1868, vol. iv, pp. 481-2).

[2] Luke, x. 23: 'Blessed are the eyes that see what you see.'

excellence and natural gifts and ability. Often, indeed, the gifts and genius of a man are out of all proportion to his qualities as a human being. All recognize this readily enough with an artist or man of letters, but all are not so clear-sighted when it comes to a man of action. Napoleon's supreme lucidity of mind as an organizer and administrator, his admirable energy, his clairvoyance in campaign or on the field of battle, his daring in conception of great schemes—all these and many other qualities reached in him to the point of consummate genius. Yet the character behind this, as seen in his personal relations, in his diplomacy, and in his spoken and written words, seems to lack a corresponding generosity and nobility, as it also lacks warmth and grace and sincerity. In Caesar, on the other hand, the contrast is not so sharp. His realist vision, his unhesitating decision, his drastic swiftness, the sureness and resolution with which he broke through obstacles at which three generations had blundered and baulked, have behind them a character that is of a piece. To say this, however, is not to say that Caesar was a good man, or that his strength of spirit could be ranked with that of Socrates.

Very similar to the trap of genius or success in action is the snare provided by what we call charm and an earlier generation thought of as urbanity: that indescribable quality which, like physical beauty, can dazzle the mind's eye and blind the judgement. Charm, save when allied to wit, is capricious and fitful in its survival. Contemporary witness makes it clear that Napoleon could exercise it, though Talleyrand remained impervious, and Napoleon's contemporary, Charles James Fox, possessed it to a degree that led his friends to forgive his considerable faults and pay his immense debts, yet in both these cases the historian finds it difficult to recapture. Caesar, on the other hand, even at this distance of time, is clearly seen to have had it, and in more recent centuries men of such different character as More and Montrose; we can still understand why Nelson drew out a personal devotion not given to Wellington, and feel the spell that Newman cast over so many minds, and which clings, like Virgil's, to a casual phrase, or a broken line of his writings. When wit is added to charm the draught is potent indeed. Even Macaulay could not judge Charles II altogether unmoved by that exquisite urbanity which, in the historian's unforgettable phrase, was 'so often found potent to charm away the resentment of a justly incensed nation'. We cannot think of George Canning without a lingering indulgence, and the cool audacities of Disraeli have disarmed more than one critic, while the world has never forgiven the high seriousness of Gladstone. Wit is a rapier, in history as in life, that can often successfully deflect true judgement.

The historian must also beware of confusing a man's cause or party or religion with his character. We have been warned once and for all to distrust the Whig interpretation of history, and the danger runs through all parties and religions. There are, indeed, many figures of the past who embody or represent a cause so clearly that it is next to impossible to dissociate their personality from the set of principles they held, and when the principles are ours also the confusion is very great. The historiography of Wyclif and Luther throughout the centuries shows this unmistakably, and when the man is also a reputed martyr there is the double consequence—he must sanctify his cause, and his cause must sanctify him. Hence, with such men as Thomas Becket, Sir Thomas More and Archbishop Cranmer both the character and the status of martyr are impugned or defended together. Say what we will, our attitude to their lives will be coloured by our decision as to what they died for. Who would dare to say that he could approach the study of Cranmer's life without prejudice or, having approached it, that he had presented Cranmer's actions in their true light?

We have left to the last the greatest of all potential difficulties, the profession of a religious ideal. Christianity, among its many results upon mankind, introduced a new scale of values in human action and laid emphasis upon virtues which we need not seek in a Cicero or a Pericles. The historian is therefore often faced with a dilemma which cannot perhaps ever be fully escaped: whether to judge a man's achievement by his ideals and professions and religious obligations, or by the generally accepted standards of human behaviour. Even this does not end our difficulties. When the profession of religious fervour has become a convention in a class or a whole society—in a religious order, for example, or during the heyday of Puritanism or

6

the Evangelical movement—conscious or unconscious hypocrisy is peculiarly difficult to recognize. The novelist or dramatist can easily unmask a Tartuffe or Trusty Tomkins or the Rev. Mr Stiggins, but Torquemada and Oliver Cromwell and Henry Edward Manning and Mr Gladstone are far more difficult problems.

If he has successfully avoided all these pitfalls, the historian must assemble all the available evidence before he draws his portrait, and he must suppress nothing, even though a detail seems to be inconsistent with all else that he knows. Sir Thomas More, who has been mentioned more than once, might at first sight seem a fairly simple subject; the text-books agree on his personal candour and integrity, and historians, at least since the days of Addison, have been all but unanimous as to his intellectual power, his charm, and his courage. Yet More is not quite the simple subject that he looks. We may consider that Chambers has eliminated the charge of harshness to heretics, but what of his asperity in controversy, his unchivalrous treatment of the fallen Wolsey, his occasional coarseness of language and the manner of his two marriages, seen in relation to his own hesitations and to a characteristically ambiguous phrase of Erasmus?[1] These remain to trouble the mind's eye, and it may often happen that we can do no more than register what seems to be presented to us, waiting for more to come that may help us to see the pattern.

There is, indeed, a truth far too often ignored by historians, which loosens many problems. A man's character, above all when the man is one of no common mould, cannot be analysed by picking up an action or a characteristic here and there and tying them in a bunch. No one passes through time and its accidents and remains unchanged. A man has free will and he can, indeed he must, exercise it. His nature with its characteristics remains recognizable, as do his features, but his aims, his ideals, his sense of values, and his directive strength of will may have changed entirely. The change is greatest when a moral or spiritual issue predominates in a man's life, as with St Augustine and St Francis and John Wesley, but the development is always there, even if gradual and unseen. No one remains the same in virtue or in love; not to go forward is to go back.

---

[1] Erasmus, *Ep.* 999 (ed. P. S. Allen).

The historian must recognize this, even if it seems to complicate his task. We see it perhaps more easily when the change is for the worse, for too often the radiance of the morning of life fades into cloud. Lord Acton's celebrated dictum on the corrupting effect of power, of which Napoleon is such an illustrious example, seems almost an assertion of the inevitability of a change for the worse. In our own day the saying has proved its melancholy truth more than once, though our own day, also, has shown more than one notable instance of its falsehood. In history it is the opposite progress that is more often ignored. St Bernard in 1150 is not the Bernard of 1120; in the young abbot we may detect excess, exaggeration, violence, rhetoric; in the mature saint we should use great circumspection in our judgement. With St Francis the change was still more rapid, from the gay young merchant to the eager apostle and then to the less comprehensible, but still more admirable, man of sorrows. In both these cases we are in the presence of men whose spiritual clarity of vision is as superior to ours as is the intelligence of a Newton or the poetic genius of a Dante, and we must bear ourselves accordingly. And perhaps we shall find here the answer to the enigma of More. His was a personality that developed very markedly in purity of vision, above all under the stress of renunciation and hardship and physical and spiritual solitude. A man who has moved away from and beyond all his friends, who has chosen to abandon all his interests rather than to compromise with what he sees as evil, who has known illness, treachery, the threat of a painful and disgraceful death, and the ultimate solitude of misunderstanding from those he loved most—this is not the same man as the friend of Erasmus and the centre of Holbein's family group.

This leads us to another point. Historians of a century ago were apt, as we have seen, to romanticize their heroes and their villains; even Stubbs, you will remember, trusting too much to Wendover, wrote of King John, 'he was the very worst of all our kings... polluted with every crime that could disgrace a man'.[1] In reaction, there has been in recent years a tendency to flatten the curve out at both ends. I remember once hearing a young reader curiously mis-

[1] W. Stubbs, *Constitutional History of England*, vol. II, ch. XIV, p. 17.

take a word in the Epistle of St James, where the apostle is asserting the basic humanity of Elijah. 'Elias', he read, in the Douai version, 'was a man *passable* like unto us.'[1] The phrase has often returned to my mind when historians have been busy reducing great men to mediocrity. Elijah, *passible* though he may have been, was not in other respects like us, and the historian must be prepared to meet with abnormality, whether of genius or of disease, just as he must expect to meet with the spiritual extremes of good and evil. Indeed, in some ways history resembles tragic drama in that greatness is a common, though not an essential element. For different reasons, though with a somewhat similar result, history, like poetry, when it touches men, touches them at a moment of significance, whether they are great in themselves, or, like Aristotle's tragic hero, stand in great place, or, like the men of 1914, are matched with great issues, or are merely passively great, caught

> between the pass and fell opposed points
> Of mighty opposites.

In any case the moment will bring out what is most significant in them, even if it be only great folly, and they will be seen, or revealed, in the light of greatness. For this reason the historian must be prepared to see a facet of character that might otherwise have remained obscure displayed in a lightning-flash. I do not forget the first time I read the words of Cicero when he heard of the murder of Caesar: 'ὦ πράξεως καλῆς'—'Oh noble deed';[2] or of the direction of Henry VIII to his commander in Scotland to 'sack Leith and burn and subvert it, putting man, woman and child to fire and sword without exception, where any resistance shall be made against you'.[3] It was in an extract for Latin prose, in a lecture-room at Christ's, that I was first directed to More's sudden word: 'Son Roper, I thank our Lord, the field is won',[4] and only the other day that I came upon the actual words of Lee's answer, in the midst of the

---

[1] James, v. 17. The Authorized Version has: 'Elias was a man subject to like passions as we are.'

[2] Cicero, *ad Atticum*, XIV, 12; this was written in May 44 B.C., but cf. *ad Familiares* VI, 15, written on the very Ides of March.

[3] Letter to the Earl of Hertford, end of May 1544 (ed. M. St Clare Byrne), p. 346.

[4] Roper's *Life of More* (ed. E. V. Hitchcock), p. 73.

agonizing morning of Appomattox, to a young officer who opposed surrender with the words, 'Oh General, what will history say?' 'That is not the question, Colonel,' replied Lee, 'the question is, is it right to surrender this army? If it is right, then I will take all the responsibility.'[1] The historian must therefore be prepared to meet men of no common mettle, to meet with sanctity and also with very great wickedness, both, it may be, far removed from his own experience and yet very real. One does not, here or at Oxford, meet commonly with a Joan of Arc or a Rasputin, or experience the strife when good and evil meet directly, but the historian must be aware of, though he must not seek or imagine, extremes outside his own experience.

When all the detail has been accumulated, we must be prepared for a picture that is not at first glance a simple one. Hamlet is Shakespeare's masterpiece of creation because he shows so great a diversity of motives and impulses within what is unmistakably a single personality. When we fail to understand a particular manifestation of it we feel (and feel rightly) that it is we, and not Shakespeare, who have failed. It is not Shakespeare who has failed in clarity or consistency of vision, but we who have failed in sympathy and insight. So with the real men of the past. A life is not a bundle of acts; it is a stream or a landscape; it is the manifestation of a single mind and personality that may grow more deformed or more beautiful to the end. If it appears complex to us it may be because we do not see it in all its circumstances, or because we do not allow for changes, or because the man is deceiving himself or us and acting in one way while he thinks in another. An unusually receptive or sensitive temperament readily receives an impress from others and seems to be following them long after the mind has moved in another direction. Some of the noblest minds are of this type; in recent English history there are the outstanding examples of Newman and Gladstone. With them the mind moved and the internal decision was taken some time before it was announced, and the apparent dissimulation during the interval was in each case attributed to policy or duplicity. How far in each case the lag between

[1] D. S. Freeman, *R. E. Lee*, vol. IV, p. 121.

mind and tongue was due to an unrealized unwillingness to abandon old friendships and principles even after the decision to do so had been taken, how far to a deep inhibition from announcing to others what they might not understand—this the historian can only hope to know, if ever, from the fullest indications of a biographer. Few eminent characters in modern history are as simple as that of the great Confederate leader who was mentioned a few moments ago. The life of Robert E. Lee was an open one, passed in a society where concealment of thought or motive was unnecessary; he had an unusually frank and generous nature, and he was an unusually honest, loyal, happy and unselfish man. Such a one is rarely found in high place; we have only to glance at Lee's great antagonist—if it is fair to call Lincoln such—to see the difference. Lincoln had to make his career in a harsh world and among unscrupulous men. He had no framework of beliefs and conventions; he had a very practical lawyer's knowledge of men together with a vision of what they should be and a deep sympathy for what they were. He had never found real understanding or love, and had ceased to look for them, though he had not ceased to give them in his own way to others. He is a Protean figure when he stands near Lee, though had Lincoln been spared they might well have met and understood one another.

Like all mental activities, the study of character has its technical apparatus and its purely intellectual interest, but it draws its strength from the centre of the personality, the final and most precious thing in man, his goodness of will, achieved by conscious and tenacious choice. That is of more significance than his natural characteristics or his intellectual gifts, or even the inspiration of genius. If we think thus, and if this is our deepest interest in human character, we are the inheritors, whether we advert to it or not, of a very long tradition which, like so many of our traditions, has its roots both in Greece and in Palestine. In Greece it was Plato, that insatiate seeker after justice, who first made of character and goodness his primary interest. It was he who gave us, though so enigmatically, the first full-length study of a great man who was first and foremost a good man. In the *Apology*, in the *Crito*, in the *Symposium* and above all in the *Phaedo* he adds the touches, until he reaches the conclusion: 'Such was the end, Echekrates, of our friend, a man, we might well say, of all men that we have known the best, the wisest and the most just.' 'Good', 'wise' and 'just'; are they not the epithets that recur throughout the historical books of the Old and New Testaments, from the call of Abraham to the warning of Pilate's wife?

Unless, then, we are to forget all we have ever learnt, it is impossible for us not to look for goodness and justice in a man. We cannot therefore allow ourselves to burke the vexed question of the historian's attitude to moral judgement. This, as we know, was the subject of a prolonged controversy sixty years ago between Lord Acton and Mandell Creighton, in which the future bishop of London became the apologist of the Borgia pope as against the Catholic moralist. Creighton, pleading for a greater sympathy and understanding than the conventional Victorian writer was willing to show, outraged the feelings of the champion of Liberty who wished to give to the historian the last word against those who had abused their authority. The passage of the years, and the interludes of Chaos and old Night which many of us have experienced, have given us a different outlook from both Acton and Creighton, but the problem remains and, as we know, it has been attacked again in recent years with penetration and discernment by a Cambridge historian of today. Let us hear once again Acton's words:

I exhort you [he said] never to debase the moral currency or to lower the standard of rectitude, but to try others by the final maxim that governs your own lives, and to suffer no man and no cause to escape the undying penalty which history has the power to inflict on wrong.[1]

To which Professor Butterfield, speaking of the last analysis of the most sensitive historian, replies:

Even this degree of knowledge [i.e., that which results from a combination of knowledge, insight and imaginative power] fails in that innermost region of all, which has to be reached before a personality can be assessed in a moral judgement.[2]

---

[1] Lord Acton, *The Study of History* (1895), p. 63.
[2] H. Butterfield, *History and Human Relations*, p. 117.

We must, I think, allow that Acton wished to give the historian a function that cannot be his. Even granted that he has overcome all the difficulties at which we have hinted, he cannot, as Acton wished, 'stand ready to smite once, and smite no more'. Whether his judgement is right or wrong, even if the facts seem certain, a later historian may question or reverse his verdict. When it is a question of a moral pronouncement on the act of an individual, we cannot

> take upon's the mystery of things,
> As if we were God's spies.

The degree of ignorance, the degree of malice, the degree of weakness, the degree of guilt, must always elude us. The whole concept of the historian as a judge in a trial is radically false, if only because a judge by his very office deals only with accused or impleaded persons; he condemns or acquits, he does not praise and reward. The historian's task is very different, he contemplates the whole of his world; he does not apportion guilt; he considers the quality of the whole man, seen, it may be, during the passage of many years. The man's acts will reflect this quality, they may help to confirm or change it, but a man acts by reason of what he is; as the scholastic axiom has it: *agere sequitur esse*. The historian, when conditions are favourable, can see the act and the man, sometimes more clearly than most of his contemporaries saw them, and he describes what he sees. He neither condemns nor acquits, he neither censures nor praises, but he presents what he sees. He must indeed have sympathy, for, in the words of one of the greatest of modern historians, the 'highest justice is found in the deepest sympathy with erring and straying men',[1] but he must have sympathy also with those who do not err and stray, and if we can see when a man is erring, we can also see when he does not. Those who refuse to pronounce on a man for evil seem sometimes to forget that by this they abdicate their right to approve him for good.

So, we may repeat, the historian is not a judge, still less a hanging judge. He watches the stream of events and the actions of men, and

---

[1] Stubbs, *Constitutional History*, vol. III, ch. XXI, p. 639. These are the final words of the great work.

records them as best he may. As he watches, he looks to see whether a man, by and large during his life, shows any evidence of acting according to a divine or moral law outside himself, whether he ever sacrifices his own profit or pleasure for the sake of a person or a principle; whether he shows evidence of loving other men, where by love we understand the classical definition of wishing them well and doing well to them; whether he puts justice before expediency; whether he is sincere and truthful. In so doing, the historian is not trying the men and women of the past; he is contemplating them; he has to see them as in truth they were and to present them as such to others, and a man, as a man, cannot be seen truly unless his moral worth, his loveworthiness, is seen. There is no flat rate here; all are different; and though in many, perhaps in most, the qualities are mixed, there are oaks great and stunted, pines majestic and storm-riven, and the historian must be able to judge between leprosy and leprosy, between weakness and malice, as he must also judge between uprightness and sanctity. Like the critic of art or poetry, he can illuminate a masterpiece and display beauties and subtleties and harmonies that had else gone unobserved; he does not only mark faults and errors and blemishes. Like the critic, too, he may at times rise to be 'himself the great sublime he draws'. A historian may well, in his assessment of character, show the same genius of sympathy that we recognize in a poet. I have often thought that Pollard, in his lives of Henry VIII and Wolsey, reveals a hidden depth of understanding that his own associates failed to note in the historian they knew; that the two gifted ladies, historians of the Pilgrimage of Grace many years ago, have not only, by their sense of pity and justice, revealed the truth of a forgotten page of history, but have enabled others to recapture in imagination a crisis in which the thoughts of many hearts were revealed. Certainly, if we travel far back to the greatest of all reflective historians, what should we know of the mind of Pericles, of the aspirations and cynicism of the Athenians, of the extent and limits of the sense of justice in the common man in the great age of Greece, unless Thucydides had himself felt the passions and been moved by the ideals which he records?

There is indeed no lack of material for the historian who, as a part

14

of his task, regards the lives of men and women in the past. Time and again throughout the ages a great issue has provoked a clash of character—Caesar and Cicero, Bernard and Abelard, Thomas of Canterbury and Gilbert Foliot, Doria and Gratian, Charles and Cromwell, Newman and Manning, Gladstone and Disraeli. More rarely, and yet not negligibly, the character of a single man—a St Francis, a Luther, a Henry VIII—has had a decisive influence over a multitude and has altered part of the stream of history. Long ago, when the recorded human story was in its infancy, the Greek poet saw that of the many marvels in the world none was stranger than man.[1] The psalmist also, in an age still earlier than that of Sophocles, marvelled that man had been made little less than the angels.

[1] Sophocles, *Antigone*, ll. 332–3.

THE HUMANISM OF THE
TWELFTH CENTURY[1]

The two centuries that follow the millennium, which have been so
closely studied by the historians of politics, economics and art, have
perhaps not yet yielded up all their secrets in the realm of cultural
life. It is only too easy to regard the medieval period as a prelude
and preparation for the modern world, and to consider the history of
Western civilization as that of an ordered progress towards the
material and intellectual perfection of man; within the medieval
centuries themselves it is equally inviting to discover a steady and
straightforward evolution from barbarism to enlightenment. Yet
even in constitutional, legal and economic history where such a view
is least misleading, the conception of an ordered and unhalting
progress, familiar to Victorian writers, must receive modification in
more than one respect; in the history of intellectual development
and the changes of religious sentiment any idea of an unfaltering
advance is wholly false.

This, perhaps, is particularly true in respect of the first great
flowering of culture in Western Europe which began shortly after
the year 1000. This age, save for its artistic life, had until recently
been unduly neglected by historians of thought. The great moral
and intellectual leaders—Anselm, Abelard and Bernard, and their
lesser contemporaries such as Peter the Venerable or John of
Salisbury—were indeed familiar figures, but they had been treated
only in isolation; and even during the last twenty years, when the
various schools of medieval philosophy and theology have at last
attracted something of the attention they deserve, there has been
a tendency to regard the eleventh and twelfth centuries as but a
dawning, a prelude, to the thirteenth, the 'greatest of centuries',
which opened with Innocent III and St Francis, which saw the

[1] [First published in *Studies*, vol. xxx (1941), pp. 43–58.]

earliest and purest masterpieces of Gothic architecture spring into being at Chartres, at Paris, at Salisbury and at Westminster, which embraced all the glories of scholastic theology, and which closed upon the year in which Dante, waking in the hillside forest, passed in imagination through the realms beyond the grave. In consequence, even those who, like the late Professor Haskins, have done most to extend our knowledge of the twelfth century or who, like Denifle and Ehrle and Mandonnet and Grabmann, have studied the growth of the universities, the origins of scholasticism and the pre-history of the friars—even these, when treating of earlier years, have given their attention to the seeds that were still to bear fruit rather than to the ripe ears of the summer's harvest. Yet to a careful observer the latter half of the twelfth century appears as a decline as well as a dawn, and as he looks back over the brilliant creative achievement of the hundred years between 1050 and 1150 and notes its deep and sympathetic humanism, which anticipated to an extraordinary degree much that is considered typical of the age of the Medici and of Erasmus, he becomes sensible of a very real change and declension between 1150 and 1200 which helped to make the culture of the thirteenth century, for all its intense speculative force and abiding power, less universal, less appealing and, in a word, less humane than what had gone before.

It is the purpose of these pages to direct attention to the earlier years, to the brilliant and original creative energies of the late eleventh century, and to the wide and sympathetic humanism which between 1050 and 1150 made its appearance for the first time in Western Europe. This first great re-birth—the proto-Renaissance as it has sometimes been called by historians of art and architecture—took place earlier than is generally supposed; the movement reached maturity between 1070 and 1130; it changed and declined in the fifty years between the death of St Bernard and the pontificate of Innocent III, and the intellectual atmosphere of the thirteenth century which followed, though it was in some ways more rare, more bracing and more subtle, lacked much of the kindly warmth and fragrant geniality of the past. The culture of the schools was, in fact—to drop the language of metaphor—without many of the elements that make a society fully humane, and that the preceding age had possessed for a time and subsequently lost.

The first stages of all great creative movements are hard to trace. The pre-Socratic philosophy, the sculpture which preceded the age of Ictinus and Pheidias, the constitutional legislation of Solon and Cleisthenes, though in many ways more original and admirable than the later developments in the golden age of Pericles, have but partially and recently been rescued from oblivion and reconstructed from the fragmentary monuments that survive. Similarly, few decades in European history are darker than those between 970 and 1030 in which the first generations of the new age were growing to maturity, and only those familiar with the writings and artistic achievements of the previous centuries can appreciate the change that then began. Consequently, there has been a general tendency to set the dawn too late—when, in fact, it is no longer dawn but a sunlight visible to all, at the end of the century, and in northern France. Yet it is clear that the real moving of the waters was in the decades immediately before the millennium, and in northern Italy.

That the schools of Italy, and in particular those of Lombardy, were the first by some thirty or forty years to develop new life, is clear not only from the calibre of their alumni but from the express testimony of contemporaries. How solid the literary training was may be seen from Peter Damian, who had himself been a master in the schools during early manhood. Damian after his conversion inveighed ceaselessly against secular learning and the poets, but in doing so he used, even in spite of himself, the very instruments against which his attack was turned; for all his writings are those of one who has not only been well trained in all the arts of expression and persuasion, but who is, besides, gifted with a real sense of the beauty of language in both prose and verse, and who is possessed of oratorical and poetic powers of a high order.

While the revival of intellectual life was a reality in Italy already between 1000 and 1020, the tide did not reach Touraine, Maine and the Ile de France till about the middle of the century; but, when it came, the spring there was even more brilliant than in Italy. Historians have often noted that while the Italian revival speedily developed into an intensive cultivation of civil and canon law, the French schools turned almost at once to dialectic. Neither of these developments was, properly speaking, humanistic in character; but whereas in Italy the purely literary education was soon abbreviated into a preparation for the study of law, in France, for almost a century, some of the monasteries and a group of schools, of which Chartres is the most important, kept to a purely literary culture, looking to philosophy, such as they knew it, for a general illumination of life and conduct rather than for a life-long intellectual pursuit and the key to the understanding of the deepest mysteries of the faith.

The three notes of the new humanism, which set the great men of the eleventh and twelfth centuries apart from those who had gone before and those who came after, may be put out as: first, a wide literary culture; next, a great and what in the realm of religious sentiment would be called a personal devotion to certain figures of the ancient world; and, finally, a high value set upon the individual, personal emotions, and upon the sharing of experiences and opinions within a small circle of friends.

Since the ideas and emotions thus shared were often of a religious or, at least, of a philosophical character, and since the writers were in every case men who wrote little or nothing that could be called pure poetry or secular literature, the fundamental humanism of their outlook has been overlooked or, at best, has been recognized only in those who, like John of Salisbury or Hildebert of Lavardin, were classical scholars of an eminence that would attract notice in any age. In one celebrated case, indeed, it has been obscured by the persistent attempts that have been made to romanticize the past in a totally unhistorical fashion. Nevertheless, the men of the early twelfth century, if they are regarded with attention and sympathy, show themselves as possessed of a rare delicacy of perception and warmth of feeling. It is to the sixteenth century, not to the thirteenth, that one looks for the spiritual kin of Anselm, of John of Salisbury, and of Héloïse.

The hall-mark of the revival, and the accomplishment that was most widely possessed by all whom it affected, was a capability of self-expression based on a sound training in grammar and a long and often loving study of the foremost Latin writers. The great ecclesiastics, one and all, who flourished between 1030 and 1180, could express themselves not only in fluent, correct and often elaborate language, but also in phrases and sentences of true dignity and eloquence. Peter Damian, John of Fécamp, Anselm, Abelard, Bernard, William of Malmesbury, Peter the Venerable, John of Salisbury—all these, and a hundred others, were masters of a flexible style and a wide vocabulary; they can be read with ease and pleasure; they are capable of giving adequate expression to their ideas and emotions, and do not fail to do so. Indeed, a student of the period comes to take this for granted—just as, in the use of contemporary manuscripts, he takes for granted the uniform, clear and beautiful script. Yet all this is in contrast alike to the age which had gone and to that which was to follow. Even the most learned men of the previous century, such as Abbo of Fleury, are narrow in the range of their ideas and awkward in their utterance; in England, among those who write Latin, the ideas are still less mature and the expression often laboured to the point of incomprehensibility. As for the century that came after, it may seem paradoxical to suggest that the great churchmen and thinkers of the age were inarticulate; yet those who have read in their entirety the correspondence of Adam Marsh, Robert Grosseteste and John Pecham, or who have endeavoured to pierce through to the personal experience and intimate characteristics of Albert the Great, Thomas Aquinas or Robert Kilwardby—to say nothing of the enigmatic Roger Bacon or Duns Scotus—will readily admit that in all the arts of language, in all manifestations of aesthetic feelings or personal emotions, in fine, in all the qualities of self-revealing intimacy, the great men of the thirteenth century are immeasurably poorer than their predecessors a hundred years before. And though the luminous and adequate expression of ideas and emotions does not of itself alone constitute a character which we call humanist—for neither Anselm nor Bernard, past masters of the craft of letters, are precisely humanists—yet the power of self-expression grounded upon, or at least reinforced by, a wide literary culture is a condition *sine qua non* of a humanist's growth.

The second trait of the humanism of the twelfth century was, it is suggested, a personal devotion to one or more of the great figures of the distant past. To look to the past as to an age wiser and more accomplished than the present, to imitate its masterpieces and hand on its doctrine, had been a common tendency in every country since the end of the Empire wherever any sort of enlightenment found scope. To rediscover and repeat the past had been the watchword of Charlemagne, as it was to be the watchword, differently understood, of Hildebrand, of the early fathers of Cîteaux and of the early promulgators of the newly revived civil and canon law. What was peculiar to many of the humanists, and at the same time a striking anticipation of the sentiment of leading circles in the later Italian Renaissance, was a reverence for the precepts and a conscious endeavour to imitate the lives of celebrated writers or characters of antiquity considered as human beings or sages, rather than precisely as saints or legislators. If we wish to see the more intimate aspects of this trait, we cannot perhaps do better than consider the ways of thinking and acting of three individuals, all endowed with eminent intellectual gifts and exquisite emotional sensibilities and all eager to give expression to a part, at least, of their experience.

Abelard, Héloïse and Ailred of Rievaulx are among the comparatively few personalities of the early twelfth century whose lives and words will continue to attract and move the minds of men throughout the ages. All three are, though in very different ways, essentially of their own period and remote from ours in the circumstances of their lives and in the cast of their thought. The problems, the catastrophe and the fate of Abelard and Héloïse are, quite as much as the austere monastic life of Ailred, typical of the twelfth century and remote from the experience of the twentieth. All three, on the other hand, by reason of their intense sensibility to emotions shared in some degree by all civilized mankind, and by reason also of a vivid power of self-expression, are not only of an age but for all time. With neither of the characteristics just mentioned are we concerned here, however, but with a third: the peculiar cast, that is, given to their thoughts and emotions by the humanistic training which they had undergone.

This appears, as has been said, most clearly in the reverence and devotion with which they regarded certain great figures of antiquity. With Abelard and Héloïse it is Cicero, Seneca, Lucan and St Jerome who are principally revered; with Ailred it is Cicero (at least in youth) and St Augustine. That in the case of all three the influence has a strong religious colour and that its primary object is a saint (for St Jerome is the exemplar to whom both Abelard and Héloïse turn most readily) does not affect its peculiar character. There is a world of difference between Abelard's attitude to Jerome or Ailred's to Augustine and the liturgical, quasi-feudal devotion of so many of their contemporaries to an apostle or an eponymous saint; equally, the reverence paid to the word of Seneca or Cicero is something personal, something coloured by emotion, and quite distinct from the immense but purely scientific authority given to Aristotle by St Thomas or to Cicero by the grammarians. It is Jerome the man, inveighing against marriage or counselling Paula and Eustochium; it is Cicero the friend and the philosopher as pictured (however un-historically) by the imagination of the twelfth century; it is 'my own Augustine' of Ailred, the Augustine who loved and was loved by others, the Augustine of the *Confessions*, not the Doctor of Grace. Yet we may see a difference between Ailred and the other two. He is a humanist to the extent that he chooses out and turns for counsel to those minds of the past who had felt and suffered and striven as he had. Abelard and Héloïse 'date' more clearly than Ailred because they, like their scholar-successors of the later Renaissance, take for masters and guides and models a few great men of the past chosen with a scholar's rather than with a Christian's mind, and set them on a pedestal, not indeed opposed to that on which Christ and His saints stand, but without direct reference to revealed, supernatural religion. Both, when coming to closest grips with their own tragic and most real and keenly felt problems, find their securest counsel and stay in the Stoics of the Empire—Seneca, Persius and Lucan—and in the letters of Jerome. Héloïse, indeed, who was at once the more absolute and final in her self-surrender and the one less susceptible of any spiritual influence, frankly turned for a model to Lucan and his Cornelia at the moment when she devoted herself irrevocably to the life for which she had no spiritual vocation. The passage in which Abelard describes this crisis is so vivid as to deserve quotation in full:

And she, as I remember well, when many full of sympathy for her youth were vainly endeavouring to deter her from submission to the monastic Rule as though it were an unbearable punishment—she, I say, breaking out as best she could amid her tears into Cornelia's famous lament, cried aloud: 'O most renowned of husbands! O thou deemed unworthy of my bed! Had fortune, then, power thus far over such a one as thee? Why did I marry so rashly above my star, only to make him unhappy? Accept from me the penalty which I pay of my free choice.' And with these words she hastened to the altar, and took from it the veil blessed by the bishop, and before all bound herself with the monastic vows.

It is hard to conceive a scene less characteristic than this of the monastic life of the twelfth century as commonly pictured: the despairing self-immolation of Héloïse, with the Stoic's cold phrases ringing in her ears, would be more in character in a heroine of Corneille or in some tragic story of a noble Roman house of the fifteenth century.

The third trait common to Abelard, Héloïse and Ailred, though again issuing in very different courses of action, is the importance which all attached to their personal emotions. With Abelard the crisis came comparatively late in life, when he was near his fortieth year. Previously, we may suppose, the vivid interests and brilliant successes of his intellectual life had kept all else suppressed; for the deterioration of character, due to wealth and fame, to which he attributed his fall, may supply a moral explanation, but does not of itself reveal the psychological background of the drama. In any case, his passion ran a not unusual course, though the genius of the man and the tragical *dénouement* of the affair have to some extent sublimated it in the eyes of posterity. From frank sensuality he rose to a deeper, if still wholly selfish, emotion; self-centred as he was, he must give his every mood expression (for in this, as in much else, he resembled a Newman or a Cicero), and the most acute dialectician of the schools, the successful rival of William of Champeaux and Anselm of Laon, became a singer of love lyrics which by their words and melody carried the name of Héloïse beyond the barriers of land

and sea. All have perished, but when we read the hymns which Abelard wrote in a still later phase, we are not disposed to accuse of partiality the judgement passed upon his earlier verses by the one who was the theme of their praise.

Abelard's love for Héloïse long remained selfish; the sacrifices which it entailed were, as he himself pointed out somewhat coldly, the unwilled consequences and punishments of his fault, not a willing gift of self-surrender. Only when he had become a monk and a priest and was, partially at least, 'converted' to the religious life, did his affection for Héloïse show itself in actions inspired by a genuine and selfless devotion. Indeed, it is by reason of the care shown by this strange ex-abbot for his wife who still more strangely found herself abbess, rather than by the earlier phases of his emotional drama, that Abelard stands among the humanists, in contrast to the more conventional religious sentiments of his day.

Héloïse, on the other hand, at once greater and not so great as her lover, gave all in a very real sense from the beginning. With her, motives of the intellectual order meant nothing, and those of the spiritual order little more. Héloïse in truth, so far as her own deepest utterances go, has nothing of the Christian in her. What renders her unique and gives her nobility and even sublimity is the combination of exceptional mental power and unshakable resolve with the most complete and voluntary self-sacrifice—not, indeed, the surrender of her own will and life to God or to any ethical demand, but the surrender of herself in totality to another. Clinging to this sacrifice with an intensity worthy of a heroine of Scandinavian legend—and indeed the blood of the pagan North may well have flowed in her veins—she found her model not in any saint of the Christian or even of the Hebrew centuries, but in the haughty and despairing women of ancient Rome, as they were depicted by the Stoic poet.

The life story of St Ailred, when compared with those of Abelard and Héloïse, may have appeared tranquil enough to those who saw the distinguished abbot of the Yorkshire Rievaulx only on his travels up and down England or at his appearances at court. Yet in his life's journey, too, as in that of 'his' Augustine, the heart had shared the traces with the head and if, here also like Augustine, he had found a final peace where both head and heart might rest secure, he underwent no violent change of character and retained to the end his fresh, warm, spontaneous readiness to give and to receive love—a love transmuted into a wholly benevolent and unselfish goodwill, embracing all who would accept it, yet having for each the delicate individuality of a mother's love, to which indeed his biographer, writing half a century before St Francis had made the expression familiar, did not hesitate to compare it.

St Augustine the thinker, the preacher and the theologian, had dominated and saturated the intellectual life of the West to a degree which even now is not, perhaps, sufficiently realized; Augustine 'the man', the Augustine of Monica and the *Confessions*, appears but rarely. It is the peculiar characteristic of Ailred that he was, until Petrarch's day, almost the only one to approach his Augustine through the *Confessions*, to recognize in him a fellowship of deep feeling, and to look to him as a predecessor and a guide in his own pilgrimage. To him, as to his illustrious exemplar, the April days of his boyhood, days of shine and shower in a Northumbrian school where he had for fellow and friend the Prince Henry, son of King David of Scotland, were an abiding memory, rich in moulding influence.

When I was still a boy at school [wrote Ailred later at Rievaulx], and took great delight in the charm of the companionship of those around me, it seemed good to me to give myself up unreservedly to my heart's leading and to dedicate myself to friendship. Nothing to me seemed more delightful, more sweet, or more profitable than to love and to be loved.

As Augustine had been stung to thought by Cicero, so Ailred, reading the Roman orator's *De Amicitia*, was humiliated at the contrast between his own impulsive, dominating emotions and the calm dignity, as it seemed to him, of Cicero's judgements, and though he had none of Augustine's intellectual crises, he found at the court of King David of Scotland, where he held for a time official rank, ties of ambition and affection not dissimilar to those which had held the great African shackled. When he describes his struggle to us, he falls naturally into the very rhythm of the *Confessions*, though the sincerity of personal experience is all his own.

When once he had found his spiritual home at Rievaulx, Ailred's great and in some ways unique gifts of mind and soul found full scope. To the visitor of today, who surveys the white ruins across the lawns and foliage of their exquisite setting, the past inevitably takes shape in a vision of the hard, sparing life of Cîteaux, shut out for ever from the world. The Rievaulx of St William, St Waldef and St Ailred had indeed an observant, austere and deeply spiritual life, but perhaps no greater surprise in all the varied life of the twelfth century awaits the student familiar only with feudalism, Domesday and the crusades than his first glimpse of the fermenting life at Rievaulx in its secluded dale—an overflowing household of more than a hundred monks and five hundred lay brothers, with its centre of acute intellectual debate and its interplay of eager and ardent personalities. Here indeed, far from the familiar centres of European life, is the quintessence of the humanism of the twelfth century; Ailred, the novice-master and teacher, surrounded by a small group of finely educated young minds absorbed in living debates—Ailred, the friend and guide, learning recollection and true charity from his contact with others—Ailred the abbot, in middle age and in premature old age brought on by long and sharp illness, the centre of an ever shifting gathering of his sons to whom he, with his old charm intensified by suffering and sanctity, was all things to all, now discussing the nature of the soul in a dialogue left unfinished at his death, now counselling an illiterate lay-brother with equal care, while around him the fixed life of choir and farm-work, of changeless routine and sparing diet, went on unchanged.

We his monks were around him [writes Walter Daniel of his last days on earth], now twelve in number, now twenty, now forty, now even a hundred, for he who loved us all was thus loved exceedingly by us in return...and he considered it his greatest happiness that he should be thus loved. No one ever said to us 'Depart, be off, do not touch your abbot's bed', but stepping upon his pallet or sitting upon it we spoke with him as a child speaks with its mother.

And so he died, surrounded by his monks, lying on the sackcloth and ashes of the monastic custumal, with his eyes upon the crucifix on the wall.

26

The familiarity of all educated men of the age with the master-pieces of Latin literature has often been remarked upon. The mention of Héloïse touches upon another aspect of this renaissance: the share, that is, of women in the higher culture of the day. Héloïse, indeed, was something of a prodigy, but nowhere is there any suggestion that her uncle, Fulbert, was acting in an eccentric or even in an unconventional manner when he decided to give his niece a perfect education in letters. Nor did she stand wholly alone. It may not be easy to point to individual *bas bleus* in Paris or even in the convents of France in general, but in England there was no lack of them. The daughter of Margaret of Scotland, the future Queen Maud, was given a thorough literary education at Romsey; Shaftes-bury, a little later, sheltered Marie de France, and Muriel of Wilton was not the only other poetess in England, as is shown by the numerous copies of Latin verses attached by the convents of women to the bead-rolls of exalted personages. These cloistered elegists, however, scarcely differ in kind from their sisters who, four hundred years before, had corresponded with St Boniface; Héloïse, alike in her single-minded enthusiasm, in her real literary powers, and in her devoted, even pedantic reverence for her classical models, is a true predecessor of Camilla Rucellai, Margaret Roper and Lady Jane Grey; to her, as to these, Dorothea in George Eliot's novel would have looked with admiration.

Héloïse may well have outdistanced all rivals of her own sex. In deploring the lack of letters among men, however, Peter the Venerable, in his celebrated letter to the widowed abbess, is using the language of exaggeration, for no one acquainted with the litera-ture of the age can be unaware of the wide familiarity shown by so many with Latin literature. Ailred of Rievaulx can assume a familiarity with Cicero's *De Amicitia* as a matter of course in a young Cistercian of his abbey; quotations from the poets are common in almost all the more elaborate chronicles and letters of the period; the greatest humanists, such as Hildebert of Lavardin, Abelard and John of Salisbury, quote aptly and copiously from a very wide range of Latin poetry. Rarely, perhaps, are the poets quoted solely on account of the intrinsic beauty of their words; Abelard, however, and John of Salisbury often give evidence of their appreciation of the purely poetic. For most the favourite authors are the rhetoricians and satirists of the Silver Age and the learned, artificial poets of the later Gallo-Roman culture. Though Virgil has pride of place, it may be suggested that even he may appear rhetorical to a superficial and unintuitive mind; Horace, significantly enough, is often quoted from the *Satires* and *Epistles*, rarely from the *Odes*—their beauty, it may be, was too sophisticated and too exquisite to be appreciated, their urbanity too unfamiliar, and their pagan morality and religion too obvious. For similar reasons Tibullus and Propertius rarely occur, and scarcity of manuscripts is sufficient of itself to account for unfamiliarity with Lucretius and Catullus. Juvenal, on the other hand, Lucan and the difficult Persius were, relatively speaking, more familiar to the contemporaries of Abelard than to classical scholars of today.

Nothing, perhaps, shows both the reality and the extent of the training on classical models than the facility with which numbers were able to compose sets of perfectly correct Latin verses, and that not only in hexameters and elegiacs, but in the lyric metres used by Horace and Catullus. That the inhabitants of nunneries in Wessex should have been able to write passable elegiacs, and that it should have seemed natural to a monk when composing a saint's life to break without warning or apparent reason into alcaics, hendeca-syllabics and the still more elaborate iambic and trochaic metres, are phenomena of the late eleventh century to which it would be hard to find a parallel save in the late fifteenth or early sixteenth. That only a few—a Peter Damian, an Abelard, a Hildebert—should have attained real poetry in their compositions should be no occasion for wonder; the rest fail where the most felicitous verses of a Jebb, of a Calverley, and even of a Milton fail; the remarkable fact is that so many had achieved a mastery of the language and the metre without any aid from a Gradus or dictionary. Occasionally, indeed, the level of true poetry is attained, together with perfect felicity of vocabulary; Peter Damian's Sapphic hymns to St Benedict, like the earlier hymn to the Baptist, *Ut queant laxis*, are supreme in their kind, and it would be difficult for a scholar, familiar only with ancient Latin literature, to assign their composition to the eleventh rather than to the sixth or the sixteenth century. More often, however, the nearest approach to true poetry is made in the simpler accentual metres and the lyrics that verge upon the vernacular.

The decline of this humanism, like its rise, was comparatively rapid. The phase of sentiment we are considering touched its apogee between the rise of Hildebert of Lavardin and the central years of the literary life of John of Salisbury. With Peter of Blois the decline is beginning, and though in England there was something of a time-lag, the end was reached with Walter Map, Gerald of Wales and their circle; Gerald, indeed, lived on into another world and lamented the change. By the death of King John the transformation was complete. The great figures of the early thirteenth century, whether thinkers or administrators, are all but inarticulate when not in their schools or chanceries. It is from the class of the unlettered, from a Francis of Assisi or a Joinville, that the clearest utterances come, 'the earliest pipe of half-awakened birds', heralding another dawn in Europe. Literary, philosophical, scholarly humanism was dead, and it is significant that the supreme and balanced art, the Pheidian assurance and repose of the sculptures of Chartres, of Wells, of Amiens and of Rheims, was the expression of life as seen, not by a Leonardo or a Michelangelo, but by unlettered handicraftsmen living wholly in the present and wholly ignorant of the literature and culture of the past.

This is not to say that the new age owed no debt, paid no homage, to the past. In one sense the debt of no century had been heavier; for, as recent scholarship has shown, a larger and larger portion of the corpus of Aristotelian writings and numerous dialogues of Plato and Greek philosophers of the Empire were becoming familiar to the West, together with works of science, Greek and Arabian. St Thomas rests upon Aristotle, 'the Philosopher', more completely and unreservedly than does Abelard upon Augustine or Jerome or Seneca; and, as regards language, all metal is tested upon the touchstone of Cicero. Plato, Aristotle and Augustine, in their various ways, are not merely the foundations of the fabric of scholasticism; they are its *materia prima*, the very medium in which

Aquinas works. Yet scholars of today who, when rightly demonstrating the traditional and wholly European character of medieval culture, emphasize the debt of the schoolmen to the ancients, may perhaps mislead those familiar only with modern history when they speak of the humanism, or of the classical tradition, of the great scholastics. The attitude of St Thomas towards the masters of the past differs by a whole heaven from that of Abelard and Ailred, as it does from that of Erasmus and More. The humanists, though living in times so very different from those of Greece and Rome, scrutinize the lives and emotions of the ancients, imitate their modes of expression and seek to reach the heart of their thought by long and sympathetic examination; the schoolmen revere the past no less deeply, but it is the external, visible fabric of thought, the purely intellectual, impersonal element that they absorb, and so far from submitting themselves to its moulding influence, they adapt it without hesitation to serve a wholly new system of philosophy, an utterly different *Weltanschauung*. To the schoolmen the personalities, the emotions, the external vicissitudes of the lives of Aristotle and Augustine meant nothing; the skeleton of their thought was all in all. To Ailred and to Héloïse, as to the contemporaries of Cosimo de' Medici, the joy and anguish of an Augustine or a Cornelia were a consolation and a light; they turned to them, and to the poets of the past, for guidance and sympathy. 'Then 'twas the Roman, now 'tis I.' So the humanists, but never the schoolmen, found strength in a community of feeling with those who, centuries before, had trodden the same path, and it is this consciousness of the unchanging mind of man that divides the culture of the first Renaissance from the more familiar culture of the later Middle Age.

3

SAINT BERNARD OF CLAIRVAUX:
1090–1153[1]

On 20 August of this year the Catholic world will celebrate the eighth centenary of the death of St Bernard. The occasion touches most nearly those who wear the white habit of Cîteaux, and those who are the saint's fellow-countrymen of Burgundy. There are to be exhibitions and conferences at Dijon, and an ambitious programme of editorial and biographical work has been drawn up to mark the year. But St Bernard, long before he received the title of Doctor of the Church, had become part of the common inheritance of the Church's children. A majority, perhaps even the great majority, of canonized saints are wholly unknown outside a region or a religious family; others have a world-wide clientele, but only among theologians or the devout; a few are figures in world history, whose personality and actions moulded the life of their day and attract the notice of all who read of the past. In this last group, and not among its shadows, stands St Bernard. He is indeed there on more than one title. As a great religious statesman, as the leader and spokesman of a celebrated order, as a theologian, and as a writer and speaker of genius he can make his claim.

To the historian he is perhaps most remarkable for his achievement on the stage of Church politics. It is hard to name any other, not occupying the chair of St Peter—St Athanasius is the only possible rival—who so determined the policy and the fortunes of the Church as he. He confirmed one pope and instructed another; he confounded anti-popes and revolutionaries; he put down dynasts from their seats in Church and state; he determined the agenda at Councils; he sent Christendom on a crusade. He challenged and engaged single-handed the greatest monastic confedera-

[1] [This article, written in 1953 in commemoration of the eighth centenary of the death of St Bernard, was published in *The Dublin Review*, vol. CCXXVII, pp. 104–21.]

tion that the Western Church had seen, and the acutest mind that the new dialectic had tempered. And all the time he was drawing to his abbey of Clairvaux, and sending as colonists all over Europe, a *corps d'élite* that counted among its numbers a pope, cardinals, bishops, and saints not a few. Had he been no more than a Cistercian abbot, his fame would have been secure. When, at the age of twenty-two and in the year 1112, he arrived at the gates of Cîteaux as a postulant αὐτὸς τριακοστός—with twenty-nine relatives whom he had won to his ideal—the new abbey of Cîteaux, to outward sight, was on the point of foundering. Poverty, austerity and disease had killed many and deterred more. With Bernard's arrival it was as if a great spring had been tapped. When he died the progeny of Cîteaux numbered 339 houses, and his own abbey of Clairvaux had 68 daughters and 159 lineal descendants. As for the numbers of their monks, who shall tell them? Bernard's magnetism was indeed irresistible. He could launch armies on the road to Jerusalem, and call legions to the cloister. Wherever he went, we are told, mothers feared for their sons, and brides for their husbands, as they were to do centuries later at the passage of Napoleon. The whole world, it was said, was turning into Cîteaux.

The spiritual teaching of St Bernard has never been neglected by the monastic order, and his treatises have throughout the centuries given joy to the city of God, but the historical personality of the saint has been strangely neglected by scholars and historians almost to our own day. Even now no fully satisfactory biography, no adequate critical edition of his works, exists. The classical *Life* of Vacandard, supplemented by articles in the great French *Dictionnaires*, is still indispensable, but, even apart from the precisions which every year has added to the story, it somehow fails to present the living Bernard. A *Life* to end all other *Lives* is even now in the making, but can any *Life* be adequate? A biographer of Bernard might well feel that had he a hundred tongues, a hundred mouths and a voice of iron, he could not comprehend all in his pages. A *Life* of Bernard becomes almost insensibly a history of Europe, in which dates and facts and unfamiliar names and episodes come crowding in till the sight of the wood is lost behind the endless trees.

Nor have the biographers with tightened rein fared better. St Bernard, whose own voice could kindle a fire of desire or shatter an opposing adversary, has emerged a pale shadow from the hands of apologists and expositors, and has suffered from the misunderstanding and sheer ignorance of historians. And, although we have so many of his own words, and a chain of early biographies, all are, with scarcely an exception, too studied and too polished to give us those intimate incidents and sayings that make such unique records of Eadmer's *Life of Anselm* and the early *Lives* of St Francis.

What was it in St Bernard that made him the towering figure that he was? Circumstances are no explanation of genius, but they may help it to expand, and undoubtedly one reason of St Bernard's influence was his long life as master of himself and in high place. Many saints—an Augustine, a Dominic, a Teresa, a Vincent—have spent many years or decades of their lives in finding their salvation or their vocation; others—a Gabriel or a Thérèse—have been made perfect in short space. For St Bernard the decisive struggle was over before he came to Cîteaux; he was abbot at twenty-five, and for almost forty years he could act and speak as the father of an immense and saintly family. Then, the age and the man were exactly matched. The tide of reform was still running strongly, and with all the anarchy and evils of the time there were everywhere some men at least in high office who were united in their aims. Moreover, the monastic ideal was acknowledged by the whole of western Christendom; the monastic life seemed to most the one and only ideal Christian life. Finally, Bernard was at the heart of the greatest monastic revival the West had ever seen; in his later years he had his marshals, his garrisons, his storm-troops everywhere. With one of his sons in the chair of Peter, and others in sees from York to the Mediterranean, he was at the centre of a network which he could use for intelligence, for propaganda and for execution.

Every human personality is unique, and the richer and deeper the personality, the more is it distinguished from all others. Among the saints, *ex hypothesi* the most fully developed of all human beings, the variety is infinite. Nor can the historian, whom even the play of

33

motive eludes, catch the workings of grace. Nevertheless, among the saints two broad classes appear. There are those who are roused and raised from a life of sin or mediocrity to sanctity, the so-called 'twice-born', such as St Paul and St Augustine, and there are those whose life resembles, all due proportions guarded, those of Our Lady or St John the Baptist; they seem sealed and set apart to a dedicated life from the waters of baptism. With the former we can often watch the struggle between good and evil, with the latter we can only guess how they were called and strengthened to accept and not to fail, to co-operate and to receive, as wave after wave of grace came upon them. St Bernard was clearly of this latter sort. From childhood, from infancy, he was a privileged soul. There is no hint, either in his writings or in his biographies, that he had ever closed his eyes to the light or slipped back. There was no great moral or psychological crisis in his youth. When he hesitated for a few months on the threshold of manhood, the choice was not between good and evil, God and the world, but between a life of letters and a life of solitude. Even then the hesitation was brief. For the rest his life, so far as we can observe it, was a series of responses to the demand for a love exclusive and heroic, and because such a love of God exceeds our experience and strains our sympathies, biographers of the saints take refuge either in silence or devotional exclamations. Moreover, though he wrote so much and was such an artist in words, and though in some of his sermons he professedly speaks of himself, Bernard is in a sense an extrovert. He was not interested in his own past and his own growth, as were Augustine, Ailred and the two Teresas. Even when he speaks of himself it is, so to say, Bernard speaking of the historical Bernard rather than a soul revealing itself.

It is for this reason, perhaps, that for the many who admire St Bernard, either as a teacher or as a leader, or as a master of words and worker of wonders, there are few who have for him that personal love that the four saints just mentioned can evoke. With them we feel that we have a spark of kinship, however remote; they would understand and counsel us. With Bernard it is not so. Yet this is not the true picture of him. Bernard could be all things to all men; his biographer tells us not only that his counsel was sought, by letter and face to face, all over Christendom, but that he was happiest and most himself in the daily relations with his monks. The same biographer, who knew him well, goes on to say that with his monks he was not only most himself, but that he used a simplicity of intercourse with them which the world did not know,

> Silent silver lights and darks undreamed of,
> Which we, too, shall never know in this life.

Bernard's feats of endurance and the interminable list of his wonders fill almost all the space in his biographies that is not given to his achievements as founder of Clairvaux and her many daughters, as champion of the Church, and as the hammer of heretics. Bernard the friend, even Bernard the father in God, are lost. More strangely still, Bernard's real fortitude is lost also; he becomes a champion whose victories are assured by his skill and prowess in arms. Yet fortitude, both in secret and *in facie ecclesiae*, is perhaps the most characteristic of all his virtues. Every saint is what he is through charity alone, but in every human personality some characteristics are more obvious than others. In Bernard it is his fortitude, his utter fearlessness. Fortitude is as essential a part of the Christian character as is humility; both in the last resort spring from a love of God which obliterates human apprehensions and values; but the fortitude of many saints of recent times has been shown only in secret to a few and in the private relationships of life. Bernard's was shown pre-eminently in his external dealings with men. Here again his biographers have done him a disservice. They show him at war only with open heresy and vice and tyranny. In fact, he denounced and fought against falsehood, worldliness and weakness wherever he saw them, however revered or exalted might be the object of his attack. A more faithful servant of the pope could not be found, but neither could one be found who had a clearer sense of the duties and obligations of that sublime office. Bernard did not hesitate to tell a pope what he should do, and what he should have done; he did not hesitate to tell him that he had neglected his duty. Biographers are apt to give the impression that only simoniacs and interlopers were Bernard's targets. In fact, he did not hesitate to thwart, denounce and uproot bishops who to the eyes of their contemporaries were passable, even respectable, or at least were secure and powerful. If he was convinced that a bishop or an abbot or a community was bad, he said so. Like the man in the nonsense rhyme, he said it very loud and clear, and went on saying it. He did not mince his words or pull his punches. If he was persuaded that the great Henry of Winchester, legate of the Apostolic See and brother of a king, disgraced his high office and his monastic profession by his ambition and his riches, he called him, in well chosen scriptural phrases, a whore and a wizard. The bishop's protégé, the archbishop of York, was, he said, an idol set up in the temple of the Lord. If authority was remiss in acting or punishing, Bernard lashed authority and gave it no rest till, like the judge in the parable, as if fearful of physical violence, it was driven to act. But behind the fire and the eloquence the courage was not that of a knight errant, still less that of a Quixote; it was the fortitude of Christ, despised as a Galilean and unlettered in the law, challenging and accusing the priests and lawyers because they set human respect and the traditions of men before the law of God; it was a fortitude that owed its clear sight of God's truth to a purity won in the secret conflict with pain and fatigue and physical illness.

The legendary austerity, the reputation for drastic and intolerant action, and the ceaseless activity of Bernard, suggest to the casual reader an iron constitution and physical powers that answered every call made upon them. Assuredly he came of a race of fighters, and had imposed his leadership upon the whole family while yet a young man in the world; he was tall and handsome as a youth, with a charm and grace of manner, and a gaiety which he never lost. But from his early years in the monastery, whether from unhealthy food, or excessive fasting, or from some cause which would elude medical science today as it did then, his health broke down utterly and never mended. For the whole of his adult life he was an invalid, brought more than once or twice to the edge of the grave. His earliest and most discerning biographer, William of St Thierry, who spoke from long and loving observation, gives a number of realistic details which are hardly susceptible of presentation in English, but which establish beyond all doubt the painful and humiliating symptoms which made

Bernard a burden to others as well as himself. During the greater part of his life his stomach repeatedly rejected all solid food. For a whole year in his early manhood as abbot he was forced to live apart from his monks in a hut because his physical presence was unbearable in choir or at table. He was, after his first years at Clairvaux, too weak to take part in any manual work; even walking exhausted him; and to his lifelong friends the characteristic memory was of a Bernard seated, emaciated and in pain. It was in such circumstances, which to most would seem an excuse for self-indulgence, self-pity and inertia, that Bernard guided his monks, made his foundations, wrote his treatises and journeyed across the Alps.

The influence of Bernard upon the Cistercian order was great and lasting; in the strictest sense of the words, it would be impossible to exaggerate it. His first arrival with his platoon of recruits revived and rejuvenated an abbey that was moribund in all but soul, and his subsequent sanctity and fame and multifarious activities gave to Clairvaux and the whole order an attraction and a publicity without parallel. But influence and the stimulation of recruitment, however phenomenal, are not the same as creative wisdom. By a comprehensible, but none the less regrettable process St Bernard, from being the great apologist and propagator of the order, came to be regarded as its patron, and when, in the later Middle Ages, it became fashionable for orders to take their name from their patron, the white monks were often called Bernardines. It was only a step further for men of letters and uninformed historians to speak of Bernard as the founder of the order.

Nothing could be further from the truth. Cîteaux, with its ideals and its customs and uses, was in existence before Bernard, and though the Charter of Charity was written down when he was already a monk, it owed nothing to him. Indeed, if we could see the workings of God's Providence, we might find that it was the hidden sanctity of the first fathers of Cîteaux that won for Bernard the gifts of grace that led him to their gates.

And yet in a sense Bernard did become the founder of the Cistercian order, for without directly desiring or intending it, he changed its character and destiny. Had Bernard never lived it is humanly possible that Cîteaux might have died; it is more probable that it would have remained, like Camaldoli or the Chartreuse, a small body of the spiritual *élite*. As it was, it became a great net, having within it all manner of fishes. Nor was this all. The first fathers had fled from the world, asking only to serve God and to be unknown. Bernard, at first by his controversy with the old monasticism and later by his reforming activity, made the Cistercians self-conscious and, in a sense, exploited them. Finally, his emergence as the leader of reform, as the most eminent preacher in Europe and as a writer of world-wide fame, destroyed for ever the primitive tradition of silence and obscurity. Bernard did indeed attack the learning of this world with all his force, but he used many of the resources of learning, and all the resources of literary art, in so doing. It was appropriate, but it was also one of Clio's ironies, that the great college of the white monks at Paris should bear his name.

The spirit of Cîteaux, and of Bernard himself, has often been regarded as puritanical. In part this is due to a single writing of Bernard's, perhaps the best known of all, his Apology to William of St Thierry. In part, also, it may be due to the identification often made of the spirit of Cîteaux with that of La Trappe in the days of de Rancé. Certainly there can be no doubt of the austerity and of the lack of all comfort and external grace and beauty in the monastery of St Stephen Harding. Even St Bernard shows little sign that music or poetry or even the beauty of nature were so deeply a part of his natural consciousness as they were, let us say, of the natural consciousness of St John of the Cross and St Francis of Sales. The well-known stories of his recollection, of his ignorance that he had passed by the waters of the Lake of Geneva within sight of the aiguilles of Mont Blanc need not provoke our indignation as they have provoked some historians—for what beauty can be even a reflexion of the Divine beauty present to the transluminous faith of a saint?—but we may perhaps be allowed to think that Bernard could never have described the beauties of the Alpine valleys in the exquisite phrases of the *Spiritual Canticle*. His adventures in musical reform were not his happiest achievement; and when it came to the delights of human learning and speculation, who could denounce them better? Yet here we touch what is perhaps the greatest paradox in St Bernard. For he is throughout, and in every line that he wrote, the great stylist, and his style is not that of an artless simplicity but full of the highest art of rhetoric. St Bernard persuades, not like St Thomas, by the luminous clarity of his exposition, or like St John of the Cross, by the selfless logic of his doctrine, but by arousing our excitement and our emotions, as he roused the apathetic knights at Vézelay. The torrent of his eloquence, to adapt the simile of the ancient critic, sweeps down the river bed, bearing with it stones and trees and our reluctant selves in its wake. Every line is charged with rhetoric; it is that flash of colour, that thrill of daring, that makes the style of St Bernard so individual—so inimitable, one would say, were it not that those nearest him succeeded so well in catching its echoes. This it is that makes Bernard one of the greatest orators of all time, the kin, if not the peer, of Demosthenes, of Cicero and of Tertullian. Even the greatest of stylists might well shun the ordeal of seeing fragments of their writings, cut up by blessings and responsories, exposed to the hazards of recitation in the breviary, yet how many readers of the breviary, inured to Jerome and Gregory and even Augustine himself, have suddenly found their wandering attention held by a new voice, and have recognized the accents of Bernard! M. Gilson, with his customary felicity of phrase, has said that Bernard left all except his mind—and what a mind!—before the portals of Cîteaux. But this is not the whole answer. No one would demand of a saint, be he never so austere, that his style should be impure or dull. Nor need sublimity and passion be banned. In both Old and New Testament there is enough of both, and enough even of that rare beauty that is poetry. But poetry and passion and sublimity may be, and often are, simple and direct, appealing to the deepest centre of the mind. Rhetoric has always an element of unreality; it persuades where it cannot prove; it sways by delight, when truth is not enough; it exaggerates; it colours. It is not easy to understand how a mind purified from all sensual images could use the colours of rhetoric. Even St Augustine, a rhetor by training and profession, uses indeed the forms of rhetoric to the end, but his later writings are rarely rhetorical in spirit. Bernard, on the other hand, is an orator even when he is most personal and sincere, as in the lament for his brother. Compared with the laments for Monica and for Nebridius those pages seem surely to smell of the lamp.

This feeling, it seems, is not merely a subjective one. An interesting, and in a sense disquieting, discovery of recent Bernardine criticism is that the form in which many, if not all, of the sermons and letters of St Bernard have come down to us is not by any manner of means the original one. Between the first delivery and the publication to the world the text was carefully worked over, roughnesses were smoothed out, phrases were given polish and point, and an additional touch of colour was laid on here and there. Often it was one of the saint's intimate companions, acting as his secretary, who thus brightened the master's work and gave it some of those last touches that an unsuspecting reader might think most characteristic of Bernard. This is not the picture we had of the abbot of Clairvaux, writing hurriedly in the prison-like cell beneath the day-stairs, but it is perhaps a glimpse that brings us very near to the real Bernard, more complex than we had supposed. However that may be, and whoever may have given the last rub to the metal, the genius of the master remains. St Bernard, in an age of literary imitation, created and developed a new style capable of adorning topics and conveying emotions neglected by his predecessors and contemporaries. It is a remarkable fact that Bernard is no more Augustinian in style than he is in thought. While Anselm and John of Fécamp and Ailred and many another had so steeped themselves in Augustine that they seem like a prolongation of his personality, so that some of their writings did in fact traverse the Middle Ages under his name, and while even William of St Thierry has numberless echoes of Augustine in his phrases and rhythm, Bernard, for all the similarity of subject matter, created a new style. No letter, no treatise of his, could ever be mistaken for Augustine; and his own style, while remaining pure, is so individual that no writer, save his secretaries and immediate disciples, has ever recaptured it and made it his own.

Much in recent years has been written of the renaissance and the humanism of the twelfth century. Real humanism there was indeed, both of the literary and philosophical kind, of which John of Salisbury and the masters of the school of Chartres are instances, and of the more elusive personal kind, seen in the preoccupation with self-expression, and with an individual's own destiny and emotions, and found in one form in the long drama of Abelard and Héloïse, and in another in the dialogues of Ailred of Rievaulx and many another writer of biography or autobiography. In the last analysis this humanism is an attitude of mind, a mental climate, intangible and yet recognizable, that links the twelfth century with the ages of Augustine and of Petrarch, but not with the ages of Gregory the Great and of Aquinas. To historians of the last generation it would have seemed paradoxical to describe Bernard, the ascetic, the puritan, the inquisitor, the enemy of Abelard, as a humanist. Yet so far as it is lawful to assign a great saint to this or that purely human group, Bernard is a humanist. No one who did not, on the purely human level, assign a value to emotion and feel the need for self-expression, could have composed Bernard's lament for his brother, or have expressed his own deepest feelings and experiences so frankly, and yet with such art, as did Bernard in the Sermons on the Canticle.

He is also a humanist of letters. Whoever may have been the unknown masters of the young Bernard at Châtillon-sur-Seine, their lessons were not wasted. Bernard was an *écrivain de race*, but the form of his writings was derived from his early training. Bernard indeed, as we have seen, did what no other writer of his age succeeded in doing. He created a new Latin style. His sentences lack altogether that sinuous, lilting rhythm so characteristic of Augustine's early writings. Bernard's Latin is far more nervous, more idiomatic; he has a wider vocabulary and relies upon idioms and individual phrases rather than upon the short sentences, the abrupt stops, and the repetition of phrases in themselves neutral that are so characteristic of Augustine. Bernard is a Ciceronian, not only in the sense that his thought and even his latest and deepest theological expressions owe, as M. Gilson has shown, a debt to Cicero, but also in the sense that his Latin, while lacking the intricate and masterly periods of the Roman, yet uses the words and expressions of the Ciceronian age far more than does Augustine's, and has far fewer reminiscences of Virgil and the satirists than has the Latin of John of Salisbury. And if John shows a greater virtuosity and a closer texture, the result of long exercise in a more exacting technique, Bernard excels him in clarity and directness, and, when need arises, in striking power.

Bernard does not, indeed, altogether neglect the poets. Occasional unexpected reminiscences occur, and have even crept into the breviary. But what others achieve by means of quotation from the poets, Bernard achieves by his use of Scripture. An intimate knowledge of every part of the Bible, and an ability to quote the inspired books constantly and with an appositeness that is often startling, has never been a test for distinguishing one saint from another. Augustine, Anselm, Aquinas and John of the Cross have nothing to learn from St Bernard here. Where Bernard is unique is in the daring and exquisite poetic felicity of his quotations; this is indeed a stylistic property of his which is almost a mannerism, so that it could be, and was in fact, imitated by his admirers. Bernard uses a phrase or word of Scripture as Addison or Newman might use one of Shakespeare or Milton—sometimes for its beauty, sometimes with irony or scorn, sometimes to startle the reader into attention, sometimes to hint at a comparison, sometimes to point a contrast. A whole essay in style could be written on this point alone.

Bernard has been called the last of the Fathers. The title is not inapt, if it is understood to mean that he is the last theologian of the first rank—at least till the age of St François de Sales—to treat points of doctrine great and small in self-contained monographs written in a meditative and discursive manner, without the direct appeal to logic and philosophy, and still more without the technical apparatus of question and resolution and schematic arrangement, that marks in greater or less degree all theological writing from Anselm onwards. Bernard was indeed not the last to write like this; there were lesser men, his followers and imitators, for almost a century longer, but Bernard was the last great anti-scholastic, and the form in which his works were written, comprehensible to all in any age, helped to carry them down the Middle Ages and into the epoch of the Reformation, unhindered by the changes of fashion and technique, and unharmed by the quarrels of the Ockhamists and the later Humanists.

He has also been called the Father of modern spirituality and devotion. This, perhaps, is a less defensible title. It is easy to say, but very hard to show, that any manifestation of Christian devotion or sentiment is first found in this or that saint or century. What we think is medieval can often be recognized in St Augustine, or St Ignatius of Antioch, or even in St Paul. There is a whole school immediately before St Bernard, the school inspired by St Peter Damian and the other reformers of Italy, in whose writings many of the typical Bernardine devotions may be found already treated as commonplaces. It has been repeated *ad nauseam* that devotion to Our Lady took a world-wide leap forward from St Bernard's preaching; it is not so often recalled that the feast of her Conception and her Little Office were spreading in England and elsewhere before the Norman Conquest, anterior to, and quite independent of, any Cistercian influence. Nevertheless, it remains true that (to take once again an example from common experience) the normal reader of the breviary feels a sudden sense of familiarity when he stumbles upon a set of lessons from St Bernard. Whether it is the Sacred Infancy, or the Compassion of our Lady, or her maternal advocacy, or whether it is St Joseph, or the Holy Angels, or the Holy Souls, St Bernard, when all allowance is made for the difference of tongues, speaks words which have a familiar ring for any Catholic reader of today, whereas St Ambrose or St Gregory may sound to him as Langland's poems do to the uninstructed reader of English verse. This, indeed, is one of Bernard's peculiar claims to the title of Doctor of the Church, and if his purely spiritual and devotional writings also are taken into account, it would be impossible to estimate—or to overestimate—the influence he has had in shaping the thoughts and devotions of Christendom—all the more so, since he was adopted as a master by all the schools of spirituality of the Counter-Reformation, whatever their other allegiances.

St Bernard, though he would have drawn the line as sharply as any today between the ascetical teaching of some of his treatises and the devotional matter of others, would not so readily have isolated what is now called the 'mystical' element in his teaching from the rest. Till recently, indeed, modern writers would not readily have thought of Bernard as a mystic. His life of constant activity and of intense practical energy would have seemed to them alien to the character of a mystic. Recently there has been a change of opinion, but the full understanding of Bernard's teaching on the life of contemplation has yet to come. Abbot Butler, in particular, in his pioneer appreciation, was led by the pattern of his book to treat Bernard as the direct descendant of Augustine and Gregory, and as being, like them, an example of a 'Western' mysticism which has an implied superiority over other kinds. Nor should we be too hasty in regarding Bernard as a mystic *par excellence*. If any judgement of greater or less can ever be made in this field, it must be by a mystical theologian who weighs his words. It is enough perhaps to say that if we hold (and it is surely permissible to do so) that the highest and purest mystical teaching is that outlined in the discourses of our Lord after the Last Supper, that this life was lived (among others) by many of the monks of the desert, whose sayings and teaching have been preserved by Cassian, and that this same life was lived and analysed in theological terms by St John of the Cross, then we may also say that some of the teaching and experiences recorded by Bernard are in harmony with, and are indeed a recognizable manifestation of part of that life.

To many readers of history, Bernard is known almost solely as the protagonist in three great controversies: with the Cluniac monks, with Peter Abelard, and with Gilbert de la Porrée. These indeed are among the select number of historic controversies, among which may be reckoned the not dissimilar exchanges between Mabillon and de Rancé, and between Bossuet and Fénelon, which will probably always continue to attract and to retain the interest of later generations. The issues were such as arise in one form or another in every age; the contestants were men who would give distinction to any issue. In the past hundred years the sympathies of most historians in this country have not been with St Bernard. The prevailing spirit of Liberalism reacted from anything that savoured of intransigence or intellectual dictatorship, as well as from all forms of ecclesiastical domination, and the impression of intolerance and 'cock-sureness' conveyed by Bernard's style, rather than by his thought, has had the effect, as have similar qualities in Macaulay, of prejudicing the reader in favour of his victim. R. L. Poole, in his justly admired sketch of the thought of the period, records with some glee the escape of Gilbert de la Porrée from the net that was spread for his feet.

Much of this antipathy will vanish at a closer view, which takes account of the historical circumstances. In the first place, though to us, wise after the event, Bernard appears as the aggressor, the man with the big stick, it was in fact he, in at least two of the controversies, who more resembled the boy David. When he wrote his Apologia he was the young abbot of a young community, with its future still to make, engaging the serried ranks of the oldest and most influential monasteries of Europe. When he attacked Abelard he came forward as one who had come to challenge on his own ground the most brilliant and adored master of his age. Even later, when, now venerated, he joined issue with the bishop of Poitiers, he had an opponent who was intellectually his equal, technically his superior, and inferior, if at all, only in the deepest spiritual qualities of a theologian.

Of the three controversies the first, that against the older monasticism, is the most familiar, as being of the widest human interest. According to our sympathies, we may regard the issue as one between the gospel purity and man-made laxities, or as the attack of puritanism and rigorism upon humanity and charity. Though Bernard never wrote with greater verve, he was still young, and we may be pardoned for thinking that on occasion his zeal and even his virtuosity intoxicated his more sober judgement; on the other hand, Peter the Venerable, at least in his early rejoinders, may well have mistaken kindliness for charity. Throughout the controversy, indeed, both antagonists seem to fire broadsides at a mirage rather than at the wide target that each presents to the other. Nevertheless, Bernard had the better case, and Peter's last actions, if not his words, go far to admit it.

In the matter of Abelard, much controversial dust has been blown away in the past twenty years. Abelard's radical orthodoxy of intention is now generally admitted, and his brilliance not only as a dialectician, but as a constructive thinker, has been established by recent discoveries. His was of a truth one of the acutest minds of the whole scholastic period. At the same time, there is an almost equal agreement that Bernard seized with absolute precision upon his radical weakness, his ignorance of accurate theological language and, above all, his failure to realize the essentially supernatural character of the Christian revelation. As for Gilbert of Poitiers, the fight in a sense was drawn, and as a patristic scholar the bishop showed more capacity than Bernard. Nevertheless, even if Gilbert's views were not explicitly condemned they were, both philosophically and theologically speaking, barren and perverse. They rested upon an interpretation of ancient philosophy which could not have survived later criticism, and upon a terminology which must soon have become obsolete. When the two theological controversies are regarded from the viewpoint of posterity, and personalities are allowed to disappear, Bernard's interventions are seen to have been most salutary. Probably no other influence than his would have been powerful enough at the time to prevent the diversion of theological speculation into channels which would have ended in the sands.

Few writers have attacked their fellow-Christians with more vigour than St Bernard; it is therefore worthy of notice that none of his major controversies ended in strife or hate. The first ended in the mutual respect and friendship of the abbots of Cluny and Clairvaux; the second, in the reconciliation between Bernard and Abelard brought about by Peter the Venerable, when the Peripatetic of Le Palais, now 'calm of mind, all passion spent', found in Bernard a charity which he had often failed both to find and to give in his earlier contests. As for the third debate, the two opponents parted with respect, perhaps even with sympathy, and in a well-known passage John of Salisbury, who knew and admired them

46

both, though well on this side idolatry, speaks of them as finding together beyond the grave that sole and perfect truth of which each had seen imperfect fragments here below.

Bernard's prestige, which on the whole had been steadily enhanced by all his activities and polemics, sustained one great and patent shock in his later life. The Second Crusade, which in the eyes of contemporaries and historians alike is 'his' crusade, ended not only in disaster, but in what seemed to be a material and moral débâcle. Bernard himself felt the blow severely, but with his characteristic vigour and decision he laid the blame, where indeed it rested in the realm of events, upon the moral failings and ambitions and quarrels of the crusaders. His contemporaries and admirers also felt the blow, and one of his first biographers attacks the problem with a directness and sincerity that are altogether admirable. To Bernard's contemporaries the acutest difficulty was provided by the hail of signs and wonders (Bernard himself called it a 'coruscation') that had accompanied his preaching of the crusade in the Rhineland. Had God, then, led to destruction Bernard and those who responded to His call? Geoffrey found an answer, suggested at the time by the saint himself, and still valid for us. Bernard's preaching, so the argument ran, was directed to saving men's souls, whether they stayed at home or went on the crusade. The wonders were provided as a divine assistance to the hard of heart and unbelievers. If those who went set out with unworthy motives or lost their original high resolve, that was not to be imputed either to Bernard or to God. The argument, granted the premisses, is valid when urged by a saint; it would not be if urged by a statesman. The latter must be judged by worldly results, which it is his task to foresee and to achieve; the former looks only to the spiritual issue. Yet for us, the real problem lies elsewhere. Why, we ask, did Bernard ever lend his great authority to the stimulation of a crusade, which, as both recent experience and normal foresight would have told him, must inevitably become a maelstrom of human vice and suffering? The answer given by Bernard's apologists, and alleged by himself, was, that he acted at the pope's command. It is clear, however, from other of his utterances that Bernard did not intend this as a full explanation of all that had happened, and other actions of his make it abundantly clear that had he believed Eugenius III to be issuing an unlawful command, he would not have hesitated to say so. The pope's words had sent into action one who would have preferred to remain silent, not one who believed that action to be wrong. It is easy to say that one age can never understand the crusades and martyrdoms of another. Perhaps a truer expression is that devotion to an ideal takes different forms according to the degree of purity of the soul concerned. To many, in that age, to go on crusade was their best expression of a devotion to our Lord. Those who condemn them must tell us what better form they have found of giving their lives for Him.

The interests and activities of Bernard are so varied, his writings so varied and voluminous, that the person behind it all, and in particular the personality as sanctified by abundant grace, tends always to elude us. Yet when all is said and done Bernard's sanctity, his reflexion of the beauty of Christ, is the only significant thing about him.

Sanctity appears externally in two ways: in actions which convince the beholder that they are caused by a strength of divine love surpassing anything that merely human emotion or endeavour could achieve; and in the revelation of a character which is seen as a reflexion of Christ Himself. Modern readers, and Catholic theologians, though for different reasons and in very different ways, are in agreement in diverting attention from signs and wonders as a primary manifestation of holiness. To the contemporaries of St Bernard they were its great, its most convincing manifestation, and as St Bernard was unquestionably an outstanding thaumaturge his miracles bulk large in all the accounts of his life. More unexpectedly, perhaps, signs and wonders occupy more than two-thirds of his own account of the life of St Malachy, though there (as doubtless always in Bernard's own mind, for he was well aware of his charisma) the emphasis is always upon the mighty work of God rather than upon the merit of the worker. Be that as it may, revealing details of the well-springs of Bernard's own sanctity are few. Such touches as we have are therefore precious indeed—his utter lack of self-assertion, characteristic in him from boyhood to death; his humility which would never allow him to believe that he could be of help to anyone; his reverence for all, his fear of none; his mother's love for every one of his sons. These, and the self-revelation of the Sermons on the Canticle, show us facets of the real Bernard, and we may believe that the monks of Clairvaux would have seen in their abbot a revelation of Christ which many kings and prophets (and among them John of Salisbury) would have failed to see. But perhaps it is seen best in the glimpses we have of him as the lifelong sufferer, a man acquainted with infirmity and despised, never at rest or at ease, yet never stinting either his daily task or his own demands upon his powers. Throughout his life, and from causes quite beyond his control, though not beyond his capacity for turning suffering into love, Bernard showed forth the Passion of his Master, and his Master's desire to give Himself utterly for others.

Bernard's death marked the end of an epoch. Eugenius III died only a few days before, and with that double loss the great age of Cistercian intervention, and indeed the great monastic age of the Church, the 'Benedictine centuries', came to an end. The future lay outside the monasteries, with the schools, with the universities, with the friars. The leader, whose sound had gone forth over the whole world, and whose words had reached to the ends of the earth, was no more among men. Clairvaux had lost its prophet. 'My father, my father, the chariot of Israel and the horseman thereof.' The whole Church could indeed mourn, for Bernard had been to all a helpmeet in a speedful time, and in tribulation. The Lord had given to his voice a voice of power, and silence fell when it had gone. Yet in a real sense his voice is never silent, and many among his sons today will say, as his monks of Clairvaux could say: 'Because of the words of thy lips I have kept to the hard ways; I have found the living waters, which run with a strong stream from Lebanon.'

4

CISTERCIANS AND CLUNIACS: THE CONTROVERSY BETWEEN ST BERNARD AND PETER THE VENERABLE[1]

The dispute between the white monks and the black, between Clairvaux and Cluny, between St Bernard and Peter the Venerable, is one of the controversies of history which would seem capable of arousing new interest and enlisting fresh enthusiasm in every age. For some, it is a contest literally between the white and the black, for others, it is one between fanaticism and moderation, and for others again, it is a dispute regarding the monastic ideal between two good men in which neither had the whole truth on his side, and in which the reader's sympathy will go out to this party or that according as he feels drawn either towards the zealous and impulsive reformer or to the reasonable and charitable defender of custom and tradition. Whatever may be our judgement, it is a story that will bear to be retold once more.

Throughout the controversy, it is well to recollect that two quite distinct cases were being tried, though the disputants rarely made the distinction. There was the case against the essential Cluny, the ideal Cluny, against the way of monastic life which she aimed at and had achieved, and the case against the degenerate Cluny, against abuses which, if really existent, were indefensible. The materials for the first case may be sketched in outline as follows.

The great Cluniac system, already in 1100 almost two centuries old, consisted of the mother abbey herself, her dependent priories and cells, and the affiliated abbeys with their dependencies: the whole family embraced more than six hundred houses, with a popu-

---

[1] [This article, of which a first draft was written in 1934, was delivered in 1955 as the ninth lecture of the Friends of Dr Williams's Library and published in the series of those lectures. Aspects of the same subject are treated in the author's articles on 'Peter the Venerable' (1956) and 'The Reforming Decrees of Peter the Venerable' (1956).]

lation of more than ten thousand monks, while around the periphery stood a multitude of other monasteries which had adapted themselves to the prevailing Cluniac climate. Under the long reign of St Hugh (1049–1109) Cluny had enjoyed her last phase of triumphant expansion, and at the moment of the first exodus of the monks of Molesme to Cîteaux (1098) she still stood as a second centre of Christendom.

Cluny, in common with almost all Western monasteries of the eleventh century, professed to follow the Rule of St Benedict. Like all other monasteries, she had modified the Rule, all questions of laxity apart. The threefold division of liturgical prayer, reading, and work had given place to one in which the liturgy occupied the first place not only in esteem (as in the Rule) but also in bulk, and now stood to the other two members separately in some such proportion as two to one. Moreover, the 'work' of the Rule had gradually, and perhaps inevitably, come to embrace every possible activity, but no longer stood for the uniform manual work of the whole body. While this was true of all monasteries during the tenth and eleventh centuries, Cluny, and the circle that felt her influence, had gone steadily farther in the direction of a purely liturgical life. Gradually, she and her dependencies, by multiplication of festivals and offices and by prolongation of ceremonies and chant, had come to make of service in choir the only occupation of the day, so that the choir duties at Cluny left practically no time for any other activity.[1] Of this fact, during the century 1030–1130, there can be no question; we have explicit witness over the whole period. When, about 1059, the young Anselm, full of a desire for learning, was debating where to turn in the religious life, he was debarred from Cluny by the *districtio ordinis* prevailing there—that is, not the physical severity (for he found this at Bec also) but the rigorous observance which kept the monks occupied in choir and therefore rendered study impossible.[2] Twenty years later we have the testimony of St Peter Damian. Using the precise phrase (*ordo districtus*) of St Anselm, he

[1] See article on monastic time-tables by the present writer in *DR*, vol. LI, pp. 706–25; also *The Monastic Order in England*, appendix xviii, pp. 714–15; and T. Symons, *Regularis Concordia* (Edinburgh, 1953), introd., pp. xliii–xliv.

[2] *Vita Anselmi auctore Eadmero*, I, i, in Migne, *PL*, vol. CLVIII, col. 53.

observes that when he was at Cluny the services in choir were so prolonged that even in the longest days of summer, when their sleep would have been shortest, the monks could hardly find half an hour of free time in the day.[1] Twenty years later again the customs of Ulrich tell the same tale, especially in the personal digressions, where we catch glimpses of the life as it was lived. Speaking of the same days of midsummer, Ulrich tells us of the continuous offices, of the long lessons which many new-comers felt as an intolerable burden, and of the breathless sequence of duties.[2] The multiplication of feasts and the elaboration of ceremonial had now been complicated by the vast number of monks at Cluny.[3] Finally, when the system was on its defence we hear the same story from both Peter the Venerable and the cardinal-legate Matthew of Albano. The former has more than one reference to the wearing round of daily choir duties at Cluny, and, as we shall see later, himself modified some of its extreme features. The latter, who may fairly be characterized as a Cluniac die-hard, found fault with the black monk abbots who in chapter at Rheims in 1131 had shortened some of the extra offices. Matthew frankly cannot see what they will find to do in the time thus left vacant. They do not, he supposes, desire to do hard agricultural work; therefore the time spent out of choir will be a dead loss.[4]

Cluny, then, had come to stand for—its 'message' was—a life in

[1] *Petri Damiani Opera, ep.* vi. 5, in *PL*, vol. CXLIV, col. 380: 'Porro autem, dum tam districtum, tamque frequentem sanctae vestrae conversationis ordinem recolo...sancti Spiritus magisterium inesse perpendo. Nam tanta erat in servandi ordinis continua jugitate prolixitas, tanta praesertim in ecclesiasticis officiis protelabatur instantia, ut in ipso cancri, sive leonis aestu, cum longiores sunt dies, vix per totum diem unius saltem vacaret horae dimidium, quo fratribus in claustro licuisset miscere colloquium.'

[2] *Udalrici Consuetudines*, i. 18 (*PL*, vol. CXLIX, col. 668): 'Saepius namque priusquam omnes in claustro consideant, et aliquis fratrum vel unum verbum faciat, pulsatur signum ad vesperas....Post vesperas, coena; post coenam, coena servitorum; post coenam servitorum, officium pro defunctis; post officium, collatio, et ita ad completorium.' *Ibid.* i. 41 (coll. 687-8): 'Tam prolixas lectiones, quae nimirum quibusdam nostris commilitonibus...non minus graves essent ad audiendum quam massa plumbea fore solet ad portandum.'

[3] *Ibid.* i. 18 (col. 668): 'Multitudo fratrum acervavit; a quibus dum...pax datur et accipitur...non minima pars expenditur diei.'

[4] U. Berlière, *Documents inédits pour servir à l'histoire ecclésiastique de la Belgique* (Maredsous, 1894), appendix, p. 101: 'Silentium imponere, psalmodiam decurtare, ad opera manuum non exire, quae est ista nova lex? Quae est ista nova doctrina?'

which everything—private prayer, active work, studies—had become subordinated to the liturgy, understood as the daily total of vocal prayer and ceremonial action. Such a life, it is clear, had little elasticity, and left little room for varied types of mind and soul to develop. Almost no provision was made in it for any active or creative work of mind or body, and little opportunity was given for that silent, individual communion with God which has always been recognized as a normal, if not essential, element in the life of prayer.

Meanwhile, the intellectual and religious world had developed very greatly in complexity between the first years of the eleventh century and its close. There was, first of all, the great intellectual awakening which was in time to rise to its height in the universities, in scholastic philosophy, and in theology, and which included new and vast developments in art and law. Alongside of this was the swift advance in organization and reforming activity radiating from the papal curia and known as the Gregorian Reform. And, in close connexion with this, there was the movement of monastic reform, which had issued in the birth of new orders in Italy, and which was even now beginning to stir in Cluny's own fatherland. Yet Cluny herself was making no attempt to absorb the new spirit of the age; indeed, at the very moment of its appearance she was proceeding on different, even antagonistic lines, and, in addition, when apparently at the apogee of splendour, already carried the seeds of decay that were so soon to germinate. And this is the second case against Cluny.

The exact moment when the shadows began to lengthen is not easy to mark. So far as can be judged, Cluny was still fulfilling her mission *in facie ecclesiae* when Peter Damian visited the abbey in 1063,[1] and when William de Warenne passed by shortly before the first colony was sent to Lewes soon after 1070.[2] In other words, the

---

[1] *P. Damiani Opera*, *ep.* vi. 2 (*PL*, vol. CXLIV, col. 372): 'Incomparabilis ille tuus sanctusque conventus.' *Ibid. ep.* 3 (col. 373): 'Angelicus tuus ille conventus.' *Ibid. ep.* 4 (col. 374): 'Quid aliud Cluniacense monasterium, nisi agrum Domini plenum dixerim?' *Ibid. ep.* 5 (col. 378): 'Vere sanctis, et angelica veneratione colendis Cluniacensis monasterii fratribus.' Such language from a saint—and a reforming saint—must surely carry weight, though Damian was impulsive both in blessing and cursing.

[2] The fact of Warenne's admiration is certain, even if the alleged foundation charter (Dugdale, *Monasticon*, vol. V, p. 12) is a fabrication of the early thirteenth century. Compare C. T. Clay, *Early Yorkshire Charters*, vol. VIII, pp. 59–62.

53

decade 1065–75 may be taken as a *terminus a quo* of our search. The *terminus ad quem* is given by the general opinion of succeeding ages, foreshadowed by contemporary sentiment, that the events of the reign of Pontius (1109–22) would not have been possible had all been healthy; with this conclusion Peter the Venerable would seem to agree.[1] The decay, then, set in under the last years of the rule of St Hugh. What were its causes?

Bearing in mind that the ultimate causes of decay in human institutions must ever elude our observation, and that what are the proximate occasions of final ruin may themselves be symptoms of an old disease, we may perhaps suggest that three causes beyond all others contributed to the decline of the golden age.

The first, wholly intrinsic to Cluny, seems to modern eyes at once the most operative and the least inevitable. This was the reception into the monastic family at Cluny and elsewhere of vast numbers of new recruits without adequate probation or training. Of the facts there can be no doubt; they are admitted to the full more than once by Peter himself. We know that during Ulrich's monastic life the community at Cluny had grown from manageable to unwieldy proportions; there was another enormous increase between Ulrich's day and the central period of the abbacy of Peter the Venerable.[2] Such a growth, which at any period in any religious order is a severe test, would under any circumstances have proved particularly testing at Cluny, for it made the daily routine still more cumbersome, and the unsatisfactory constitutional relations between the mother house and her dependants threw upon the abbot of Cluny an unbearable responsibility for discipline. But the problem was intensified tenfold by the readiness, to us wholly incomprehensible, with which, in defiance alike of the Rule and of common sense, novices were

[1] *Petri Venerabilis de Miraculis*, ii. 11 (*PL*, vol. CLXXXIX, col. 921): 'Succreverant paulo ante [i.e. before 1122] in magno illo et nobili monastici ordinis agro, resecanda vel potius evellenda, utilibus satis contraria, et quorumdam quos nominare nolo culpa vel desidia, nam ex majori parte jam vita excesserunt, plurima exstirpanda exorta fuerant.'

[2] *Petri Venerabilis Statuta* (*ibid.* 1040): 'Quorum [*sc.* senum et debilium] major in eo tempore [i.e. his own day] numerus CCC vel CCCC fratribus erat quam priore illo [tempore] inter fratres sexaginta, aut ad plus octoginta.' Compare charter *c.* 1149 in Bruel, *Recueil des chartes de Cluny*, vol. v, no. 4132: 'Trecenti erant vel eo amplius fratres.'

received to profession after a probation of a few months, a few weeks, and even of a few days and hours. Once such a practice had a fair hold, once the Cluniac houses were full of multitudes received without probation or training, nothing, we may feel, could have saved Cluny.

The second cause, for which Cluny was less directly responsible, may be found in the growing wealth of the great abbey and her daughters. Cluny had long been freed from material care, but the economic conditions of the tenth and early eleventh centuries had not favoured the growth or employment of great wealth. Now, however, property was increasing in value and gifts were being multiplied; artistic and architectural masterpieces were being produced in the Romanesque world, and there was a spirit of luxury abroad. We may remember the reflexions called forth among chroniclers by the loss of the *White Ship*, which stood to so many of that time as a kind of judgement upon a delicate and luxurious society.

A third cause was less the fault than the misfortune of Cluny. When an institute has ceased to lead the age, it inevitably ceases to attract to itself the individuals who by their vision, their ability, and their zeal are marked out to be the leaders of the age to come. The presence of five such is of more value to a cause, and especially to a spiritual cause, than the presence of five hundred others who choose their way without deep thought and pursue it without enthusiasm. Already in the first half of the century Lanfranc and Anselm had passed Cluny by in their search for perfection, and we cannot but suppose that even before the flood swept towards Clairvaux several of the other new orders that were its spiritual brethren, such as the Chartreuse, Tiron, and Savigny, had begun to drain away from Cluny her income of sanctity. At the beginning of the eleventh century Cluny had been spiritually at the head of the age, and even as late as the reign of Gregory VII was still there to all appearances, but in reality the tide had begun to ebb. It is a characteristic of such times of religious ferment—the sixteenth century affords a remarkable parallel—that the new life of the spirit breaks out in every direction at once, like a new and abounding and irresistible source of water, and no observer can predict which of the channels will be the stream-bed in a future age. As we watch the rise of saints and orders between 1040 and 1140—Vallombrosa, Camaldoli, the Chartreuse, Bec, Tiron, Savigny, Cîteaux, Prémontré, and the rest—we cannot help feeling that as with a vine the very fecundity of the new shoots may be a source of weakness, that many a monastery was starved by extrinsic, not intrinsic causes, and that many of the new ventures failed to survive, not because they did not satisfy the essential demands of religion, but because they failed to satisfy as completely as did some other house which came into being a decade later. In any case, whatever the fate of new plants, at such a time the old establishments suffer, justly or unjustly. The Cistercians and their cousins outbid the black monks, just as a century later monks both black and white were outbidden by the friars, and as in the sixteenth century both friars and monks failed to satisfy their age as completely as the Jesuits.

In thus discussing the causes of Cluny's decline from what had been her unassailable high estate we may seem to have prejudged the trial before we had heard the evidence and the pleading. Yet without some such statement of the question it is impossible to approach the actual controversy with any understanding. What we have said need not prevent us from hearing the advocates judicially and from treating the evidence on its merits.

The original exodus from Molesme, led by St Robert in 1098, was, it is clear, prompted by a desire to get back to a more literal observance of the Rule of St Benedict. While still at Molesme the emigrants had often discussed the question, and noted where and to what extent reform was needed.[1] The changes they desired were of three kinds. They wished for a stricter life, a more solitary life, and a life in which work of the hands had a place.[2] To give effect to these wishes they rejected all that was not allowed by the Rule in the way of clothing and food, together with the possession of churches and tithes; they chose a remote and uncultivated spot in which to settle;

[1] The Cistercian documents are cited from Ph. Guignard, *Monuments primitifs de la règle cistercienne* (Dijon, 1878). The controversies at present existing over the early Cistercian records do not affect our present subject. The reference in the text is to the *Exordium Cisterciensis coenobii*, p. 63: 'Viri isti apud Molismum positi sepius inter se dei gratia aspirati, de transgressione regule beati Benedicti patris monachorum loquebantur conquerebantur contristabantur.'

[2] For their original desires and the measures taken, see *Exordium*, pp. 71-2.

and they rejected a considerable proportion of the current monastic choir duties. Thus the first movement was towards simplicity and austerity. The note of puritanism, almost of ferocity; the avoidance of any aesthetic satisfaction, not merely of the costly and the superfluous; these seem to have come in later under St Stephen Harding, perhaps under the influence of the young Bernard; they are familiar features of St Bernard's early letters.

The aims of the early community of Cîteaux cannot have been at all widely known; the documents in which they have come down to us are either later compositions or semi-private letters. But when the *Carta Caritatis* and the Constitutions of 1119 were framed it was clear to all who were interested where the white monks intended to differ from the black.[1] These two documents, each a masterpiece of lucid and practical legislation, aimed at establishing and securing the ends for which the exodus had been made: the Rule observed (*ad apicem litterae*) to the last dot; the office (*Opus Dei*), spiritual reading (*lectio divina*), and manual work (*labor manuum*) each in the place assigned by St Benedict; simplicity and seclusion of life, together with the silence of the Rule; and the constitutional safeguards to guarantee absolute uniformity and reciprocal control among the various houses of the new movement.

Neither of these two documents is couched in provocative language. They are addressed as laws to the subjects of Cîteaux, not as propaganda to all and sundry, and no reasonable exception could be taken to them by others. Inevitably, however, feeling in monastic circles ran high. The natural impulse of resentment among the unreformed, increased by the *succès fou* of the white monks after Bernard's arrival amongst them, was intensified by the self-satisfaction expressed by some of the new body. But the particular turn taken by the nascent quarrel was due to the action of St Bernard.

Among the members of his family who had accompanied or followed him into religion was a cousin, Robert, whose parents had many years previously promised to offer him as a monk at Cluny. Finding life at Clairvaux more than he could stand he took refuge at Cluny, where he was received as a prodigal son; it was argued that

---

[1] For these documents see Guignard, pp. 79–287.

his vicarious oblation took precedence over his Cistercian clothing, and on appeal to the pope the claim was upheld. Meanwhile Bernard, to whom the fugitive had been bound by ties both of blood and of spirit, followed him up with a passionate letter,[1] wholly characteristic of the young abbot both in its fervent pleading and in its exuberant attack on his opponents, which the original editor of the saint's epistles chose, with singular felicity of judgement, to stand first in the long and magnificent series. It is undoubtedly a literary masterpiece. Whether it is at all points a saint's letter and one that the mature Bernard would have written; whether, that is, the passionate hatred of laxity flames unjustly against a whole great body of religious, and is expressed in words which satisfy the ear rather than the heart, the natural instinct rather than the spiritual, must remain a question for each reader to answer. But the main charges are clear enough. The food and clothing of the black monks were luxurious, their life delicate; sloth and idle talk had taken the place of prayer and silence; repugnance to manual work and even to the slightest exertion had made them slothful, tender, and fastidious.

The letter was a private one, and there is no evidence that its contents became public property at the time. When, a few years later, the formal debate is opened, Cluny has found a champion and Bernard is prepared for a frontal attack.

In default of precise dating, we cannot say with certainty whether the first letter of the recently elected abbot of Cluny, Peter of Montboissier, to the abbot of Clairvaux was written before or after Bernard's Apology to his friend William of St Thierry.[2] It is indeed

---

[1] *Bernardi epistola*, I (*PL*, vol. CLXXXII, coll. 67 ff.). The following passage (col. 73) is typical; Bernard is speaking of the grand prior of Cluny. 'Attrahit, allicit, blanditur, et novi evangelii praedicator commendat crapulam, parcimoniam damnat; voluntariam paupertatem miseriam dicit; jejunia, vigilias, silentium, manuumque laborem, vocat insaniam: e contrario otiositatem contemplationem nuncupat; edacitatem, loquacitatem, curiositatem, cunctam denique intemperantiam nominat discretionem.'

[2] We cannot fix a certain date to Peter's letter. The inscription *Bernardo humilis Cluniaci abbas* is presumably genuine, so it must be posterior to 1122. For every other reason we should wish to put it as early as possible. E. Vacandard, *Vie de S. Bernard* (Paris, 1895), vol. I, p. 101, argues that it precedes Bernard's *Apologia*, pointing out that the conclusion of the letter—'erit modo tuum, si aliter senseris'—suggests that Bernard had not yet intervened.

remarkable that neither of these two manifestoes contains any allusion, however remote, to the other, though that of Peter is directed to Bernard's address. All that can be said is that the abbot of Cluny had not seen the Apology when he wrote. In his long defence of Cluny he tells us that he has not yet met Bernard, much as he has desired to do so, but nevertheless ventures to tell him of a series of charges brought against the black monks by certain of the Cistercians, and to give his answers to them. The charges, which fall under some dozen heads, are sufficiently sweeping and serious, though they are so general in their form as to suggest that they are deduced from the official Cistercian documents. There is no hint of any moral delinquency, but in every case it has been argued that the Cluniacs have set aside the authority of the Rule.

Peter opens his case with spirit, accusing the Cistercians of pharisaical self-complacency. They boast of keeping the Rule to the letter, but seem to have overlooked the chapter on humility.[1] He then proceeds to answer the charges one by one; in almost every case he admits the facts and defends them. Readers at all acquainted with the religious life and with the Rule may feel that his answers ring true only on one or two points out of the dozen; more often they take the form of special pleading, not infrequently supported by quotations from the Gospel which are remarkably inappropriate. We may take as an example the first charge, a serious and well-founded one: that the Cluniacs receive a novice to profession after a few months or even days, instead of allowing the year's noviciate of the Rule to take its course. Peter replies at great length without facing the spiritual issue that is at stake. Who are we, he says, to keep novices waiting a year when the Lord told the young man to sell all and follow Him without delay, and told another that he was to follow Him, leaving the dead to bury their dead? Do you accuse us of not keeping the Rule when we keep the greater rule of charity? If we refused an early profession the novice might fall away and go back to the world. Such a fashion of argument does not need dis-

[1] *Petri Venerabilis, ep.* i. 28 (*PL*, vol. CLXXXIX, col. 116): 'O, o, Pharisaeorum novum genus, rursus mundo redditum!...dicite, veri observatores Regulae, quomodo vos eam tenere jactatis, qui nec breve illud capitulum...servare curatis, quo dicitur ut monachus omnibus se inferiorem et viliorem...credat?'

cussion; if it did, we should need to do no more than point to Peter's own reforming regulations on the subject a few years later.

An even less convincing reply is given to the charge that whereas the Rule allows only two cooked dishes (with a third of fresh vegetables) at dinner, the Cluniacs have added many more. Peter argues that if St Benedict allowed a choice of two through consideration of the weak, it was equally logical of the Cluniacs to give a choice of three or four.[1] Finally, to the charge of possessing wealth and landed property and serfs Peter, after a lengthy rehearsal of canonical arguments which do not touch the substance of the charge, ultimately replies that monks are the children of light, and that it is far better that they should possess wealth of which they will give a good account than that the children of this world should have it to use to their damnation.[2] As for the serfs, they are so happy and well treated that they exactly resemble St Paul's ideal Christians, 'as having nothing, and possessing all things'.[3]

After dealing in this *sic et non* fashion with all the objections Peter proceeds to a lengthy apology for the Cluniac ideal. Put in brief his case is that while some divine commands are alterable, such as the details of legal observance, others, such as the precept of charity, are not. The Cluniacs prefer charity to the religion of the Pharisees, and since times have changed and men are weaker than they were in St Benedict's day, it has been Cluny's ideal to change many things, but to keep charity, while the Cistercians, while professing to keep the Rule, fail to keep the first and greatest commandment. Peter, indeed, endeavours to impale Cîteaux on the horns of a dilemma.

[1] *Petri Venerabilis, ep.* i. 28, col. 126: 'Si ergo quisquam infirmitatis propriae causa ex duobus illis non potuerit edere, non oportet eum ex tertio refici? Quod si nec ex tertio, non debet ei quartum offerri?' Half a century later, the Cluniacs put forward a more subtle defence. In the *Dialogus inter Cluniacensem et Cisterciensem monachum*, ed. Martène, *Thesaurus novus Anecdotorum*, vol. v (ed. 1717), col. 1637, we find the point discussed: 'CIST. Quare ergo vos habetis tria aut quatuor [fercula] contra praeceptum Regulae? CLUN. Absit hoc. Nos enim duo tantum regularia habemus, quia quod ex caritate inter duos et duos datur, pro ferculo non computatur.'

[2] *Ibid.* col. 145: 'Quis non judicet rectius, melius et utilius esse, ut cuncta illa superius sigillatim posita illi possideant, quos assumptus ordo et religionis propositum cogit legitime possidere, quam illi qui et negligentia et minoris propositi securitate...incongruenti circa ipsas res amore...seipsos interimunt?' The monks, in fact, have the best of both worlds.

[3] 2 Corinthians vi. 10.

All admit (he argues) that many popes and monastic legislators (and, he might have added, St Benedict himself) have reversed and revised previously existing laws. The Cistercians dare not say this was wrongly done, and if right, why are the Cluniacs condemned for having done in their turn what saints and rulers of old had done before?

It should not have been very difficult to escape between the horns of such a dilemma as this. The radical vice of the first Cluniac Apology is its obliteration of all distinction between essentials and accidentals in the life of evangelical perfection. It is certainly true that customs and circumstances change and demand new legislation, and it may be that regulations of extreme severity are not essential for religious perfection, but it is not true that a fervent religious life can exist without a constant invitation to a spiritual, supernatural ideal. No talk of charity can make the mediocre into the holy. The virtue of close adherence to an authorized Rule lies precisely in the guarantee it gives that the life so lived does not fall below the lowest level necessary for those who wish, in the technical phrase, to tend towards perfection of life. The wholly supernatural end which the Christian proposes to himself, namely, perfect imitation of Christ, demands that the religious life should have on it a stamp not of this world.

It is a curious fact of religious history that neither St Bernard nor Peter the Venerable, at least at the period of their first controversy, was able to formulate this truth. Bernard and the early Cistercians felt it and lived it—it was indeed their *raison d'être*—but they did not express it in so many words. As for the Cluniacs, instead of endeavouring to show, as Lanfranc and Anselm might with justice have shown, that accidental modifications of the Rule did not result in any essential lessening of fervour, they used arguments which, pressed to their logical conclusion, would have implied the wholesale abandonment of high ideals.

We cannot say with any certainty at what date Peter's letter was written, and there is no trace of its reception by St Bernard. The first great *pièce justificative* of Clairvaux, Bernard's celebrated Apology to William of St Thierry, may have been written almost

61

simultaneously, or as much as two or three years later.[1] In any case, it contains no direct reply to Peter, and was perhaps not aimed directly at Cluny herself but at other great monasteries, such as Suger's St Denis, whose way of life was not greatly different. It is a masterpiece of impassioned pleading, and once again the reader may feel that it only falls short of the highest eloquence because it uses, however successfully, some of the devices of rhetoric rather than the more persuasive, if less brilliant, language of the spirit.[2] Bernard opens, most skilfully, in a low and neutral tone of self-accusation, deprecating strife and exalting charity, gently rebuking his followers for attacking others. He, at least, is free from that charge. Who would dare to accuse him of belittling the Cluniacs? Whatever others may do under the cloak of zeal, he will not say a word against them. Even if the charges against Cluny are true, even if she breaks the Rule upon the wheel, we must remember that charity and piety are far more important to religion, and that those relaxations which we deplore were doubtless introduced by the holy men of old to save more souls. Doubtless: but that those saints of old would have tolerated for an instant what we see around us today— no, that we cannot believe. And now Bernard has the scent, red-hot, and is tearing off along the line, while the hills re-echo. The words come foaming out, as it might be Juvenal or Tertullian. *Semper ego auditor tantum?* Did someone beg me to fear the scandal? Better scandal than that the truth should be hid.[3] And the vials are poured

---

[1] Vacandard (vol. i, p. 115 n.) dates the *Apologia* 1123–25. In the *Dictionnaire de théologie catholique*, art. *Bernard* (1910), he dates it 1127. Bernard's first epistle to his cousin probably dates from 1115–19.

[2] When these words were first written I was unaware that even Cistercian apologists of the twelfth century had passed a similar judgement on the *Apologia*. Thus the Cistercian in the Dialogue already quoted, col.1577, makes the following candid admission: 'CIST. [Epistolam ad Willelmum] legi et relegi, et diligenter consideravi; in prima lectione idipsum quod tibi, visum est mihi [*viz.* that St Bernard's rebuke to his followers and praise of the Cluniacs were both entirely unaffected]; nec mirum, quia...loquitur eo dicendi genere, in quo simplices et minus diligenter legentes falluntur lectores. CLUN. Quod est illud dicendi genus?...CIST. Rhetores appellant illud Insinuationem ...tunc enim advocatus accusati in principio orationis cum detestantibus detestatur... postea vero mira verborum arte, quae firmaverat infirmat, quae accusaverat excusat.'

[3] *Apologia*, ch. VII (*PL*, vol. CLXXXII, col. 908): 'Melius est ut scandalum oriatur, quam veritas relinquatur.' It is a quotation from St Gregory, *Homilia*, i. 7 *in Ezechielem* (*PL*, vol. LXXVI, col. 842), often used by St Bernard and his school.

out one by one. The rich meats, baked, boiled, and stuffed—the eggs, the fishes, the pigments—honeyed wine, soft beds—silks, furs, and fine array, bought of rich merchants in booths of regal splendour—abbots with their pomp and state. Did Basil live thus, and Antony and Odo and Odilo? But these are trifles compared with what lies behind. We will not stigmatize the preposterous vast churches of the Cluniacs.[1] We will look rather at the sumptuous ornaments encrusted with gems and gold, put there that money may breed money and pilgrims may give to monks alms that should be bestowed upon the true poor. We will look at their cloisters with their monstrous capitals and arabesques, fit only to distract the idle from their books. Just heaven! Even if they are not shocked by their impropriety, they might at least blench at their cost.[2]

This is, I think, not an unfair précis of the Apology. One or two reflexions will suggest themselves to the mind of almost every reader of its pages. The first is, that St Bernard must undoubtedly have had truth on his side. Charges of luxury, at once so sweeping and so detailed, must have been well founded. Bernard's character is alone sufficient guarantee that there is no direct falsification, and the entire absence of any charges of immorality—always the first refuge of calumny—gives more weight to the serious indictment that remains. Two other impressions, however, are not so favourable to Bernard. No one, I imagine, can read the Apology without hearing as a kind of undertone the words of the Pharisee in the parable.[3] It is not only that Bernard denounces laxity; others besides Pharisees may do this; if real laxity is there, it deserves to be branded, be the critic who he may—and in this case the critic's own life was a sufficient justification of his action. It is rather that Bernard, even when urging his followers to tolerance, implies that the best and most

---

[1] *Ibid.* ch. XII (col. 914): 'Omitto [!] oratoriorum immensas altitudines, immoderatas longitudines, supervacuas latitudines, sumptuosas depolitiones, curiosas depictiones.' The four last words somewhat weaken the tremendous force of the previous six; the reference to the great church of Cluny is unmistakable.

[2] *Ibid.* ch. XII (col. 916): 'Proh Deo! si non pudet ineptiarum, cur vel non piget expensarum?'

[3] At least, many will feel thus when they read the *Apologia*, though it is the work of such a brilliant mind that it is quite impossible to isolate a sentence and pronounce it to have a pharisaical ring.

sincere Cluniac is a less faithful follower of Christ than the average Cistercian; that every Cistercian, simply because his life is more austere, is therefore more holy than a Cluniac. The Cluniacs were exacerbated by his attitude, and with reason. The second point is perhaps still more characteristic. St Bernard, at least during the earlier part of his life, often fails to distinguish between what is strictly within the realm of morality, and what is only so indirectly. In the Apology he thunders with equal vehemence against the pride of life and artistic achievement. He is now the true reformer, now the Puritan. When, in the Apology, he passes from small things to great, and the reader prepares himself for a list of gross moral delinquencies, it is only to hear of the splendid churches and cloisters of the Cluniacs, which a generation appreciative of Moissac, and following with admiration the excavations of Dr Conant at Cluny itself, is inclined to regard with a certain tenderness of affection. No doubt, as a recent Cistercian scholar has reminded us, Bernard had in mind the nullity of all man-made beauty in face of the beauty of God to which a Cistercian's gaze was directed, but he does not say this in the Apology.

When next we find Peter the Venerable corresponding with St Bernard the tone is very different. They are now friends and know each other well;[1] Peter's one desire is to get at the root of the quarrel between the two bodies of monks and end it. He is much less eager to make a formal defence of the Cluniacs, and struggles manfully to come to grips with the real problem, though with indifferent success. Let each of us, he writes, abound in his own sense. We both follow the Rule, and we both admit that the Rule without charity profits nothing, while with charity, all things are lawful. We both wish to save souls—you, for example, by a strict and full noviciate, we, by taking aspirants as easily as possible. You, with a pure intention, keep all the regular fasts; we, with an intention equally pure, drop half of them.[2] Why should we quarrel or abuse

[1] *Petri Venerabilis, ep.* iv. 17 (*PL*, vol. CLXXXIX, col. 321): 'Singulari veneratione colendo, totis charitatis brachiis amplectendo, individuo cordis mei hospiti, domino Bernardo, &c.'

[2] *Ibid.* col. 329: 'Simplici oculo tu [Cisterciensis] uteris, qui absque exceptione aliqua regularia jejunia...observas....Simplici oculo et tu [Cluniacensis] uteris, qui et hos dies, quos praedixi, et omnem authenticam duodecim lectionum solemnitatem ab hac regularium jejuniorum consuetudine excipis.'

each other? May we not fear that the real reason is that the black monks envy the popularity of the white, while the white are contemptuous of the milder rule of the black? And Peter ends with a sincere and moving exhortation to charity.

Yet once again we feel that he has missed the point. The quarrel was not at root concerned with the accidental differences between two equally good ways; nor between different customs and traditions; still less did it spring merely from envy and pride, however much these failings may have animated individuals on either side. The basis of the whole Cistercian programme was that the Cluniacs had so relaxed the Rule that it was no longer for them a way of perfection.

As the years passed the two great representatives of the old and the new were drawn closer together. It is clear enough that Peter was not slow to recognize the hand of God in Bernard's work, and that he grew both to reverence and to love Bernard himself; it is no less clear—and perhaps more significant—that Bernard came to love and to admire Peter, to whom indeed he gave the surname by which he is known to history.[1] But what is perhaps most significant of all is that in the course of a few years Peter changed from being an advocate of Cluny to being its reformer. The stages of this change are hidden from us; we do not know whether it was caused by a progressive deterioration of Cluny or, as would seem more likely, by a growth in the abbot's spiritual insight. We have seen that Peter recognized a certain falling-off at Cluny before his assumption of office; we are told by St Bernard himself that he took steps to enforce the Rule from the first years of his abbacy.[2] In any case, when

[1] Compare the letter (*ep.* 277) of Bernard to Eugenius III (*PL*, vol. CLXXXII, coll. 482-3), written *c.* 1146: 'Stultum videtur scribere ad vos pro domino Cluniacensi, et ei quasi velle patrocinium ferre, quem omnes sibi patronum habere desiderant.' *Ep.* 282 (col. 489), written *c.* 1150, also to Eugenius: 'Venerabilis abbas Cluniacensis....' Compare also Peter's letter (vi. 29, *PL*, vol. CLXXXIX, col. 443) written in 1149, where he declares he would prefer living with Bernard to ruling Cluny.

[2] Peter himself tells us (*De Miraculis*, ii. 11; *PL*, vol. CLXXXIX, col. 922) that on becoming abbot he appointed Matthew prior to assist in restoring observance. 'Nam noxia vel superflua quaeque in cibis, in potibus, in moribus quam maxime persequens ...ea...ad congruum finem...meque cum quibusdam aliis pro viribus juvante, perduxit.' Bernard may be alluding to this in *ep.* 277 (see last note): 'Pene ab introitu suo in multis Ordinem illum meliorasse cognoscitur; verbi gratia, in observantia jejuniorum, silentii, indumentorum pretiosorum et curiosorum.' Both these letters increase the difficulty of dating Peter's first letter much later than 1122.

the silence is broken again Peter has crossed the ditch once and for all; he has grasped the difference between tolerable customs and intolerable relaxation.

The document in question is a circular letter to all the priors and wardens of Cluniac houses wherever situated, and opens at once in a very different style from the two earlier letters we have been considering.[1] Peter has been to school to Clairvaux, and has caught some of its abbot's prophetic style. 'Shall I speak or remain silent?' he begins, 'Shall I open my lips or keep them shut? Do I wish to be one of those of whom it is written: O my people, they who call thee blessed, the same deceive thee and destroy the way of thy steps?' And he proceeds to denounce the luxurious feastings of Cluny in language which clearly owes its peculiar flavour to Bernardine influence, though Peter moves a little heavily and lacks that ultimate perfection of style—that transmission of personality— that makes Bernard one among many thousands.

Pork boiled or baked [he declaims], fat heifers, rabbits and hares, geese chosen from out the whole tribe of their fellows, hens and every quadruped and fowl that man has domesticated, cover the tables of the holy monks. And now even these pall, and we turn to strange regal delicacies. The forests must be drawn; we need our huntsmen. Fowlers must trap for us pheasants, partridges and turtle-doves, lest the servants of God die of hunger. Is this how we follow the Rule?

And then, conscious that he had himself in the past been responsible for some questionable exegesis, he hastens to add: 'Let no one say these changes were not made without good cause by our fathers. I myself argued in this way when writing of other matters to the abbot of Clairvaux, but for eating fleshmeat no excuse will serve.'[2] And he ends on a note of solemn warning.

Within a few years of this letter the influence of Cîteaux was making itself felt throughout black monk circles in France. The

---

[1] *Petri Venerabilis, ep.* vi. 15 (*PL*, vol. CLXXXIX, coll. 418 ff.).

[2] *Ibid.* (col. 420). A curious passage. 'Si enim de novitiis suscipiendis, &c.,...a bonis Patribus post sanctum Benedictum mutatum est, non dubia, sed certa et rationabili causa factum est. Et causa vel ratio, quia bis a me in duabus epistolis olim domino abbati Claravallensi directis, studiose descripta est, hic iterare superfluum judico. Si adeo studiosus fueris, ibi plene reperies. At hujus capituli [*sc.* that prohibiting fleshmeat] praevaricatio, qua ratione excusabitur?'

justice of many of the criticisms levelled against Cluny, and the obvious success of the Cistercian reform, could by 1130 be gainsaid by no one, and some decline in the quality, if not in the quantity, of Cluniac recruitment must have followed. In any case, we pass from conjecture to fact in 1131, when we find a number of Benedictine abbots of the province of Rheims, not directly depending upon Cluny, holding a chapter and passing a series of reforming resolutions, all clearly framed with one eye upon Cîteaux.[1] The office is to be said more slowly; some accretions of psalmody are to be shorn off and the scale of the ceremonial mounting of the liturgy is to be reduced. Fleshmeat is forbidden; the daily winter fast of the Rule is to be honoured; there is to be no recreative conversation in the cloister.[2]

These seemingly reasonable proposals met with immediate and severe criticism at the hands of the cardinal-legate Matthew of Albano. This distinguished prelate, a monk of Saint-Martin-des-Champs, had risen to be prior of Cluny and the trusted assistant of Peter the Venerable, who describes his career and edifying death in some detail. Observant himself, he had always striven to raise the level of religious life around him. His criticisms, therefore, are not those of a lax monk but of one who stood wholeheartedly for the Cluniac system as it was and deplored any infiltration of Cistercian ideas. He begins by criticizing the regulations regarding silence. Silence is good, but he would not have it pharisaical and perpetual (clearly a glance at Cîteaux); he fears that the abbots by closing the door on moderate charitable conversation, such as Cluny permits, will throw it open for clandestine and scandalous talk. But Matthew is touched more nearly by the shortening of psalmody and ceremonial. What are the abbots about? Do they mean to put manual labour in the place of prayer? And if not, how will they justify their existence?[3] Do they think ceremonies are vain? Are they not a

---

[1] Printed by Molinier, *Obituaires français au moyen âge* (Paris, 1890), pp. 288–9; reprinted by Dom U. Berlière in *Revue Bénédictine*, June 1891, pp. 260–1, and in *Documents inédits &c.*, vol. I, pp. 92–3.

[2] Berlière, *Documents inédits*, pp. 93–102.

[3] *Ibid.* p. 100: 'Quid est hoc pro Deo, fratres? Alterum horum eligite, vel ad agriculturam...exite, quemadmodum multi [*sc.* Cistercienses] faciunt, vel in claustris vestris cum silentio vestro ampliori et prolixiori psalmodiae studete.'

mortification, and of the best? And the cardinal gives a feeling description of the fatigue and discomfort of standing for hours bareheaded in an alb on a winter's night.

The abbots did not permit this reply to end the matter. They met the legate's letter with a spirited rejoinder.[1] Our efforts, they said, were all directed to true liberty of spirit. We took our vows to the Rule, not to the customs of Cluny, and though we do not claim to keep to the letter every line of the Rule,[2] yet when we try to keep it as nearly as reasonably may be, we should be encouraged, not abused, by the true friends of religion. When you were prior of Cluny, you had the name of one zealous for observance; has the spirit of the monk been extinguished by the mitre and the ring? Say, in all earnestness, why do you wish to hinder our attempts at reform? You are perfectly aware that your talk of spiritual conversation at Cluny is wholly out of touch with reality; talking in the cloister always in practice has a relaxing effect. Your words about the psalmody are equally disingenuous; we wish to reduce it, as you know, to avoid irreverent haste; no one is ignorant that we have at present far more than the Rule allows for. As regards ceremonies, whatever may be said of them in the abstract, we are few in numbers compared with Cluny, and simply cannot manage them. The abbots end with an appeal which is unquestionably sincere. The times are evil, they write, and we are struggling manfully in the darkness and the tempest. If attacks from our friends are added to those from our enemies who will blame us if we cease from our endeavours to save the sinking ship?

Whatever may have been the motives and desires of Matthew of Albano, St Bernard was never one to leave his sentiments concealed.[3] At almost the same moment that the Rheims abbots were answering

[1] Berlière, p. 94: 'Ces abbés, il faut le reconnaître, lui rendirent la monnaie de sa pièce.' He prints their letter, pp. 103–10.

[2] The abbots have not got their programme quite clear on this point. At the beginning of the letter (p. 103) they make the full-blooded Cistercian statement: 'profitemur nos non in consuetudines Cluniacenses jurasse, sed in legem et regulam Sancti Benedicti.' At the end, however, they protest (p. 110): 'Nos enim Cluniacenses consuetudines non dampnamus, non abicimus...sed adoramus vestigia pedum eorum [sc. consuetudinum].' But at bottom it is the old controversy of Rule versus Cluniac Uses.

[3] Bernard, ep. 91 (PL, vol. CLXXXII, coll. 222–4).

the cardinal-legate, a similar gathering at Soissons received a most heartening letter from the abbot of Clairvaux.

Have nothing to do [he told them] with those who say 'We would not be better than our fathers'. The prophet whom they profess to quote did not use those words. He stated a fact; he did not express a desire. While we are in this life we must either go up or go down; if we stand still we shall find ourselves precipitated into the abyss. Let others say what they will. Do not believe them. They are blind, and leaders of the blind.[1]

Meanwhile, quite independently of these gatherings at Soissons and Rheims, the main Cluniac family was now being urged in the direction of reform. In 1132 Peter the Venerable summoned no less than two hundred priors from France, Italy, and England to Cluny *ad audiendum verbum*, and their meeting was attended by representatives of other bodies, the newspaper men of the day, such as Ordericus Vitalis the historian of St Évroul.[2] Peter's reforms, like those of the abbots of Rheims, were directed mainly towards an increase of fasting and silence, and provoked from the *corpus vile* the usual reminiscences of the days of Maieul, Odilo, and Hugh, with reflexions upon the wisdom of treading the well-worn paths of sanctity without experiments. In the event, Peter had to modify the force of some of his edicts.[3]

The meeting of 1132 was not, however, the great abbot's last contribution to the movement of reform. In 1147, when he had been abbot of Cluny for twenty-four years, he drew up a long list of seventy-six changes that had been introduced in his time, adding in each case the reason that had prompted the change.[4] This most interesting compilation, especially if read in conjunction with

---

[1] Bernard, *ep.* 91 (col. 223): 'Recedant a me et a vobis qui dicunt: nolumus esse meliores quam patres nostri...sanctus Elias, Non sum, inquit, melior quam patres mei [Vulgate, 3 Kings xix. 4]: et non dixit se nolle patribus esse meliorem. Vidit Jacob in scala angelos ascendentes et descendentes, nunquid stantem quempiam, sive sedentem?' The whole of this short letter is in Bernard's happiest vein.

[2] Ordericus Vitalis, *Hist. Ecc.* XIII. 13 (ed. Société de l'histoire de France, vol. v, pp. 29 ff.): 'Fervor quoque abbatum metas antecessorum suorum transcendere praesumpsit, et priscis institutionibus graviora superadjecit, satisque dura imbecillibus humeris onera imposuit.' The whole passage is both interesting and amusing. More than 1200 monks were present, so Orderic tells us.

[3] *Ibid.* p. 31: 'Perplura de gravibus institutis quae proposuerat intermisit.'

[4] *PL*, vol. CLXXXIX, coll. 1025–48.

Ulrich's *Customs*, throws a flood of light on the conditions of daily life at Cluny. Taken as a whole, it may be said to supply a complete vindication of St Bernard's Apology. Many of the charges so strenuously resisted by Peter twenty-five years before are now not only conceded with both hands, but picked out and underlined. The general impression given by the *Statuta* is undoubtedly a saddening one. We feel that the water is coming in at every seam and that it is a desperate business to caulk the chinks. We feel too, as perhaps we felt with Peter's earlier circular letter, that there is an undertone of sadness and harshness in his words; that his pride in Cluny has gone and that he has something of the bitterness of an officer whose men have disgraced themselves under fire, and who lashes them into the familiar movements of routine rather as a punishment than with any hope of the recovery of honour.

Of the seventy-six changes nine concern the psalmody, six luxury in food, three luxury in clothes, and four silence. The first of all imposes a moderate pause in each verse of the psalmody. Short and apparently innocent as the change appears, it resumes a whole generation of controversy. It is, to begin with, a concession to Cistercian influence. Next, it is an admission that the Cistercian changes in the mode of reciting were needed, for Peter gives as his reason for the change the haste and irreverence that previously prevailed. Thirdly, it consciously adopted a mean between the old haste and the extreme slowness of Cîteaux: the monks, says Peter, are to make a moderate pause only, not one in which three *Paters* can be said, as at some houses he has visited.[1] Fourthly, Peter remains a Cluniac, even if a pessimistic one, at heart, for he remarks that the extra hour or so spent in choir is better spent thus than in the useless occupations practised hitherto. Fifthly, a rider is added that this change does not apply to Cluny itself, for there it is simply not possible to find the extra hour either in the day-time or night-time.

A similar commentary could be made on very many of the *Statuta*,

---

[1] *PL*, vol. CLXXXIX, col. 1026: 'Mediocrem vocavi [repausationem] ad distinctionem illius quam quidam facere solent, in cujus intervallo orationem dominicam, hoc est Pater noster, saepe bis, quandoque ter, olim ipse consummavi.'

did time permit. For the present we can do no more than glance at a few of the most significant decrees. Those concerning silence are particularly frank: one of the two daily periods of talking is abolished, and the reason given is that the time was not merely wasted, but spent harmfully;[1] the cloister at Cluny has become a public thoroughfare; servants bawl along the passages and carry provisions filched from the infirmary to support their relatives in the town. Manual labour is ordered in another decree, because many, and especially the *conversi*, spend the whole day gossiping or asleep against the wall of the cloister. Incidentally, we are told that the numbers at Cluny have risen from seventy-odd to between three and four hundred. But it is when dealing with cells that the language takes the hardest tone. Where less than twelve brethren are together they must at least sleep and eat together: if they cannot or will not keep the full observance they must at least preserve a shadow, a vestige, a particle of it, and not spend the whole day in sheer waste of time.[2] The language of disillusion could hardly go farther, and we note that in the statutes referring to priories there are suggestions, if no more, that grave scandals are not uncommon there.[3]

When the severity of many of these charges is borne in mind, Peter's legislation on the all-important question of the noviciate is curiously hesitant, and seems to reflect the presence of some deep-seated difficulty in the way of what seems to us perfectly reasonable practice.[4] Certainly, there is no longer that facile defence of things as they are that we noted in the first letter to St Bernard; it is now decreed that no one is to be clothed as a novice under the age of twenty. This seems at first sight to be as drastic a reform as could be wished, especially as the reason given is the evil results of the previous system. But the very next decree enacts that the noviciate

---

[1] *Ibid.* col. 1037: 'Otiositas...in tantum magnam partem nostrorum, eorum maxime qui conversi dicuntur, occupaverat, ut...aut adhaerentes claustri parietibus dormitarent, aut ab ipso, ut sic dicam, ortu solis usque ad ejus occasum... totam pene diem vanis, otiosis et (quod pejus est) plerumque detractoriis verbis consumerent.'

[2] *Ibid.* col. 1037: 'Saltem aliquam umbram vel vestigium vel particulam ordinis retinerent, ne integra die nugacibus verbis aut rebus vacantes in nullo a saecularibus differre viderentur.'

[3] For example, nos. 46 and 47 (col. 1038).

[4] *Ibid.* nos. 36 and 37 (col. 1036).

71

must last at least a month, and we are told that hitherto a novice had often been professed on the very day of his clothing. Doubtless a month is better than the inside of a day, but no one with any experience of judging and training character in any walk of life would attach much value to a single month. St Benedict six centuries before, and the universal Church in her subsequent legislation, put the minimum period of probation at a year, leaving it to individual orders to extend or double this space of time. That Peter the Venerable could legislate so easily on this point leads us to wonder whether Cluny did not regard the religious life as a routine, a profession, a task of work for which one signed on, and then performed *tant bien que mal*, rather than as a vocation, a way of life, a spiritual discipline and ascent.

With this, the last utterance of Peter the Venerable, the immediate controversy ends. There can be no doubt who has won. Peter, in the end, is so far from opposing St Bernard that he is using every effort to impose upon his own subjects not only that closer observance of the Rule for which Cîteaux stood, but even many details of Cistercian practice. We may feel perhaps that whereas the abbot of Clairvaux was working in and with a susceptible medium, the abbot of Cluny was attempting the impossible by imposing from outside what must always, in the last resort, spring from within. *Spiritus intus alit.* Yet, though we may admit to the full the deficiencies of Cluny and give full weight to Peter's unwilling witness for the prosecution, we must in honesty give equal weight to him when he speaks, as he does in his treatise *De Miraculis*, of the graces the Cluniac body has received from the Lord before his eyes, and of the saintly lives and deaths of which he has been witness. No one can read the book without acknowledging that even within the Cluniac framework and in Peter's own day sanctity was to be found. Peter himself, who won and retained the affection and admiration of St Bernard, and who said the last word of love to both Abelard and Héloïse, is no unfit epitome of all that was most typical of twelfth-century Cluny at its best. It may be that he lacks, alike in his early pleadings and his later railings, that expansive warmth of wisdom, that lucid light of truth, that are the hall-mark of Christian sanctity, and are present in such large measure alike in the black monk Anselm and in the white monk Bernard. But he is an admirable and amiable figure, and when he passed the star of Cluny set for ever. It is not without significance that the great Benedictine annalist, when he reaches that day, leaves for a moment the severe style of the chronicler to mark, in words of solemn if unstudied pathos, the end of an epoch.[1]

We have spoken of the *Statuta* of Peter the Venerable as if they formed the last document in the dossier of the controversy. This is strictly true if we regard the dispute as an ordered movement from the outbreak of the quarrel to the harmony of its resolution, and if we study it in the writings of the two great men who alone could give to it a dignified expression. If things are thus regarded, we may say that nothing was added—that nothing new could be added—after the deaths of Bernard (1153) and Peter (1156). But in point of fact there is another document, not without an interest of its own, in the shape of a fictitious dialogue between a Cluniac and a Cistercian composed by a German Cistercian apparently about 1160–70.[2] The author, who had become a black monk on what was thought to be his death-bed, lived in the house of his profession for some ten years and then migrated to the white monks. His *Dialogue* somewhat belies its title, for the fiction of an exchange of views is soon abandoned and the piece becomes little more than a tirade, supported by quotations, against the Cluniacs. The enthusiastic convert, who is clearly a man of acute but somewhat superficial intelligence, trained in the latest dialectical methods, is surprisingly well read in all the literature of the controversy. He adopts an intolerant and hectoring, not to say a grossly abusive, attitude which alienates the reader's

---

[1] *Annales O.S.B.*, ed. Lucca, 1745, vol. VI, pp. 518–19, where, after recording Peter's death, the annalist adds: 'Quo ex tempore sacra illa congregatio priscum splendorem, haud scio an aliquando ex integro rediturum, amisit.' This volume was produced after Mabillon's death by Martène.

[2] Martène, *Thesaurus* (see above, p. 60, n. 1). In his introduction the editor shows (coll. 1570–1) from internal evidence that the dialogue was written after St Bernard's death in 1153 and before his canonization in 1174. The argument seems peremptory, yet the style and mentality of the writer, and especially his scholastic, Aristotelian background, would suggest a later date. If he wrote before 1170, he must previously have fallen under the influence of the most progressive intellectual circles in Europe (cf. Otto of Freising).

sympathies,[1] and, as the Cluniac defence is never seriously presented, we do not get as much insight as we should wish into the real thoughts that were at this time occupying the minds of the rival orders. Rather, we gather with surprise that the terrain of the conflict has shifted very little from the first exchange of letters between Cluny and Clairvaux, and the charges made against the black monks give no hint that there has been a Peter the Venerable to defend or to reform.

The basic thesis of the Cistercian is once more the necessity of a complete return to the Rule as the only safe course. The Cluniac customs, the moment they are not according to the Rule (*secundum regulam*), are against it (*contra regulam*) and so evil and of no binding force. Descending to particulars, he brings before us the old list of charges—the long and frivolous conversations, the reception of novices to profession after a month's probation, the lack of manual work, the dislocation of St Benedict's time-table, the unbearably long psalmody, the luxuries of every kind. St Bernard's Apology is clearly the text-book used, and the flavour of Puritanism is clearly perceptible, with the same strange confusion of intellectual and sensual perceptions and gratifications. The black monks are accused of pandering to their five senses and examples are given (piecemeal and at long intervals) of five noxious pleasures—beautiful paintings and stained glass; melodious bells; sweetmeats and seasoned foods; incense; and soft garments.[2] We cannot resist the impression that in circles distant from Burgundy the dispute had lagged behind the times, and that the Cistercians did little more than take out the old weapons from the arsenal so well stocked by St Bernard. The only novel contribution on either side is the incidental retort of the Cluniac that his way of life is the contemplative Mary's, whereas the agricultural Cistercian has chosen Martha's part—a retort which throws no little light on the general confusion of thought prevailing

---

[1] Even the judicial Martène (in his introduction to the letter) remarks: 'Cluniacenses aliquando plus aequo perstringit, Cistercienses vero suos mire nec sane immerito extollit.' For a defence of traditional monachism, see A. Wilmart, 'Une riposte de l'ancien monachisme', in *Revue Bénédictine*, vol. XLVI (1934), pp. 296–344.

[2] For the pleasures of sight see Martène, col. 1584; hearing (bells, &c.), 1586; taste, 1628; smelling (e.g. superfluous incense), 1638; touch (soft garments), 1638.

in the author's circle. As a whole, the *Dialogue* leaves us with the same impression as Bernard's Apology, written fifty years before, that the Cluniacs were luxurious and the Cistercians intolerant. It is aesthetically unsatisfactory, though perhaps wholly in accord with human psychology in all spiritual and moral controversies, that, after more than half a century of wrangling, the combatants should disappear from sight belabouring each other with weapons forged and discarded by great men now dead. Yet, though a later generation might fail to realize it, Bernard and Peter had not failed to seize the great issue and proclaim the answer, and their experience and their words remain for all who, in the fitful fever of monastic history, have met, or may again encounter, the crisis that divided the first white monks from the black.

5

THE CASE OF ST WILLIAM OF YORK[1]

The complicated series of disputes which followed the York election of 1140–41 is familiar in broad outline to all students of the period. From a small beginning the strife came to involve almost every person of importance in England, and many on the continent, and lasted, in its ramifications, for some twenty years. Yet the history of this controversy, though it could not fail to receive some notice in any detailed account of the times, has not hitherto been set out in full with complete accuracy. This failure has been due in part to the nature of the records, which are scattered among English chronicles, papal documents and Cistercian sources, and can only be fully used by one who has them all before his eyes simultaneously; many of those who have treated the episode *obiter* have failed thus to assemble them with completeness. In part also it has been due to gaps in the evidence at more than one crucial point, which have thrown all historians back upon conjecture. These gaps, in part, still exist, but it so happens that within the last few years a number of independent studies have reconstructed much of the narrative that was hitherto dark, and some important documents have come to light; it is therefore possible to arrive at something approaching to a clear view of the whole business.[2]

Thurstan, the zealous and energetic archbishop of York who had vindicated the claims of his Church against Canterbury and had welcomed the Cistercians to Rievaulx and Fountains, breathed his last on 6 February 1140. Had he died a few years earlier, the see would in all probability have been filled by a successor of the king's choice, and no controversy would have arisen, but the political and ecclesiastical situation in England had recently undergone a great

---

[1] [First published in *The Cambridge Historical Journal* [now *The Historical Journal*], vol. v, no. 2 (1936), pp. 162–77, 212–14.]

[2] For Bibliography, see Appendix A, p. 94.

change. Politically, the country was divided by the struggle for the throne between Stephen and the empress, and the king's power had in consequence greatly declined. Ecclesiastically, the situation had since early in 1139 been dominated by the king's brother, Henry of Winchester, who was also papal legate. Henry's policy was fully Gregorian, but, as in all his actions at this time, there was in it a strong element of opportunism; he stood for a free Church, and in the matter of episcopal elections this implied the canonical procedure, that is, the free choice by the cathedral chapter assisted in their deliberations by other ecclesiastical notabilities of the diocese; but the exigencies of the time and his own temperament often led him to interfere with this freedom. Thus in the elections of these years the chapter, though nominally playing a large part in the proceedings, found its freedom limited in practice by more than one circumstance.[1] Freedom of election was a new thing, and the chapters of the great cathedrals often included several members of influential families unconnected with the diocese, together with a number of young ecclesiastics with great patrons. With such a personnel, division of opinion was inevitable, and if unanimity were not attained the minority could appeal to Rome. This in fact was what happened in the Salisbury and London elections, as later in those of York and Durham.[2] Secondly, although the legate might proclaim, and the king permit, a free election, neither refrained from putting forward candidates of his own choice and frequently also of his own kin. This, as we shall see, occurred at York, as it had occurred at Salisbury and elsewhere. The whole situation at York, however, was novel, for the York electors acted under the eyes of a group of men who held opinions on the qualities essential to a bishop and on the freedom of election which were far more exacting than those held by Henry of Winchester.

This group, formidable by reason of the high character and fearlessness of those who composed it, consisted of the heads of the

[1] See Voss, *Heinrich von Blois* (Berlin, 1932), pp. 41–5, and sources there cited.
[2] At Salisbury the legate proposed Henry de Sully, his and the king's nephew; Stephen, however, wished for Philip de Harcourt, the Chancellor. See Voss, p. 42, and Böhmer, *Kirche und Staat in England und in der Normandie* (Leipzig, 1899), p. 376.

77

newly founded Cistercian abbeys, together with the priors of the northern houses of Augustinian canons who were in sympathy with their programme of reform. Only three years previously St Bernard had provided a model for his followers by his conduct of the election at Langres, and it was scarcely a year since the Lateran Council of 1139 had reasserted the right of *viri religiosi* of the neighbourhood to assist the chapter at an election; the monks and canons were therefore in a position to know what was going forward and anxious to exert their influence.

The leader of the group was William, first abbot of Rievaulx, an Englishman by birth and subsequently a monk of Clairvaux and the intimate disciple of St Bernard. During his fruitful period of office he won the affection and reverence of all who knew him, and numbered among his spiritual sons Ailred and Waldef.[1] It is clear, however, that he had his full share of that fiery zeal characteristic of Clairvaux; this was well known to St Bernard, who on at least one occasion felt it necessary to utter a word of warning.[2] Richard, second abbot of Fountains, was of a different mould. He had been the spiritual leader of the body of monks who seceded from York in 1132; from first to last complete retirement from the world was his one desire, and we may suppose that on this occasion only a sense of strict duty led him into action.[3] Ailred, at this time a monk of fairly recent standing at Rievaulx, doubtless acted wholly according to the wish of his abbot. His friend Waldef, prior of the neighbouring Augustinian house of Kirkham, was a stepson of King David, a brother of Simon, earl of Northampton, and half-brother of Henry, earl of Northumberland; his high connexions and his own ability made him, as we shall see, a candidate for the vacant archbishopric, but, though widely known and trusted, he was still a young man and, as events were to show, had not yet found his true vocation. Thus

[1] All the sources agree in their praise of William, especially Walter Daniel, *Vita Ailredi* [ed. F. M. Powicke, Nelson's Medieval Texts, 1950, pp. 32–3], and John of Hexham, p. 317 (see Appendix A). Among the white monks he was venerated as a saint, though never formally canonized. Compare Sir Charles Peers in *Archaeological Journal*, vol. LXXXVI (1929), pp. 24 ff.

[2] Bernard, *ep.* 353 (autumn, 1143): 'Propterea sciens zelum vestrum, ne forte plus justo ferveat, temperamentum scientiae non admittens', etc.

[3] See especially the tribute of Serlo in *Memorials of Fountains*, vol. I, pp. 73 ff.

THE CASE OF ST WILLIAM OF YORK

these four men, all members of a circle inspired by the most rigid ideals of St Bernard, were by character or antecedents disposed to make a resolute stand whenever they conceived that a principle was at stake; three at least were of great energy of temper, and all were quite fearless. They were indeed a formidable group of opponents, and when to their cause were added Henry Murdac and St Bernard himself, it may be doubted whether there could have been found in all Europe another half-dozen so tenacious and so indefatigable.

As they had absorbed undiluted the ideals of Clairvaux, they naturally held the most extreme opinions not only upon the canonical freedom of elections as a part of the high policy of the Church, but also upon the exalted spiritual qualifications needed in its pastors; they were thus by no means prepared to co-operate unreservedly with Henry of Winchester, who was willing to make concessions not only to expediency, but also to the needs of secular policy, and whose plurality of offices and military adventures must have been a standing scandal to the reformers.[1] During the canvassing at York their apprehensions could not fail to be intensified by a recollection of what had happened in recent episcopal and abbatial elections. The legate and the king between them had appointed or put forward relatives at Winchcombe in 1139 and at Salisbury in 1140. Early in the latter year the monks of Malmesbury had succeeded in obtaining a free election by means of a large gift of money to Stephen, only to see the election quashed as irregular by his brother, who proceeded to appoint a candidate of his own.[2] To these instances must be added the abbatial appointments of a royal relative at St Benet's of Hulme and of a worthless illegitimate son of Stephen's at Westminster. Thus the prospects of a near relation of the king being thrust upon the electors of York were antecedently very probable; and indeed it was what actually took place.

---

[1] Besides holding the abbacy of Glastonbury while bishop of Winchester, Henry during 1139–41 was administering the sees of London and Salisbury; cf. Voss, p. 44. Henry of Huntingdon, p. 315, calls him 'novum quoddam monstrum...monachus et miles'. Bernard's adverse opinion may be seen in his letter to Lucius II (see Appendix B, p. 96).

[2] See Voss, pp. 42–5, and references.

The negotiations at York were protracted. Even if the judgement of John of Hexham be considered harsh,[1] the sequence of events makes it clear that the York electors failed to act with dispatch or decision. At one moment Waldef of Kirkham was a favoured candidate; he would naturally rally to himself both the party of reform and the supporters of the empress, and this circumstance would account for much that happened during the election and afterwards. He was vetoed by Stephen on political grounds, as being a relative of the Scottish royal house, but the earl of 'York' (or Aumâle), so we are told, who himself was related to Waldef, offered to remove the veto if rewarded for his pains by the life interest in an estate of the see. Waldef indignantly refused.[2] Finally—whether before or after this we do not know—agreement was reached upon a nephew of the king, Henry de Sully, abbot of Fécamp. Henry had the support of the legate,[3] who had put him forward unsuccessfully a year before at Salisbury, and was to repeat the move seven years later at Lincoln. The elect, however, was unwilling to relinquish his hold on his abbey, and although his uncle and patron was in no position to criticize this, Innocent II, possibly acting under the influence of St Bernard, refused to allow him to hold the two offices. The business had therefore all to be done again, and it is permissible to suppose that the miscarriage did not strengthen the morale of the electors. It was at this stage that William le Gros of Aumâle, earl of York, once more, so it was alleged, intervened in the election with a message from the king to the dean of the chapter that his nephew,

---

[1] John of Hexham, p. 306: 'Clerici Eboracenses secundum desideria cordis sui varia et vaga sententia circumacti fuerant toto anno super electione facienda.'

[2] 'Vita S. Waltheni' in *Acta Sanctorum*, August, vol. I, p. 257. Attention was first called to this important passage by Professor Powicke (*Bull. John Rylands Library*, vol. VI, 1921–22, p. 346 n.). The writer was Jocelin of Furness, *c.* 1210, but there is no reason to question his statement; he clearly had Cistercian records before him, and could have no motive for fabricating an incident which he only mentions in passing, and of which he gives precise details which, so far as they can be checked, are entirely accurate. Thus he refers to William le Gros as *consanguineus* of Waldef, a circumstance alluded to by no contemporary source. Waldef was great-grandson of Adelaide, sister of the Conqueror, by Lambert, her second husband. William, earl of Aumâle, was her grandson by Eudes, her third husband. See *Complete Peerage*, ed. V. Gibbs (revised edition), vol. I, pp. 350–3, s.v. Aumâle.

[3] John of Hexham, p. 306. Hexham wrongly calls Henry de Sully abbot of Caen.

William the treasurer, was to be chosen.[1] It was also subsequently alleged that the treasurer furthered his prospects out of his considerable wealth. The majority, therefore, in January 1141, proceeded to elect him, but a minority stood out, supported by the group of Cistercian abbots and Augustinian priors.[2] Among those who thus resisted were the senior archdeacon, Walter of London,[3] his brother archdeacons, and William the precentor. Clearly feeling had long been running high, for Robert Biseth, prior of Hexham, resigned office when the election was announced, as one despairing of the republic, and proceeded to Clairvaux where he asked for admission as a novice.[4]

William the elect was, as it seems, a son of Herbert of Winchester and Emma, an illegitimate daughter of Stephen, count of Blois, and half-sister to King Stephen. His father, himself an illegitimate son of Herbert II, count of Maine, had been chamberlain to King Henry I, and William, besides being nephew to Stephen and Henry of Winchester, was related in more than one way to a number of Norman and French noble houses, including that of Roger, king of Sicily.[5] He had been brought up from boyhood in pleasure and wealth, and while still extremely young had been given the lucrative treasurership of York.[6] His contemporaries and those who wrote before his

[1] John of Hexham, p. 313: 'Summa vero querelæ eorum [sc. the appellants] in hoc niti videbatur, quod Willelmus comes Eboracensis in capitulo Eboracensi praecepit ex ore regis hunc Willelmum eligi.' For the account given by Innocent II see below, p. 83, n. 1.

[2] We are not told if the minority still held to Waldef as candidate. Roger Howden (ed. Stubbs, RS), vol. 1, p. 198, says that Henry Murdac was William's rival, but it is clear that he is amalgamating and confusing the two elections of 1141 and 1147. Dr R. L. Poole, 'St William' [cited below, p. 95], p. 277, notes this as probable, which Tout had failed to do in *D.N.B.*, but continues: '[Bernard] exerted himself strenuously in favour of Henry and did not spare his denunciation of William.' This is to anticipate in 1141 the situation of 1147.

[3] He appears in John of Hexham, p. 307, as 'magister Walterus Lundoniensis archidiaconus'. For the erroneous identification of him with archdeacon Osbert see Appendix C, p. 97 [and the works of Sir Charles Clay there cited].

[4] John of Hexham, p. 311. Compare Ailred in Raine, *Priory of Hexham* (Surtees Society, 1864), vol. 1, p. 193.

[5] For William's genealogy see Dr R. L. Poole's 'St William', where it is set out very fully.

[6] If we may trust two Selby charters William was treasurer of York under Archbishop Thomas II, i.e. *ante* 1114 (*Selby Coucher Book*, ed. J. T. Fowler, Yorks. Arch. Soc. Record Series, no. x, 1891, vol. 1, pp. 290, 300). [Compare Sir Charles Clay, *Yorks. Arch. Journ.*, vol. xxxv (1940), pp. 8–10.] Compare John of Hexham, p. 317.

canonization agree that he was amiable and generous, though unused to exertion of any kind, or to a serious employment of his time.[1] His opponents, including the Cistercians of the north and St Bernard, accused him of unchaste living, and stood to this accusation for two years and more, maintaining it in the Roman trial before the pope.[2]

Upon his election, William went straightway to the king at Lincoln and was confirmed in the temporalities of his See; Walter the archdeacon, also on the way to Lincoln, was waylaid by the earl of York and imprisoned for a while, so John of Hexham tells us, in his castle of Bayham. Meanwhile, a few days later, on 2 February 1141, Stephen was unexpectedly taken prisoner at the battle of Lincoln, and the whole political situation was radically altered. Henry of Winchester, now the decisive influence in both Church and state, was the natural authority to whom the appellants against the election would address themselves, especially as it appears certain that Theobald of Canterbury designedly held himself aloof.[3] We do not know when the meeting with the legate took place; it was for him a year of great stress and activity, and he executed more than one political *volte face*; whatever may have happened between the parties, the appellants were ultimately directed to Rome.

By this time they had a powerful ally. We do not know how St Bernard first heard the news, but without a doubt he would have been kept informed by William of Rievaulx throughout the year. In any case, he addressed the pope in a number of vigorous letters,

---

[1] John of Hexham, p. 317; William of Newburgh, vol. I, p. 80; *Memorials of Fountains*, vol. I, p. 80. The last passage, however, bears traces of interpolation.

[2] Compare letter of Innocent II in Voss, p. 169, and W. Holtzmann, *Papsturkunden*, II, ii (Berlin, 1936), no. 32: 'Quidam religiosi viri illius terre [i.e. the Cistercians and Augustinians] in presentia nostra viva voce asseruerunt, quod in provincia illa celebris fama est de ipsius incontinentia et incestu.' Bernard, *ep.* 235, speaks of him as one 'quem rumor publicae opinionis et operis veritas detestatur'. Compare *ep.* 240, and above all his statement to Eugenius in 1145 that Imar of Tusculum 'tanta jam ut accepimus de homine illo audivit et cognovit ea, ut non possint nares ejus fetorem horribilem sustinere [ni]si tamen desuper ei fuerit data potestas' (see Appendix B, p. 96). The judgement of Vacandard (*Vie de S. Bernard*, vol. II, p. 326) that all this was calumny seems unjustifiable.

[3] So Gervase of Canterbury (ed. Stubbs, RS), vol. I, p. 123. Gervase wrote *c.* 1190, but his reference to William as 'cuidam clerico' shows that he was copying an earlier document.

of which only the last has been preserved, carried to Rome, apparently, by one who had a first-hand knowledge of the affair.[1] Soon after, the first deputation from York arrived, furnished with a commendatory letter (*ep.* 347) from Bernard. Besides Walter of London, Ailred was of the party, acting for William of Rievaulx, and his conduct of the business won him great credit.[2] The elect, accompanied by his friends, was there also, and prolonged discussion took place, for both parties had influence in the college of cardinals. Finally, the pope cited all to appear before him again on the third Sunday of Lent in the following year, that is, 7 March 1143.[3] This time the opposition mobilized its full strength. Besides Walter the archdeacon and William the precentor of York, there were William, abbot of Rievaulx, Richard, abbot of Fountains, Waldef, prior of Kirkham, and Cuthbert, prior of Guisborough. We learn from Innocent's ultimate pronouncement that the appellants brought all three charges—of unchaste life, of simony and of intrusion—against the elect, but relied chiefly on the last, for which they produced witnesses.[4] We can see clear traces of divided sympathy among the cardinals, and the testimony as to the precise circumstances of the alleged *démarche* of the earl of York was not above criticism, at least on a technical point. The rules governing the giving of witness in a canonical court were rigid, and their rigidity was not infrequently exploited by a judge (in this case the pope himself) who wished to escape the onus of a decision. Innocent therefore was able to refer the matter back to Henry of Winchester and Robert of Hereford as judges-delegate.[5] Their instructions were precise. If the dean of

[1] Bernard, *ep.* 346: 'Archiepiscopus Eboracensis venit ad vos, ille de quo saepenumero scripsimus sanctitati vestrae, homo qui...speravit in multitudine divitiarum suarum...a planta pedis usque ad verticem non est sanitas in ea [*sc.* causa ejus].'

[2] Walter Daniel, *Vita Ailredi* [ed. Powicke, p. 23]. Dr R. L. Poole ('St William', p. 277), not having noticed this passage, does not distinguish between the two legations to Rome, which are confused also by Mr W. Williams (*St Bernard of Clairvaux*, Manchester, 1935, p. 168).

[3] John of Hexham, p. 311.

[4] Dr R. L. Poole, 'St William', p. 278, writes: 'probably the critical matter was a charge of simony.' Innocent's letter (see next note) makes it clear that uncanonical intrusion was the main charge. For the personnel see John of Hexham, p. 313.

[5] Innocent's letter to the legate, first published by Voss, pp. 168–9, and since by Holtzmann, *Papsturkunden*, II, ii, no. 32, has not hitherto been used in any full account of the affair. It greatly strengthens the case against William. The pope writes: 'Utriusque

6-2

York (William of Ste Barbe), who, it was alleged, had been the recipient of the king's message, was willing to swear that the election had been free, it was to stand. Opportunity should then be given for the other two charges to be preferred. If no accuser came forward, the elect was to be allowed to clear himself on oath—the normal method in canonical procedure of rebutting *diffamatio*.[1]

This was all that the papal letter contained, and Bernard states more than once that even this was a concession to the elect: not a judicial pronouncement of the court, but an answer to a personal appeal.[2] The abbots and their company presumably quitted Rome forthwith;[3] what William did does not appear, but shortly after he arrived in England he was in possession of a second document, purporting to be an authorization to the court to substitute other witness for that of the dean. As it has been very generally assumed by historians that such authorization was duly issued by Innocent, and as much hangs upon the matter, it will be well to examine the evidence closely.

Until the publication a few years since of the original (first) letter of the pope, it was possible to suppose that this contained a clause providing for an alternative to the dean, and the suggestion was made that Innocent, knowing when he wrote that William of Ste Barbe would soon be bishop of Durham, had prepared for all contingencies

partis rationes et testes una cum fratribus nostris [i.e. the cardinals] diutius examinavimus. Gualterus siquidem archidiaconus...duos testes produxit, qui asserebant, quod dilectus filius noster S[tephanus] rex Anglorum, frater tuus, per comitem Eboracensem decano [i.e. William of Ste Barbe] mandaverat, ut G[uillelmum] thesaurarium in archiepiscopum sibi assumerent. Qui cum secundum sanctorum patrum institutionem et ecclesiasticam consuetudinem a fratribus nostris diligenter examinarentur de loco, in quo prefatus comes supradictum verbum ex parte regis decano dixit, discordes inventi sunt.' The reference in the last sentence is doubtless to Dan. xiii. 51–9 (Vulgate). Many cardinals, it must be remembered, were anti-Cistercian.

[1] Innocent's words are: 'Communi fratrum nostrorum consilio judicavimus, ut, si decanus cum duabus vel tribus idoneis personis ipsius ecclesie...juraverit...ipsa electio proprium robur optineat.' No alternative is given.

[2] Bernard, *ep.* 235: 'Hoc autem non ex judicio, sed ex misericordia: sic enim rogaverat ipse.' *Ep.* 236 (to the cardinals): 'Nec vos latuit quam plena esset sententia, non judicii, sed misericordiae; nimirum cum hoc Willelmus ipse quaesisset.' This last letter, written to members of the court which had tried the case only some six months previously, must be accepted as a true account.

[3] The trial began on 7 March, and we know that Richard of Fountains returned home, after visiting St Bernard, on the eve of Pentecost, i.e. 23 May (*Memorials of Fountains*, vol. I, p. 75).

when drafting his letter.[1] The publication of the text of the letter has eliminated this hypothesis, and full weight should therefore be given to the assertion, made by Bernard at the time, when writing to the Curia which had tried the case, and repeated two years later to Eugenius III, that the second letter was either forged or the outcome of double dealing at Rome.[2] This assertion was in the event supported by the formal statement of Eugenius, in his letter to the clergy of York on 21 February 1146, that he can find no trace of such a letter in the papal register.[3] As Eugenius wrote when surrounded by a number of cardinals who had been members of the Curia in 1143, and still favoured William, we can scarcely suppose that failure to find traces of the letter was due to secretarial carelessness in registering it, or that Eugenius would have formally declared, as he did, that William's consecration had been illicit, if he had had knowledge of the letter having been issued, even though unregistered. John of Hexham, whom previous writers have followed, does indeed state that permission was given for an alternative witness to appear, but he wrote some twenty years later, and may well be only recording a version of the story that had reached him.[4] Moreover, the full significance of what happened at Winchester may perhaps have escaped the notice of modern writers. Instead of a witness (the dean or another) appearing to swear to the freedom of election, the elect was apparently allowed to apply to the very question which was *sub judice* the procedure only allowed in the case of *diffamatio*, that is, *compurgatio* by means of an oath. It is scarcely credible that such a permission was formally given by

[1] So Dr R. L. Poole, 'St William', p. 278: a suggestion which Mr W. Williams assumes as a fact in his narrative, *St Bernard*, p. 169.

[2] Bernard, *ep.* 236 to the Curia (October 1143): 'Quid enim de eo dicam, quod occultas et vere tenebrosas litteras habuisse se gloriatur Willelmus ille?...Et ecce, audierunt filii incircumcisorum: subsannant Romanam curiam, a qua post datam tam manifestam sententiam, furtim datas esse aiunt contrarias litteras.' *Ep.* 240 to Eugenius III (1145): 'Qui sibi possessionem vindicat furtivarum commercio litterarum, nonne fur est et latro?...Si pro se [*sc.* Innocentio] respondere liceret, procul dubio diceret huic, quia Ego palam in te dedi sententiam, et in occulto locutus sum nihil.'

[3] Compare his words (Voss, pp. 169–70): '...causam diligentius inquirentes ex literis predecessoris nostri.'

[4] John of Hexham, p. 313, after giving a very correct summary of Innocent's letter, adds: 'Impetratum etiam fuit, vice decani aliam approbatam personam ad sacramentum posse substitui.'

Rome. That a second document of some kind existed seems clear, for Henry of Winchester would scarcely have ventured to act without it, but that it was either forged or (as would seem more likely) issued informally and dishonestly, and not by Innocent himself, seems equally clear from the evidence which we now possess, and it may well be that the legate allowed himself more latitude than was permitted even by this second letter.

Soon after the parties had quitted Rome, the dean of York was elected and consecrated (20 June 1143) bishop of Durham, and found himself under the necessity of forcing his way into the see, which was occupied by the intruder, William Cumin. Meanwhile, Henry of Winchester held his court as judge-delegate in his episcopal city in September 1143; there is no mention of Robert of Hereford. Henry had consecrated the new bishop of Durham three months before and doubtless knew how he stood with regard to the proposed oath; according to Bernard's contemporary statement he utterly refused to swear and even offered to give evidence in a contrary sense,[1] and it may have been the previous knowledge of this that led to the production by William's party of the second letter. When the trial actually came on, he sent a message (so, at least, John of Hexham tells us) that he was prevented from attending by his own troubles. The Cistercians also kept away, perhaps realizing that protest could now achieve nothing.[2] The people of York desired William; the legate favoured him. The elect appeared, together with a suffragan, the bishop of Orkney, and the two abbots of York and Whitby (the two black monk houses, it may be noted, hardest hit by the Cistercians), and these three took some kind of oath in his support, though probably not as witnesses to the election but as *compurgatores* to William.[3] The legate therefore proceeded to

---

[1] Compare Bernard's letter to Lucius II (Hüffer, *Der heilige Bernard von Clairvaux*, p. 234): 'Decanus namque ab ipso [*sc*. Henrico] ad prefinitum invitatus iuramentum non solum in publico iuramentum renuit sed et in contrarium iurare paratus fuit.'

[2] John of Hexham, p. 315. Actually, unless dispensed *ad hoc*, the Cistercian abbots would have been at general chapter.

[3] John of Hexham, p. 315, uses the vague words 'satisfacturi cum electo et pro electo'. *Compurgatores* did not swear to the innocence of the accused, but to his (general) reliability. Compare Paul Fournier, *Les Officialités au Moyen Age* (Paris, 1880), p. 266.

consecrate him, Theobald still holding aloof.[1] Two days previously Innocent II had died in Rome, and on the very day (26 September) of William's consecration a successor was elected, Celestine II, an enemy of the king and of the legate.[2] With the news of his election the legateship of Henry of Winchester expired.

To the new pope, and to the whole college of cardinals, St Bernard, who had heard what had happened, poured forth his indignation in letters which must rank among the most vehement he ever wrote. William is an incubus upon the Church, twice intruded into the See, once by the king, now by the legate; the abbot of Clairvaux finds life a burden in a world where such things go unpunished.[3]

Celestine was an old man, and so far as can be ascertained made no move. But this, under the circumstances, was equivalent to acting against William, for the archbishop of York had not yet received his pallium and so could not exercise full jurisdiction. Meanwhile, at about this time, the party of his opponents in the north had received a great accession of fighting strength in the person of Henry Murdac, ex-abbot of Vauclair, whom Bernard had sent to be elected abbot of Fountains in place of Richard, lately dead.[4]

Celestine died after a short reign of six months on 8 March 1144. His successor, Lucius II, was of the opposite party in the Curia; in spite of this Bernard addressed to him an invective against Henry of Winchester, in which he begged the pope to refuse any application for the pallium.[5] Lucius, however, received Henry with warmth in Rome, though he did not renew his legateship, and after some months dispatched Imar of Tusculum, a Cluniac, as legate to

[1] Gervase of Canterbury, I, 123, asserts this, but he may be merely safeguarding any possible claims of Canterbury.

[2] John of Hexham, p. 315.

[3] Bernard, ep. 235 (to the pope), calls William 'homo bis intrusus, primo quidem per Regem, deinde per Legatum'. In ep. 236 (to the cardinals) he is 'incubator ille'. Bernard writes 'urimur assidue, dico vobis, urimur graviter nimis, ita ut nos taedeat etiam vivere'. It is not without piquancy that only a short time before he had written to William of Rievaulx (ep. 353, see above, p. 78, n. 2) begging him to curb his zeal.

[4] The date of Murdac's election cannot be fixed with certainty; cf. Bernard, ep. 320: 'dudum misissem'. The most likely date is c. January 1144. Richard's obit in the President Book of Fountains is 12 October (1143). He died at Clairvaux.

[5] For this letter see Appendix B, p. 96.

England, bearing with him the pallium for William.[1] Imar passed through France, where he met Bernard, who extracted from him a promise not to bestow the pallium unless the whilom dean of York, now bishop of Durham, should be willing to swear the oath as originally prescribed by Innocent II.[2] Imar seems not to have reached England before the beginning of 1145, and was engaged in several pieces of business in the south. William of York, for his part, either because of indolence, as a chronicler tells us,[3] or because he knew of the condition to be exacted by the legate, made no movement, while the bishop of Durham wrote to Imar that the election of 1141 had been uncanonical.[4] Added to this, Theobald continued hostile,[5] and activity may have been resumed among the Cistercians.[6] Thus the legate in any case would presumably have refused to take a decisive step; as it was, Lucius II died shortly after his arrival in England (15 February 1145); when Imar returned, therefore, he carried the pallium back with him.

The successor of Lucius II was Eugenius III, the disciple of St Bernard and the friend and fellow-religious of Henry Murdac, abbot of Fountains. In his very first letter to the new pope Bernard demanded prompt and drastic action against William, and directed the attention of Eugenius significantly to the brief reigns of his predecessors.[7] The pope was in a difficult position. The majority of the

[1] Imar would seem not to have left Rome till December 1144; see Poole, 'St William', p. 279. H. Tillmann, *Die päpstlichen Legaten* (Bonn, 1926), p. 50, *note*, seems to favour an earlier date. [See now *EHR*, vol. LXIII (1948), pp. 526–7 and n.]

[2] Bernard, *ep.* 360. 'Laboravimus, quantum potuimus, adversus pestem communem …suggessimus domino Tusculano episcopo…et omnino promisit nobis se, nisi aliquid melius fecerit nobis, id saltem omnimodis observaturum, ne tradat ei pallium quod portat, si non juraverit decanus ille, nunc vero episcopus, &c.'

[3] John of Hexham, p. 317. Dr Poole, 'St William', p. 279, assumes that Imar visited York, and Mr W. Williams, *St Bernard*, p. 173, takes it for granted that he held an inquiry, but Tillmann, *Päpstlichen Legaten*, pp. 50–1, gives no reference to his presence in northern England, and I have found no allusion to it in the sources.

[4] So Bernard, *ep.* 240: 'Exstant denique litterae ipsius de eo ad apostolicae Sedis legatum [i.e. Imar, not, as Mr W. Williams, *St Bernard*, p. 174, supposes, Henry], in quibus manifeste manifestam asserit intrusionem, electionem negat.' Compare also the letter quoted above, p. 86, n. 1.

[5] Bernard, *ep.* 238, to Eugenius III (March 1145).

[6] So John of Hexham, p. 318: 'Resumpta itaque confidentia…[et] instantibus in appellatione [Cisterciensibus].' Compare *Memorials of Fountains*, vol. I, pp. 99–100. I have not, however, found mention of any in England making a move, save Murdac.

[7] Bernard, *ep.* 238. Mr W. Williams, *St Bernard*, pp. 173–4, confuses *epp.* 238 and 239.

cardinals favoured William; his consecration was a *fait accompli*, and the deposition of an archbishop was a very serious affair. But Bernard gave him no rest; in letter after letter he cried for action. The Church, he told him, is sighing for a pastor who will extirpate the stock of Ananias and Simon Magus; the pope alone can depose bishops. In whatever way seems good to him let him strike, or rather blast, the iniquitous archbishop of York. It is not for the abbot of Clairvaux to say, nor does he greatly care, which way the barren tree should fall, provided that fall it does.[1]

At this juncture, towards the end of the year, William of York, either as a forlorn hope or trusting in reports received from his Roman friends, proceeded to Rome to ask for the pallium. The case was once again examined at great length; a majority of cardinals seems still to have favoured the archbishop,[2] but the pope, supported by Bernard and taking his stand upon Innocent's original letter, declared that the required oath had not been sworn and that the consecration of William had therefore been illicit.[3] It was doubtless owing to the influence of William's friends that Eugenius did not depose the archbishop there and then; he compromised by suspending him until such time as the bishop of Durham should have sworn the oath. That, however, at this stage, was the equivalent of defeat for William; he gave up the struggle and betook himself to the court of his kinsman Roger, king of Sicily.

When the news of the papal decision reached England the patience of William's supporters in the north broke down, and some of his relatives, regarding all the recent obstruction as the work of Henry Murdac, raided Fountains intent on vengeance, and inflicted a considerable amount of damage on the abbey.[4] News of this was

[1] Bernard, *epp.* 238–40 (all of 1145): 'idolum illud Eboracense...Quo autem impetu, non dico ferienda, sed fulminanda fuerit...vestrae conscientiae derelinquo' (no. 239) ...'Nec multum interest qua parte arbor infructuosa cadat, dummodo cadat' (no. 240).
[2] John of Hexham, p. 318: 'Astipulabantur ei instanter suffragia Romani senatus.'
[3] Compare the pope's letter to the clergy of York (21 February 1146) announcing William's suspension (Voss, p. 169; Holtzmann, *Papsturkunden*, II, ii, no. 50): 'nequiter et maliciose contra formam iudicii...predecessoris nostri consecratus est.'
[4] *Memorials of Fountains*, vol. I, p. 101: 'Abbatem de Fontibus Henricum...strictis gladiis perimere moliti sunt.' The attack on Fountains is then described. John of Hexham, pp. 318–19, speaks of the attack as on a grange of Fountains, but Serlo, a monk at the time, can scarcely be in error on this point, and he is supported by the *Chronicon de Melsa* (ed. E. A. Bond, RS), vol. I, p. 115.

duly transmitted to the pope, and the mutilation by the same body of men of Walter the archdeacon, who fell into their hands about this time, called forth another urgent appeal from Bernard to Eugenius for a final sentence upon William.[1] This was at last pronounced early in 1147, and at the same time the pope issued letters authorizing another election. It was duly held at Richmond in Yorkshire on 24 July, and once again the votes were divided; the king's party, led by nominees of William, were for Hilary, sometime protégé of Henry of Winchester; a weightier group, including the suffragans William of Durham and Æthelwulf of Carlisle, were for Henry Murdac. The matter was referred back to the pope who, giving the vacant See of Chichester to Hilary, confirmed the election of Murdac, whom he himself consecrated on 7 December 1147. At the council of Rheims in March 1148, William was once more solemnly declared to be deposed.[2]

By this time he had returned to England. All hope now seemed lost, and the final disgrace caused, so we are told, a great change in him. He proceeded to Winchester, where his uncle the bishop loyally received him with all honour, and lived in the cathedral monastery with the monks in regularity and retirement, uncomplaining and without a word of reproach against his opponents.[3] So matters rested for six years till, in 1153, within a few weeks of each other, Eugenius (8 July), Bernard (20 August) and Henry Murdac (14 October) died.

---

[1] William of Newburgh, I, 56–7: 'Propinqui quoque depositi...seniorem archidiaconum qui forte in manus eorum incid[it] abscidere minime vere[bantur].' This outrage, which only Newburgh records, doubtless helped to provoke Bernard's *ep.* 252 to Eugenius III, which hitherto has been taken as referring only to the attack on Fountains, and has been branded by many (following Walbran) as violent and exaggerated. But his words do not necessarily imply that murder had been committed.

[2] John of Hexham, pp. 320–1, who says he was consecrated at Trèves. John of Salisbury, *Historia Pontificalis*, ed. R. L. Poole (Oxford, 1927), p. 6, says it was at Auxerre. For Murdac's activity at the council and the earlier decision of Eugenius, supported by a minority of the cardinals, see Gervase of Canterbury, I, 134.

[3] John of Hexham, p. 320; a passage written before there was any question of canonization, and supported by the account in *Annales de Wintonia* (ed. H. R. Luard, *Ann. Monastici*, RS, vol. I, p. 54). For a somewhat embroidered version, which however refers to Winchester testimony, see *Historians of the Church of York* (ed. J. Raine, RS), vol. II, pp. 272–3.

When his opponents had thus all been removed by death, and the See to which he had been consecrated was again vacant, William once more took action, though it is impossible to be certain as to the exact sequence of his movements. William of Newburgh, the only quasi-contemporary source of information, states that he set out from Winchester on hearing of Bernard's death, while Murdac was still alive, but his statement in the same sentence that he proceeded to Rome to ask for mercy, not justice, seems, as Dr Poole noted, to involve confusion, for a plea for mercy could have no meaning while Murdac still occupied the See.[1] The late and usually untrustworthy *Life* of St William, and other late sources, relate that he went to Rome only after another election at York,[2] and this may well be the true version, for we know that he did not return to England till April 1154, six months after Murdac's death. In any case, when he arrived in Rome, he found the new pope, Anastasius IV, and the leading cardinals friendly;[3] everything, in fact, both at Rome and in England, would clearly be simplified by his appointment; and it was effected. He returned to his diocese in May 1154, and took especial pains to visit Fountains, to which he promised compensation, and Meaux, the Cistercian foundation of his sometime supporter, the earl of York.[4] The Cistercians had now undoubtedly decided to forget the past,[5] but the personal feud of so many years was not yet dead among the restless higher clergy of York. The Archdeacon Osbert and others appealed to Theobald of Canterbury as legate, bringing presumably the old charges against the personal character of William, and against actions of his during his previous tenure of the See. Before further steps could be taken the archbishop was dead. Shortly after his triumphal entry into

[1] William of Newburgh, vol. I, p. 79: 'Tertio [*sc.* Henrico] adhuc superstite...spe recuperationis concepta...judicium non accusans, misericordiam humiliter postulavit.' Compare Poole, 'St William', p. 280.

[2] *Historians of the Church of York*, vol. II, pp. 274, 396. See also *Chronicon de Melsa*, vol. I, p. 116.

[3] Anastasius had been one of his chief supporters (*Historians of the Church of York*, vol. II, p. 274); the powerful Cardinal Gregory of St Angelus favoured him (Will. Newburgh, vol. I, p. 79).

[4] *Memorials of Fountains*, vol. I, pp. 109–10; *Chronicon de Melsa*, vol. I, pp. 116–17.

[5] I can find no authority for the statement of Voss (p. 69), 'doch der Fanatismus des Cisterziensertums glühte noch im geheimen fort.'

York, having solemnly celebrated mass before entertaining a number of the clergy, he was on the same day taken ill, and died a week later, on 8 June; whereupon the dean, Robert, and Osbert the archdeacon succeeded (by questionable means, it was said) in bringing about the speedy election of Roger of Pont l'Évêque, archdeacon of Canterbury, who was duly approved by Theobald as legate and consecrated by him on 10 October.[1]

Meanwhile, a charge had been preferred against Archdeacon Osbert of having murdered the late archbishop by means of poison administered in the chalice at mass. The matter came before King Stephen at a council, no doubt that held at Westminster at Michaelmas, when the York election was discussed.[2] The accuser, one Symphorian, a chaplain of William, professed himself ready to undergo any of the various trials by ordeal; the accused, Osbert, protesting his innocence, demanded to be tried in an ecclesiastical court. Before any decision was reached, Stephen died; Henry II took cognizance of the case, and only with great difficulty could Theobald succeed in withdrawing it from the royal to his own jurisdiction.[3] When at last, in 1156, the archbishop began the trial the case went through all the familiar stages. Symphorian could not produce the necessary witnesses;[4] Osbert was therefore given the opportunity of clearing himself on oath of *diffamatio*, if his three brother archdeacons and four other clerics were ready to act as *compurgatores*. For whatever reason he failed to give satisfaction

[1] William of Newburgh, vol. I, pp. 81–2: 'Robertus decanus et Osbertus archidiaconus...Rogerium...elegerunt, magnisque suffragiis atque terroribus Eboracense capitulum ad consentiendum induxerunt.'

[2] Compare the letter of (Theobald to Adrian IV, written by) John of Salisbury, ed. Giles, vol. I, p. 170, *ep*. cxxii [*Letters of John of Salisbury*, ed. W. J. Millor, H. E. Butler and C. N. L. Brooke, I, Nelson's Medieval Texts, 1955, no. 16; *q.v.* for the date]: 'In praesentia regis Stephani et episcoporum et baronum Angliae in quodam conventu celebri.'

[3] John of Salisbury, vol. I, pp. 170–1 [*Letters*, no. 16]: 'Vix cum summa difficultate in manu valida, cum indignatione regis et omnium procerum, iam dictam causam ad examen ecclesiasticum revocavimus.' This is an interesting confirmation of Dr Z. N. Brooke's judgement as to Theobald's strength (*The English Church and the Papacy*, Cambridge, 1931, p. 189).

[4] G. Foliot, *ep*. cxiv (ed. Giles, vol. I, pp. 152–3), says: 'nullis fulta testimoniis verba funde[bat].' Theobald, however, implies a mere technical flaw (John of Salisbury, vol. I, p. 171 [*Letters*, no. 16]): 'Cum...actor...secundum subtilitatem legum et canonum accusationem non posset implere.'

and appealed to Rome,[1] and so the case disappears from our sight[2] with the formal letter, written for Theobald by John of Salisbury, his secretary, acquainting Adrian IV with the facts. A fortunate chance gives us the personal views of two acute contemporaries, but they are at variance. John of Salisbury, writing on private business to Adrian about this time, adds in what is almost a postscript to his letter that, whatever anyone may say, Osbert failed in his purgation.[3] It is natural to suppose that the *quisquis* of the letter alludes to Gilbert Foliot, bishop of Hereford, who for some reason had constituted himself Osbert's advocate with the pope. Foliot, who had read Theobald's letter, writes to inform Adrian that Symphorian had been bold in his challenges to the ordeal and in his appeals to the king's court only because he knew that ecclesiastical law forbade clerics to have recourse to either; he therefore begs the pope to keep an open mind and protect the innocent.[4]

No record is extant of what happened at Rome, but every indication goes to show that no formal judgement was ever given, either there or in the court of a judge-delegate.[5] The episode has its importance in view of what happened so soon after in England. It has not, so far as I am aware, been remarked that the spectacle of this case, relinquished by the king at the demand of the primate, passing through a series of fruitless delays and ultimately failing to reach an issue, may well have given Henry an incentive or an excuse for his demands at Clarendon in 1163. However this may be, if a formal process had ever been concluded we should scarcely find William of Newburgh thirty years later endeavouring—not, we may think, very

[1] Salisbury says he failed; Theobald that he preferred to appeal; Foliot is silent.

[2] [Dom Adrian Morey has since shown that there is evidence of the later stages of the case in a decretal of *c*. 1175–80: this proves that Osbert appeared both before Adrian IV and before Alexander III; he claimed to have been acquitted by Adrian, but this may not have been the truth, or the whole truth (*CHJ*, vol. x, pp. 352–3, 1952). It was probably in or soon after 1157 that Osbert was removed from his archdeaconry and retired into secular life (cf. Clay, *Yorks. Arch. Journal*, vol. XXXVI, 1944–47, pp. 277–9, 286).]

[3] John of Salisbury, *ep.* cviii (I, 158 [*Letters*, no. 18, Autumn 1156]): 'Osbertus Eboracensis archidiaconus in purgatione defecit. Quisquis vobis suggesserit aliud, non credatis.'

[4] Foliot, *ep.* cxiv: 'Has quidem [litteras Theobaldi]...diligenter inspeximus.' It is interesting to find Foliot warmly supporting Osbert's refusal to submit to the king's court.

[5] [But see above, n. 2.]

efficiently—to elicit for himself and for posterity the truth of the matter from isolated survivors of the circle of archbishop William.[1] He had spoken, he tells us, with an aged, invalid and dying monk of Rievaulx, who had been a canon of York, and who denied the possibility of foul play having escaped the notice of himself and others. On the other hand, he quotes with approval the statement of Symphorian (with whom also he had spoken) that William had taken an antidote to poison. Strangely enough, he gives no hint in his narrative that Symphorian was the leading spirit of the accusation, which he refers to as *mera quorundam opinio*, nor does he indicate Osbert as the accused, though he animadverts with severity upon his other activities. Indeed, taken as a whole, his evidence does little to clarify the question. He convinced himself, though it can scarcely be said that he proved, that the charge was without foundation; but before he wrote miraculous cures had been reported at the archbishop's tomb. They continued, and in 1227, after due inquiry, William was canonized by Honorius III. Thus ended, in a manner not wholly free from enigma, the story of William Fitzherbert, which had throughout its course abounded in unexpected changes of fortune and in episodes which, to us at least, must remain in some measure enigmatic.

APPENDICES

A. BIBLIOGRAPHY

The principal sources of the narrative, in chronological order of composition, are: St Bernard's *Epistolae* (quoted from Mabillon's edition, reprinted Paris, 1839); John of Hexham's continuation of Symeon of Durham's *Historia Regum* (ed. T. Arnold, *Symeonis Opera*, RS, II), composed *c.* 1160–70; William of Newburgh's *Historia Regum* (ed. R. Howlett, *Chronicles of the Reigns of Stephen etc.*, RS, I, II), *c.* 1195; the *Narratio Fundationis* of Fountains (ed. J. R. Walbran in *Memorials of Fountains*, vol. I, Surtees Society, 1863), dictated *c.* 1203 by an aged monk Serlo, who had been a witness of the years 1132–54. John of Hexham, the fullest and most consecutive of these, is on the whole reliable and well informed; he

---

[1] William of Newburgh, I, 80–2.

is slightly biased against both the York clergy and Bernard, but sympa-
thizes with the party of reform; it should, however, be remembered that
he is not strictly contemporary. From 1141 onwards he gives dates
wrongly a year in advance. His editor corrects in the margin, but not all
students have noticed this, and confusion has resulted.

Among the more important recent contributions by specialists may be
mentioned: 'Ailred of Rievaulx and his Biographer Walter Daniel', by
Professor F. M. Powicke (*Bulletin of the John Rylands Library*, vol. VI,
1921–22, pp. 310–51, 452–521, reprinted separately in 1922 [and later
revised in *The Life of Ailred of Rievaulx by Walter Daniel*, Nelson's
Medieval Texts, 1950]), a most valuable essay, in which is printed the
greater part[1] of Walter Daniel's *Vita Ailredi*, an addition to the original
sources; *Die päpstlichen Legaten in England*, by Helene Tillmann (Bonn,
1926); 'The Appointment and Deprivation of St William, Archbishop of
York', by Dr R. L. Poole (*EHR*, vol. XLV, 1930, pp. 273–81); *Heinrich von
Blois*, by Lena Voss (Berlin, 1932). [In 1950 Dr C. H. Talbot published
some recently discovered letters of St Bernard in an article in which he
showed that they threw new light on the case of St William, while con-
firming the main lines of the present article (*CHJ*, vol. X, pp. 1–15).
'They showed, for instance, the cause of the failure of the first legation to
Rome in the early part of 1142 [Ailred of Rievaulx and Walter of London
could not prove their charges, because they lacked *first-hand* evidence],
who were the main supporters at the Roman Curia of the opposing party,
the dangers run by the Cistercians and Augustinians in presenting their
case, and several other details of a like nature' (see also above, p. 93, n. 2,
and below, p. 97).]

Hitherto no account of the affair has taken notice of the two papal
letters printed by Voss (pp. 168–70) from a MS. (137; ff. 84 and 93) of
Corpus Christi College, Oxford, and since reprinted by Dr Walther
Holtzmann, *Papsturkunden in England*, II, ii (Berlin, 1936), nos. 32, 50.
Innocent's letter is of March 1143, Eugenius's of 21 February 1146. Nor
has any notice been taken of a letter and part of a letter of Bernard's
bearing on the case, which are not contained in the editions of his works
and were printed from the same Corpus MS., 137 (ff. 82v, 89v) by
G. Hüffer, *Der heilige Bernard von Clairvaux. I. Vorstudien* (Münster,
1886; no more parts appeared), pp. 234–7. For these see below,
Appendix B.

The first to make a serious attempt to piece the narrative together (if we
except Mabillon's notes to Bernard's letters) was J. R. Walbran in his

---

[1] [In the revised edition of 1950 the *Life* is printed complete.]

annotations of the early Fountains documents referred to above. Since then the story has been told by T. F. Tout, *s.v.* William Fitzherbert in the *Dictionary of National Biography* (1889), by the late Abbé E. Vacandard in his *Vie de S. Bernard*, ch. XXVIII (4th ed., Paris, 1910, vol. II, pp. 314–27), by H. Böhmer, *Kirche und Staat in England* (Leipzig, 1899), pp. 377 f., by Dr R. L. Poole in the article already referred to, and, most recently of all, by Mr Watkin Williams in *St Bernard of Clairvaux* (Manchester, 1935), pp. 167–76. No account is free from all error, and the articles on St William in standard works of reference contain numerous inaccuracies.

B. Two unfamiliar letters of St Bernard

Use has been made in the text of the article of the two letters of Bernard published, as stated above, by G. Hüffer. To the best of my knowledge, they have not appeared elsewhere, and no English writer has noticed them.

The first letter is addressed to Lucius II soon after his election, i.e. it was written perhaps early in April 1144; it is Bernard's only letter to that pope known to exist. It is typical of the writer both in its vehemence and in the inimitable and daring felicity of its scriptural reminiscences. In it Henry of Winchester is fiercely denounced for acting against the Roman decision of Innocent II. 'Expectabamus' (writes Bernard) 'ut vitis illa Wincestrie, immo ut vulgo canitur vitis secunde Rome, faceret uvas, sed conversa in amaritudinem vitis aliene fecit labruscas' (p. 234). Further on, Henry becomes the Philistine who sets up the idol Dagon near the ark of the Lord, and the harlot who sells herself to all who pass by the way. Finally, the pope is warned against 'seductor ille vetus Wintoniensis' (p. 236). Bernard's letter did not prevent Lucius II from giving a warm welcome to Henry in Rome, but it may have had influence in preventing the pope from renewing the legateship he had held under Innocent II.

The second letter is in reality the second half of *ep.* 239 to Eugenius III, of which previous editors had given a greatly shortened text. It belongs to the group of letters dispatched to the pope soon after his election by Bernard, and as it refers to Imar of Tusculum as still legate in England ('legatione fungitur') it must have been written in the very early weeks of the new reign.

Hüffer in his notes (p. 226, n. 1; p. 228, n. 2) tells us that he received the letters of English provenance from Edmund Bishop (those in the British Museum) and Dr Plummer (those at Corpus, Oxford). The text of the Oxford letters is far from satisfactory, and a new edition of them would be welcome.

C. WALTER AND OSBERT, ARCHDEACONS OF YORK

As mentioned in the narrative (p. 81), the leader of the opposition to William's election in 1141 was Walter 'of London' the archdeacon. He was imprisoned for a short time at Bayham by the earl of York, but was soon at liberty, for he was one of the deputation at Rome in 1142 and again in 1143. In 1147 the 'senior archidiaconus' of York was mutilated in revenge by the relatives of William (Newburgh, vol. I, pp. 56–7); he is clearly to be identified with Walter, and is 'senior' in distinction to the archdeacons of Richmond, Cleveland and Nottingham. There is no further mention of him.

At some period under Henry Murdac Osbert took his place; he appears as active during the short interregnum after Murdac's death (October 1153), when he restored Elias Paganel, recently deposed by the archbishop, to the abbacy of Selby (*Selby Coucher Book*, ed. J. T. Fowler, vol. I (Yorks. Arch. Soc., Record Series, no. x, 1891), p. [45]), expelling Germanus. The latter, a monk of St Albans, retired thither, and the abbot lodged a protest on his behalf at Rome, as a result of which Elias was restored by Theobald as legate and Osbert rebuked (so *Historia Selebeiensis*, p. [45], and *Gesta Abbatum S. Albani*, ed. H. T. Riley, RS, I, 120). Osbert, as related in the article, opposed William in 1154, took a leading share in electing Roger, and was accused of poisoning William.

The two archdeacons are quite distinct, and are doubtless the Walter and Osbert in the following of Thurstan who witness a charter, *c.* 1139 (*Hist. York*, vol. III, p. 65). The editor, however, of the *Vita* of St William (*Hist. York*, vol. II, p. 271), perhaps misled by the late *Vita* of Henry Murdac (*Hist. York*, vol. II, p. 389), identifies Osbert with William, in which he is followed by Tout, Voss and others. There is no warrant for this.

[On these archdeacons see Sir Charles Clay, *Yorkshire Archaeological Journal*, vol. XXXVI (1944–47), pp. 277–9, 283, 286, and *York Minster Fasti*, vol. I (Yorks. Arch. Soc. Record Series, no. 123, 1958), pp. 33, 46, who confirms that Walter was archdeacon of York or the West Riding, and shows that Osbert, who was Archbishop Thurstan's nephew, was probably archdeacon of Richmond.]

6

ARCHBISHOP THOMAS BECKET:
A CHARACTER STUDY[1]

The long controversy between Henry II and Archbishop Thomas of Canterbury is probably the most familiar episode in the history of the twelfth century, and the great protagonist in the drama is certainly the most celebrated Englishman of his age. Yet, for all that historians and hagiographers and poets have written and sung, the character and personality of St Thomas elude us like a wraith each time that we start forward to grasp them. Judgements have been made, and pictures drawn, in plenty; but with scarcely an exception they appear unreal when narrowly scanned; they are words, not life; the being they describe might tread the stage, but certainly never sat in the archbishop's hall at Canterbury. The most assiduous medievalist is often the first to admit that he can get no clear sight of the great archbishop.

This is not the fault of the age in which he lived. We feel that we have a clear and just, if necessarily imperfect, conception of Anselm, of Abelard, of Bernard, and of Ailred of Rievaulx, of John of Salisbury, and Hugh of Lincoln—and, indeed, of Henry II and Gilbert Foliot. Nor is it due to lack of material. The nine volumes of the Rolls Series devoted to the subject are far from containing all that there is to find. And yet the difficulty remains, and it was because a deepening acquaintance with the subject increased my appreciation of this difficulty that I set myself the task, by deciding the title of this lecture, of setting out the evidence once more.

The difficulty does not lie in a lack of material, but it is, perhaps, intensified by the quality of that material. There are at least eleven lives in print,[2] all written by contemporaries who were in many

[1] [The Raleigh Lecture on History, 1949, published in *The Proceedings of the British Academy*, vol. XXXV, pp. 177–205.]

[2] By John of Salisbury, William of Canterbury, Benedict of Peterborough, Alan of Tewkesbury, Edward Grim, William FitzStephen, Herbert of Bosham, Guernes of

instances acquaintances and in several cases intimate companions of the archbishop. These lives present, indeed, critical problems of great complexity; their relationships are manifold and often greatest when least suspected, and the problems of their interdependence have given occasion for discussion and research comparable to the critical studies devoted to the lives of St Francis of Assisi. But they do not, like the Franciscan documents, present various interpretations of the personality of their object; their defect is rather that they were written by men who had experienced the shock of the murder and had been subsequently dazzled by the coruscation of wonders, by the influx of pilgrims, and by the official canonization. They were also, without exception, clerks or monks committed professionally in greater or less degree to the cause sponsored by the archbishop, even had it not been approved by miracles. They were therefore in every way, and above all in their analysis of character, committed to the ultimate sanctity of their subject. Yet it may be said that there are innumerable letters extant of the archbishop himself, and of such acute observers as Gilbert Foliot and John of Salisbury. This is true, but it is also true that all these letters, without a single notable exception, are letters written for some practical end connected with the great controversy. With very few exceptions, more apparent than real, they are official or business letters, and this is especially the case with the letters written by the archbishop himself. Yet even this is not the whole story. Neither Anselm, nor Bernard, nor John of Salisbury could write a letter, however occasional, without revealing his personality. Not so Archbishop Thomas.

This is in itself characteristic. Archbishop Thomas felt no need for self-expression of a literary kind. While elaborate personal letters and considerable literary work have come to us from so many

Pont S. Maxence, Anonymous I (the so-called Roger of Pontigny), Anonymous II, and the anonymous author of the Icelandic Saga. The best discussion of the dates of composition and mutual relationships of these is by E. Walberg, *La tradition hagiographique de S. Thomas Becket* (Paris, 1929). The two fullest, most original, and best authenticated are those of William FitzStephen and Herbert of Bosham, both clerks of the archbishop, but several of the others contain much, and all contain some, original matter. In addition, of course, there are the many letters contained in the last three volumes of the Rolls Series *Materials for the History of Archbishop Thomas Becket* (ed. J. C. Robertson and J. B. Sheppard). All references with no further indication are to the last-mentioned work, cited by volume and page.

of his contemporaries, there is no suggestion that Thomas ever wrote anything save his official letters. There are, as history and our own experience teach us, men whose personality and charm seek an outlet and reveal themselves in every page they write or word they speak. Such were Cicero and Augustine in the old world, Anselm and Bernard in the twelfth century, Cromwell, perhaps, Abraham Lincoln, and Newman in the modern world. The charm and power of others were felt by their contemporaries; we see it in their influence and their achievements; but their surviving words are not conductors of the magnetic spark. Such in the recent past was David Lloyd George, such was Cardinal Manning, such, perhaps, with certain reservations, was the great Napoleon, such, in the twelfth century, was Archbishop Thomas.

Yet one further observation may be made before we approach his life. The canonization of St Thomas was due directly to his murder and to his posthumous fame, not to his personality. Whether in his latter years his life showed any clear marks of dawning sanctity is a question which it is certainly possible, if not plausible, to answer in a different sense from his biographers, and most certainly he was not an example of that type of sanctity which recurs throughout the ages, where the predestined spirit seems to walk from childhood with unseen reality. Nor was he of those who pass at a definite moment, with Paul, with Augustine, and with Francis, from the world of other men into a new world of the spirit. Whatever we may think of the change of life that Thomas made in 1162, it was not for him the clear-cut beginning of a mystical or heroic existence. In other words, whatever be the difficulty of interpreting his words and acts, it does not arise because their author is himself transcending the limits and categories of common experience.

Whatever may have been the patriotic imaginations of earlier historians, there can be no doubt that Thomas was of Norman blood through both his parents.[1] He had therefore as the basis of

[1] II Anon. IV, 81: 'Gilbertus...Becchet, patria Rothomagensis...habuit autem uxorem nomine Roesam, natione Cadomensem, genere burgensium quoque non disparem.' W. FitzStephen, III, 15, is more definite: 'ortu Normannus et circa Tierrici villam (i.e. Thierceville).'

his character the Norman temperament, different both from that of the Englishman and the Frenchman. The Englishman of the Anglo-Saxon centuries had certain recognizable, if indefinable, character-istics, seen at their finest in an Alfred, a Dunstan, a Wulfstan, and an Ailred; there was a certain warmth and ripeness and sympathetic gentleness, that had in it the seeds also of weakness and boorishness. The Normans, as seen in the Conqueror and many of his knights, bishops, and abbots, as also in their cousins in Italy and Sicily, had a drastic, hard directness, a metallic lustre of mind, highly coloured and without delicacy of shading, together with a fierce efficiency that easily became brutality. We begin, then, with these two general observations upon St Thomas. He was a Norman and, as his most familiar and characteristic actions show, true to his race; and he was by nature one who did not seek or find self-expression in reflective or intimate writing.

Psychologists reiterate, what indeed normal experience and obser-vation teach, that the very earliest impressions and environments of infancy are the most influential. Thomas's father was of knightly class,[1] but had taken up with trade, first, perhaps, in Caen and later in London, and by the time his son was born had become a pros-perous citizen, well known in the public life of London and of standing to give entertainment to men of rank connected with the court.[2] He was older than his wife,[3] and misfortunes overtook him in his latter years, which straitened the family fortunes.[4] There is no suggestion—rather the reverse—of sympathy and under-standing between father and son, and if the widespread tradition that the boy stammered[5] rests on fact, it is possible that Gilbert in some way dominated or repressed him. His mother, on the other

---

[1] W. FitzStephen, III, 15: 'ut ille [sc. Theobaldus]...de equestri ordine.'

[2] II Anon. IV, 81: 'in commerciorum exercitio vir industrius.' W. FitzStephen, III, 14: 'vicecomes aliquando Londoniae'...(he and his wife were) 'cives Londoniae mediastini neque foenerantes neque officiose negotiantes sed de reditibus suis honorifice viventes.' For his guests v. Grim, II, 359. J. H. Round, *The Commune of London* (Westminster, 1899), p. 101, published a charter of 1137 witnessed by Gilbert Becket.

[3] Grim, II, 359: 'Pater jam senuerat (when his wife died in Thomas's twentieth year).'

[4] *Ibid*.

[5] Compare *Thómas Saga Erkibyskups*, ed. Eiríkr Magnússon, ch. VII (RS, vol. I, p. 29). The editor remarks (vol. II, p. xcvii) that this trait is mentioned in all the Icelandic accounts.

hand, was a strong influence for good. To her he owed his early piety, his devotion to the Blessed Virgin, his lavish generosity to the poor, and, we may suppose, his purity of life.[1] It was for her sake that he pursued what were to him at the age of twenty ungrateful studies, and when she died his home, even with a surviving father, was cheerless.[2] She is indeed the only person, save the two kings, old and young, whom Thomas is recorded to have loved. Strangely enough, though we have many details of his early life, there is no mention of his sisters. He had at least two—the one a citizen's wife, exiled with the other relations, the second a nun and later Abbess of Barking[3]—but there is no suggestion and little likelihood that they held in the boy's emotional life the place so often taken by a sister. It is, indeed, noteworthy that, apart from his mother, no woman had any place in Thomas's life, and save for an official letter or two to the old empress and such, there is only a single letter addressed to a woman in his correspondence.[4]

Though it was long before intellectual interests meant anything to Thomas,[5] the boy, and later the man, had many gifts of body and mind. He was tall, handsome, and vigorous, with dark hair, pale complexion, and aquiline nose.[6] All who knew him remarked on his

[1] I Anon. IV, 7: His mother used to give to the poor food and clothes and money equal in weight to her child. She taught him: 'sicut ipse referre solitus erat, timorem Domini, et ut beatae Mariae Virgini post Christum spem suam committeret.' Compare John of Salisbury, II, 302–3.

[2] I Anon. IV, 8: 'Mater, quae sola ut erudiretur instabat, defuncta est, et exinde circa studia Thomas se remissius coepit habere. Paternam igitur domum quasi vacuam et desolatam sublata matre fastidiens, &c.'

[3] His sister Agnes founded the hospital of St Thomas of Acre on the site of his birthplace (Dugdale, *Monasticon*, vol. VI, pp. 646–7). For Mary, Abbess of Barking, *v.* Gervase of Canterbury, I, 242; Guernes knew her well (ed. Walberg, 1922, pp. 210–11).

[4] The single example is a characteristic letter (*ep.* 672, VII, 307) to one Idonea, 'dilecta filia sua', whom he charges with serving a papal letter on Roger of York. She was under a vow of virginity and the archbishop proposes Judith and Hester as her models, and wishes her 'perseverantem in virtute obedientiae et iustitiae zelo vigorem'. It would be attractive to identify her with the daughter of Baldwin de Redvers, 'viriliter agens et zelum habens obedientiae Dei', who according to W. FitzStephen, III, 102, refused to take the oath against the archbishop in 1169.

[5] II Anon. IV, 82: 'Seriis discendorum omissis saecularium ineptiis meditationum inhaesit.'

[6] Grim, II, 359–60: 'venustus aspectu, forma satis elegans.' J. Salisbury, II, 302: 'statura procerus.' W. FitzStephen, III, 17: 'naso eminentiore et parum inflexo.' The Thomas Saga (*loc. cit.*) vouches for his pallor and dark hair, but Herbert of Bosham notes his occasional high colour in later life.

abnormally keen sight and hearing, and on the acuteness of his other senses;[1] they also note his marvellously retentive memory, with which he could recall without effort and with absolute accuracy words heard or read long before.[2] All remark, in addition, on his readiness of speech and his address in argument—qualities exemplified at more than one critical moment of his life.

We have glimpses also of his moral characteristics. He was, from childhood, devout. Whether or no we may believe one biographer who tells us that he was from infancy dedicated to the priesthood,[3] it seems quite clear that he never passed through a period of religious negligence or a crisis of doubt. Similarly, all agree that, though as a youth he may have complied with the speech and manners of his companions, he was throughout his life entirely pure.[4] It is significant that neither Henry II nor Gilbert Foliot, when using all available ammunition against him, ever make the slightest charge in this respect. Chaste and devout, he had therefore in a sense less excuse for his faults of vanity and extravagance and ambition, for he had not forfeited his spiritual clarity of sight.

Though living in a bourgeois home, circumstances gave Thomas an early glimpse of another world. Richer de Laigle, a Norman baron of note, was in the habit of staying in his father's house and often took the boy out riding with hawk and hound.[5] Sport became a passion with him; his devotion to it and his knowledge of the fine points of hunting and fowling is noted by all his biographers and cast in his teeth by Foliot and his other enemies.[6] Even after his change of life and in the midst of misfortune, as a tired wanderer his

---

[1] W. FitzStephen, III, 17. I Anon. IV, 6: 'Quod nos quoque in majori ejus aetate multotiens probavimus.'

[2] I Anon. IV, 5: 'memoriae vivacitas.' II Anon. IV, 82: 'tenacis...memoriae'; cf. J. Salisbury, II, 302.

[3] II Anon. IV, 82: 'Parentes eum ecclesiasticae militiae servitio devoverunt.'

[4] H. Bosham, III, 166: 'Juvenis amplexus prae honesto [i.e. on account of his good looks] tamen castitatis semper amator vehementissimus fuit.' Compare J. Salisbury, II, 303.

[5] Grim, II, 359–60; I Anon. IV, 5–6; Guernes, 206–30. For Richer, see note of E. Walberg in his edition of Guernes, p. 219. He lived to be one of the signatories of Clarendon (Materials, IV, 207) and died in 1174. He may well therefore have given his reminiscences to the Canterbury monks and others.

[6] W. FitzStephen, III, 20; H. Bosham, III, 165; Grim, II, 360.

keen appraising glance at a falcon on the wrist of a loitering knight all but betrayed his disguise.

It may have been his aversion from learning and his attraction to the pursuits of a class to which he did not belong that delayed the recognition of Thomas's unusual gifts. His talents were not precisely those best fitted to take him through the schools to a brilliant ecclesiastical career; his genius was for action, for organization, for leadership, and for debate. In any case, when he returned from Paris at the age of twenty-one[1] to find his home desolate he drifted into a career that could scarcely have satisfied him, that of a financial clerk to a relative in the city.[2] It was only after three years that he came almost by accident into the household of Theobald of Canterbury, his father's fellow countryman,[3] and joined that brilliant society of eager and ambitious young clerks among whom were some of the keenest minds of Europe, men destined to high places in the churches and counsels of many lands, to archbishoprics and bishoprics, to the cardinalate, and even to the papacy itself.[4]

We can gain a fairly clear picture of the young Thomas of twenty-five. Reserved and even repressed, yet possessing unusual gifts of which he must have been fully conscious, he was at first uneasy in the exclusive circle of Theobald's curia.[5] He won his way by being all things to all men, and by humouring and becoming indispensable to the old archbishop.[6] Gradually, as he found his feet, he took still

[1] Will. Canterbury, I, 3: 'Vigesimum secundum aetatis annum...agebat.'

[2] Grim, II, 361: 'Osbernus, Octo-nummi cognomine, vir insignis in civitate...cui carne propinquus erat.' W. FitzStephen, III, 14, says Thomas became 'vicecomitum clericus et rationalis'. J. H. Round, *Geoffrey de Mandeville* (London, 1892), pp. 374–5, and *The Commune of London*, pp. 113–24, have shown that Osbern Huit-Deniers was justiciar of London *c.* 1140–41, i.e. while Thomas was his clerk.

[3] W. FitzStephen, III, 15: 'Gilebertus cum domino archipraesule de propinquitate et genere loquebatur...natu vicinus.'

[4] The society has been celebrated by Stubbs in a well-known lecture. Humbert, archdeacon of Bourges and later Urban III, was a member of Thomas's household in France (H. Bosham, III, 529).

[5] This is implied by the twice-successful hostility of Roger of Pont l'Évêque, noted by W. FitzStephen, III, 16; cf. *ibid.*: 'Horum respectu Thomas minus litteratus erat... rudis et pudoratus.'

[6] H. Bosham, III, 168: 'Eo plus gratum quo plus fidum et devotum pontifici impendisset obsequium.' I Anon. IV, 9: 'Nullum illi [*sc.* Theobaldo] familiariorem, nullum...haberet cariorem.'

more the tone of his surroundings. He helped others to preferment and expected the like help in return.[1] He accepted revenues from many sources and began to indulge the taste and talent for magnificence and display that was a part of his natural character and to court popularity with those above and below himself—a trait that perhaps reveals the void left by a lonely childhood, starved of love and encouragement, and his consequent abandonment to the attractions of the new glittering world. All the biographers are agreed on a few salient characteristics—his charm,[2] his generosity, his gentleness,[3] his infinite desire to please and to be applauded, his strict truthfulness.[4] One trait—or rather the absence of one—should surely be noted. In all the mass of biographical material there is scarcely a single reference to personal affection given or received. Thomas was admired, listened to, and followed, but not loved; for his part, he delighted in directing or controlling or pleasing men, but not in friendship. John of Salisbury, a very sensitive witness, has respect and admiration, but not the fire of personal devotion. Not even his clerks who had followed him so long and admired him so sincerely make mention of affection. The only two human beings (apart from his mother) who are recorded to have loved him are the two masters, Theobald and the king,[5] whom in different ways

[1] Compare his pact of mutual assistance in obtaining benefices with Roger of Pont l'Évêque and John (later of Poitiers) in Will. Cant. I, 4.

[2] Grim, II, 359–60: 'Venustus aspectu, forma satis elegans, gratum sese omnibus et amabilem exhibebat.' Compare John of Salisbury, II, 302; W. FitzStephen, III, 17: 'omnibus amabilem.'

[3] I Anon. IV, 8: 'superexcellens ejus mansuetudo et liberalitas.' Compare ibid. 9, 'mansuetudinis sinceritas'; 10, 'solita mansuetudine'; 12, 'mansuetudo'.

[4] For the desire of esteem, cf. Will. Cant. I, 5: 'popularis aurae flatibus delectari'; John Salisb. II, 303: 'supra modum captator aurae popularis'; I Anon. IV, 13: 'favori populari supra modum deditus videretur'; H. Bosham, III, 166: 'popularis aurae, quam juvenis captabat, sequens spiritum.' No doubt there is literary interdependence here, but all these writers knew Thomas personally. For his love of truth, cf. W. FitzStephen, III, 17: 'fallere vel falli praecavens'; Grim, II, 360: 'Vix aut nunquam joco vel serio quicquam protulerit contrarium veritati.'

[5] For Theobald see above, p. 104, n. 6. For the king's affection, Grim, II, 372: 'quem supra omnes homines [rex] adamaverat.' Thomas for his part certainly loved Henry; cf. H. Bosham, III, 276, 294: 'qui adeo regem [i.e. in 1164] diligebat quod eo exacerbato laetus et hilaris esse nequivisset'; cf. also the archbishop's letters: 'dilectissime domine' (V, 267); 'domino carissimo' (V, 282) and, writing to Robert of Hereford in 1166 (V, 453): 'Unum est, quod sine multa animi mei amaritudine sustinere non valeo. Fleo super dilectissimo domino nostro rege.'

he strove to please by concealing his real self, and it is worth noting that both were, though in different ways, disillusioned at the last.

In 1154, at the age of thirty-six, the archdeacon of Canterbury was appointed chancellor. The prime agent in this was Theobald, and his principal aim was to protect the Church against encroachment; he may also have hoped to make the succession to Canterbury possible for his protégé, for with rare exceptions all chancellors since the Conquest had become bishops. The archdeacon certainly did not shrink from the appointment; he may even have paid for it.[1] Hitherto the chancellorship had not been a major office, nor was Thomas immediately successful, but when he found his feet his ability and energy and magnificence made his seven years' tenure memorable. Conscious of his own powers he now had for the first time great responsibilities and great opportunities. Moreover, for the first time in his life the mature Thomas, whose young manhood had been spent in narrow circumstances, could now meet the great on an equality and prove to himself and to them that he could excel and surpass them in their own accomplishments and pastimes. Prescient though he was in many ways, Theobald assuredly did not anticipate the torrent of energy and the blaze of splendour that followed the arrival of his archdeacon at court. The attention of historians has been so concentrated upon the later controversy that few have paused to record the achievement of those seven years, distorted in perspective as they have often been by the quotation of a few highly coloured incidents from the biography of William Fitz-Stephen. Nevertheless, they are essential to an estimate of Thomas's character. The extent of his achievement and celebrity is unquestion-

---

[1] Foliot roundly asserts this to be public knowledge; cf. his words (v, 523–4): 'quis toto orbe nostro, quis ignorat, quis tam resupinus ut nesciat vos certa licitatione proposita cancellariam illam dignitatem multis marcarum millibus obtinuisse?' That no notice of this payment appears in the relevant pipe roll does not necessarily prove the falsehood of the assertion, and the words of W. FitzStephen (III, 18) that payment for the chancellorship is equivalent to simony because the office is a stage to ecclesiastical preferment may well have been intended to explain how it was that the election as archbishop of such a reluctant candidate as Thomas could be regarded as tainted.

able; it is vouched for by chroniclers, biographers, and cool critics such as John of Salisbury and Arnulf of Lisieux;[1] some of it can be checked from the earliest pipe rolls. Not only did the chancellor display remarkable powers of organizing and executing with exceptional speed every kind of undertaking, whether civil, military, or architectural; not only did he show clearly for the first time the indefinable but unmistakable stamp of greatness—greatness in conception, greatness of manner, greatness in execution[2]—but he showed also a tact, a charm, and a prudence which overcame the prejudices and rebuffs of his first months and won the respect and support of all save the envious and the discontented.[3] This tact, this charm, this prudence should be noted. They are not the qualities associated with Archbishop Thomas in most men's minds, but they are attested by the most reliable contemporary witnesses. The same witnesses, moreover, agree that the archbishop readily listened, and was prepared to defer, to serious criticism.[4] He had none of the sensitive vanity or blind egoism or domineering, demanding ways which usually distinguish the fanatic, the despot, and the dictator. It is worth bearing this in mind; when in later years Thomas acted tactlessly, stubbornly, or harshly, it was not because of an old character-fault, but because he judged, rightly or wrongly, that the time had come to dismiss conciliation and neglect criticism.

As he grew in self-confidence he displayed his magnificence and

---

[1] Compare their letters, v, 13–15, 20–1.

[2] W. FitzStephen, III, 20: 'Tanta tamen animi magnitudine...magnanimus magna perquirebat.' *Ibid.* 24: 'animi magnitudinem.' H. Bosham, III, 172–3: 'in adversis magnanimum, in apparatu magnificum'; cf. also his eloquent outburst, *ibid.* 176: 'supra omnes et prae omnibus apparebat magnificus, sicut magnus corde magnus et corpore, magnus et apparatu. Nihil circa eum nisi magnum, nihil nisi magnificentia.' The I Anon. IV, 22 refers to his 'magnanimitas'.

[3] W. FitzStephen, III, 23: 'Ut cuique erat aetas, ita quemque facetus adoptabat.' Will. Cant. I, 5: 'conformans se regiis moribus...idem coenandi dormiendique tempus observare.'

[4] Compare the sharp rebuke of Alexander Llewellyn after Clarendon, and the many examples of the freedom of speech allowed to John of Salisbury. Nor is the request to Herbert of Bosham to act as his constant monitor, though related by Herbert himself (III, 186), to be dismissed as apocryphal; Herbert gives many instances in his narrative of advice given by Robert of Merton and other clerks at moments of crisis, and not infrequently the archbishop followed the course proposed to him.

versatility in every direction. Sweeping in all the many emoluments that came his way, not excepting those from vacant abbeys and bishoprics, he poured out all lavishly on entertainment, on gifts, on his establishment and its furnishings—plate, clothes, beasts, and provisions. His hounds, his hawks, and his horses were a marvel; no subject of the English king before, and none again till Wolsey, so dazzled the eyes of Frenchmen. Over all there was a gaiety, a gallantry, an irresistible blend of high spirits and panache[1] joined to solid work and keen foresight.[2] He must even show that he could have been a *preux chevalier* of the best; his personal men-at-arms and his trumpets were the cynosure of the host; he himself, now chancellor and still archdeacon, donned armour and overthrew his foe, while at the same time, with that steady drive towards the end with a disregard of the means that characterized him, he would have taken Toulouse out of hand untroubled by the feudal scruples of his master.[3] To Henry himself—young, imperious, gifted, impulsive, and gallant as yet—Thomas showed once more his powers of adaptation and comradeship. To the experience and counsel of an older man he joined the sympathy and gaiety of a comrade. Indeed, to the young Henry, with the freshness of youth added to the charm of royalty as it appeared to the son of a burgher family, Thomas felt drawn by the magnetism of personal devotion, intensified as it was by the fifteen years of age that lay between them.[4]

Yet for all the high-spirited *camaraderie* this was not what his life should have been, and he knew it. Modern apologists have palliated his extravagance and even his military exploits on the score that he was no more than a deacon. His contemporaries neither

[1] W. FitzStephen, III, 24: 'colludebant rex et ipse, tanquam coaetanei pueruli, in aula, in ecclesia, in consessu, in equitando.' The whole celebrated passage might be cited.

[2] John Salisb. II, 305: 'experientissimus, et bene solitus plusquam facile dici posset futura metiri.' Compare Will. Cant. I, 77 (the literary source of John's words) and, in another context, H. Bosham, III, 436: 'Novimus quippe omnes dominum nostrum archipraesulem virum valde industrium in multis exercitatum et expertum multa, a quo etiam praedicta evenerunt saepissime.'

[3] W. FitzStephen, III, 33–4.

[4] W. FitzStephen, III, 25: 'magis unanimes et amici nunquam duo aliqui [*v.l.* alii] fuerunt temporibus Christianis.'

made nor would have accepted such an excuse,[1] and, beyond this, he knew that he had 'devoted his life to the Church; it was for that that he had been advanced by Theobald, and he must have known well that when he tired of all this business he would find a bishopric ready to hand—for which he would be how ill prepared! Beyond this still there was the call of Christ, which has been the same in all ages. The promises of the gospel are not made to the rich, to the worldly, to those clad in soft garments who are in the houses of kings. Thomas knew this, and his lavish almsgiving may have been in part a compensation. Nor was it enough that his chastity was proof[2]—here at least he did not follow Henry—and we may believe that there is little if any exaggeration in the accounts of his efforts— again a psychological compensation—to maintain the rights of the Church[3] and to multiply his secret penances and prayers. Throughout his chancellorship there is this tension, this reserve; we hear of decisions taken alone and of the exterior unwilling compliance with others. But whether hiding himself or revealing himself he could not fail to be a master of men.

In one quarter, however, he did not succeed in being all things to all men. The sober Theobald could not be won by extravagance or display, and there is evidence that, as he saw his end approaching, he examined his conscience still more strictly, and found things amiss. He sent more than one urgent summons to his archdeacon, calling him to his spiritual father's death-bed and even threatening anathema. But the chancellor could not serve two masters; he did not come, and he never saw Theobald alive again.[4]

---

[1] W. FitzStephen, III, 25–6; H. Bosham, III, 185–6. H. Bosham, III, 183, quotes the opinion of many that 'nimis foret absonum, et omni divino juri adversum, hominem militari potius cingulo quam clericali officio mancipatum, canum sectatorem et pastorem avium, ovium constituere pastorem'; cf. the judgement of Thomas himself (III, 290): 'superbus et vanus de pastore avium factus sum pastor ovium; fautor dudum histrionum et canum sector.'

[2] The biographers are unanimous here; I Anon. IV, 14, cites the testimony of those who had served him for twenty years; W. FitzStephen, III, 21, quotes that of his confessor, Robert of Merton.

[3] I Anon. IV, 12–13: 'pravam regis voluntatem...caute et quasi ex occulto, ne suspicioni pateret, frustrante.'

[4] Compare the letters of Theobald and John of Salisbury, V, 9–15.

There is no hint in any biography that Thomas had been expecting or desiring the archbishopric in the long months of Theobald's decline. There was an unexceptionable candidate to hand in Gilbert Foliot. Nor is there any reason to doubt the sincerity of his resistance.[1] Certainly he never shrank from high office or responsibility, but the chancellor's life was sweet and he knew, from his past training and from his conscience, that he could never be a worldly and pliant archbishop. He knew the king also[2]—for Thomas never misjudged men though he may sometimes have misjudged the effect of his actions upon them—and he knew well, as did another chancellor, his namesake, four centuries later, that no appeal to the past would weigh with his lord. He, Thomas, could hide his own deepest personality and meet Henry on another level, but the king would not follow him if he gave freedom to his true self. What he did not, perhaps, realize yet was that whereas he could retain his loyalty and affection for Henry throughout a bitter quarrel, Henry's love would vanish once and for all like morning mist when his will was thwarted.[3]

Once he had made his decision Thomas became the servant of the Church, whose laws he knew well. His change of life was startling and real, but it was not yet in the deepest sense a conversion. As chancellor he had given free play to his natural, worldly tastes and talents; as archbishop he moulded his life on the lines which he had always inwardly admitted to be those of his vocation. But the deeper conversion, the real surrender of his life to the unseen, the break with the world he had loved, was not yet.

Thomas was by nature thorough, drastic, and masterful. The ordering of his life as archbishop was therefore physically stern and austere. There is no reason to doubt the substantial accuracy of Herbert of Bosham when he details the day's horarium with its vigils, its maundies, its haircloth, and its scourgings. But in a more

---

[1] Will. Cant. I, 7. H. Bosham, III, 181–2, vouches for having heard the exiled archbishop often tell of his resistance.

[2] Compare his remark to the prior of Leicester (W. FitzStephen, III, 26): 'dominum meum regem intus et in cute novi.'

[3] H. Bosham, III, 294: 'Jam [*sc.* at Woodstock in 1163] deprehendit archipraesul, qui regem ex multo tempore et familiaritate eximia noverat, cor regis elongatum ab eo.'

subtle way the archbishop had not put off the old man. The magnificence, the expense, the panache were still there.[1] Thomas might wear haircloth and wash the feet of the poor, but in the splendour of all his appointments, in the lavishness of his gifts, and in his commanding presence he was a very different archbishop from the calm Theobald and the gentle Anselm.

The storm which the chancellor had foreseen was not long in breaking. Again and again the archbishop withstood the king or acted in opposition to what he knew to be his policy. But his very audacity and lack of hesitation seem to show that while he knew there would be strife he thought of it as a tournament rather than as an issue that would break the ties that held him to his old brilliant life with the king. As is familiar to all, the first crisis that revealed the gravity of the contest developed at Clarendon, where the king, after frustration at Westminster, demanded assent to what soon became the celebrated sixteen constitutions. The archbishop knew that they ran starkly counter to the requirements of a free church in direct canonical relations with the papacy, and for long he stood out. He was in the end overborne by a crescendo of pleas, persuasions, and promises; by anxiety for his colleagues, fear for himself, and affection for the king.[2] Popularity, the favour of others won by compliance, had often been his aim in the past, and it would seem that he yielded at the last because he was unable to bear the bitterness of the reproaches of the king and his friends. As always, his decision was sudden and uncounselled.[3] He repented almost as soon as he had yielded,[4] and the following months must have been

[1] H. Bosham, III, 228: 'Mensa haec splendida tota; splendida in discumbentibus, splendida in adstantibus, splendida in ministrantibus et in epulis splendidissima... nihil in domo adeo pontificis faciem reddebat demissam ut mensa inops.' The whole passage, with its description of the archbishop's piercing scrutiny of the dining hall, is very characteristic both of the author and his subject.

[2] H. Bosham, III, 276, 277, twice strongly asserts this sense of personal loyalty, and though various other motives—fear, compassion for threatened colleagues, &c., are alleged by other biographers—he is possibly correct. The archbishop's own admission (given by W. FitzStephen, III, 67), 'caro enim est infirma', is ambiguous.

[3] Gilbert Foliot, writing to the archbishop himself (V, 528), can scarcely be falsifying the facts: 'Dicatur itaque quod verum est...a fratrum suorum collegio simul et consilio dominus Cantuariensis abscessit, et tractatu seorsum habito, &c.'

[4] H. Bosham, III, 289 (on the evening of the meeting at Clarendon): 'archipresul in via supra modum conturbatus videbatur, &c.'

among the most unhappy of his life. He had lost every advantage of a firm stand; he had antagonized some of his colleagues and betrayed others, yet he had failed utterly to recapture the confidence and affection of the king.[1] The months that followed were the only period of his life in which he acted inconsistently and imprudently at every level, and his indecision and inconsistency no doubt reflected his lack of strength to stand alone in his conviction and his need for support either from his king or from the pope. His attempts to leave the country against his undertaking given at Clarendon were unwise and ineffective, and his subsequent attempts at reconciliation ineffective and humiliating. Meanwhile he continued to provoke Henry and to disobey his summons.

In consequence of this, the critical meeting at Northampton in October 1164 opened with the primate at a disadvantage, and as the early days passed his difficulties, his danger, and his indecision increased. Had Henry known when to hold his hand the victory would have been his, and Canterbury would have lacked its most precious shrine. But Henry knew neither pity nor moderation. The archbishop, deserted by his colleagues, now had in the king not an adversary in an equal struggle, but a ruthless enemy, bent on his ruin. He was face to face with pain, imprisonment, perhaps even death, and that not for a principle but in a feudal, personal quarrel; he would pass into oblivion and pope and king would pick up the threads of their old life while he lay in prison or in the grave. His mental agony was joined to physical fear such as the battlefield had not brought,[2] and that in its turn brought on an illness that was possibly the result of the mind's attempt to escape from its dilemma.[3] It was at this crisis that the decisive change in his personality was

[1] Grim, II, 383: 'Nam regi quidem et ex parte paruit, et regis tamen irreparabiliter animum amisit.'

[2] Grim, II, 392, describing the incident: 'indicem anxietatis sudorem ostendit.' Compare Guernes, l. 1546: 'Quant il l'oï, la char l'en prist tute a fremir.'

[3] It is naturally impossible to be certain whether the archbishop's illness was wholly or in part somatic. The fact of its frequent recurrence and its sudden disappearance would suggest a psychological element, and all agree that it was brought on by his anxiety. It is worth noting that Grim tells us that it was illness that prevented Thomas from answering the king's first summons in the case of John the Marshal, and that then, as at Northampton, Henry suspected the archbishop of using his illness as a pretext (Grim, II, 390–1).

achieved—the result, so his biographers relate, of the advice of his confessor, Robert of Merton.

If you wished [Robert told him] you could easily escape from all danger and not only mitigate the king's anger, but make him your friend. You refuse to do so because you choose rather to seek the will of God. The affair, then, is no longer in your hands, but in God's, and He will be with you. Stand fast in your just cause.[1]

The events of the following day are familiar to all—how the archbishop, having said a votive Mass of St Stephen, carried his own cross into the hall of the castle, how he refused to hear judgement pronounced and forbade his colleagues to take part in his trial, how he regained the initiative he had long lost by lifting the quarrel to the high level of a spiritual issue, and how he broke from the circle of his enemies. It was the first of the two occasions when, for a whole act's length, he stood in the centre of the stage of English history.

Yet, though he now carried his cross with a realization of its power and of its message, he was no Anselm. As he strode out through the hall the knights raised the cry of traitor, among them the king's illegitimate half-brother Hamelin. Thomas turned fiercely on him and called him bastard. 'If these were not a priest's hands', he exclaimed, 'you would feel their strength.'[2] Late that night, in a storm of wind and rain, he rode out of Northampton in disguise.

The incidents of the archbishop's short Odyssey throw a welcome light on his personality. His assumption of the dress of a simple lay-brother of Sempringham would seem to have been as effective a disguise as the hat and cloak assumed to give a stage incognito to a Garrick or an Irving. Unaccustomed to walking on rough ground, he stumbled over the shingle on the Flanders beach or rode uncomfortably on a pony with a wisp of hay for bridle. His commanding presence, his fine hands, and the air with which he gave presents of food to children convinced cottagers and innkeepers that they were entertaining one of the great. A biographer records his courteous acceptance from a warm-hearted fisherwoman, dimly

[1] I Anon. IV, 45.   [2] Will. Cant. I, 39; I Anon. IV, 52.

perceptive of his eminence, of a staff that had lain in the chimney-corner, heavy with soot and with the grease of fish, and we are told how he looked with the quick glance of a judge at a falcon on a knight's wrist, remembering perhaps

> that long-distant summer-time,
> The castle, and the dewy woods, and hunt
> And hound, and morn on those delightful hills.

And, as he looked, the knight said to his friend: 'That's the archbishop of Canterbury or the devil.'[1] Nor had his sense of the magnificent left him; by the time he arrived at Sens he was accompanied by 300 horsemen,[2] and his friends had difficulty in persuading him to moderate his style even at Pontigny.[3]

The six years of exile are a sharply defined period in the life of the archbishop in which he found himself in circumstances entirely novel to his experience. To the student of the present day they are a stumbling-block, for the scanty evidence of his personal life must be derived either from the accounts, often repellent to modern ears, of his austerities, or from the severe and even harsh tone of his letters. When, in November 1164, Thomas retired with a small group of clerks and servants to the celebrated and observant abbey of Pontigny, he withdrew, for the first time in his adult life, from the activities of administration, travel, and lawsuits. Granted, he had with him the nucleus of a household, with whom he continued a skeleton curial routine; no doubt, also, correspondence and visitors occupied some of his time. Nevertheless, the period as a whole, and especially the earlier years before the great conferences began, was a time of retreat and enforced inactivity. The excitement of the struggle had passed; the uncertainties of the issue remained; responsibility for the Church in England was his and his alone, for he could at any moment have put an end to the deadlock by a single word of submission,[4] and now he had to bear the attacks of his

---

[1] I Anon. IV, 56–7; H. Bosham, III, 326–9. I have adapted the neutral phrase 'aut ei simillimus'.

[2] W. FitzStephen, III, 74.

[3] Compare the letter of John of Poitiers, v, 196 ff.

[4] Compare his words in consistory to the cardinals, given by H. Bosham, III, 352.

enemies, the criticisms and impatiences of his friends,[1] and the searchings of heart, the seasons of doubt, and the physical discomforts of a temporary lodging. The psychological strain which such conditions imposed on such a temperament as his must have been great. The evidence that we possess indicates that he met the trial with equanimity. He had wished, he said, for years for such a time of retreat and study, in which to repair the omissions of other days,[2] and John of Salisbury who, though not now in his household, was in constant communication with him, bears witness to the change for good which the new conditions had upon him.[3] Exiles are naturally and notoriously discontented, jealous, and quarrelsome, and some of the archbishop's clerks failed to persevere. Others, however, of no less distinction, joined themselves to him, and the majority held fast, even under great temptation; numerous small indications show that what held them was the leader's grasp, which the archbishop never lost, together with his gallantry of spirit and the loyalty which he inspired.[4]

The mental and physical rigours of Pontigny were increased by the archbishop's resolve to adapt himself to the monastic life. He assumed the habit, lay on a rough pallet, followed the offices, ate sparingly, and even for a season endeavoured to follow exactly the coarse dietary régime of the monks. To these austerities he added frequent scourgings, long vigils, the wearing of haircloth, and immersion in the cold stream that flowed through the offices.[5] It is not

[1] Compare the opinion of the Archbishop of Rouen in 1166, quoted by a correspondent (v, 420): 'Totum quoque quod agitis aut extollentiae imputat aut irae.' John of Salisbury was particularly outspoken, e.g. v, 216 (1165): 'Sicubi vero aut exorbitare a justitia, aut modum excedere videbatur, restiti ei in faciem'; ibid. 545: 'Novit enim cordium Inspector...quod saepius et asperius quam aliquis mortalium corripuerim dominum archiepiscopum.'   [2] II. Bosham, III, 358.

[3] v, 545: 'Et proculdubio domino Cantuariensi quod ad litteraturam et mores plurimum profuit exsilium istud.'

[4] H. Bosham, III, 374: 'Semper tam aequalis, tam compositi, tam erecti animi esset, ut in omni pressura sua vix adverti posset ullam se sentire pressuram...semper hilaris, semper jocundus, jocundus mente, jocundus facie, jocundus semper et aequalis.'

[5] Compare in particular Grim, II, 412-13 (Pontigny); 417-18 (Sens). For an almost contemporary parallel to his penitential immersions, see the austerities of Ailred of Rievaulx (Walter Daniel's *Vita Ailredi*, ed. Powicke [Nelson's Medieval Texts, 1950, p. 25]), and for a modern example, *Father William Doyle, S.J.*, by A. O'Rahilly, 3rd ed., pp. 306 ff. Fr. Doyle, a heroic chaplain of the Irish Guards, fell at Ypres in the First World War.

surprising that his health deteriorated. A modern reader may first smile and then turn in revolt from details that must be left in Latin. No doubt the twelfth century was less delicate than the twentieth, but it is worth remarking that even the monks of Canterbury regarded Thomas's mortifications with marvel. Saints as well as fanatics are on occasion extravagant, and each reader may make his own pronouncement on the great archbishop; those who, with another saint and namesake of Thomas, are 'of nature so shrinking from pain that they are almost afeard of a philip'[1] may be allowed to respect his sincerity and high courage.

The first weeks of his exile had been something of a moral triumph for the archbishop. Not only had the King of France hailed him as a confessor for the cause of Christ, but Alexander III, after full examination and hearing the envoys of Henry II, had solemnly condemned the greater part of the constitutions and publicly recognized Thomas as the Church's champion. It might well have seemed that the phase of mental and moral strife was over for him. Logically, the procedure would have been for the pope to co-operate with the archbishop in bringing growing pressure to bear, first upon the bishops of England and then upon the king. Thomas, indeed, maintained throughout, first, that nothing but the threat of excommunication and interdict would break the king, and secondly, that such a threat, seriously made, would be effective. All that happened in the struggle vindicated his judgement. The difficulty was that with a man of the calibre of Henry II nothing but firm, continuous, and relentless pressure would have availed. This difficulty, hard enough for a pope to overcome at any time, was rendered peculiarly formidable by a number of reasons which historians have enumerated, and which need not delay us here.

Not the least of these reasons was the past and present bearing of the archbishop. The early months of exile at Pontigny had undoubtedly deepened his earnestness, but his greatest handicap from his life as chancellor was the wrong relationship it had created between himself and the king—a relationship tolerable enough

---

[1] Sir Thomas More to his daughter Margaret Roper, *Correspondence of Sir Thomas More*, ed. E. F. Rogers (Princeton, 1947), letter 211, p. 506.

between a young king and a chancellor younger than his years, but one quite intolerable between a mature monarch and his spiritual father. The archbishop's first attempt to change this relationship had been to assert the primacy of spiritual authority. Now that the quarrel had deepened, he made a valiant attempt to establish a purely spiritual, personal, and paternal relationship with the king. In the three celebrated letters of 1165 he strikes a deeper and more intimate note than anywhere else in the correspondence.[1] But he lacked the background, the acknowledged wisdom, and the experienced sanctity that had given strength to Lanfranc and Anselm. Henry did not deign to answer; and the note is rarely heard again.

The biographers, who dwell in some detail on the life at Pontigny, tell us little of the remaining four years of exile. Nor have we any intimate letters of those years. Our judgement, therefore, of the archbishop's personality is influenced, at least unconsciously, by the impression given by his public actions and official letters. The struggle was a dour one, between men of exceptional tenacity and power, and both parties soon realized that it could be ended only by the capitulation or annihilation of one of them.

Each was possessed of a weapon of great efficacy: Henry could eject and keep out of his dominions the archbishop and his supporters; the archbishop could cast his opponents out of the society of Christendom and suspend his clerical foes from office. As we have seen, Thomas had as archdeacon and chancellor been noted for his ability to be all things to all men that he might win all. From Northampton onwards another man appears—rigid, stubborn, even ruthless. These qualities are not virtues; an Anselm or a More could be unyielding and immovable enough without them, but neither Anselm nor More had a sense of past guilt and weakness. One who has long yielded to human respect and worldly compliance—one whose gentleness has been mistaken for whole-hearted sympathy—may easily, from self-distrust or by way of compensation, turn from gentleness to uncompromising rigidity.

[1] These are the letters *Loqui de Deo*, *Exspectans exspectavi*, and *Desiderio desideravi*, v, 266–82.

More than one of his biographers note that Thomas, throughout his life, was gentle to the toward and harsh to the froward.[1] The phrase is a commonplace of medieval morals and lives, but it has a relevance here. When once Henry, by exiling the archbishop's relatives, began total warfare Thomas showed himself every whit as relentless. He was a masterful man, and it may be that the somewhat capricious treatment he received from the pope drove him to act swiftly when he could. Certainly whenever his hands were freed he used the whip, and its lash fell most sharply on those of his opponents who were most exposed. Drastic he had always been; he took his great decisions swiftly and without counsel,[2] and it may be that some of them were ill-advised—the Vézelay excommunications, for example, the first excommunication of Jocelin of Salisbury, and, four years later, the sentence against York and London. In each case he had strict justice on his side, but in each case he lost, externally at least, more than he gained.

The tone of the archbishop's utterances during these years has met with adverse judgement from his own day to this, and an appraisal is essential for those who would have a complete view of his personality. It is, perhaps, allowable to remark that no one can fairly pass judgement who has not read more than once and deeply pondered the whole long series of letters. Moreover, it must be remembered that we have before us nothing from the archbishop and his staff save official or semi-official pieces from the dossier of the struggle. The public pleadings and rejoinders of either party to a protracted and bitter controversy must always seem overbearing, or at least one-sided and opinionated. Also, readers in a later age, to whom the controversy has no actuality, and who have been educated in a social tradition of toleration and gentle speech, may too readily be repelled by firmness and severity and consistency which the circumstances of the time fully justified. The utterances of Socrates at his trial have not escaped this criticism, and it is even

---

[1] W. FitzStephen, III, 39: 'affabilis mansuetis, se efferentibus severus' (he is referring to the monks of Christ Church); the phrase is an echo of the Rule of St Benedict.

[2] H. Bosham, III, 417: 'virum velocem in opere suo.' He notes (III, 392) that the Vézelay excommunications were resolved upon 'nobis inconsultis' (i.e. his familia).

probable that many, if they were to be frank, would confess to receiving something of a shock at the action of Christ Himself in expelling the traffickers from the Temple enclosure, or at His stern and biting denunciation of the Pharisees. Certainly such utterances can only be justified if the words are true and there is necessity for speaking them. So with the words of Thomas. His severity is only justifiable if the essential justice of his case, and the impunity which the forces of evil enjoyed, made it necessary for him to use whatever force of word or sanction he could command. In such matters, each student or reader must make his own judgement with a due sense of the grave issues involved.

The first excommunication of Jocelin of Salisbury is certainly a case where he would appear to have acted with formal justice, but severely and, perhaps, unadvisedly. Jocelin, by permitting and assenting to the election as his dean of the justly excommunicated John of Oxford, had certainly deprived himself of any canonical foothold. There was, however, much to be said in his defence. He had, at considerable personal risk owing to the king's old grudge against him, been the archbishop's loyal supporter at Clarendon, and had remained his sincere well-wisher at Northampton.[1] Since Thomas had been in exile, the king had mercilessly extracted from him the sums for which he had gone bail on the archbishop's behalf.[2] Now, still in danger, he had been subjected to strong pressure by the king in order to force him into agreeing to the appointment of a useful royal clerk. Weak he doubtless was, but he had not acted from either contempt or enmity towards the archbishop. John of Salisbury thought the sentence just, but severe, and used all his influence to procure its revocation.[3] Jocelin's excommunication

---

[1] For these incidents, and the sources from which they are drawn, I may, perhaps, be allowed to refer to the account given in the Ford Lectures of 1949 [*Episcopal Colleagues of Thomas Becket*, pp. 111-14].

[2] John of Poitiers to Archbishop Thomas (?1165), V, 223: 'Dominum Saresberiensem in tantum praegravasse dicitur, ut nec uno bove hodie dominium ecclesiae Saresberiensis excolatur.'

[3] Compare his letters to the bishop's brother, Richard de Bohun, VI, 186-7, his son Richard, *ibid.* 187-90, and the bishop himself, *ibid.* 191-3. His final counsel to the last-named is submission: 'Nihil aliud consulere possum quam. . .quod Deo potius oportet obedire quam hominibus.'

had the result of throwing him finally into alliance with Gilbert Foliot, while it had no great effect as a piece of justice.

Another important occasion on which the archbishop's severity is open to criticism is more crucial. It is his fulmination against the archbishop of York and his companions, the bishops of London and Salisbury, of the papal excommunication and suspension with which he had been furnished in 1170. These bulls, it will be remembered, he sent across the Channel immediately before returning to England in November, and they were served upon the three prelates when they were about to take ship to visit the king. It was their bitter statement of their grievance, and the allegation that the archbishop had returned to bring, not peace, but a sword, that provoked Henry into the outbursts of passion that gave the impulse to the four knights, and it was the demand of these knights for the revocation of the sentence against the bishops, firmly and repeatedly refused by the archbishop both in his hall and in the cathedral, that served as a pretext for the final act of violence. Certainly the missive sent from Witsand as a harbinger, and the manifest satisfaction of the archbishop at having driven the blow home,[1] startle the reader as a sudden and unexpected cut of the whip across the face. We cannot refrain from asking, not only was it wise, but was it charity? Would Anselm or even Gregory VII have acted thus?

There are, however, some considerations to be borne in mind. The first is, that the bishops concerned—and especially Roger of York—had acted with full knowledge that they were trespassing upon a traditional preserve of Canterbury. The second is, that the three prelates were actually crossing to the king for the express purpose of taking part in an election to the vacant English Sees and abbacies—a flagrant reassertion by Henry of one of the uncanonical decrees of Clarendon and a direct and grave insult to the archbishop[2] on the part of the prelates. Lastly, it should be noted that the

---

[1] H. Bosham, III, 472: 'Quod cum audiret archipraesul, gaudio magno gavisus est, laetante justo eo quod vindictam desideratam jam vidisset.' It should, however, be noted that the cause of the archbishop's rejoicing was not, in fact, the infliction of punishment, but the recognition of papal authority by the bishops concerned.

[2] Compare the letter of Archbishop Thomas, VII, 406, written in December 1170; also Will. Cant. I, 106.

archbishop's move, stern as it was, was all but successful. The best-informed biographers agree that Foliot and Jocelin were for submitting and asking for absolution; they were overborne by the less scrupulous Roger of York. Had they been reconciled with the archbishop, events might have taken a very different course.[1] As for the refusal of the knights' demand that the censures should be cancelled, Thomas's reply was just and true. He had no power to remove the papal ban from Roger of York, who was not his suffragan; as for the other two, he was willing to exercise his right of conditional absolution if they would sincerely ask him.

As the struggle wore on, the precise object for which the archbishop fought had changed its appearance to his eyes. At the beginning it had been the forensic rights of the Church and the clerical order; then it had become at Clarendon the freedom of the English Church as part of the universal Church in its relations with Rome; finally, it had broadened into a defence of the rights of God as against Caesar. There is no question that Thomas's conception of the issue deepened and became more spiritualized, and that his attitude acquired thereby a dignity and a strength which it had lacked before. As early as 1165 he had told the hesitant cardinals that even if they failed to defend the rights of the Apostolic See he would stand unmoved amid the ruins of their world.[2] Four years later, when his old colleague, John of Poitiers, publicly rebuked him for pride and obstinacy and for destroying the Church, he replied: 'Have a care, brother, lest the Church of God be destroyed by thee; by me, by God's help, it shall never suffer destruction.'[3] Later still, when Henry at a conference broke out with a longing for agreement: 'If only you and I were together again, if only you would do my will, I would give you all power', the archbishop saw in the words the supreme trial of the Tempter: 'All these things will I give thee, if

---

[1] W. FitzStephen, III, 121; H. Bosham, III, 480 et al.

[2] H. Bosham, III, 351–2: 'Etsi vos in praesenti ex qualicumque causa...ruitis, ego tamen inter vestras quasi orbis ruinas, Domino manum suam supponente non ruam.... Ego summi pastoris vester qualiscumque...conservus...pro ecclesia sustineo crucem confusione contempta et velit nolit probet vel improbet mundus, sustinebo.'

[3] H. Bosham, III, 428: '"Frater", inquiens, "cave ne destruatur ecclesia Dei per te; per me favente Domino non destruetur."'

falling down thou wilt adore me.'[1] There can be no reasonable doubt, to one who reads and ponders the letters and the lives, that Thomas was not deceived at the final concord. He had hoped to return to his Church secure; he was now willing to return without the formal guarantee. It was with his eyes wide open that he assented to the final agreement without the kiss of peace.[2]

During those last months of 1170—perhaps even earlier—he had become convinced that only by his death would a solution be found. From whatever more intimate and hidden sources this conviction may have arisen, his own experienced knowledge of Henry and the men about him would have been enough. The consistent refusal of the kiss of peace was sinister in the extreme. There are abundant indications that even had the four knights not acted, men and forces were in motion that would have borne the archbishop away.[3] It was to his death that he was going in England; he accepted and in a sense he desired it; during the last weeks of his life he was fey.[4] But to say, with some recent historians, that desire for the glory of martyrdom made him fatalistic or reckless, courting death, is to go beyond the evidence and the bounds of human nature. The archbishop's last weeks and days and hours are full of the vitality that characterized him all his life. He delighted in his homecoming,[5] and would, as he said, willingly live in peace at Canterbury.[6] But, as he saw it, the forces of evil were around him in pride, and it was the part of an archbishop to strike at them.[7]

---

[1] H. Bosham, III, 470: 'Inter alia dixit rex, "O", inquiens, "quid est quod voluntatem meam non facis? Et certe omnia traderem in manus tuas."...Archipraesul hoc regis verbum retulit discipulo qui scripsit haec, adjiciens: "Et cum rex", inquit, "mihi dixisset sic, recordatus sum mox verbi illius in evangelio, *Haec omnia tibi dabo, si cadens adoraveris me*."'

[2] H. Bosham, III, 466: 'Sciens et prudens pacem talem qualem suscepit.'

[3] Compare, especially, the account of the well-informed FitzStephen, III, 113–14, 123 ff.

[4] Compare his words to his clerk Gunter, who tried to prevent him from embarking at Witsand, whence the distant line of the English coast could be seen: '"Certe", inquit, "Gunteri, terram video, et favente Domino terram intrabo, sciens tamen certissime quod ibi mihi immineat passio."' H. Bosham, III, 476.

[5] Herbert of Bosham (III, 479) describes his appearance as he entered the cathedral: 'In ipso ecclesiae Salvatoris ingressu tanta faciei gratia, roseo sic subito perfusa et venustata colore.'

[6] W. FitzStephen, III, 135: 'Si liceat mihi in pace fungi sacerdotio meo, bonum est mihi.'

[7] H. Bosham, III, 484: 'Tam ardens, tam audens...gladium in medio inimicorum non reponit, sed audacter et fiducialiter exserit.'

The four weeks that passed between the landing of the archbishop at Sandwich and his death were full of dramatic incidents that displayed every facet of his personality. The popular welcome on his journey to Canterbury, in the city itself, and on his subsequent visit to London was such as no subject had ever before enjoyed. If many of the scriptural parallels drawn by his biographers in their narratives offend modern sentiment, few readers of William FitzStephen's glowing pages could fail to recall, without his suggestion, the welcome given to Christ as He entered the holy city, and the jealous anger of His enemies. As for the archbishop, he recaptured once more the high spirits of other years. Flushed with emotion, brilliant and generous as ever, his progress to London to do homage to his old pupil, the young king Henry, and the princely gift of bloodstock that he took with him recalled the palmy days of the Chancellorship.[1] And then, when his overtures were met with sullen, implacable enmity and insult, he used the festival and crowds of Canterbury as he had used those of Vézelay to hear and to publish his comminations. It was clear to all—it is clear to us as we read—that the bitter sarcasm of Henry was true: England was not a bush that could hold two such robins as the archbishop and himself—unless they were joined in purest amity.

There is probably no hour in medieval history of which the details are so well known, and so revealing of character, as is the last hour of the archbishop's life, from about half-past two to half-past three on that dark December afternoon.[2] There are at least nine

---

[1] W. FitzStephen, III, 122.
[2] The indications of time, though precise, are at first sight contradictory. When the knights arrived, the archbishop had dined, but his servants were at dinner. The archbishop usually dined at the ninth hour, 'circa diei nonam' (H. Bosham, III, 225; cf. 219), so this could scarcely be earlier than three o'clock. W. FitzStephen (III, 132) says: 'hora diei erat quasi decima'; Ben. Peterb. II, 1: 'circa horam diei undecimam'; I Anon. IV, 70: 'circa horam nonam'. It was already dusk when the archbishop entered the cathedral; cf. W. FitzStephen, III, 140: 'Vespera erat, nox longissima instabat', and the monks had begun vespers. The reckoning followed is that by which light and darkness are divided into twelve hours each, sixty minutes in length at the equinoxes. On 29 December the sun sets at 4 p.m.; the ninth hour of the day would therefore begin at 2 p.m., the tenth at 2.40, the eleventh at 3.20. Probably, then, the knights arrived at the outer gate shortly before three, but did not immediately obtain access to the archbishop.

major accounts, of which four are the work of eye-witnesses.[1] Here we are concerned not with the series of incidents as such, but solely with the light they throw on the archbishop's personality at this consummation of his life.

The knights arrived intent on murder; though they may, with Lady Macbeth, have confirmed their resolution with strong drink, they were certainly not drunk;[2] there was no disorder or noise at their first arrival and they made their way to the inner room, where the archbishop, having confessed himself after the High Mass, had dined and was seated with his monks and clerks. For a few moments he did not notice the new arrivals, who seated themselves sullenly on the floor at his feet. When he saw them, he looked long at them in silence with his keen and penetrating glance, and flushed scarlet at the first malediction of FitzUrse.[3] In the argument which followed over the excommunication of the bishops he spoke fearlessly but with restraint; when at length the knights turned the argument into a wrangle and began to rail at him he replied:

It is useless to threaten me. If all the swords of England were over my head, your threats would not shift me from God's justice and obedience to the pope. I will dispute every inch of ground with you in the Lord's fight.[4]

---

[1] William FitzStephen, Edward Grim, and John of Salisbury were present throughout at the interview with the knights and in the cathedral. William of Canterbury was a witness of the murder. Herbert of Bosham, unfortunately for us, was not present, having been sent abroad by the archbishop a few days previously. It has often been remarked that a detailed and stereotyped vulgate version of the whole afternoon's doings must speedily have become the property of everyone connected with the cathedral, but it is noteworthy that the narratives both of eye-witnesses and others differ very considerably in detail. No doubt the official showmen had a patter, but, when it came to writing, the contemporary mixture of plagiarism and individualism resulted.

[2] The suggestion that the knights committed, when drunk, a crime from which they would have recoiled if sober has received wide currency from a phrase in Mr T. S. Eliot's play which does not, in fact, imply so much. The dramatist was no doubt recalling the words of one party of the archbishop's clerks (W. FitzStephen, III, 137), which are supported by no other evidence. The conversation and deliberate behaviour of the knights, who had at first intended to brain the archbishop with his own cross (I Anon. IV, 71), forbid the suggestion that they were in any way *non compotes*.

[3] Grim, II, 430–1: 'Diligentius singulorum considerans vultum, pacifice salutavit... salutantem continuo maledictis aggressi....Ad quod verbum amaritudinis et malitiae vir Dei incredibili rubore perfunditur.'

[4] W. FitzStephen, III, 134: 'Frustra mihi minamini....Pede ad pedem me reperietis in Domini proelio.' The last sentence defies translation; it is in Grim also (II, 433).

I left England long ago in fear; I have now returned to my church at the pope's behest; I will not again abandon her. If I may hold my office in peace, well and good; if not, may God's will be done.

An uproar followed, and the knights left the room calling on those present to defy the traitor and prevent his escape. The archbishop started up and followed them to the door, where he heard them telling his servants that the king released them from fealty to the archbishop. 'What do you say?' he exclaimed. 'Speak! speak! I shall not fly. I shall be here. Here you will find me.' And he raised his hand to his head.[1]

He then turned calmly back and sat down once more.[2] John of Salisbury, as always the candid friend, made complaint. 'You have always been like that. You always act and speak entirely on your own, without taking advice.'[3] The archbishop took him up good-humouredly. 'What would you then, master John?' 'You should have summoned your council. You must realize that those knights simply want an excuse for killing you.' 'We must all die, master John,' replied Thomas, 'and we must not let the fear of death make us swerve from justice.[4] I am ready to accept death for the sake of God and of justice and the Church's freedom—far more ready to accept death than they are to kill me.' 'It is all very well for you to say that,' was John's reply, 'but the rest of us are sinners and not so ready for death. Not a soul here except yourself is asking to die.'[5] 'God's will be done', said the archbishop quietly. It was the last moment of familiar talk.

Even as they were speaking the knights, now fully armed, began to batter their way into the archbishop's lodging, and the monks implored him to take refuge in the church. He refused: 'What are

[1] Guernes, l. 5358: 'Huge, qu'as tu dit? Di!' Grim, II, 433: '"Quaerite, qui vos fugiat....Hic, hic reperietis", posita supra cervicem manu.'

[2] Grim, II, 433: 'Imperterritus residebat.' I Anon. IV, 74: 'Sedit supra lectum suum.'

[3] Guernes, ll. 5364–5: 'Sire, tuzjurs avez nostre conseil desdit, Fors ço qu'avez tuzdis en vostre quer eseit.' I Anon. IV, 74: '"Haec", inquit, "consuetudo tua semper fuit, et est, ut quod tibi soli videtur, illud semper et dicas et facias."'

[4] Guernes, ll. 5371–2: 'Tuz nus estuet murir. Ne pur mort de justise ne me verrez flechir.' I Anon. IV, 74: '"Omnes", inquit, "mori habemus, nec timore mortis a justitia flecti debemus."'

[5] Guernes l. 5379: 'N'un sul ne vei, fors vus, qui muire de sun gré.' I Anon. IV, 74: 'Neminem video qui gratis mori velit praeter te.'

you afraid of, my fathers?' and when they insisted he still sat on: 'You monks never have any spirit in you.'[1] Then as the din increased they began to drag him, resisting and expostulating, towards the church.[2] Thrice he forced them to halt and at last, breaking loose, he refused to move till his cross-bearer was found. Then, driving the others before him, and walking slowly behind his cross, he entered the minster.[3] In the panic the door was shut in the face of some of his clerks who had been left behind; the archbishop returned and opened the door for them.[4] The monks began to bar the door to the cloister, but Thomas forbade them: 'Christ Church is not a fortress. Let anyone who wishes enter.'[5] Then, as a cry was raised that armed men were in the cloister, 'I will go to meet them',[6] he said; but the monks once more seized him and carried him towards the high altar. The aisle was full of monks and townspeople, and as the knights strode in they collided in the dusk with those rushing hither and thither. 'Where is the traitor Thomas Beketh?', they shouted. Then, when no reply came, 'Where is the archbishop?' Thomas came forward. 'Here am I, no traitor, but a priest ready to suffer in my Redeemer's cause. God forbid that I should flee from your swords or depart from what is just.[7] But do not dare to touch any of my people.'[8] He then retired a few steps and stood by a pillar, with a few monks and clerks by him. 'Reginald, Reginald,' he said to FitzUrse, 'is this your return for all that I have done for you?'[9] The knights rushed at him and endeavoured to hoist him on the

---

[1] W. FitzStephen, III, 138: 'Plerique monachi plus justo timidi sunt et pusillanimes.'

[2] Grim, II, 434: 'Arripiunt monachi, trahunt, portant, et impellunt, nec attendentes quanta convitiando opponeret ut ipsum dimitterent.'

[3] W. FitzStephen, III, 138: 'Lento passu postremus vadit, omnes agens ante se, quasi oves pastor bonus.'

[4] Ben. Peterb. II, 11.

[5] W. FitzStephen, III, 139: 'Absit ut de ecclesia Dei castellum faciamus.'

[6] Will. Cant. I, 132: '"Armatos in claustro." "Ad ipsos", ait, "exeo." Prohibentibus autem fratribus, &c.'

[7] Grim, II, 435–6: '"Ubi est Thomas Beketh, proditor regis et regni?"..."Ecce praesto sum in nomine Ejus pati qui me sanguine suo redemit; absit ut propter gladios vestros fugiam, aut a justitia recedam."'

[8] W. FitzStephen, III, 141: 'Auctoritate Dei interdico ne quempiam meorum tangatis.'

[9] Will. Cant. I, 133: 'Reginalde, Reginalde, multa tibi contuli beneficia. Ingrederis armatus ad me?'

shoulders of William Tracy to carry him outside the church.[1] The first to touch him was FitzUrse. 'Unhand me, Reginald,' exclaimed the archbishop, 'you are my sworn vassal',[2] and then, struggling with him, 'Unhand me, pander!'[3] He shook himself loose, seized FitzUrse by the mail coat and sent him reeling back.[4] 'I will not leave the church. If you wish to kill me, kill me here.'[5] Then, as they delayed to strike, he covered his eyes and bowed his head: 'To God and blessed Mary, St Denis, and St Alphege I commend myself and my Church.'[6] These were not, as is often said, his last words. After the two first blows he was still standing, and FitzStephen heard him say: 'Into thy hands, O Lord, I commend my spirit.'[7] At the third stroke he fell upon his hands and knees, and said in a low voice, 'I accept death for the name of Jesus and for the Church.'[8] Then at the fourth stroke he fell at full length, with his hands outstretched as if in prayer, and his cloak covering his whole body to the feet.[9] 'Great he was in truth always and in all places,' wrote Herbert of Bosham, 'great in the palace, great at the altar; great both at court and in the church; great when going forth on his pilgrimage, great when returning and singularly great at his journey's end.'[10]

[1] Guernes, ll. 5547-9: 'Sil comencent forment a traire e a sachier, E sur le col Willaume le voldrent enchargier; Car la hors le voleient u oscire u lier.' I Anon. IV, 76: 'Coeperuntque eum fortiter trahere, nitentes eum imponere humeris Guillelmi, et de ecclesia ejicere.' Compare Grim, II, 436.

[2] Grim, II, 436: 'Non me contingas, Reinalde, qui fidem ex jure debes et subjectionem.' Compare I Anon. IV, 76.   [3] Grim, II, 436: 'A se repulit, lenonem appellans.'

[4] I Anon. IV, 76: 'Excutiens se vir Dei impegit eum a se, ita quod fere corruit super pavimentum.' H. Bosham, who was not present, recounts this incident (III, 492-3), adding: 'Willelmus de Traci hic erat, sicut ipsemet postea de se confessus est.' The archbishop may, of course, have shaken off two assailants, but Tracy in retrospect made the most of his confused recollections; thus he boasted that he had cut off the arm of John of Salisbury (Will. Cant. I, 134).

[5] W. FitzStephen, III, 141: 'Nusquam ibo; hic facietis quod facere vultis.'

[6] I Anon. IV, 77: 'Junctis manibus operuit oculos suos, caputque inclinans percussori, dixit: "Deo et beato Dionysio sanctoque Elfego me commendo."' Compare Guernes, ll. 5577-80; H. Bosham, III, 499, adds the name of Our Lady.

[7] W. FitzStephen, III, 141.

[8] Grim, II, 437: 'Tertio vero percussus martyr genua flexit et cubitos...dicens submissa voce, "Pro nomine Jesu et ecclesiae tuitione mortem amplecti paratus sum."'

[9] W. FitzStephen, III, 141-2: 'Curam habuit vel gratiam ut honeste caderet, pallio suo coopertus usque ad talos, quasi adoraturus et oraturus.'

[10] H. Bosham, III, 471: 'Et revera semper et ubique magnus; magnus in palatio, magnus in sacerdotio, magnus in aula, magnus in ecclesia, magnus in peregrinatione, magnus in peregrinationis reversione, maximus vero in peregrinationis consummatione.'

The church had been full of noise and eddying crowds. Now, for a space, it was empty and silent, under the gathering thunderstorm, save for distant shouting as the knights pillaged the dead man's lodging. In the dark church, neglected for the moment by all, lay the tall form of the archbishop, majestic and motionless.

Κεῖτο μέγας μεγαλωστί, λελασμένος ἱπποσυνάων.[1]

---

[1] *Iliad*, Book XVI, l. 776: 'He lay...mighty and mightily fallen, forgetful of his chivalry' (trans. Lang, Leaf, and Myers).

7

THE CENSURED OPINIONS OF
UTHRED OF BOLDON[1]

The name of Uthred of Boldon, monk of the cathedral priory of Durham and master of theology at Oxford, has always been familiar to students of monastic and academic history of the mid-fourteenth century. The stages of his long career are known with some accuracy, even to the day of the year on which the notable changes occurred, and his activities both at his monastic home, at Durham College, and in the wider field of service to his order and to the king, can be traced in a number of sources.[2] Hitherto, however, his work as a theologian has remained unexplored, and no attempt has been made to assess his significance or to define his position with regard to the philosophical and doctrinal issues of his day. Bale, indeed, in his list of medieval authors, duly noted a controversy between Uthred and

---

[1] [First published in *The Proceedings of the British Academy*, vol. XXXVII (1951), pp. 305–42.]

[2] The most complete account of Uthred (this would seem to be the most correct of the many ways of spelling his name) is in 'Uthred de Boldon, Friar William Jordan, and Piers Plowman', a thesis by M. E. Marcett privately printed in New York, 1938. There is, however, a longer and in some ways more accurate study in 'Uthred of Boldon, a study in fourteenth-century political theory', by C. H. Thompson (1936), a typewritten thesis for the Ph.D. degree at Manchester University. A chronological skeleton of Uthred's life, entitled *Vita compendiosa Uthredi monachi Dunelmensis*, probably composed by Prior Wessington of Durham early in the fifteenth century, has been printed from Brit. Mus. Addit. MS. 6162, fo. 31 v in the *Bulletin of the Institute of Historical Research*, vol. III (1925–26), p. 46, and in default of other evidence this may be accepted as giving correct dating, though the other information it supplies is meagre. Mr W. A. Pantin has a biographical note and many references to Uthred in *Chapters of the Black Monks* (Camden Soc. 3 ser., LIV, 1937), vol. III (see p. 318), and has assembled a number of other notes which he has kindly allowed me to use. The article written *c.* 1898 for the *Dictionary of National Biography* by Professor A. F. Pollard, though using the accepted sources, is surprisingly inaccurate in detail. See also R. B. Hepple, 'Uthred of Boldon' in *Archaeologia Aeliana*, 3 ser., vol. XVII (1920), pp. 153–68, and Appendix D, below, p. 170. [See now also Knowles, *Religious Orders in England*, vol. II (Cambridge, 1955), pp. 48–54; W. A. Pantin, *The English Church in the Fourteenth Century* (Cambridge, 1955), pp. 166–75.]

a Dominican named William Jordan,[1] and the succession of historians and bibliographers dependent upon Bale repeated the information, but the matter had not been taken up till some eighteen years ago, when an American scholar printed, almost incidentally, a short work of Uthred in which he gives a list of errors imputed to him, and adds disclaimers or justificatory comments.[2] Miss Marcett, however, was primarily a student of Middle English and did not attempt a theological commentary. Moreover, she did not notice that the propositions cited by Uthred bore a very close resemblance to a list of propositions censured by Archbishop Langham and printed by David Wilkins.[3] This resemblance had been noticed, before Miss Marcett's book appeared, by Mr W. A. Pantin, who had read the work of Uthred in another and less complete manuscript,[4] but after drawing the present writer's attention to the fact he took no further action. A closer inspection has made it clear that Uthred's treatise and Langham's articles, when studied carefully in conjunction, throw a welcome light not only on Uthred's opinions but on the whole climate of thought prevailing at Oxford shortly before the emergence of Wyclif as a disturbing element, and as the period is otherwise so dark, any glimpse of light is of value to students of the intellectual and theological life of Oxford between the death of Bradwardine (1349) and the inception of Wyclif as doctor c. 1372.

---

[1] J. Bale, *Index Britanniae Scriptorum*, ed. in *Anecdota Oxoniensia* (Oxford, 1902) by R. L. Poole and M. Bateson, p. 463: 'Utredus Dunelmensis, Oxonii multas opiniones novas et subtiles invenit per studii laborem scolastici exercitii gratia. Et adversarium molestissimum habebat Guilhelmum Iordan Dominicanum doctorem, calumniatorem, qui eum ab ecclesie unitate proscindere nitebatur. Sed minime claudicabat Utredus', &c.

[2] This is the tract *Contra injustas fratrum querelas*, printed by Miss Marcett, *Uthred de Boldon*, pp. 25–37, of which the relevant parts are printed below, pp. 332–40, from a fresh collation of the manuscript.

[3] Wilkins, *Concilia*, vol. III, pp. 75–6 [now printed in *Registrum Simonis de Langham*, part 2, ed. A. C. Wood, Canterbury and York Society, 1950–52 (1954), pp. 219–22].

[4] The tract exists in full and legible in a single manuscript, Brit. Mus. Royal 6. D. x (c. 1390–1400), fos. 283–5. It is complete, but much damaged by reagents and thus partially illegible, in Oxford, Bodl. Wood Rolls 1 (25277) (c. 1400). Bodl. Tanner MS. 408, fo. 83v, contains part of the introduction, and MS. Balliol 149 (fifteenth century), fos. 63–64v, has a fragment containing the introduction and a discussion of the first article.

Although we are not concerned with the monastic life and other activities of Uthred, a few dates must be recorded to give precision to his academic career. Born *c.* 1320, he was at Oxford, doubtless studying arts, from 1337 to 1341; in the latter year he became a monk at Durham, and in 1344 was sent to the cell of the cathedral priory at Stamford, where he may have continued his studies. In 1347 he returned to Oxford, where he studied theology, proceeding B.D. in 1354 and incepting as Doctor in October 1357. Thenceforth for ten years he was Prior or Warden of Durham College and Regent Master for much of the time.[1] Uthred was thus almost exactly contemporary with Wyclif, who also was born *c.* 1320 and from *c.* 1340 had been permanently resident at Oxford. Unlike Uthred who, as a monk, studied divinity from the earliest possible age, Wyclif remained for many years a master in arts, lecturing and determining in philosophy. It was not till 1373-74 or a little later that he incepted in divinity: that is, some five years after the date with which we are principally concerned.

The fifty years 1325-75 are, as has just been noted, a dark period in the history of Oxford thought. There, as at Paris, it was an age of dissolution and individualism and eclecticism. The age of the great syntheses and systems—the age of Bonaventure, Albert the Great, Thomas Aquinas, and John Duns the Scot—had ended with the death of the last-named in 1308; there had followed a short period in which, while the rank and file adhered more or less closely to the school of their order or choice, a number of acute and critical minds were striking out new theories on a number of particular points of metaphysics, ethics, psychology, and theology. Then, unexpectedly, the existing streams of thought were invaded by a potent flood of new ideas released by William of Ockham. With the opinions of the Nominalists or, as they may be more fittingly called, the Ockhamists, we are not directly concerned; it is enough to note that almost all the essentials of the 'new way', as it was termed, were present in the writings composed by the young Franciscan before he left Oxford in 1324, and that his first and most ardent disciples were

---

[1] The dates are in the main those of the *Vita compendiosa*, which does not, however, give the year of his birth. Uthred died at Finchale in 1396.

among the English Franciscans. Ockhamism, however, soon ceased to be the monopoly of any order, school, or country, and was to be found, in stronger or weaker solution, in the thought of the majority of theologians and philosophers. Thenceforward, for more than half a century, both at Paris and Oxford, it was by far the most pervasive influence, but it is characteristic of the period that few, if any, thinkers were entirely faithful to any one system, whether Thomism, Scotism, or Ockhamism. In this they bore some resemblance to their predecessors of 1200–50, with the important difference that while those of the earlier period were groping their way towards a state of order and equilibrium, those of the later age were chiefly engaged in criticizing and destroying the works of the past, and chose their instruments of art from whatever quarter they might wish.

To this general lack of balance the peculiar circumstances of time and place contributed other factors making for confusion at Oxford. Until the age of Ockham there had remained a solidarity in European intellectual life; persons, ideas, and doctrinal pronouncements circulated freely throughout north-western Europe, and in particular there was constant interchange of men and ideas between Oxford and Paris. From about the middle of the century, however, a great change began to take place. While the University of Paris became increasingly nationalistic in outlook, the Hundred Years War and later the Great Schism isolated English thought and the two English universities both from Paris and from what may be called the theological climate of continental Europe. As a consequence of this, individual theologians are found putting forward and pressing to their logical conclusion novel opinions which, if aired at Paris or Oxford a century earlier, would have come under such a heavy fire of criticism that they would have been withdrawn, or at least seriously modified. Ockham himself is one of the most striking examples of this, both in the instant reaction of criticism to his early works at Oxford, and in the ready acceptance of the same teaching both at Paris and Oxford a few years later. Almost at the same time, Thomas Bradwardine, himself influenced by certain features of Ockham's teaching, erected his system of determinist theology which departs from orthodoxy in one direction almost as clearly as do the

132

'Pelagians', whom he was attacking, in another. Thirty years later again, Wyclif laid a whole series of theological opinions upon a basis of logical and metaphysical theories of which he himself was the author, and which had never been adequately criticized by adversaries conversant with the great syntheses of the past. Between Bradwardine and Wyclif came, as we shall see, the pronouncements of Uthred of Boldon, which have rippled the waters of history less violently only because they were concerned with topics less explosive and were the work of a thinker who was intellectually less powerful than the Mertonian, and more radically orthodox than the Reformer.

In the fifth and sixth decades of the fourteenth century, therefore, a number of influences were at work at Oxford. The most pervasive of all was Ockhamism, Protean in its many manifestations, now appearing as terminism, now as secularism, now as extreme voluntarism and semi-Pelagianism, now as fideism.[1] Next, there was the influence of Bradwardine, most strongly felt by Wyclif, which unduly depreciated human liberty, and regarded God as the necessitating cause of all things, human acts included.[2] Thirdly, there was the legacy of the immediate predecessors of Ockham, remarkable particularly for their preoccupation with the definition of grace and with the nature of the beatific vision and the requisites for salvation, as also with the distinctions between the absolute power of God and the laws ordained by Him, and between rules and moral judgements made by human beings and the decisions of God known only to Himself.[3] Finally, there was the influence of Wyclif himself on his

[1] No detailed and authoritative study of the thought of the fourteenth century has yet appeared. The main streams of doctrine and the names of the principal masters are to be found in M. de Wulf, *Histoire de la philosophie médiévale*, vol. III (6th ed., Louvain, 1947), E. Gilson, *La Philosophie au moyen-âge* (2nd ed., Paris, 1944) and F. Ehrle, *Der Sentenzenkommentar Peters von Candia* (Münster, 1925). See also the articles *Nominalisme, Occam, Thomas Bradwardine*, and others in *Dictionnaire de théologie catholique*. The scattered articles and notes of C. Michalski, though valuable, need close control.

[2] No full-length study of Bradwardine and his system exists. The article referred to in the preceding note gives no more than an outline, and that in the *Dictionnaire d'histoire et de géographie ecclésiastique* is short and purely biographical. [See now G. Leff, *Bradwardine and the Pelagians* (Cambridge, 1957); H. A. Oberman, *Archbishop Thomas Bradwardine* (Utrecht, 1958).]

[3] For this the important study of P. Vignaux, *Justification et prédestination au XIVe siècle* (Paris, 1934), should be consulted.

contemporaries. This, as all available evidence shows, was very great. Wyclif, indeed, though the subject of innumerable studies, has yet to be assessed as a philosopher,[1] when all the purely philosophical writings of his pre-theological period have been printed. Hitherto his English critics have almost without exception failed to relate his thought to that of his predecessors, while continental scholars, hampered by their scarcely disguised hostility, have usually, as trained Thomists or Scotists, experienced a kind of repulsion from the crudity of his opinions, and have failed to do full justice to the originality—or at least to the idiosyncrasy—and to the logical power of his mind. He was, it would seem, the only teacher of the first rank in the faculty of arts in his day to take an interest in meta-physics; his two eminent contemporaries Heytesbury and Strode were primarily logicians. He was also the principal teacher to react strongly against Ockhamism, and in particular he elaborated a system of Realism more extreme than anything the schools had hitherto seen. According to this the *genus substantiae* was actually present in the individual as its *pars quidditativa*; annihilation was therefore impossible, and even substantial change unthinkable.[2] Wyclif's universe—the universe of things past, present, and future— was in consequence a rigid, static whole which in the last resort could scarcely have been separable in thought from God. At the same time, the determinism which he inherited from Bradwardine gave a similar rigidity to his ethical teaching. In the general lack of firm metaphysical thinking in an age penetrated by the Ockhamist depreciation of its value, Wyclif's obstinate but logical persistence in his coherent scheme must have attracted those minds that felt the need for a stable philosophical outlook.

While speculation at Oxford was thus both active and fluid, untrammelled by the axioms of an earlier age and in consequence shifting and confused, circumstances of another order were influ-

---

[1] [See now J. A. Robson, *Wyclif and the Oxford Schools* (Cambridge, 1961).]

[2] Wyclif's logical and metaphysical systems still await detailed and accurate examination [see n. 1]. For the main features of his realism the tracts by him and his opponents, and the extracts from other works printed by W. W. Shirley a century ago in *Fasciculus Zizaniorum* (Rolls Series, 1858), are still the most convenient introduction.

encing the alinement of the various groups in the academic society. The controversy between the mendicant friars and the 'possessioners', as the property-owning monks and canons were called, had its roots in the past and its aggravating circumstances in the present. It derived, though not directly, from the series of controversies set in motion by the claim of the early Franciscans to follow an ideal of poverty superior to that taught by the monastic orders, a series which had culminated in the important theological issue of the Poverty of Christ. A second strand of dissension was the allied issue of 'Dominion and Grace'.[1] This, which originated in the simple if radical thesis that only the just man had a right to the ownership of property, was complicated by the application of the theory in opposing senses by two parties: the papalists and the clerical party in general, who held that the visible, organized Church, and, above all, its rulers and ministers, as being spiritual and holy by definition, alone had a right to all dominion; and the radical party, of which the extreme right wing of the Franciscans was an early, and Wyclif a later, representative, who saw in the simple, just man the lord of all under God, and who regarded the wealthy prelates and ecclesiastical corporations as the very antitheses of justice, deserving only to be deprived of their property. When this controversy reached the schools and in particular Oxford, perhaps originally in the form given to it by Archbishop Fitzralph, it was natural that the friars and the old propertied orders should take opposite sides, and a brisk academic and pulpit warfare broke out between them. The secular clergy, though counting among the 'possessioners', offered a less attractive target than the rich abbeys and for a time remained in the background, and the secular masters took little part in the fray, save for Wyclif, who, at first from reforming zeal and later from political associations, lent vigorous support to the radical friars. The issue was embittered by its near relation to the anti-clerical, secularist attacks of Marsilius and Ockham on the wealth of the Church, and it was given actuality in England by the financial crisis and consequently burdensome taxation resulting from the long and now unsuccessful war with France. A proposal to tax the clergy heavily,

[1] For this, see in particular A. Gwynn, *The English Austin Friars* (Oxford, 1940).

and even to confiscate some of their wealth, was in the air. With this we are not concerned, but it is important to note that before the purely theological issue arose between them, Uthred and the friars were old enemies; the eminent monastic theologian was the protagonist of the 'possessioners' and had written and determined on behalf of his order against the Franciscans, while Wyclif had taken part in the controversy against Uthred, though treating him with great respect.[1]

Uthred had been at Oxford for some twenty years as student and teacher when the controversy with which we are concerned began. As we have seen, he had often found himself ranged against the friars, especially in the years after 1360, but it is not clear whether the attack on him by the Dominican, William Jordan, was made with the intention of discrediting an old enemy, or whether it was a purely theological dispute in which a somewhat combative man felt it his duty to defend the traditional teaching. Such facts as can be ascertained seem to suggest that the two men had long been opponents, and that the appeal to authority was the climax of a long academic strife.

William Jordan,[2] a northerner by birth, had been at the papal court at Avignon in 1355, and was prior of the Preachers' house at York in 1358, in which year he was again at Avignon, where he was one of the friars who argued against Fitzralph. At about the same time he was engaged in a controversy at York with Mardisley, the provincial minister of the Minors, on the subject of the Immaculate Conception of the Blessed Virgin; in this the two friars took up each the position traditional in his order. It is not known when his opposition to Uthred began; a letter written to the latter by a confrère shows that the two were at odds at the end of 1366,[3] and the titles of

[1] Wyclif's *Determinatio ad argumenta magistri Outredi de Omesima* (= Uthredi de Dunelmia *or* Oxonia) *monachi* is in *Opera Minora*, ed. J. Loserth (London, 1913), pp. 405-14.

[2] For Jordan's career see M. E. Marcett, *Uthred de Boldon*, pp. 49-56.

[3] The letter (Pantin, *Chapters of the Black Monks*, vol. III, p. 309) is written by a monk of St Mary's, York, most probably to Uthred, and can be dated *c*. 8 December 1366. In a sentence only partly decipherable the writer asks for information 'de modo accessus et recessus fratris Willelmi Iordan de Oxonia'. The date would fit in with all the other

three works attributed to Jordan[1] suggest that he had attacked Uthred both on the question of the mendicants' poverty and on his theory of the vision of God at the moment before death, of which much will be heard in the sequel. Soon after this, perhaps in 1367, the friars, no doubt led by William Jordan, drew up a list of propositions taken from various academic pronouncements of Uthred which they held to be contrary to sound doctrine. This list, according to Uthred, they published in many places, and spoke against the errors alleged to be contained therein before general audiences, without coming forward in due form at Oxford. To defend his reputation, therefore, Uthred himself published the list, together with his own corrections and replies. We do not know what provocation he had received, but his abuse of the friars certainly equalled in violence that of any serious English theologian prior to Wyclif. On the doctrinal issue, he stood in the main firmly to his guns, and his corrections and explanations do not bear out his complaint that he had been seriously and maliciously misrepresented. The friars, therefore, may on every account be excused for pressing their attack, and early in 1367–68 the list of Uthred's propositions was delated to the Archbishop of Canterbury. Simon Langham, ex-abbot of Westminster, though he himself had never been a student at Oxford, had recently taken decisive action in re-establishing Canterbury College on a wholly monastic basis,[2] and must have known Uthred well, both as an Oxford master and as a frequent member and agent of the provincial chapter of the black monks. For this reason, and because he would naturally have been unwilling to take strong measures against one of his own habit on behalf of the friars, the business must

indications. Uthred was apparently still at Oxford (i.e. it was before his departure for Finchale in the late autumn of 1367) when matters came to a crisis, for he complains that he had been 'per ipsos [sc. fratres] in diversis provinciis nequiter diffamatus' (Marcett, p. 26), and that these attacks had been launched 'non in scolis nec in locis aliis aptis pro veritate discucienda...ubi eorum mendacia per audientes non poterunt reprehendi' (*ibid.* p. 27; below, pp. 158–9).

[1] J. Quetif and J. Echard, *Scriptores Ordinis Praedicatorum*, vol. I (Paris, 1719), p. 695, give *Tractatus de clara uisione Dei, Tractatus de libera electione ante mortem* and *Apologia Fratrum Mendicantium aduersus Utredum Boldun monachum*...as works by Jordan: cf. Antonio Senensi Lusitano, *Biblioteca ordinis fratrum praedicatorum* (Paris, 1585), p. 99.

[2] For this see W. A. Pantin, *Canterbury College, Oxford* (Oxford Historical Society, New Series, vols. 6–8, 1947–50).

137

have been distasteful to him. He nevertheless wrote on 18 February to the Chancellor of Oxford, ordering him to silence both parties and their adherents, who were continuing to dispute upon the articles delated.[1] The matter, the archbishop added, was about to be judicially decided. The examination duly took place that same year, and on 9 November, less than three weeks before his resignation of the see, Langham censured thirty propositions, which he forbade to be defended in the schools.[2] The names of Uthred and Jordan do not appear in the decree, but twenty-two of the propositions repeat with small verbal changes propositions on the list quoted and defended by Uthred. The remaining eight are entirely different from their predecessors, and may represent propositions delated by Uthred from the utterances of his opponents.

In theological matters, it has almost always happened that when an attack is made on a distinguished teacher no serious attempt is made to isolate his cardinal error, but a collection, as complete as possible, is made of the questionable propositions that he has maintained in order to make the condemnation as comprehensive as may be. It is not therefore surprising that the 'schedule' reproduced and commented upon by Uthred is a disorderly list in which the various items seem at first sight to have little logical connexion with one another. Langham's theologians, however, who were clearly an able body of men, shook the list out and rearranged the propositions which they retained for censure in a logical sequence. It will be convenient, therefore, in discussing the points, to follow the order of the censured articles rather than that of Uthred's list.

The first article[3] is clearly the key to many of the others, and was probably the stimulant that set the whole process in motion. This was the opinion that all human beings, whether Christians, Jews, Saracens, or pagans, whether adults, children, or still-born infants, enjoyed at the moment immediately preceding death a clear vision

---

[1] Printed below, p. 168, from Lambeth Reg. Langham fo. 60v. I owe the transcript of this to the kindness of Mr Pantin.

[2] The censure and the articles are printed in Wilkins, vol. III, pp. 75–6 [and *Reg. Simonis de Langham*, pp. 219–22].

[3] This is the third article of the schedule; see below, p. 160.

(*clara visio*) of God. In the light of that vision the soul chose or rejected God, and by that choice its lot was determined for eternity. It is to be observed that the supposed vision took place while the soul was still in the body and the person was therefore still a *viator*, the technical theological term for one who is still in a state of probation, with the consequent capability of meriting eternal life.[1] Furthermore, the 'clear vision' is to be distinguished from the 'beatific vision': in the latter the glorified intelligence sees directly, though without full comprehension, the Divine Being, its last end and the object of complete beatitude; the 'clear vision', though never defined by its proposer in his extant writings, is to be understood as resembling the 'intellectual vision' of God which some scholastics and many later mystical theologians have thought to have been experienced by Moses, Elias, and St Paul.[2]

---

[1] It will be remembered that the attention of theologians had recently been attracted to the nature of the Beatific Vision by the unusual view put forward with much vigour by Pope John XXII in 1331, that the souls of the just do not attain to bliss until the end of the world. The pope's opinion, however, which he expressly stated to be a private and personal one only, and which he himself in large part retracted before his death, had little support save from a few interested associates, and the traditional teaching was formally defined by his successor, Benedict XII, in the Constitution *Benedictus Deus* of 29 January 1336 (Denzinger–Bannwart, *Enchiridion Symbolorum*, no. 530). For the whole episode and its literature see G. Mollat, *Les Papes d'Avignon* (9th ed., Paris, 1950), pp. 54 ff. Though no doubt this had repercussions on the schools, there is no resemblance between Uthred's view and that of John XXII.

[2] Theological pronouncements on this point were in the Middle Ages (and still in part are) made with reservation. While it has always been the common teaching, based both on a number of familiar Scriptural texts and on the theological presentation of the transcendence of God, that the human intelligence, while still united to the mortal body, cannot see the Divine Essence, there was a tendency among the schoolmen, due largely to the deference paid to Augustine, to admit a few rare and momentary exceptions, and in particular Moses and St Paul, to whom were sometimes added Elias and St Benedict. Compare *Summa Theologica*, 1a, xii, 11; 11a, 11ae, clxxv, 4–5 (Moses); clxxv, 3–4 (St Paul); clxxx, 5 (St Benedict). This tendency received support from the claims of the mystics to some kind of mental contact with God in Himself, and Aquinas, while clearly enunciating the principle that no man can see God here below, hesitates to rule out the transitory and rare exceptions. Three centuries later St John of the Cross takes a similar doctrinal position, but in several places enunciates the opinion which has since become common, *viz.* (1) that the Beatific Vision is incompatible with mortal life save in the altogether unique case of the human intelligence of Christ; (2) that the experiences of Moses, St Paul, and others are preferably to be reckoned as exceptionally exalted 'intellectual visions' and examples of the gift of 'prophecy' (i.e. the sight of a particular aspect or attribute of the Divinity under the influence of a special and transient illumination); (3) that the mystical attainment of God, though real and immediate, is experiential and obscure. (Compare *Ascent of Mount Carmel*, bk. 11, chs. 24, 26, trans. P. Silverio de

So far as can be ascertained, this opinion was an original proposition of Uthred, and as such it entitles him to a place in the history of dogma; it has been revived, apparently as an entirely novel proposition, in modern times.[1] To appreciate both Uthred's intention and the zeal of his critics it should be remembered that the problem with which he was wrestling was a serious and a real one. Eternal life with Christ in the Beatific Vision was the goal of all Christian hope and endeavour, and in the mid-fourteenth century religious sentiment was becoming at once warmer and more personal and at the same time more social in its expression; it was the age of Richard Rolle, of Langland, of Suso, of Ruysbroeck, of Juliana of Norwich, and of the poet of *The Pearl*. There was a general preoccupation with the problems of grace and salvation, and a concern for the multitudes, not only of Jews and Saracens, but of unbaptized infants—in fact, of the majority of mankind in the past—who were generally thought to be excluded from all hope of salvation through ignorance of the message of Christ and lack of baptism. Yet, on the other hand, the gratuity, the uncovenanted mercy, and the mystery of that call and choice might not be challenged without endangering the fundamental belief that Christianity was a revelation and a supernatural life. Uthred himself seems to have defended his opinion principally as being most consonant with God's goodness and justice, and he used as a supporting text from scripture 'All flesh shall see the salvation of God'.[2]

Santa Teresa and E. A. Peers, *Complete Works of St John of the Cross*, vol. I, London, 1934, pp. 188–90, 195–6.) Uthred's 'clear vision' would seem to be reducible to the second class above, as is made clear by his explanation apropos of the seventh article; there he states that the object of the clear vision is the body of Christian revelation, no longer *believed*, but *seen* and *known*. He never asserted, as some of his opponents appear to have suggested, that its object was the Divine Essence.

[1] Hatton, indeed (Worc. Cath. MS. F. 65, fo. 7), says: 'solet...dici et specialiter per Utredum...', but this can scarcely be taken as proving that others held this opinion. It was revived early in the last century, but only for unbaptized infants, by the German Catholic theologian H. Klee, and has since been entertained by a series of Catholic writers, as well as by many others (cf. *Dictionnaire de théologie catholique*, art. 'Persévérance', vol. XII, col. 1303). It is in some ways a resurrection of the Origenist opinion that all would attain bliss at the end of the world (cf. Denzinger–Bannwart, *Enchiridion*, no. 211, and *Dict. de théol. cath.*, arts. 'Augustin', vol. I, col. 2443–5, 2450–2, 'Enfer', vol. V, col. 74–7). Still more recently it has been put forward by P. Glorieux in *Nouvelle Revue Théologique* (1932), pp. 865–92, and attacked by E. Hugueny in *Revue Thomiste* (1933), pp. 217–42, 533–67. I owe this reference to Fr. D. Callus.

[2] Isa. xl. 5, as quoted in Luke iii. 6.

It will be seen at once that he thereby excluded the possibility of a 'limbo', a place either of mitigated suffering or 'natural' happiness for those who, though innocent of personal sin, had not been cleansed from original sin by any kind of baptism. The application of the vision is, however, much wider than this; it is, indeed, a two-handed engine. While it opens heaven to vast numbers excluded by the majority of patristic and medieval theologians, it effects this, not on the supposition that God has, so to say, a second unseen method of opening heaven to the harmless or good unbeliever, but by giving a normal and critical choice to all at the moment that they have passed for ever from human observation, but have not yet left their mortal life.[1] Not only the infidel and the unbaptized child have this moment of testing, but the saint and the baptized infant also. Not only does Uthred give no hint that the final choice is decided, or all but decided, by the previous moral conduct of the person, but he positively makes it clear that in what is the test case, that of the baptized infant, the wrong choice may be made although the soul is in a state of both innocence and grace. It is symptomatic of the theological climate of the age that a trained divine of considerable distinction should have committed himself so hardily to a position so open to attack. When in modern times a similar view has been put forward by a theologian of any standing, some of the more obvious and serious difficulties have usually been forestalled by supposing, not a clear vision, but a kind of private revelation of the faith in a confused manner, and by restricting this to unbaptized infants or to a relatively small class of unbelievers who have not misused the oft-repeated 'actual' assistance (i.e. short of sanctifying grace) given by God.

Uthred's view led also to a series of further difficulties, one of which was duly dealt with in the second proposition selected by the panel of his judges.[2] As the choice made in the moment before death was *ex hypothesi* decisive, the sin of rejection, so he held, was without remedy or possibility of remission; it was indeed so heinous, as being committed by one with a clear sight of God, that it resembled

---

[1] As one of Uthred's critics (Worc. Cath. MS. F. 65, fo. 11 v) pertinently remarks: 'Si visio talis sit ponenda...sequitur quod in necessariis ecclesia defecit, eo quod latuit ecclesiam et apostolos ante ista tempora unum quod fuit necessarium ad salutem.'

[2] Arts. 4 and 5 of schedule; see below, p. 161.

that of the devil; therefore the Passion of Christ was unavailing to satisfy for it, though of itself all-powerful. This limitation of the efficacy of the Passion of Christ was duly censured. Uthred nowhere says why he took up this position. He might have avoided it, as Christian theology avoids a similar difficulty regarding the final impenitence of a sinner, by making final perseverance an individual grace, not necessarily differing in species from other graces, but special by reason of the moment and purpose of its bestowal.[1]

The next article of the 'schedule' is one of the very few that seem to justify Uthred's complaint of unfairness.[2] It has been held by many theologians in all ages of the Church that explicit faith in Christ, either as the Messiah or the Redeemer, is, according to the common dispensation of God, an essential condition for the bestowal of eternal salvation.[3] Yet according to Uthred an infidel might pass from human contact without giving the assent of faith, and yet might choose God in the clear vision and be saved. The censure imposed was nevertheless doubly unfair: first, because Uthred in fact had safeguarded himself by placing the clear vision *before* death. The moribund person was therefore still technically a *viator*. Moreover, an explicit faith in Christ (not merely a faith in God as a provident Father and rewarder) had never and has not yet been defined as a necessity *sine qua non* for salvation for an unbaptized person.[4]

If the third censured proposition was treated unfairly, the theologians were on firmer ground with their fourth.[5] If all alike were to have the opportunity of choosing God in the clear vision, the sacrament of baptism, always regarded by Christians as a necessity *sine qua non* by Christ's law, became otiose. This indeed was the most serious consequence of Uthred's theory. Those who have revived it in modern times have escaped the difficulty by restricting the

---

[1] Compare the Canon of the Council of Trent, *De Justificatione*, can. 22: 'Si quis dixerit, iustificatum vel sine speciali auxilio Dei in accepta justitia perseverare posse, vel cum eo non posse, A.S.' (F. Cavallera, *Thesaurus doctrinae catholicae* (1920), no. 892, p. 493).

[2] Art. 7 of schedule; see below, p. 161.   [3] *Summa Theologica*, IIa, IIae, i, 8, ii, 7.

[4] The contrary, indeed, might be inferred from the words of a proposition condemned by Innocent XI in 1679: 'Nonnisi fides unius Dei necessaria videtur necessitate medii, non autem explicite Remuneratoris' (Cavallera, *Thesaurus*, no. 176, p. 95).

[5] Art. 8 of schedule; see below, pp. 161–2.

opportunity of a final choice to those who during life had had no opportunity of hearing of the Christian faith. Uthred, in this as logical *à outrance* as Wyclif himself, had made no such reservations. Moreover, in his reply to the *cedula* he had burnt his boats by elaborating his views. After making the unexceptionable statement that baptism of desire was as efficacious as baptism by water, he continued with what appeared to be the equally orthodox statement that as with excommunication, so with all external judgements as to whether a person was in the right disposition for salvation, the Church might err. His further words, however, as the restriction of the case to infants shows, make it clear that he applied this principle not only to the judgement of the authorities of the Church as to a question of fact in individual cases, but to the judgement of the Church *qua* Church on a question of the law of Christ and the necessities for salvation. The Church, so his argument seems to run, is influenced in her legislation and theology by the visible circumstances of life. As the choice in the clear vision took place invisibly, it could not be taken into account by the legislator. Therefore baptism had been declared necessary by the law of the Church, which regarded the visible things of life only, but it was not so according to the hidden law of God. Here Uthred seems to have been under the influence of a distinction, developed by Ockham and exploited by his disciples, between the external, phenomenal plane, and the hidden, spiritual ordinances of God. It is a distinction profoundly true if understood in the traditional way with the traditional safeguards, but disruptive of all external organization and doctrine if taken to imply the co-existence of mutually exclusive levels of truth and law. That Langham's theologians were well aware of the issue, and that they were also acquainted with Uthred's defence, is clear from the addition of a single word made by them to the relevant article of the *cedula*. While this ran: 'Quod sacramentum baptismi non est de lege alicui parvulo', thus giving Uthred the loophole of escape he had taken by distinguishing between the *lex ecclesiae* (concerned with appearances) and the true judgement of God, the proposition as censured contained the word *Dei* after *lege*, thereby equating the law of God with the law of the Church. Possibly also they intended to imply, what Uthred strangely enough had omitted to consider, that the precept of the necessity of baptism rested in fact upon divine, and not merely upon ecclesiastical, authority.[1]

The next proposition[2] is a logical extension of the last, and also has an Ockhamist tinge. It is concerned with the still-born infant dying without baptism. On Uthred's theory it also had the clear vision and choice, whereas the Church had always, both in theory and practice, sharply divided the baptized from the unbaptized child, committing the former to the grave with the white robe and flowers of the blessed, and relegating the latter to limbo and unconsecrated ground. To the latter class the still-born infant of necessity belonged. Uthred's clear vision gave a chance—one might even say a good chance—even here, and consequently one was justified in reserving one's judgement as to the eternal lot of the infant concerned. Here, therefore, once again Uthred distinguished between the external judgement of the Church and the true judgement of God, adding, however, that baptism did in fact help both infants and others to choose aright in the clear vision.

The next proposition caught Uthred on the other horn.[3] If one could hope that an unbaptized infant might be saved after all, one might equally be apprehensive of the damnation of a child who had been baptized. Here again Uthred's answer was ready. The article in the *cedula* ran: *est catholice dubitandum*. This, he said, he had not taught in the sense alleged. *Catholice*, in his technical use of the term, would mean 'according to the judgement of the Church in the world of visible things', and he had never denied that the Church was in this sense justified in considering a baptized infant to be saved. What he had held was that a man could not say what God might do out of the range of human vision. The theologians therefore changed *catholice* to the unambiguous *a catholico*, thus precluding that way of escape.

The next proposition[4] was based upon one in the *cedula* which attributed to Uthred the doctrine that any infidel, even though

---

[1] John iii. 5.   [2] Art. 9 of schedule; see below, pp. 162–3.
[3] Art. 10 of schedule; see below, p. 163.
[4] Art. 11 of schedule; see below, pp. 163–4.

destined never in his lifetime to believe the Christian creed, might attain salvation, and that therefore it was right for a Catholic to express doubt as to his future state, rather than to say that he would be lost. Uthred had taken exception to the wording of this article as committing the logical fault of ambiguity (the fallacy of the *sensus compositus* and the *sensus divisus*), for if understood *sensu diviso* all would admit that it was *possible* that a given infidel might be saved by conversion, even if *de facto* he never came to the Christian faith; however, even if one took the proposition, as was presumably intended, *sensu composito*, i.e. that a particular infidel, who in fact was never going to be converted, might still be saved, it was still, so Uthred held, tenable, for in the clear vision the soul attained the object of Christian belief by intelligence, if not by faith. If, on the other hand, the article were taken to mean that those who never attained the object of faith in any way could yet be saved, Uthred would agree in reprobating it. Langham's theologians duly censured the proposition, and the terms they used make it clear that they had seen Uthred's defence, for they inserted the words *intelligendo in sensu composito*.

The eighth and ninth articles[1] condemned another consequence of the theory, which was that it rendered original sin meaningless. If all were to have the opportunity of choosing at the moment of death, no one could be lost through original sin alone. Uthred had accepted this without demur.

The ninth article had completed the series connected with the clear vision.[2] The theologians then proceeded to deal with Uthred's views on grace. Once again they reshuffled the numbers of the schedule, and their treatment of the question is, perhaps, from the historical point of view the most interesting part of the process.

The nature of sanctifying grace—the grace, that is, by which a soul is admitted by God into a 'state of grace', and which is a 'habit' of grace enabling it to perform actions deserving of eternal life—had been debated at length by the great scholastics of the previous

---

[1] Arts. 12 and 13 of schedule; see below, p. 164.
[2] Save for an article that went uncensured; below, p. 164.

century. The Master of the Sentences, Peter Lombard, had committed himself, in an almost casual pronouncement, to the opinion that the Holy Spirit Himself was the formal principle of sanctifying grace,[1] but this found little acceptance. Aquinas, whose teaching on the subject ultimately prevailed and has been partially adopted in official formularies, held that sanctifying grace was a quality, an accident of the soul, the principle of the supernatural love of God by which a man could merit; it was strictly and truly the beginning, the seed, of eternal life.[2] A different opinion was held among the Franciscans. Bonaventure had asked himself the question whether grace in the sanctified soul was something created or uncreated, and had preferred the former.[3] Scotus, while not following the Lombard, held that charity and sanctifying grace were not distinguishable; grace was therefore the infused supernatural love of God.[4] The Franciscan Pierre Auriole adopted this opinion with an important addition. Grace for him was the infused love of God, in which God of necessity was well pleased, and therefore of necessity rewarded this love with eternal happiness.[5]

Ockham, who on this question seems in all sincerity to have intended to remain fully and traditionally orthodox, defended the position of Scotus against that of Pierre Auriole;[6] he defined grace as a form by which a soul is acceptable to God; he did, indeed, with a characteristic appeal to the 'absolute' power of God, maintain that God could accept a soul which was, and remained, graceless, but he

---

[1] Pet. Lombard., II Sent., dist. xxvii, c. 6.

[2] *Summa Theologica*, Ia, IIae, cx, 1 and 2, e.g.: 'Aliquod habituale donum a Deo animae infunditur...et sic donum gratiae qualitas quaedam est.' *Ibid.* 3: 'Lumen gratiae, quod est participatio divinae naturae.'

[3] *Dict. de théol. catholique*, vol. VIII, col. 2117 (art. 'Justification').

[4] Compare in II Sent., dist. xxvii, n. 35: 'Habitus...quae est gratia, et ipsa est caritas.' He seems to have held, however, that grace does not sanctify precisely as a physical entity, but in virtue of the acceptation of the soul by God.

[5] *Dict. de théol. catholique*, vol. XII, pp. 1870–1: 'Auriol soutient que l'âme justifiée porte en soi une forme où Dieu se complaît nécessairement au point de lui donner la vie éternelle....Cette forme est un amour de Dieu que l'âme ne produit pas naturellement, mais que Dieu lui infuse....La charité infuse nécessite donc Dieu, d'après Auriol, à donner la béatitude' (A. Teetaert).

[6] See art. 'Occam' by P. Vignaux in *Dict. théol. catholique*, vol. XII, coll. 876 ff., esp. 878–9 and 886–7, and the same writer's *Justification et prédestination au XIVe siècle* (Paris, 1934).

held that according to the present dispensation grace was necessary. As against Auriole, he rejected the conception of grace as a created form necessitating God's acceptation of the soul; but he does not seem to have rejected the idea that grace was a real entity in itself.[1] It does not seem clear who was the first theologian to extend Ockham's reaction from Auriole, and his insistence on the absolute power and freedom of God, so as to make of grace not a quality or a gift, but a relationship, an attitude towards God, established by God Himself and not necessarily implying any new principle or quality or spring of action in the soul concerned. Grace was thus simply a right relationship of man towards God consequent upon God's acceptation of man's love.[2] The concept of grace as a real but essentially supernatural entity, a sharing of the life of God, was gone entirely. Uthred, indeed, had committed himself to the forthright statement that grace as defined by most contemporary theologians was bunk.[3] He defended this by stating that grace, if said to be an infused entity distinct from the soul, was (on Ockhamist principles) a superfluity and therefore meaningless. The theologians were here on delicate ground, for there was little agreement among contemporaries at Oxford as to the nature of grace. They therefore ignored Uthred's explanation and made a significant exception to their otherwise invariable formula 'this is an error' by adding the words 'because it sounds ill'.

In the eleventh article they came to the essential point.[4] The seventeenth proposition of the schedule had asserted that man could merit by his merely natural powers. That opinion, of course, if acknowledged, would alone have sufficed for the condemnation of

---

[1] For example, I Sent., dist., q. i E: 'Forma qua anima fit accepta est quaedam Dei habitualis dilectio quae ab ipso infunditur, nec ex puris naturalibus generatur.'

[2] Compare Uthred's words (below, p. 164): 'the word grace does not primarily denote an entity, but a relationship, not something absolute but what has reference to another; so that a man may be in due relationship to God, and then he is "acceptable" and "in grace" with regard to God, and in a state where he can merit eternal life.'

[3] 'Gratia juxta communiter ponentes est truffa' (below, p. 165). *Truffa*, from the Old French *trufle*, *truffe*, whence English *trifle*, = 'trick', 'mockery', 'worthless thing'. Fr. Callus has drawn my attention to a passage in the writings of the Franciscan Olivi disclaiming a somewhat similar opinion (*Quodlibeta Petri Joannis*, Venice, no date, fo. 63).

[4] Art. 17 of schedule; see below, p. 165.

its supporter as a heretic, for the definition to the contrary was as old as the Pelagian controversy.[1] Uthred had therefore disclaimed any intention of holding it, whether the merit was for eternal life or for some temporal reward from God. Besides the human act there was needed, so he said, a right relationship to God such as he had explained in a previous article. It will be noted that Uthred clearly had no conception of sanctifying grace as bestowing an essentially supernatural life and principle of action to man. Langham's panel, however, were proceeding warily. They took no notice of Uthred's explanation, and contented themselves with censuring the proposition 'that a man can merit eternal life by his merely natural powers'. To describe this as an 'error' was certainly an economy of words.

The twelfth article[2] dealt with an allied topic. One of the propositions charged against Uthred stated that human nature provided man with everything requisite for attaining his natural end. Uthred had accepted and endorsed this. The statement is in fact ambiguous: is it a general one for human nature as such, or does it regard human nature in its fallen state, with original sin? If the latter, it is certainly an error. Furthermore, does 'natural' mean purely natural happiness, i.e. the philosopher's paradise, with a recognition of God as the Creator, or does 'natural' here mean 'the end for which man is in fact created', i.e. the vision of God as He is, the sharing of the divine life? Strictly speaking, and probably also in Uthred's intention, the former meaning was implied,[3] but the theologians, to be on absolutely safe ground, added: 'if by the natural end of man final and eternal happiness is meant.' They then censured the article as thus amended.

[1] Compare canon 5 of the Council of Carthage (A.D. 418) approved by Pope Zosimus (Denzinger–Bannwart, no. 105): 'Quicumque dixerit, ideo nobis gratiam iustificationis dari ut, quod facere per liberum iubemur arbitrium, facilius possimus implere per gratiam, tanquam et si gratia non daretur, non quidem facile, sed tamen possimus etiam sine illa implere divina mandata, A.S.'

[2] Art. 19 of schedule; see below, p. 165.

[3] The proposition as thus understood was held as a philosophic thesis by the unorthodox Aristotelians such as Boethius of Dacia (late thirteenth century; the *Opusculum Magistri Boetii Daci de Summo Bono sive de Vita Philosophi* was published by M. Grabmann, *Mittelalterliches Geistesleben*, vol. II (München, 1936), pp. 209–16), and had been adopted by some of the 'Pelagians' of Ockham's day.

The thirteenth article went a stage farther.[1] Uthred had accepted as his the thesis that man in this life has it always in his power to regain the degree of grace lost by sin. This by itself would have been sheer Pelagianism; Uthred therefore hastened to add that supernatural assistance might also be needed. The explanation was ambiguous; if such assistance were a necessary condition, the proposition would cease to have a meaning; if not strictly necessary, the article would remain Pelagian.[2] In any case the theologians censured it.

The next article[3] returned once more to Uthred's *Lieblingsidee*. He had accepted as his the thesis that no one could justly be deprived of his heavenly inheritance for any sin short of the rejection of God in the clear vision, adding that all sins previous to that, even if mortal, were of their nature remediable (*remediabile in natura*) on account of the ignorance of the sinner (i.e. as lacking clear knowledge, such as that provided in the clear vision). Here again the terminology of Uthred is ambiguous; he seems to have acknowledged the possibility of a sin being mortal (which by definition implies the loss of sanctifying grace despite a lack of clear knowledge) and yet not in fact punishable by the loss of heaven. The commission ignored his explanation and censured the article.

With that they passed to another topic, but in doing so they left uncensured and unrecorded three of the propositions objected against Uthred.[4] The first of these stated that sanctifying grace was not something infused into the soul from without; the second, that infused grace of such a kind would be of a superior nature to the recipient; the third, that created grace, if understood as a created or infused entity, was an impossibility. Uthred had accepted all these, and explained that in his view the words grace (*gratia*) and pleasing to God (*gratus*) denoted a relationship, not an entity; a man was 'in grace' if he stood in the right relationship to God, and without

---

[1] Art. 20 of the schedule; see below, p. 165.
[2] Compare the anathema in p. 148, n. 1 above, and the canon of Trent (Denzinger–Bannwart, no. 812): 'Si quis dixerit, ad hoc solum divinam gratiam per Christum dari, ut facilius homo iuste vivere ac vitam aeternam promereri possit...A.S.'
[3] Art. 21 of the schedule; see below, pp. 165–6.
[4] Arts. 14–16; see below, pp. 164–5.

the right relationship to God a man could not merit. This was not the same, he maintained, as saying that grace was a non-entity, and he added that, so far from being Pelagian, this thesis clearly disposed of the Pelagian heresy.[1] Here Uthred was proposing a development of Ockham's 'voluntarist' emphasis on liberty, both human and divine, and was also making use of the Ockhamist development of the theory of relation. The meaning of the second article, that if grace were an infused entity it would be superior to the subject (man) in which it resided (i.e. the greater would be subordinated to the less), seems to be an argument directed against the view of Auriole that infused charity necessarily drew upon itself the love and acceptation of God.[2] Once again Uthred ignores the Thomist view that grace intrinsically elevates and renews man so that he can become the living, free agent moved by God. The third article, asserting that grace was not a positive entity, merely enlarged the first. Doubtless the theologians of the Council of Trent and since would have stigmatized these articles along with the others, but the question of the nature of grace was still so fluid that the theologians, having censured what they held to be Pelagianism, were chary of entangling themselves in controversial niceties. They also left uncensured another alleged proposition to the effect that ignorance of fact (as opposed to ignorance of law) could not excuse from sin. This Uthred disclaimed altogether and his judges apparently accepted his disclaimer.

They then proceeded to another small group of propositions. In these Uthred appears somewhat unexpectedly to react firmly against an ethical view held (to a degree) by Scotus and in a more extreme fashion by Ockham, that no (or few) actions are intrinsically good or evil, but receive their moral character according as they are commanded or forbidden by the free choice of God. Even the anti-Pelagian Bradwardine had affinities with Ockham here. Uthred, on

---

[1] It is difficult to see how Uthred would have escaped the Tridentine anathema: 'Si quis dixerit, homines iustificari...exclusa gratia et caritate quae in cordibus eorum per Spiritum Sanctum diffundatur atque illis inhaereat, aut etiam gratiam, qua iustificamur, esse tantum favorem Dei, A.S.' (Denzinger–Bannwart, *Enchiridion*, no. 821).

[2] Ockham specifically raised this objection, e.g. III Sent., q. v (cited *Dict. de théologie catholique*, vol. XI, col. 878).

the other hand, reacted so strongly as to deny that God could ever forbid an act which was not evil either in itself or in its effects. He therefore accepted the proposition that nothing could be evil solely because it had been prohibited.[1] This was censured as it stood; it would indeed be unacceptable to theologians in the sphere both of revealed and natural theology, and would have serious repercussions on all man-made legislation. The further articles dealt with the same question. The classical instance of a divine precept for which no obvious reason existed was that given to our first parents in paradise; Uthred had therefore maintained[2] that the forbidden fruit, excellent in other respects, was unfit for human consumption and banned for that reason. This was censured, as was also another asserting that an assignable cause existed for every effect brought about by God, and that to shirk explanation of an event by saying that 'God had willed it thus' was an old wives' trick. The theologians branded this as erroneous, but were careful to explain that the proposition was only censurable if applied universally in the sense that God of necessity, by analogy with human beings, adapted cause to effect.

The next two propositions were of an entirely different kind, and dealt with the divine 'names' and the 'attribution' of particular functions to particular Persons of the Trinity.[3] Several such attributions had been normal ever since the Trinitarian controversies of the patristic age, and others had been accepted by the great scholastics, such as Aquinas. In the fourteenth century there had been here, as in other fields, a great deal of ingenious and reckless speculation. Uthred had propounded the view that the Holy Spirit was, so to say, the term of the personal activity of the Divine Persons in the same way as the Father was the source; therefore, since it was allowable to say that the Father alone had no principle, while the two other Persons had one, so it might be said that in the Divine Life the Holy Spirit as the 'completeness' of the Father and Son was alone infinite, whereas the other two Persons were finite as being 'completed' by Him. Besides its intrinsic unsuitability, this way of speaking did in

[1] Art. 22 of schedule; see below, p. 166. This is the opposite extreme to Ockham (e.g. II Sent., q. xix). [2] Art. 23 of schedule; see below, p. 166.
[3] Arts. 26 and 27 of schedule; see below, pp. 166–7.

fact seem to contradict the Athanasian Creed.[1] Neither Uthred nor his censors seem to have adverted to this fact, but the proposition was duly censured, as was another appropriating to each Person different stages in the process of creation.

Langham's articles ended with three which had no clear connexion with any other group. The first was the thesis that God cannot annihilate anything.[2] This Uthred maintained that he had always taught and still held. The proposition became celebrated a dozen years later as the philosophical basis of Wyclif's refusal to accept transubstantiation, and we know that he had held it at least some time before 1368. He derived it from the peculiar version of extreme realism of which he seems to have been the originator. According to this the *genus substantiae* (e.g. the *humanitas* of man) which formed the *pars quidditativa* of every individual would be annihilated if the individual were annihilated, and this in turn would imply the annihilation of a divine idea.[3] Wyclif may have been drawn to his opinion, or at least confirmed in it, by passages in Fitzralph's *De pauperie Christi*, a book from which he is known to have derived his theory of dominion and grace. The position taken up by Fitzralph is, however, radically different; he maintained what is indeed common Christian teaching, *viz.* that it would be contrary to God's goodness to destroy that to which He had given being.[4] Whatever be Wyclif's relationship to Fitzralph, it can hardly be supposed that he derived this characteristic doctrine from Uthred, who makes no claim to have originated it; we are justified, therefore, in seeing here evidence of the commanding position of Wyclif at Oxford in philosophical matters, and of a relationship of dependence between the leading monastic theologian and the secular master.

[1] For example 'Immensus Pater, immensus Filius, immensus Spiritus Sanctus.'

[2] Art. 2 of schedule; see below, p. 160.

[3] Compare *De Logica*, ed. M. H. Dziewicki (Wyclif Society, London, 1896), vol. II, p. 192; also cf. *De Ente, Libri Secundi Tractatus Sexti Fragmentum*, ed. M. H. Dziewicki (London, Wyclif Society, 1909), p. 289.

[4] For example, 'Anichilacio non foret accio sed conservacionis desinicio, quod repugnat vero domino' MS. Vienna, Pal. 4307*b*, fo. 106*a*, cited by S. H. Thomson, 'The Philosophical Basis of Wyclif's Theology', in *The Journal of Religion*, vol. XI (1931), pp. 86–116. Compare the decisions of St Thomas, *Summa Theologica*, Ia, civ, 3–4, where he avoids answering the question of possibility, but maintains that God does not in fact annihilate anything.

Langham's theologians censured the proposition as erroneous, presumably on intrinsic grounds, as limiting the omnipotence and freedom of God. Had we no evidence at all we should be justified in supposing that Wyclif knew of this condemnation; actually, there is in a work of his what seems clearly to be a reference to it.[1] His utter indifference to what was certainly a pronouncement of authority, even if not of the most solemn kind, is worthy of remark.

The twenty-first article,[2] that God cannot punish anyone directly, because He cannot be a rackmaster, was, with its maladroit wording, scarcely worthy of serious attention from the theologians. It is of interest as being another instance of the humanitarian frame of mind which had prompted Uthred's speculations on the clear vision.

The twenty-second and last of the articles directed against Uthred is that which appears first in his *cedula*.[3] It is another piece of Trinitarian speculation. It was a commonplace that power was 'appropriated' to the Father, wisdom to the Son, and goodness to the Holy Spirit. Since Christ referred to sins against Himself and against the Holy Spirit, which were commonly taken to be sins of ignorance and malice respectively, Uthred argued that there was consequently no third type of sin, from impotence, against the Father. In his lengthy explanation he shows himself radically orthodox, and he charges his accusers with falsifying his thought by implying him to have said that any sin against God the Father was impossible. The theologians nevertheless censured the proposition, which was certainly novel and ill-sounding,[4] without any warrant in Scripture or tradition, but they were at pains to insert the word

[1] This occurs in a citation from the *De potentia Dei* by W. W. Shirley in his introduction to the *Fasciculus Zizaniorum* (RS, 1858), pp. lvi–lix, where among the arguments quoted by Wyclif against his own view is the following: '...ut patet ex multis damnationibus positionum negantium possibilitatem annihilationis et communi testimonio loquentium modernorum, qui omnes dicunt concorditer quod Deus non esset plenus dominus creaturae nisi ipsam posset annihilare.'

[2] Art. 28 of schedule; see below, p. 167.

[3] See below, pp. 159–60.

[4] It was an unlucky departure from the tradition rendered classic in the schools by Peter Lombard (Lib. II Sent., dist. xliii, *PL*, CXCII, coll. 754–6, §§ 2–4): 'Peccatum enim in Patrem id intelligitur quod fit per infirmitatem, quia Patri Scriptura frequenter attribuit potentiam.' Uthred, whose phraseology implies acquaintance with the Lombard's words, directly contradicts his position.

appropriate, thereby depriving Uthred's complaint of its force, for he had certainly held what was now censured. The most interesting part of his explanation is that in which he equates sin against the Holy Ghost with sin committed in the clear vision. It may well have been meditation on this difficult text of Scripture that prompted his theory.

Finally, mention must be made of another article which escaped censure,[1] to the effect that the *lumen gloriae* (as opposed to the *lumen fidei* or *lumen gratiae*) was not required for the Beatific Vision. Here Uthred was again following the common Ockhamist opinion (resisted by the orthodox Thomists and others) that no supernatural light of any kind was necessary as a medium in or by which revealed truths or God Himself might be seen. The revelation, according to this view, was made directly by God's power. For this reason, therefore, as in the other articles dealing with the nature of grace, the theologians refrained from censuring what was the opinion of a large number of the masters of the day.[2]

Langham's articles, in which no name occurs of the person aimed at in the censures, proceed without a break or rubric to brand eight more articles of a totally different character, which are not found or implied in Uthred's schedule.[3] These, it might naturally be supposed, were samples of undesirable utterances attributed to Uthred's opponents, and brought before the tribunal as a counter-charge. The probability becomes a certainty from a letter contained in Langham's register, stating that friar William Jordan has disclaimed ever having held such opinions.[4] If Langham was willing to record this protest in his register, it may be supposed that he accepted Jordan's disclaimer; in that case, the articles were probably a perverted or garbled version of what Jordan and his fellows had said. In themselves, the articles are extravagant and without theological

---

[1] Art. 6 of schedule; see below, p. 161.
[2] The Council of Vienne (1311–12) had indeed asserted the necessity of *lumen gloriae* when censuring a proposition of the Beguards: 'Quod quaelibet intellectualis natura in se ipsa naturaliter est beata, quodque anima non indiget lumine gloriae, ipsam elevante ad Deum videndum' (Denzinger–Bannwart, no. 475).
[3] See below, p. 169.   [4] See below, pp. 168–9.

interest. In default of any comment or context it is not easy to decide whether they reflect 'terminist' logic, following Gregory of Rimini, or the still more extreme Nicholas of Autrecourt, according to whom affirmation and negation are mere combinations of logical terms, without any meaning in reality,[1] or whether they may not rather be expressions of extreme Wyclifite realism, according to which a being cannot change either its nature or its qualities. The propositions themselves, e.g. that men always remain mortal, even when in heaven, that the Blessed Virgin always remains potentially sinful, the devils always convertible and forgivable, and the like, perhaps suggest the latter interpretation. It was part of Wyclif's teaching that whatever has being exists already in God's thought, and is therefore immutable, since the connexion between the *esse intelligibile* and the *esse actuale* is so close that no change in the latter is possible. The trend of the articles suggests that one or two at least may reflect arguments brought forward by Jordan and his associates against the doctrine of the Immaculate Conception, in the controversy which is known to have taken place between Jordan and the Franciscan Mardisley.

There is no record of the composition of the panel of theologians convened by Langham, as there is of the various groups summoned a few years later to examine Wyclif's doctrine. In the latter case those taking part were chiefly friars, drawn as a rule, and sometimes in equal proportions, from the four orders, with both universities adequately represented. Undoubtedly the Dominicans must have been of the number when one of their habit was on his trial. More cannot be said, save to note that they were an able group who, whatever the academic fashions and extremes might be, could when need arose distinguish novel and dangerous theological opinions from the traditional teaching of the Church. Langham forthwith, only a few days before his retirement from his see, wrote to the Chancellor of Oxford prohibiting teaching and disputation in the

---

[1] For these see M. de Wulf, *Histoire de la Philosophie médiévale*, vol. III (1947), pp. 99–100, 144–9, and the propositions of Autrecourt condemned by Clement VI in 1348 (Denzinger–Bannwart, *Enchiridion*, no. 555): 'Quod propositiones: Deus est, Deus non est, penitus idem significant, licet alio modo.'

sense of the articles condemned,[1] but Uthred was not mentioned by name and there is no indication that a recantation and confession of faith were required of him, as they were shortly to be required of Wyclif. Nevertheless, the troubles into which he had run, and the ban placed upon him with regard to so much of his most individual teaching, may well have been the reason why, in the late summer of 1367, he was recalled from Oxford to become prior of Finchale.[2] It is true that he succeeded a prior who had died, and that therefore there is no clear evidence that the appointment was anything more than a matter of routine, but the post was not a distinguished one for an eminent scholar in the prime of life, and in fact Uthred soon became sub-prior of Durham,[3] the most dignified post in the gift of the prior and convent, and one which had more than once in the past received lustre from the literary or academic eminence of its holder. The monks were not going to regard Uthred's misfortune in a serious light.

The whole episode is of interest in many ways. In the first place, it shows clearly how eclectic and personal theological teaching at Oxford had become, and how easily a master could leave the paths of traditional doctrine to pursue some favourite theory of his own. Fortunately, there is additional evidence both of the novelty of Uthred's views on the clear vision and of the notice taken of them in academic circles. There are in the library of the Dean and Chapter at Worcester several determinations and other notes attributed to one Hatton or Hayton whose identity has not yet been established, in which the clear vision and some other articles are attacked in academic form.[4] Here the theory is appropriated to Uthred, and his

---

[1] See below, p. 168.

[2] Compare *Vita compendiosa* (above, p. 129, n. 2): 'Item anno etc 67 primo prior de Fynchall ad festum Laurencii' (i.e. 10 August).

[3] *Ibid.*: 'Item anno etc 68 Supprior post festum purificacionis' (2 February).

[4] Fr. Daniel Callus, O.P., has suggested to me that 'Hatton' may be John Hilton, the Franciscan opponent of Uthred. Worcester Cathedral MS. F. 65 contains several pieces relating to Uthred:

   (a) Fo. 1v. Determination of 'Hatton' dealing with the nature of grace and the impossibility of the clear vision—which, however, is misunderstood as being one of the Divine Essence.

opponent brings forward a series of reasons, both from authorities and from quasi-medical and practical sources, against it.[1] These disputations contain no clear reference to Uthred's defence, and may either form part of those asserted by Langham to have taken place, or refer to a still earlier phase of the dispute.

Next, the form and consequences of Langham's censure should be noted. No name is given and no kind of abjuration is imposed. The propositions are simply branded as erroneous and as not to be taught or disputed upon in the schools. The contrast between this and the more severe and personal proceedings taken against Wyclif only a few years later is noteworthy, but readily explicable. Uthred, however erroneous or fanciful or rash his opinions may have been, was clearly speaking as a theologian among theologians, and was as clearly desirous of following authentic tradition. He could plead with justice that he had spoken only in the schools, and that it was his adversaries who had carried his theses into the pulpit. He was likely, therefore, to take his quietus in good part, if with surprise and chagrin. Wyclif's attack on transubstantiation, on the other hand, implied a novel attitude of mind towards traditional teaching, with corollaries of novelties in practice and preaching which did in fact occur among his followers. Moreover, his obstinate and opinionated temperament must long have been well known to all concerned. In his case, a censure without sanctions would scarcely have had even the force of a gesture.

Thirdly, in this episode as in others of the period, the friars appear as an energetic and competent reservoir of theological teaching, to whom the bishops could look in the last resort for effective pronouncements on novelties of opinion. The odium incurred by them in the eyes of some modern historians for their resolute opposition

(b) Fo. 7. Anonymous arguments against the clear vision and the doctrine that nothing can be evil merely because prohibited by God.

(c) Fo. 11v. The reply of the same (? Hatton) against Uthred, especially on the clear vision, but referring also to sins against the Father (art. 22), God the torturer (art. 21), and natural beatitude (art. 12).

(d) Fo. 19v. A statement of some of Uthred's positions. I owe a transcript of these to the kindness of Mr W. A. Pantin.

[1] For example, it is argued that sudden death (such as that of Lot's wife, or by public execution) gives no time for the clear vision; that the vision itself would cause death or the suspension of powers by reason of its delight, &c.

to Wyclif and Lollardy is seen to be largely undeserved. Neither in that episode nor in this of Uthred do they appear as pressing for condemnation in the interests of an obscurantist or party policy, but as defenders of what was certainly the traditional doctrine of the Church.

Finally, an altogether new view is obtained of Uthred himself. Hitherto much has been known about his activities and reputation, but nothing concerning his opinions in philosophy and theology. Consequently, the student of the times has probably received the impression that in these matters the Durham master was eminently sound but, to modern readers, eminently dull. With his propositions and defence before us we can see him as one influenced by all the currents of the age, with an interest which seems peculiarly modern in the salvation of what may be called the theologically depressed classes—unbaptized infants, Jews, and unbelievers—and, above all, we can see him as a man of strong and daring views, which he was ready to hold till the very moment when they were shown to be, and were censured as being, rash, novel, and unorthodox.

APPENDIX A

Uthred's tract *Contra querelas fratrum* has been printed in full by M. E. Marcett, *Uhtred de Boldon*, pp. 25–37. The greater part of this is taken up by Uthred's presentation of the alleged heretical propositions drawn from his teaching, together with his disclaimers and defence. The text as printed, however, contains a number of errors of transcription, some of them on points of doctrinal interest. The whole has therefore been collated with the British Museum MS. Royal 6. D. x, fos. 283–5. At the beginning and end of the tract are lengthy but quite irrelevant passages of abuse of the friars; these, which Marcett printed, have been omitted here as adding unnecessarily to the length of the paper. The only other manuscript which covers a large part of the tract, Bodleian Wood Rolls 1, has been used in places to check a doubtful reading, but the few and insignificant variants have not been noted. After each article of the *cedula* the relevant censure is printed in italics from Wilkins, *Concilia*, vol. III, pp. 75–76. [Now printed in *Reg. Simonis de Langham*, pp. 219–22, by which the text has been checked.]

fo. 283 v (line 8)

...Isti vero fratres maledicti non in scolis nec in locis aliis aptis pro veritate discucienda set a tergo resistunt veritati scolastice, ubi eorum mendacia per audientes non poterunt reprehendi. Illi magi[1] saltem ad perpetranda quedam mirabilia sensibiliter fecerunt suis privatis incantacionibus, set isti fratres maledicti nullam evidenciam faciunt, set solum obnubilant veritatem suis perversis compilacionibus. Compilaverunt enim ipsi quandam cedulam falsissime fabricatam, quam dicunt a dictis meis scolasticis verissime reportatam. Que cedula, cum sit libella famosa, iam in diversis mundi partibus divulgatur, unde et fama mea penes personas graves ex eorum malicia denigratur. Quare tam auctores huius cedule quam fauctores sunt canonice excommunicandi, set iuste forent secundum leges civiles propter suas nequicias decollandi.

Ut autem expressius eorum latens falsitas convincatur et ab omnibus qui in domo dei sunt veritas cognoscatur, ipsorum scripturam tam detestabilem quoad puncta singula recitabo, et ubi mentiti fuerint et ubi vera miscuerint declarabo. Incipiunt quidem isti falsi fratres suam mendacem cedulam isto modo. 'Isti', inquiunt, 'sunt articuli quos dominus Uthredus, monachus Dunelmensis, sacre theologie professor in Universitate Oxoniensi, pro veris tenuit et contra impugnatores defendit, in suis determinacionibus et lecionibus publice affirmando.'

I. 'Quod impossibile est contra patrem in divinis peccare, eo quod non est possibile aliquem ex inpotencia peccare.'

Ad hunc primum articulum respondeo antequam recitem aliquem aliorum, quia sic intendo ad omnes alios in recitando per ordinem respondere ad singulos singillatim. Et dico ad istum articulum quod est falsus, sicut et fundamentum quod adducitur pro eodem. Verumptamen ut cunctis fidelibus ostendantur ipsi falsi fratres quod sunt filii diaboli, pleni omni dolo et fallacio; ideo a mendacio, quod est proprium patris eorum, incipiunt scriptum suum. Nec articulum hunc tenui, set dixi et persuasi quod nulla natura sit peccabilis nisi natura cognitiva et libera. Set omnis huius cognicio aut est obscura, sicut pro statu fidei, aut est clara, sicut pro statu sciencie. Et iam non sunt nec esse possunt nisi duo prima genera peccatorum, scilicet, peccatum ignorancie, quod conservat statum fidei, quomodo peccant homines quousque claram habuerint visionem, et ideo sunt reparabiles a peccato; et peccatum malicie, quod conservat statum clare sciencie, quomodo peccaverunt angeli, propter quod sunt irreparabiles a peccato.

Peccatum autem quod dicitur ex inpotencia non est nec esse potest aliquod primum genus peccati. Set quodcumque peccatum inpotencie oritur ex altero duorum predictorum, et naturam sue radicis semper sapit ac est debita pena eius. Ideo dixi quod est impossibile aliquem peccare

---

[1] The reference is to the Egyptian magicians of Exod. vii. 11; cf. 2 Tim. iii. 8.

ex inpotencia, que constituat novum genus peccati; set omnis huius inpotencia, vel est in genere ignorancie aut in genere malicie, et a suo genere peccatum commissum caperet nomen suum; unde dixi consequenter quod cum patri in divinis approprietur potencia, filio sapiencia, et spiritui sancto bonitas, peccatum ex ignorancia commissum est appropriate contra filium in divinis, peccatum ex malicia commissum est appropriate contra spiritum sanctum; set nullum est nec esse potest peccatum appropriate contra patrem in divinis, quia tale peccatum foret omnino in genere tercio peccatorum, scilicet in genere peccati ex inpotencia. Verumptamen, sicut essentialiter loquendo una est potencia una est sapiencia una bonitas, personarum tamen, immo singule persone, est potencia, sapiencia et bonitas, et omnes tres una persona; et sic de aliis sic eciam loquendo omne peccatum contra omnes personas equaliter est commissum, quamvis appropriate sit peccatum contra filium in divinis et aliquod contra spiritum sanctum, et nullum penitus appropriate contra patrem, sicut patet ex evangelio, Mt xii Mc iii Luc xii, ubi dominus Iesus sufficienter dividens peccatum, loquitur de peccato appropriato contra filium, quod est remissibile, et de peccato appropriato contra spiritum sanctum, quod est irremissibile, et de peccato contra patrem nullam faciens mencionem. Unde dixi quod impossibile est peccare appropriate contra patrem in divinis, ex quo non sequitur quod impossibile est peccare contra patrem in divinis, sicut non sequitur pater in divinis non est sapiencia appropriate, igitur pater in divinis non est sapiencia.

> *xxii. Nullus potest peccare appropriate contra Patrem in divinis, eo quod nullus potest peccare ex impotencia nisi peccet ex ignorantia vel malitia. Error.*

II. 'Quod deus non potest aliquod adnichilare.' Hunc articulum sepius tenui et persuasi, et adhuc dictat mihi ratio quod sit verus.

> *xx. Deus non potest aliquid adnihilare. Error.*

III. 'Quod viator quilibet, de lege communi in via, tam adultus quam non adultus, habebit claram visionem ipsius dei.' Hunc eciam tenui et persuasi et reputo verum esse. Notandum tamen quod hoc complexum 'de lege communi' non est restringendum ad solam legem ecclesie, set est generale ad omnem legem competentem homini ut est homo.

> *i. Quilibet viator tam adultus quam non adultus, Saracenus, Judaeus et Paganus, etiam in utero materno defunctus, habebit claram visionem Dei ante mortem suam; qua visione manente habebit electionem liberam convertendi se ad Deum, vel divertendi se ab eo: et si tunc elegerit converti ad Deum salvabitur, sin autem, damnabitur. Error.*

IV. 'Quod peccatum commissum in huiusmodi clara visione, per malam electionem, non est remediabile nec remissibile.' Hunc semper tenui et persuasi, eo quod peccatum sic commissum est peccatum malicie, et ideo contra bonitatem, et sic in spiritum sanctum, et ideo irremissibile iuxta sentenciam salvatoris, loquendo de finali electione.

V. 'Quod aliquod peccatum est commissibile in via quod non est remediabile nec remissibile, et sic pro illo christi passio non potest satisfacere.' Hic articulus quantum ad primam partem sequitur ex precedenti. Quantum ad secundam partem, quod pro tali non [fo. 284r] potest christi passio satisfacere, verum est quantum ad efficienciam, sicut nec pro peccato diaboli, potest tamen quantum ad sufficienciam a parte passionis christi.

ii. Peccatum commissum in huiusmodi clara visione per malam electionem non est remediabile nec remissibile, et sic pro illo passio Christi non potest satisfacere, quantum ad efficientiam, si intelligatur de clara visione viatoris, sicut primus articulus. Error.

VI. 'Quod stat aliquem viatorem clare videre essentiam divinam sine lumine glorie creato ipsum elevante.' De isto articulo non recolo me tractasse, quia ut communiter non tractamus de lumine glorie quoad viatores, set solum quoad comprehensores. Conceditur tamen quod nec in viatore nec in comprehensore requiritur aliquod lumen glorie quod sit aliquid absolutum creatum distincte a vidente, set sufficit in eo sola habitudo debita quoad deum, sicut de gratia hic pro via. Ad articulos de gratia post dicetur.

This article receives no mention in Langham's register.

VII. 'Quod stat aliquem adultum sine fide christi in se de communi lege salvari, ut si sarascenus in illa clara visione meretur per electionem.' Hunc non dixi, set contrarium tenui, quia talis sarascenus haberet eandem fidem tunc quam nos habemus quantum ad materiam fidei, set non quoad actum credendi, quia ipse haberet actum sciendi, ubi nos habemus iam actum credendi respectu eiusdem materie subiecte.

iii. Stat aliquem adultum sine actu vel habitu fidei Christi in se de lege communi salvari, si intelligatur de viatore adulto, sicut primus articulus. Error.

VIII. 'Quod sacramentum baptismi non est de lege alicui parvulo decedenti requisitum ad salutem.' Pro isto articulo et aliis sequentibus de eadem materia declarandum: primo, notandum est quod triplex est baptismus, scilicet flaminis, fluminis et sanguinis, set tam in parvulo quam in adulto solus baptismus flaminis necessario requiritur ad salutem; etiam est notandum quod sicut habetur extra *de sentencia excommunicationis, a nobis est sepe*: 'Iudicium dei veritati, que nec fallit nec fallitur, semper innititur; iudicium autem ecclesie nonnunquam opinionem sequitur quod et fallere sepe contingit et falli; propter quod contingit interdum ut qui ligatus est apud deum apud ecclesiam sit solutus, et qui liber est apud deum ecclesiastica sit sentencia innodatus.'[1] Tercio est notandum quod iudicium privatum est iudicium dei, set iudicium per evidencias et signa apparentia est iudicium ecclesie. Similiter, iudicium catholicum, cum catholicus sit idem quod generalis vel universalis, est iudicium ecclesie. Et quamvis multa requirantur ad salutem secundum iudicium ecclesie que non sic requiruntur secundum iudicium dei privatum, non tamen est iudicium ecclesie umquam erroneum, set semper verum, quia iudicans secundum quod sibi constare debet, ut alias declaravi. Ideo tam de parvulis quam de adultis, tam de infidelibus quam de christianis decedentibus, est secundum ista iudicia aliter senciendum, nec de aliquo moriente scimus quid de eo secundum privatum iudicium Dei fieret, set solum de talibus credimus cum ecclesia matre nostra. Unde istum articulum nunquam tenui set negavi, eo quod articulus asserit sacramentum baptismi de nulla lege requiri talibus parvulis ad salutem. Et ego contrarium asserens dixi et dico illud sacramentum requiri pro talibus ad salutem secundum iudicium et legem ecclesie matris nostre.

iv. Sacramentum baptismi non est de lege Dei alicui parvulo decedenti requisitum ad salutem aeternam, si intelligatur universaliter, quod nullum sacramentum, &c. Error.

IX. 'Quod de quolibet parvulo in utero materno decedente, ac aliis parvulis decedentibus sine baptismi sacramento, est a catholico dubitandum nunquid talis aliquis dampnatur aut salvatur.' Quamvis iste articulus peccet in logica, tamen ad mentem articuli veniendo dixi et reputo esse verum de nullo parvulo sic decedente esse dubitandum secundum iudicium catholicum et ecclesiasticum quin dampnatur, set de quolibet tali secundum iudicium dei privatum est dubitandum an dampnetur sive aut salvetur, sicut erat in proximo declaratum. Persuasi enim tam de parvulis quam de adultis, quod quilibet eorum ante separacionem anime a corpore haberet claram visionem et consequenter liberam electionem, et qui debite tunc elegerit salvabitur quamvis non fuerit in flumine baptizatus, quia solus baptismus flaminis tali sufficiet ad salutem. Baptismus tamen aque multum valet, tam parvulis quam adultis, primo,

---

[1] *Decretals*, v, 39, 28.

quia removet difficultates que electionem debitam impedirent; secundo, quia delet omnia peccata precedencia; tercio, quia confert graciam debite eligendi.

v. De quolibet parvulo in utero materno decedente, ac aliis parvulis decedentibus sine sacramento baptismi, est a quolibet catholico dubitandum an damnetur an salvetur. Error.

X. 'Quod de parvulo baptizato decedente est catholice dubitandum nunquid talis salvetur.' Hunc non tenui, set negavi et nego, sicut ex precedentibus satis patet, quia de nullo tali est catholice, hoc est secundum iudicium ecclesie catholicum, dubitandum quin salvetur, quamvis quid tam de baptizato quam de non baptizato fiat secundum privatum dei iudicium postquam hinc transierit, sit a nostrum quolibet dubitandum.

vi. De quolibet parvulo baptizato decedente an salvabitur seu damnabitur, est a quolibet catholico dubitandum. Error.

XI. 'Quod saracenos, iudeos ac paganos adultos et discretos, qui non crediderunt, nec credunt, nec credent fidem christi, possibile est de lege communi salvari, immo de quolibet eorum decedente an salvatur, est catholice dubitandum.' Ponens hunc articulum, ut videtur, logicam non cognovit; ideo non mirum si dicta mea scolastica non sicut scolasticus, set tamquam inscius, reportavit; nescivit enim sensum divisum a sensu composito distinguere, ut apparet. Tales tamen in patria clerici reputantur, et inter scolasticos sunt laici idiote, quia minimus sophista Oxoniensis concederet in sensu diviso quod saracenos, iudeos, immo quoscumque infideles, qui nunquam salvabuntur, possibile est de lege communi salvari, sicut concederet quod illud quod est album et semper erit album possibile est esse nigrum, set in sensu composito negaret quod possibile est illud quod est album et semper erit album esse nigrum. Et similiter negaret quod possibile est infideles qui nunquam [fo. 284v] salvabuntur salvari. Huius nihilominus articuli primam partem eciam acceptam in sensu composito, ut est dictum, ad verba respondendo, concedere possum satis quia possibile est quod illi qui non crediderunt, nec credunt, nec credent fidem christi, habebunt fidem christi, quia materiam fidei habebunt etsi non actum, ut supra ad vii articulum est responsum. Set tenendo primam partem articuli ad hunc sensum, quod sit possibile illos qui non habuerunt, nec habent, nec habebunt fidem christi de lege communi salvari, sic utramque huius articuli partem et negavi per antea et iam nego.

vii. Sarazenos, Judaeos, ac Paganos adultos et discretos, qui numquam habuerunt, habent, vel habebunt actum seu habitum fidei christianae, possibile est de communi lege salvari, intelligendo in sensu composito, et de quolibet tali decedente, an salvabitur, est a quolibet catholico dubitandum. Error.

XII. 'Quod non est possibile de lege communi aliquem precise pro peccato originali dampnari.' Hunc tenui et persuasi propter peccatum committendum a quocumque dampnando in electione finali habita clara visione, et adhuc reputo esse verum.

> *viii. Non est possibile de lege communi aliquem pro solo originali peccato damnari, si intelligatur pro solo originali sine actuali, ut proximus articulus sequens. Error.*

XIII. 'Quod impossibile est de lege communi aliquem dampnari, sine peccato actuali ab ipso commisso.' Hunc tenui sicut proximum precedentem.

> *ix. Impossibile est de lege communi aliquem damnari sine peccato actuali ab ipso commisso. Error.*

XIIII. 'Quod nulla gratia in viatore ad vitam eternam promerendam est ponenda que sit aliud infusum distinctum a creatura merente.' Hunc dixi et reputo quod sit verus, eo quod hec vocabula 'gratus' et 'gratia' et huiusmodi sunt relativa seu respectiva. Nec notant principaliter aliquid, set ad aliquid, non absolutum set respectivum; ut viator sit in debita habitudine quoad deum et tunc est 'gratus' et in 'gratia' quoad deum, et in statu promerendi vitam eternam. Non tamen tenui quod gratia nichil est, sicud nec de aliquo relativo vel respectivo dicerem simpliciter quod est nichil, eo quod nichil, cum sit simpliciter negativum, negat tam pro substancia ſbã gracia.[1] Hoc est sine grata et debita habitudine nostra ad patrem nostrum celestem nunquam mereremur, immo nec mereri possemus, hereditatem celestem. Ut hec positio mea non solum sit contraria heresi pelagiane, set eciam sit satis evidens ad illam heresim destruendam.

This article receives no mention in Langham's register.

XV. 'Quod si gratia esset quid infusum a deo, qua aliquis viator esset gratus, huiusmodi gratia esset superius in natura quam homo gratus.' Ad hoc deduxi tanquam ad inconveniens dato primo.

This article is not mentioned.

---

[1] *Sic* MS. It is not clear what the writer intended as the final text of this obscure clause.

XVI. 'Quod nulla potest esse gratia creata que sit aliquid positivum creatum vel infusum, gratificans viatorem.' Hunc ad sensum iam proxime limitatum tenui et persuasi.

This article is not mentioned.

XVII. 'Quod quis potest mereri ex puris naturalibus, ita quod nichil requiritur a parte merentis preter naturalia ad eliciendum actum meritorium.' Hunc non tenui nec intendo tenere, sive intelligatur de actu meritorio vite eterne, quia in tali actu requiritur insuper habitudo debita quoad deum sicud ad articulum xiiii est responsum, sive intelligatur de actu temporaliter meritorio, quia adhuc aliqualis habitudo quoad deum et passiva preservacio et huiusmodi requiruntur.

xi. Aliquis potest ex puris naturalibus mereri vitam aeternam. Error.

XVIII. 'Quod gratia iuxta communiter ponentes est truffa.' Hunc dixi, eo quod iuxta communiter ponentes gratia ponitur aliquid esse absolutum, creature superinfusum, et ab ipsa creatura absolute distinctum, quod videtur esse in natura superfluum et sic truffa.

x. Gratia juxta communiter ponentes est truffa, eo quod non est possibile aliquam talem esse. Iste articulus est erroneus, quia male sonat.

XIX. 'Quod est medium sufficiens in natura ad attingendum finem hominis naturalem.' Hunc tenui et persuasi et reputo esse verum.

xii. Est medium sufficiens in natura ad attingendum finem hominis naturalem, si intelligit per finem hominis naturalem beatitudinem ultimam et aeternam. Error.

XX. 'Quod pro quolibet peccato commisso in statu fidei est remedium sufficiens in natura per quod redire potest viator ad gradum deperditum per peccatum.' Hunc eciam tenui et persuasi pro omni statu fidei citra claram visionem, set non ultra. Verumptamen per istam sufficienciam naturalem non exclusi adiutorium supernaturale fore insuper requisitum, set persuasi supernaturale adiutorium requiri ad viam hominis debitam, tam pro statu innocencie, quam pro statu hominis post peccatum.

xiii. Pro quolibet peccato commisso in statu fidei est remedium sufficiens in natura, per quod redire potest viator ad gradum deperditum per peccatum. Error.

XXI. 'Quod pro nullo peccato commisso citra claram visionem dei est aliquis iuste privandus hereditate celesti, sic nec puer ex ignorancia peccans est hereditate privandus.' Hunc tenui et persuasi, eo quod omne tale peccatum quantumcumque sit mortale, et immo deiciens peccatorem de statu filii in statum servi, est tamen remediabile in natura propter ignoranciam concomitantem.

> *xiv. Pro nullo peccato commisso citra claram visionem Dei est aliquis juste privandus hereditate caelesti, sicut nec puer peccans ex ignorantia est hereditate privandus. Error.*

XXII. 'Quod nichil est nec esse potest malum solum quia prohibitum.' Hunc tenui et persuasi, et adhuc reputo verum esse.

> *xv. Nihil est nec esse potest malum solum quia prohibitum. Error.*

XXIII. 'Quod pomum vetitum quod primus parens comedit non solum fuit malum homini quia prohibitum, set sibi prohibitum quia malum.' Hunc eciam tenui ut priorem, non tamen dixi quod pomum illud in se fuit malum, immo bonum in se et bonum homini quoad multos usus, set solum malum inconveniens homini quoad esum.

> *xvi. Pomum vetitum, quod primus parens comedit, non solum fuit malum sibi quia prohibitum, sed sibi prohibitum quia malum. Error.*

XXIIII. 'Quod ignorancia facti non excusat, nec excusare potest quempiam a peccato.' Hunc non dixi quin ignorancia facti sepius excusat in partibus, et poterit contingere in diversis casibus quod in toto.

> *This article is not mentioned in Langham's register.*

XXV. 'Quod quocumque effectu signato oportet quod sit aliqua causa quare Deus vult illum effectum, et dicere finaliter quia Deus vult est responsio vetularum.' Hunc sepius dixi, quia Deus nichil vult nisi quod procedit ex ratione.

> *xvii. Quocunque effectu signato oportet quod sit aliqua causa, quare Deus vult illum effectum, si intelligatur universaliter de omni effectu, quod oportet ponere aliquam causam ex parte effectus. Error.*

XXVI. 'Quod pater in divinis est finitus, filius in divinis est finitus, et solus spiritus sanctus infinitus.' Hunc eciam tenui, et eo sicud pater est primum principium in divinis, ita spiritus sanctus est finis ultimus in divinis, ideo sicud solus pater in divinis est inprincipiatus, et alie due persone principiate, sic a simili, solus spiritus sanctus est infinitus et alie due persone finite.

> *xviii. Pater in divinis est finitus, Filius in divinis est finitus, et solus Spiritus Sanctus est infinitus. Error.*

XXVII. 'Quod solus pater efficit, solus filius format, solus spiritus sanctus finit quamlibet creaturam.' Hunc articulum sic tractavi quod, [fo. 285 r] tenendo hec verba essentialiter, quelibet persona in divinis efficit, format et finit quamlibet creaturam, set tenendo hec verba appropriate, tunc solus pater efficit, solus filius format, solus spiritus sanctus finit quamlibet creaturam. Quomodo beatus Augustinus in quadam meditacione de spiritu sancto, modicum infra principium, alloquens animam suam peccatricem quomodo ex sola misericordia que spiritus sanctus est salvatur, sic dicit inter cetera: Vide quod sola ista persona Trinitatis, scilicet spiritu sancto, indiges ad reformacionem. Iusticia quidem, que opus Dei patris, et iudicium quod opus filii, ex reatu tuo te trahunt ad dampnacionem et cetera. Et docet quomodo ex sola misericordia spiritus sancti erit salva, cum tamen essencialiter loquendo quelibet persona in divinis sit misericordia equaliter sicud persona tercia in divinis.

xix. Solus Pater efficit, solus Filius format, et solus Spiritus Sanctus finit quamlibet creaturam. Error.

XXVIII. 'Quod Deus non potest punire, eo quod non potest esse tortor.' Quantum ad hunc articulum dixi et dico quod Deus non potest immediate quemquam punire, habet tamen regno suo plurimos tortores; sicud in isto seculo, ad torquendum et ad purgandum fideles suos, habet innumeros falsos fratres.

xxi. Deus non potest aliquem immediate punire, eo quod non potest esse tortor. Error.

Post hos articulos specificatos iidem falsi fratres in genere sic concludunt: 'Preter autem istos articulos unum librum edidit in quo non solum isti set multi alii continentur errores.' Ad quod respondeo quod librum nondum edidi, set plura dixi et scripsi que fortassis a clericis poterunt inpugnari, set ab omnibus falsis fratribus quantumcumque malivolis non poterunt infirmari. Pro quorum tamen malicia insuper et stulticia declarandis cedulam istam scripsi, tam ecclesiasticis et prelatis reverendissime exhibendam ut caritative me corrigant, dato quod in hiis vel quibuslibet aliis senserint me errasse, quam scolasticis graduatis ob exercitium ostendam, ut contra hec si velint arguant ubi eorum opinionibus me viderint repugnasse.

APPENDIX B

(i)

(Lambeth)   (18 Feb. 1367–8)

Reg. Langham, fos. 60v–61 [*Reg. Simonis de Langham*, p. 184].

Simon etc', reverende discrecionis viro, cancellario universitatis Oxon', salutem etc'. Cum in quodam negocio occasione quarundam conclusionum,[1] que in cedula presentibus annexa plenius sunt descripte, quod vertitur coram nobis inter fratres Willelmum Iurdan ordinis predicatorum et Umfridum[2] monachum ecclesie Dunelmensis, sacre pagine professores, processimus legitime ad nonnullos actus iudiciales, ac ut audivimus huiusmodi negocio pendente coram nobis, ipsi fratres Willelmus et Ughtredus huiusmodi conclusiones in scolis et alibi publice disputant et determinant, unde de facili homines ex huiusmodi disputacione duci poterunt in errores, ac scandala quamplurima exinde verisimiliter provenire; vobis igitur mandamus, quatinus eisdem fratribus Willelmo et Ughtredo et eorum cuilibet ac quibuscumque aliis, quibus in hac parte fuerit inhibendum, inhibeatis et faciatis per alios inhiberi, ne huiusmodi negocio indiscusso coram nobis, sub pena excommunicacionis maioris in eos et eorum quemlibet, si inhibicionibus huiusmodi non paruerint cum effectu, per nos canonice fulminand*e*, de huiusmodi conclusionibus disputent, predicent, sive eas determinent, vel alias quomodolibet tractent, quousque dictum negocium coram nobis determinatum fuerit plenarie et discussum. Et quid feceritis in premissis, certificetis nos etc' citra festum pasche prox*imo* futur*um*. Dat*um* apud Cherryng xij kal. Marcii anno Domini M°CCC^mo lxvij^mo.

(ii)

(Lambeth)   (17 Nov. 1368)

Reg. Langham, fo. 72 [*Reg. Simonis de Langham*, p. 226–7].

Litera testimonialis pro fratre W[illelmo] Iurdan super negacione certorum articulorum.

Universis Christi fidelibus presentes literas inspecturis, Simon etc' salutem etc'. Dampnatis per nos pridie sub certa forma, prout in registro nostro plenius continetur, diversis conclusionibus, quarum alique dicebantur venerabilis viri fratris Willelmi Iordan, ordinis predicatorum, sacre pagine professoris, supplicavit nobis idem frater Willelmus, quatinus cum ipse al*ias* tam in iudicio coram nobis, quam extra, conclusiones predictas

---

[1] *In margin*: Conclusiones sunt in quaterno actorum.
[2] *sic, for* Ughtredum: *cf. below.*

negaverat esse suas, dignaremur de negacione[1] sua huiusmodi[2] veritati testimonium perhibere. Unde nos predicti fratris Willelmi in hac parte supplicacionibus inclinati, universitati vestre tenore presencium intimamus, quod prefatus frater Willelmus dixit pluries coram nobis conclusiones predictas suas non esse nec fuisse, neque se easdem aliqualiter tenuisse. In cuius negacionis[3] testimonium sigillum nostrum fecimus hiis apponi. Da*tum* apud Lamheth[4] xv kal. Decembr. anno Domini supradicto.

APPENDIX C

The following are the censured propositions, not found in Uthred's schedule, and attributed in the text to his opponents. They are taken from Wilkins, *Concilia*, vol. III, pp. 75–76 [*Reg. Simonis de Langham*, pp. 221–2].

xxiii. Quam necessario homo est animal tam necessario homo est mortalis, si intelligatur universaliter pro omni statu hominis, non obstante gratia competente. Error.

xxiv. Quod Christi beata mater Maria,[5] et omnes homines beati adhuc veraciter sunt mortales, si intelligatur de lege ordinata. Error, quia contrariatur dictis apostoli et sanctorum.

xxv. Quod virgo beata est adhuc peccabilis et damnabilis pro peccato, si intelligatur quod ipsa beata virgo non sit facta impeccabilis et etiam indamnabilis per eiusdem gratiam confirmationis finalis beatitudinis ordinate. Error.

xxvi. Quod omnes beati tam angeli quam homines, excepto Christo, sunt peccabiles et damnabiles, si intelligatur ut proximus praecedens. Error.

xxvii. Quod omnes homines damnati in inferno sunt reparabiles et beatificabiles, si intelligatur quod sint reparabiles et beatificabiles non obstante eorum finali reprobatione, quorum ignis est inexstinguibilis secundum evangelium. Error.

xxviii. Quod omnes daemones sunt et semper erunt reparabiles ad beatitudinem consequendam, si intelligatur ut praecedens. Error.

xxix. Quod Deus de potentia sua absoluta non posset facere creaturam rationabilem impeccabilem, si intelligatur simpliciter, sicut verba sonant, quod non posset creaturam rationalem impeccabilem facere per naturam nec per gratiam confirmationis. Error.

xxx. Quod beati sunt mortales et immortales. Error secundum intellectum xxiv[ti] articuli.

v id. Nov. 1368 Lamheth.

[1] negociacione MS.   [2] *Erasure follows.*   [3] *Erasure follows.*   [4] Repeated in MS.
[5] [*Christus beata Maria* MS.—so printed ed., p. 221, cf. n. 1.]

APPENDIX D

When this paper was about to go to press I was able, through the kindness of Mr W. A. Pantin, to read a thesis for the B.Litt. degree at Oxford written by Fr. Stephen L. Forte, O.P., and entitled 'A Study of some Oxford Scholars of the middle of the fourteenth century, with special reference to Worcester Cathedral MS. F. 65'. Part of this thesis consists of an edition of the manuscript in question, and Uthred's opinions also are considered, though from a different angle and perhaps somewhat less fully than in the present paper. The whole is of considerable interest and will probably be published at some future date. For this reason, and because there is little disagreement between Fr. Forte's conclusions and those here set out, it has seemed better not to attempt to make any use of his thesis, but to draw the attention of those interested to its existence.

8

THE LAST ABBOT OF WIGMORE[1]

Almost a century ago James Anthony Froude, in a magazine article soon to be reprinted among his *Short Studies*,[2] threw upon the world two documents of the Tudor period which he conceived to be good evidence of the prevailing corruption of monastic life shortly before the Dissolution. Each in time attracted the attention of other writers and became the nucleus of a controversial literature in which fresh material came to hand piecemeal; various hypotheses were put forward or attacked, but in neither case has a satisfactory and final critical discussion appeared. In consequence, students of the religious life of the period, who can scarcely fail to come upon the two cases, must, if they are not prepared to accept the first account they find, allow themselves to be led on from reference to reference and from article to article without attaining final satisfaction. The more important of these two episodes is the celebrated case of Archbishop Morton's charges against Abbot Wallingford of St Albans. The ends of the thread of that tangled skein have yet to be found: to the very end of his life the late Dr G. G. Coulton was searching for them.[3] The other and slighter episode concerns the career of John Smart, abbot of Wigmore from 1518 to the dissolution of the house by surrender in 1538. Of this a brief review, giving as clear a narrative as the available evidence will permit, may not be out of place.

The gravamen of Froude's indictment was provided by a paper of charges against the last abbot of Wigmore, forwarded to Thomas

---

[1] [First published in *Essays in History presented to Rose Graham*, ed. V. Ruffer and A. J. Taylor (Oxford, 1950), pp. 138–45.]

[2] 'The Dissolution of the Monasteries' first appeared in *Fraser's Magazine* in 1857; it was reprinted thence in the first series of *Short Studies on Great Subjects*; these went through many editions, with different pagination; in the 1905 reprint of the eighth (1890) edition the essay is on pp. 401–42 of vol. I.

[3] [See Knowles, *JEH*, vol. III (1952), pp. 144–58.]

Cromwell by John Lee, one of the canons of the house.[1] It is a long and most comprehensive list, containing accusations of simony on the grand scale, of extortion, violence, and forgery of all kinds in dealing with tenants and lessees, of alienation of valuables to purchase papal bulls, of manifold incontinence, rape, and robbery, of the murder of one corrodian by harsh treatment and of another by poison, of the murder of yet a third person, John Tykkyl, of superstition, violence, and in general of scandalous misgovernment; altogether there are some thirty articles, which the writer asserted to be true in substance and offered to prove to satisfaction if Cromwell would appoint him or any unprejudiced party to sit in commission at Wigmore.[2]

When Froude wrote, this document lay among the unprinted manuscripts at the Rolls House, and remained unpublished for some forty years, till its turn came among the *Letters and Papers* of the reign of Henry VIII. Froude regarded his find as 'a genuine antique, fished up, in perfect preservation, out of the wreck of the old world', and he presented it for consideration as 'a choice specimen out of many' similar examples of the consequences of papal rule; he rendered it still more scandalous by attributing to the abbot of Wigmore 'a faculty to confer holy orders, though there is no evidence that he had been consecrated bishop'.

Gasquet took the matter up in the first volume of his *Henry VIII and the English Monasteries*,[3] and from an examination of the then unprinted episcopal registers of Hereford was able to give something of a background to the abbot of Wigmore by noting his election and confirmation, as well as his appointment by the pope, at the bishop's request, as coadjutor to Booth of Hereford. He also discovered the articles of a visitation of Wigmore made by order of Bishop Edward Fox in the autumn of 1536, and put forward the suggestion that this was a result of Canon John Lee's letter; he even went on to maintain that 'the visitation really discredits the charges and base insinuation of John Lee', and that 'the injunctions must fairly be con-

---

[1] *Short Studies*, vol. I, pp. 418–24.
[2] Froude, *loc. cit.* reads 'direct your commission to men (or any man) that will be indifferent, &c.' Gasquet and Gairdner read 'me' for 'men', possibly rightly.
[3] Pp. 365 ff. (1888).

sidered as a verdict in favour of the abbot'—an opinion which was not shared by Dr Coulton.[1]

Some years after Gasquet wrote, James Gairdner summarized Lee's paper in three slightly different versions,[2] together with Fox's visitation articles, which he had from Gasquet, without pronouncing on their mutual relationship. Finally, the registers of Booth and Fox were printed in Latin by Canon A. T. Bannister, who was inclined to adopt Gasquet's view that the visitation was subsequent to, and a result of, Lee's letter. This, as will be seen, cannot be maintained.[3]

Wigmore, a small abbey of Augustinian canons in the broken country of the Welsh border in the north-west corner of Herefordshire, after a distinguished beginning[4] came to have a peculiarly unsatisfactory record, and caused endless vexation to successive bishops of Hereford.[5] In 1518, when a vacancy occurred, the community asked Wolsey to nominate an abbot; his choice fell on John Smart, then a canon of St Augustine's, Bristol.[6] Smart had probably applied to Wolsey for the office, as he applied to Cromwell later for a greater one, and it was afterwards asserted that he had paid heavily for it; this also is possible, if not probable; Wolsey settled many elections, and was not the poorer in consequence.[7] It was common, in the last century before the Dissolution, for diocesan bishops to employ as coadjutors the superiors of religious houses within their diocese, and in 1523 Charles Booth of Hereford, in whose territory Wigmore was the only non-exempt abbey, selected Abbot Smart,[8] who continued for some eighteen years to act for him and his successors, and for part of the time for the bishop of Wor-

[1] Gasquet, p. 370. G. G. Coulton, *Medieval Studies* (First Series, London, 1915), pp. 88–9.

[2] *Letters and Papers* (henceforward *L. & P.*), XII (i), no. 742.

[3] *Registrum Caroli Bothe* (Cantilupe and Canterbury and York Societies, 1921); selections from Fox's short register are included.

[4] For its origins see B. Smalley in *Recherches de théologie ancienne et médiévale*, vol. X (1938), pp. 358–73.

[5] For past disorders at Wigmore see Registers of Richard of Swinfield, Adam of Orleton, and John Trefnant (Canterbury and York Soc., 1909, 1908, 1916); consult indices s.v. Wigmore.

[6] For the official documents of the election see *Registrum Caroli Bothe*, pp. 36–41.

[7] For Wolsey's practice, see A. F. Pollard, *Wolsey* (London, 1929), pp. 200–2.

[8] *Reg. C. Bothe*, p. 145.

cester as well. Smart was consecrated bishop of Panada *in partibus*, and could only continue abbot by being given his house *in commendam*. This rendered him irremovable save by a canonical process in the papal courts.

No evidence remains to tell us when first Bishop Smart got into trouble, but in August 1529 an agent of Wolsey's had been deputed to offer him a pension of 40 marks if he would resign the abbey. A few years since, we are told, such an offer would have been accepted, but now Smart knew that Wolsey himself was insecure, and refused to go. Wolsey's correspondent remarks that the alternatives are for the abbey to be destroyed by Smart or to take action against him by canonical process.[1] Smart's forecast proved correct, and Wolsey fell before taking action, but early in 1530 the bishop of Hereford took the administration out of the abbot's hands and handed it over to a canon of Hereford, John Cragge, and one of the community of Wigmore, Canon John Lee, the future delator of the abbot to Cromwell.[2] Richard Cubleigh, another member of the community of Wigmore, was up in London at the time; when he returned to find the abbey in the hands of Cragge and Lee a quarrel ensued, in the course of which some of Lee's henchmen set upon Cubleigh, who forthwith dispatched one of them, John Tykkyl, with a sword which he happened to have by him on his return from the road.[3]

How long Smart remained out of power we do not know; he regained control at least within a couple of years, and used as his factotum the truculent Cubleigh, for whom a dispensation from irregularity was obtained at Rome.[4] Lee, therefore, had from 1530, at least, been ranged against the abbot, and now had both resentment and rivalry as possible motives for action. Meanwhile, domestic upheavals had apparently failed to weaken either the reputation or the assurance of the bishop of Panada, for in 1534 he was appointed by the Ordinary as visitor for the diocese of Hereford,[5]

---

[1] *L. & P.* IV (iii), no. 5898 (31 August 1529).
[2] *Reg. C. Bothe*, p. 232 (17 January 1530).
[3] *Ibid.* p. 271: 'vim vi repellendo...ense quo tunc forte pro itinere munitus erat quemdam Johannem Tykkyl...interfecit.'
[4] *Ibid.* The dispensation is dated 25 March 1532.
[5] *Ibid.* p. 286 (11 March 1534).

and a year later, when the see of St Asaph became vacant, he is found writing to Cromwell to suggest himself as a candidate: 'If I were a man of sufficient qualities I trust you would help me to succeed him.'[1]

Nevertheless, all was not well at Wigmore. The abbey was visited, in an ordinary visitation which was probably also the bishop's primary, by the vicar-general of Edward Fox on 19 September 1536. The visitor was Dr Hugh Corwen, who had recently been ordained by the abbot of Wigmore in his own church; he was also employed, perhaps at the same time, to serve on Smart the king's injunctions, sent to all houses in 1536.[2] Fox did not issue his own injunctions for more than six months, and when they came at the end of the following March the phrasing was cautious, but certainly implied that the abbot had been guilty, or at the least defamed, of incontinence[3] and dilapidation, besides treating his community in an overbearing manner, and pawning the abbey's treasure. Grave suspicions attached to some of the canons also, and Richard Cubleigh, the abbot's chaplain, was clearly a law unto himself, and when not out hunting and hawking was as likely as not to be scuffling and brawling in the precincts.[4] Wigmore, in fact, in the last years of its existence was, as it had been for a great part of the past two centuries, a thoroughly disorderly house.

Canon John Lee may well have contributed some of the more notable *detecta* at this visitation; if so, he would have been dis-

[1] *L. & P.* VIII, no. 1073 (20 July). Gairdner had already printed this on the same date in the previous year (*ibid.* VII, no. 992).

[2] For Corwen's ordination see *Reg. C. Bothe*, p. 381, n. 1, cf. p. 377, n. 1. In the reference to the royal injunctions Gairdner, *L. & P.* XII (i), no. 742, has 'Dr Cave'. Gasquet, vol. I, p. 366, has 'Core'. In any case, the vicar-general, Dr Coren or Corwen, is clearly indicated.

[3] See the injunctions in *Reg. C. Bothe (Foxe)*, p. 373: 'Mandamus quatinus consortium quarumcumque mulierum suspectarum, illarum maxime si que sint cum quibus de incontinencia accessu [*sic*] notatus existis, vitare studeas *sub penis contra incontinentes a jure editis, quas*, si nostris in hac parte non obtemperaveris injunctionibus, *nulla expectata monitione te noveris incursurum.*' To those familiar with the language of visitations and with the circumstances of this one, the above (of which the significant words have been printed in italics), written by a bishop to his coadjutor, will appear tantamount to a declaration of guilt. Gasquet (vol. I, p. 369), by isolating the words *si que sint*, stresses them more than the context allows.

[4] *Reg. C. Bothe (Foxe)*, p. 374: 'Ricardus Cubley...ab aucupatoribus, venatoribus [*sic*; ? *-ionibus* in both cases], rixis, pugnis et id genus exercitiis illicitis abstineat.'

appointed by the dilatory and inconclusive action of the bishop. In the sequel, no great changes had taken place at Wigmore when Fox died on 8 May 1538, a year after the injunctions had been issued. By that time the proximate surrender of the monastery must have been clear enough to all interested parties, clerical and lay; two of the latter had already settled down at the gates: Thomas Croft, son of Sir Edward Croft of the Welsh Council, and a protégé of Cromwell, was deputy constable of Wigmore Castle and had obtained from the abbot at Cromwell's request a life interest in the abbey's tithe, while the fortunes of a certain John Bradshaw were being pushed by Rowland Lee, whose niece he had married;[1] he also had for a time a portion of the tithe, and by the summer of 1538 was farming the demesne.[2] With the bishop of Hereford out of the way and surrender imminent, Canon John may have thought that it was worth while having a throw at tripping the bishop of Panada at the last hurdle. Whatever his motive, early in September he obtained permission from the administrator of the diocese to delate his abbot to Cromwell, on the grounds that he had gravely infringed the royal injunctions.[3]

Smart had not failed to get wind of this, and ransacked the canon's room in the abbey on the pretext of recovering a stolen vestment; there he discovered correspondence which appeared to him and his allies among the local justices to give a handle for a charge of treason.[4] He therefore applied to Croft at Wigmore Castle, with whom John Lee had taken refuge, but Smart's agent Brydges was for some reason personally objectionable to the constable, who therefore refused to surrender the canon.[5] Instead, he took him to his

---

[1] For the unsuccessful attempt of Rowland Lee to obtain all the tithes for his niece's husband see *L. & P.* XIII, i, nos. 958, 1231.

[2] *Ibid.* no. 1331.

[3] *Ibid.* XIII, ii, no. 329 (11 September 1538). Thomas Croft to Cromwell. He writes that John Lee had been to Hereford to obtain licence of his ordinary. At the moment (since 8 August) Bonner, then ambassador in France, was bishop-elect of Hereford; the 'ordinary' was presumably his administrator. This conclusion to the Wigmore affair has hitherto escaped notice.

[4] *Ibid.* no. 333 (12 September). Smart and justices to Cromwell. It is noteworthy that John Lee is referred to (in Gairdner's abstract of the letter) as 'one of the late brethren'. Smart had with him the bailiff of Ludlow in addition to several local justices.

[5] *Ibid.* nos. 329, 333. Croft says he told Brydges that the abbot had no judicial powers; according to Smart he offered 'to break the same Brydges' head and set him by the heels'.

father, Sir Edward, and when the charge of treason was not pressed, sent him at his own request up to Cromwell to press his accusation of the abbot. This visit allows us to date with precision the sheet of charges against Smart originally published by Froude.

Such moves as may have followed remain hidden. If Lee's accusations could have been easily substantiated they might have been used to accelerate and cheapen the surrender by disqualifying Smart; probably, however, the canon had missed his chance, and the abbot had already shown himself amenable to authority. Were this the case, points of justice and morality would have made little appeal to the Lord Privy Seal. In any case, the surrender of Wigmore was taken on 18 November by Bishop Rowland Lee and Sir William Sulyard, and notification was carried up to Cromwell by 'cousin Bradshawe' with a recommendation from the bishop that the bearer should have the place to farm.[1] The abbot, he added, had not yet answered the charges made against him.[2] Three weeks later, however, when Lee was again at Wigmore to execute the dissolution of the abbey, his namesake the canon appeared before him and was unable to prove his serious charges, whereupon he renounced in writing all intention of proceeding further. Smart, therefore, at Cromwell's bidding, received 'his goods'[3] and subsequently a lavish pension.[4] Rowland Lee was an efficient administrator and an energetic and at times a drastic magistrate; there is no obvious reason why he should have wished to shield Smart, and in default of further evidence we must regard his decision as an acquittal of the more heinous of the public crimes charged against the abbot.[5] Nor is

---

[1] *L. & P.* XIII, ii, nos. 861 (18 November), 868, 1007.

[2] *Ibid.* no. 868 (19 November). 'As to the abbot's matter, he has not yet made his answer, and I doubt not he will make suit to you.'

[3] *Ibid.* no. 1007 (8 December). Rowland Lee to Cromwell. 'As touching the late abbot, the canon renounced any further to proceed, as appeared by his writing sent' (as the enclosure is not printed it has presumably disappeared). *Ibid.* p. 1008 (same date; the same to the same): 'At your letters we have delivered to the late abbot of Wygmore his goods; the canon could prove nothing.'

[4] *Ibid.* XIV, i, no. 1355 (p. 600). Smart received a grant of £80 per annum, the equivalent perhaps of £2000 of our money. A year later he is found paying the first subsidy on this pension (*ibid.* XVI, Appendix I).

[5] G. Baskerville, *English Monks and the Suppression of the Monasteries* (London, 1937), p. 74, states that 'Smart was afterwards employed as assistant by Rowland Lee'. He

there any reason for giving credit to the accusation of promiscuous ordination in the diocese of Llandaff. The ordination lists of that diocese have not been printed and perhaps are no longer extant, but those of Hereford show ordinations of normal numbers to have been canonically performed by Smart. With the abbot's moral delinquencies, now somewhat stale, Rowland Lee would have been less concerned, and faults against the regular life had ceased by now to have any significance.

Thus the whole episode, so far as it can be reconstructed, affords one more instance of the last days of a religious house passed in the midst of a complicated and often sordid web of personal intrigue. It is only when some part of the involved pattern has been revealed that the charges and exculpations can be seen in something of their true colours. The list of accusations against Smart, which Froude treated as proven crimes, was the work of an irresponsible and malicious man, and was doubtless in many of its articles and details either pure fabrication or reckless gossip. On the other hand, Smart was as clearly an ambitious, dishonest, and unworthy man, and his innocence is not established merely by noting that neither his bishop nor Cromwell wished to proceed to extremes in his regard.

gives no reference, and I have not been able to identify his authority. Baskerville, on the same page, accepts without question John Lee's assertion that Smart ordained a thousand priests in seven years *motu proprio* in the diocese of Llandaff.

9

THE MONASTIC BUILDINGS
OF ENGLAND[1]

During the greater part of the nineteenth century the history of the religious orders in England, and in particular the history of monastic remains, was widely regarded as the province of the learned antiquary rather than of the professional historian; in consequence, the greater part of the work done was unco-ordinated and scattered up and down the publications of national and regional antiquarian societies. The interest of these antiquaries in their topic was often derived from enthusiasm aroused either by the Romantic movement in literature or the somewhat later Oxford Movement in religion.[2] For both reasons, their work was largely neglected by the new school of critical historians in the second half of the century, whose concern with monastic history was limited to its connexions with political or institutional history. Meanwhile, critical methods of discussion and a scientific technique in excavation, largely derived from the associated fields of prehistoric and ancient archaeology, were influencing the antiquaries who were at work on monastic remains, and since the beginning of the present century, largely owing to the pioneer achievements of St John Hope, their activities have in the majority of cases reached a high standard of excellence, being based both on a study of relevant documentary evidence and on field work conducted on the lines laid down by the great archaeologists who have

[1] [This article, which has not been published before, was written as a concluding chapter to vol. III of *Rel. Orders*. An asterisk (*) after the first reference to a monastery signifies that an illustration of it can be found in Knowles and St Joseph, *Monastic Sites from the Air*.]

[2] It is interesting to note, in all this very considerable literature, how the earlier generation (1820–60) emphasizes in particular the 'romantic' and 'melancholy' aspect of the sites, while later writers (1860–1900) are almost all of Anglo-Catholic sympathies, deploring the destruction and sacrilege, and regretting what they consider to have been an age less materialistic than their own. Ruskin and his disciples form something of a link between the two schools.

laid bare classical and prehistoric sites.[1] Nevertheless, historians as a body have gone their own way without glancing over their shoulders, and a real danger has arisen that here, as elsewhere, the divergent paths of specialists might take them out of each other's sight; while the antiquary became more and more an archaeologist or a historian of architecture, the academic historian would neglect more and more the material and visual remains of the society whose records he was studying. Admittedly, the historian of monasticism must abandon to the historian of art and architecture the form and decoration of monastic churches and buildings, with which the monks themselves had very little to do, and which form a part of a much wider province, but the developments of the plan and complexity of the monastery, the increase of elaboration and comfort, the relations of these to the external history of the orders concerned and the spread of a particular change throughout the monastic body are a part of the domestic history of the monks which can scarcely be neglected without peril. It is proposed therefore in the present chapter to glance at the chief modifications in the plan and equipment of the religious houses between the Conquest and the Dissolution, and to note the moment at which these changes occurred. As in these matters each order had from the beginning its own characteristics and needs, it will be best to treat the half-dozen leading orders separately, even though the developments in each followed a parallel course, but attention will chiefly be concentrated on the two bodies responsible for the largest and most regularly planned groups of buildings, the black monks and the white.

[1] Sir W. H. St John Hope (1854–1919), the son of a clergyman and himself a devout High Churchman, was secretary to the Society of Antiquaries from 1885 to 1910, and for more than thirty years spent several weeks in the late summer excavating monastic and other medieval sites. His very numerous articles, containing historical and architectural accounts of the buildings concerned, accompanied by exact plans and based on documentary sources, remain indispensable to the student of monastic life; as he gradually acquired a wide and unrivalled knowledge of monastic remains he was able to formulate general conclusions. Second only to Hope was his friend and colleague Sir Harold Brakspear (1870–1934), a professional architect who used and in some respects developed Hope's technique. The method was taken over and made available to H.M. Commissioners (later Office and now Ministry) of Works by Sir Charles Peers (1868–1952) and Sir Alfred Clapham (1883–1950), both distinguished antiquaries and public servants.

All organized religious life in community clearly stands in need of certain essential buildings of some size, where the members may come together to pray, take counsel, eat and sleep, but the early Christian monasticism, which never stereotyped, so to say, its planning to the extent common in the West, gave no typical plan to the first monks of Italy and Gaul, and the Rule of St Benedict neither presupposed nor established any fixed relations between the component parts of the monastery such as did, in a later century, the Cistercian *Consuetudines* or the statutes of the order of Sempringham. Nevertheless, by the beginning of the ninth century and probably earlier still a plan had been evolved which contained all the main elements of the monastic complex and which became the basis of the monastic plan and of that of many of the religious orders throughout the Middle Ages and beyond; indeed, it is still recognizable in many of the monastic buildings of the modern world.

The nucleus, which gave its peculiar character to this complex, and became in time a synonym for the monastery itself and for the life lived there, was the broad passage or gallery surrounding an open rectangular space and giving direct access to all the buildings and apartments. This, known as the cloister, was, so far as can be discovered, not primeval in Italian and Gallic monasteries of the days of St Martin and St Benedict, but appeared first (as did the elaborate liturgical observance) in the so-called basilical monasteries of Italy from the late sixth century onwards. It was derived, according to the opinion now in favour, not from the atrium of the Roman house, but from the atrium or narthex usually found at the west end of the Roman and Lombardic city churches of the period; this was transferred from the west end of the nave to a site alongside, thus filling, when the church had transepts, one of the angles between nave and transept. As a circulating and ventilating area at the centre of a mass of buildings wherein lived a large family secluded from the external world its convenience is obvious, and in a Mediterranean climate it provided also a large area, lighted and partially warmed by the sun in winter and shaded from its heat in summer. Although its suitability in these latter respects was less marked in more northerly climates, the convenience of the cloister for economic and regular planning, and the conservatism that was a mark of all medieval institutions, led to the spread of the architectural form throughout Europe.

The plan of the abbey of St Gall (*c.* 820) shows that, as early as the ninth century, the location of the principal apartments of the monastery had also been settled.[1] The cloister, a covered passage, backed, as has been said, upon the nave of the church, and upon one of the transepts when these existed. Near to the choir of the church, and therefore in the eastern range of the buildings, lay the assembly room or chapter house, whither the monks proceeded each day from the church at the end of Prime, and whence they returned when the regular business had been done. In the eastern range, also, but at first-floor level, lay the dormitory (or dorter), whence they proceeded to the night offices in the church by a direct stair usually debouching in the transept. In the range opposite to the church lay the dining-hall (refectory or frater), with the kitchen at the west end, furthest from the entrance to the church. Along the west range were the store rooms, and at the end of this range nearest the church lay the entrance to the monastery from the outer world. To the west of church and cloister lay, in the ideal plan, the great outer court of the monastery. Two other buildings remain that were a necessary part of every great religious house: the infirmary (or farmery) and the guest house. The former found a convenient site outside the cloister either due east of the dormitory or east of the angle between dorter and frater, a site which was at once the most remote and quiet; the latter lay to the west of the western range for reasons directly contrary.

It will have been noted that while eastern and western ranges have been mentioned, the terms northern and southern have been avoided. The reason for this is that the position of the cloister in this respect was by no means constant. Speaking very generally, it lay

---

[1] This plan has often been reproduced, usually in reliance on F. Keller, *Bauriss des Klosters S. Gallen von Jahr 820* (Zürich, 1844). This and all other discussions of the plan have now been superseded by the full-scale facsimile colour-photograph published by the Historical Society of St Gall (St Gall, 1952) with a monograph on historical and archaeological aspects of the plan by Dr Hans Reinhardt and others. Dr Reinhardt establishes conclusively that the plan is an ideal one, sent to St Gall (possibly by Benedict of Aniane) to serve as an exemplar for the contemplated rebuilding of the abbey church.

to the north of the church in southern lands, where shade is most desirable, and to the south in the northern countries, where the need is warmth. This practice, however, cannot be elevated to the rank of a rule, or even of a convention. Whenever in northern countries a cramped site, steep slope or even considerations of drainage affected the planners, they had no hesitation in siting the cloister to the north of the church.

There is no evidence or likelihood that the developed claustral plan was introduced into Britain before the general collapse of the monastic life in the eighth and ninth centuries. It had, indeed, even been generally assumed, owing to a lack of full knowledge of the history of the tenth-century revival, and to the small scale and irregularity of plan in surviving Anglo-Saxon architecture, that the pre-Conquest monasteries as a whole were simply a congeries of small rooms similar to those revealed by excavations of earlier Northumbrian monastic sites.[1] Discoveries, however, on the site of St Augustine's abbey at Canterbury gave clear indications that a small cloister had existed,[2] and the knowledge that the three leaders of the revival were all familiar with great continental houses, and adopted a ceremonial presupposing the existence of a monastery with a cloister and community rooms, would make it extremely likely that the buildings of their abbeys would conform to the arrangements normal on the continent. Recent excavations at Glastonbury* have made it certain that a cloister existed there also, and it is probable that at Westminster and elsewhere the same arrangement existed, though it is also certain that buildings everywhere were on a very small scale compared with those of Burgundy, the Rhineland, Lorraine and Normandy.

In the last-named region in particular the newly founded abbeys had created a type of monastic architecture which both in scale and regularity surpassed the older abbeys of the south. The Normans of

---

[1] For example at Streneshalc (Whitby): cf. C. R. Peers and C. A. Ralegh Radford, 'The Saxon Monastery of Whitby', in *Archaeologia*, vol. LXXXIX (1943), pp. 27–88.

[2] C. R. Peers and A. W. Clapham, 'St Augustine's Abbey Church, Canterbury', in *Archaeologia*, vol. LXXVII (1928), pp. 201–18, and for Westminster, *Lives of Edward the Confessor* (RS, London, 1858), p. 90.

the eleventh century were not always great architects, and rarely great artists, but they were ambitious and energetic constructors. Above all, their monastic churches were conceived on a generous scale and almost always provided with a very long nave, which necessitated a lofty roof and transepts and presbytery of ample dimensions. The immediate purpose of the large church was probably to give space for the ritual processions which were a feature of the ceremonial in monasteries deriving from Cluny, but it soon became an architectural form with no direct relation to need or utility, and as such was transplanted to England, where it influenced all ecclesiastical architecture. A large church inevitably gave amplitude to the cloister and other buildings, and the Norman monasteries of the epoch of the Conquest were spacious, well-arranged blocks of building, without comfort, finish or decoration, but providing models easy of imitation on any scale.

The veritable fury of building that possessed the Norman churchmen of the first and second generations after the Conquest has been remarked by every historian. In this, the newly appointed abbots vied with the bishops, and so thorough was their reconstruction that in no abbey or priory of any size does a stone remain above ground from the pre-Conquest monastic buildings. The rebuilding usually began with the transepts and presbytery of the church. Rarely was the site of the minster transferred; Glastonbury is almost a unique exception, but here the *vetus ecclesia* was too sacred to be tampered with, and in consequence the new church was sited on a clear space to the east of all existing buildings, which were, in the sequel, entirely destroyed by a disastrous fire a century later; normally, the high altar of the existing church was taken as the guiding mark, and the new fabric built around it.[1] Only in the rarest of cases did the Norman planners enjoy the freedom of a virgin site; the majority of the old abbeys were at the centre of a town, or at least within the ambit of its walls, and the houses and streets surrounded a precinct that was already irregular. Sometimes indeed, as at Gloucester*, Melton* and Bury St Edmunds, the public graveyard adjoined the

[1] Examples of this may be seen at Bury St Edmunds*, Much Wenlock* and Muchelney*.

minster, and itself enclosed one or more of the small churches that abounded in pre-Conquest towns. These encumbrances were responsible for the northern position of the cloister at the three places just mentioned, and probably the same reason influenced the site at Canterbury. Facilities for a supply of water and the outflow of drainage were also taken into the reckoning, but they were not yet the overriding considerations that they were to become later. The Normans, in short, usually found the site of their monastery fixed for them in advance, and their flexibility was reduced to a manœuvre within the limits of a few yards.

The black monk plan in England was never regulated by any instrument or authority, and therefore reflected in its variety the independence which every house enjoyed. Convention, however, and the monastic observance dictated a certain order in the buildings, which was generally observed unless local difficulties stood in the way. The eastern range, of which the western wall continued the line of the western wall of the transept, was of two storeys. On the ground level, running from the transept, there occurred the following buildings: a passage to the monks' cemetery, usually lying east of the church; the chapter house; a parlour, sometimes adjacent to, and sometimes used as, a passage leading to the apartments east of the cloister; and a large room, forming the pillared undercroft of the dorter and devoted to various uses, of which the most common were that the part nearest the chapter house should serve as a store for muniments, while the remainder, equipped with a hearth, was the monks' warming house. Over the whole wing, at first-floor level, ran the dorter, which communicated with the church by a night-stair debouching in the transept, and with the cloister by a day-stair opening on the cloister between the chapter house and parlour. The dorter range was prolonged at the far end by the latrine (rere-dorter), which usually stood over the main drain at right angles to the range; beneath it on the ground floor further space was available, used sometimes by the infirmary.

Opposite the church lay the frater, which usually occupied the whole of the range on the ground floor; the kitchen sometimes stood at the western end and sometimes outside the range to the south-west, as at Durham*. The frater, especially in early days, stood as a rule on cloister level, and was entered by a large doorway, near which, either along the wall of the cloister or more rarely in a small building in the garth, were troughs or a laver with running water for washing.

The western range was never in early times in England allotted so precisely as the others to a particular use; normally it contained the cellarage and storage on the ground floor, and accommodation for guests above; at the end nearest the church and the general entry the cellarer had his checker, and between this and the nave lay a passage leading to the outer world. The cloister garth was seldom used for burials in a Benedictine or Cistercian monastery, though the chapter house served as a burying place for abbots; the community worked and read in the alley backing against the church, while the novices and children of the cloister had their schools in other walks.

Outside the claustral range lay outposts to the east and to the west. To the east lay the infirmary, and as this provided accommodation not only for the sick, but for the aged and for those undergoing the periodical 'cure' of blood-letting, it was a building of some size, which usually took the shape of a large rectangular hall, divided by columns into three aisles, with an altar at the east end. To the west, round the outer court, stood the offices serving the material needs of the community: bake-house, brewhouse, stabling and the rest. Round the whole precinct, which included vegetable and herb gardens, ran a wall pierced by gateways which were later enlarged to become an architectural feature of some magnificence.

The not unusual transference of the whole complex to a site north of the church has already been mentioned, but modifications in the arrangement of buildings round the cloister were also not unknown. Thus at Worcester* lack of water and drainage facilities for the rere-dorter, which always formed part of the dormitory block, as well as the proximity of the city, led to the construction of a large dorter on the western side of the cloister, below which ran the Severn, and in its final shape this occupied a unique position at right angles to the western range, a position apparently dictated by the sanitary arrangements of the time; a supply of water to flush the great drain could only be obtained from cisterns on the roof, whence a steep fall within the building took the sewage into the river; the lower storeys beneath the dorter were used as the infirmary.[1] At Durham also, where the lie of the land was not dissimilar, the dorter was ultimately transferred to the western range, though it lay in the normal position parallel to the cloister. At Gloucester, another abbey with a northern cloister, the dorter stood at right angles to the eastern walk beyond its northern end, and parallel to the large chapter house which met the range at right angles. Sometimes, as at Durham and Chester*, the chapter house adjoined the transept, elsewhere, it was separated from it by a passage; it was usually rectangular, but at Durham and elsewhere it had an eastern apse, and at Worcester a circular building was internally polygonal. The infirmary, which usually lay well outside the claustral area to the east, approached by a long gallery, lay abnormally at Worcester, as has been said, and at Gloucester it stood parallel to the dormitory and beyond it to the north. The eastern site had the advantage of allowing the infirmary to make use of the great drain after it had passed beneath the kitchen and the rere-dorter in its flow from west to east; it was no doubt this consideration that brought about a transference of the infirmary as a frequent concomitant of a transferred dorter, as at Worcester and Gloucester, both eccentric houses, and at Malmesbury*, a site comparable to Gloucester, where the infirmary ran from east to west along the same axis as the frater and to the east of it.

The great outer court, surrounded by offices, found its ideal position west of the church and between it and the great gateway of the precinct. In practice, however, local conditions often modified its situation. Thus at Durham and Worcester physical features and the position of the town alike forbade a western siting, and in these two cases the court is found due south of the monastic complex, with its great gateway to the east. At Chester it lay west of the church, but shared with all the other buildings a northern site; at Bury St Edmunds the existing town and church of St James blocked the normal site, and the great court lay some distance due north of the

---

[1] Compare H. Brakspear, 'On the Dorter Range at Worcester Priory', in *Archaeologia*, vol. LXVII (1916), pp. 189–204.

west end of the church and of the monastic buildings. At Ely*, where it originally lay in the normal position, the situation was entirely changed by the action of the first bishop, who claimed for himself all of the precinct that lay to the west of what is now the road named The Gallery, running due south from the west end of the cathedral. It was left for the monks to improvise a court, smaller than was customary for a monastery of the size of Ely, due south of the monastic complex. These instances, which could be multiplied, may serve to show the need for great flexibility in planning when the Norman abbots approached their task.

In almost every monastery one of the first tasks of the Norman superior was to build or rebuild on the grand scale. Speed was essential, in order to provide the large and growing communities with the accommodation needed for a regular life, and the first outfit of buildings was often completed before the end of the century. Thus at Westminster Gilbert Crispin ran up the dorter, rere-dorter, frater and much of the cloister before the end of the eleventh century;[1] at St Albans* Paul of Caen, the first Norman abbot, built the cloister and many of its adjoining rooms;[2] at Bury the cloister and its surrounding ranges were the work of Abbot Robert II in the first decade of the twelfth century;[3] at Worcester the conventual buildings nearest the church were the work of Wulfstan.[4] The fabric was un-decorated, and often insecurely built, as the event proved, but the scale at least was usually adequate. This was fortunate, as for obvious reasons it would have been well-nigh impossible to enlarge the cloister later; though rebuilt in almost every case, the dimensions of the garth remained those of the first Norman architect, and again in almost every case they were adequate for all subsequent needs. One

[1] For this and subsequent references to Westminster buildings see *Westminster Abbey* vol. of R[oyal] C[ommission on] H[istorical] M[onuments], and H. F. Westlake, *Westminster Abbey*.

[2] For the buildings of St Albans, see C. R. Peers in *Victoria County History, Herts*, vol. II, pp. 483–570, and in RCHM, *Hertfordshire*.

[3] For all Bury buildings see A. B. Whittingham, 'Bury St Edmunds Abbey', in *Archaeological Journal*, vol. CVIII (1951), pp. 168–89. For Abbot Robert see *Memorials of St Edmund's Abbey* (RS, London, 1890–96), vol. I, pp. 356, lxii.

[4] H. Brakspear in *Victoria County History, Worcs*, vol. IV, pp. 394–408.

contributory cause of this was the long Norman nave, which encouraged the planning of an ample cloister; another was the rapid growth of numbers, which within half a century of the Conquest reached a maximum, thus ensuring that the various buildings were in early days constructed on a generous scale.

Nevertheless, enlargements and additions and rebuilding in another style began early, and continued to the end. The various modifications of the plan of the church concern the historian of architecture rather than the monastic historian. Speaking very generally, the early rebuilding chiefly affected the eastern limbs, and was directed towards providing greater space for ceremonies at the high altar, for sung Masses at other altars, for the provision of a chapel of some magnificence dedicated to the Blessed Virgin, and for more spacious choirs. The cloister itself and the surrounding buildings were rebuilt from time to time according as the lapse of time, accident of storm and fire, growth of numbers, development of a standard of comfort, or merely the desire of an abbot or official to expend ready money on buildings of a more modern and sumptuous style, might dictate. At each house particular circumstances influenced the procedure, but if we regard the abbeys as a whole, there would seem often to have been three great rebuildings of the cloister and its rooms: the first at the middle of the twelfth century, when the primitive Norman work was renewed in more solid and richly ornamented style; the second in the thirteenth century, when the Early English vaults and tracery supplanted the Norman; and the third towards the end of the fourteenth century, when the whole was rebuilt in the late Decorated, or the early Perpendicular fashion. These rebuildings often extended over a generation or a monastic lifetime: thus at Westminster, after the disastrous fire of 1298, reconstruction proceeded round the cloister, beginning with the dorter in 1300 and completed in the western range only in 1370, while at Evesham the whole cloister and its adjuncts were rebuilt by Abbots John of Brockhampton and William of Chirton between c. 1290 and 1344.[1]

---

[1] *Victoria County History, Worcs*, citing abundant detail from *Chronicon de Evesham* (RS, London, 1863).

It would be tedious to examine more than a very few instances. For our present purpose it may be best to consider some parts of the monastery where a steady development can be seen in almost every house, reflecting the social changes in the country as well as the modifications of the monastic life; such parts are the lodging of the superior, the provision for the sick, and the arrangements for the daily life of the monks of the cloister.

The requirements of the superior and of the guests were closely related, for by the Rule and monastic tradition the abbot or prior was directly and personally responsible for the guests, who shared his table and with whom he alone was allowed free converse. The abbot's table had therefore been from the first apart from the community, and even when there were no guests, he still dined apart and took as his companions a few of the monks. What began as a safeguard of regular life and fare became in the sequel an abuse, and spiritually minded abbots in the Middle Ages often made a point of taking meals in the frater in order both to share the regular diet and to preserve their sense of solidarity with their community. These, however, were the exceptions, and the social position of the feudal abbots rendered such a way of life all but impossible. Similarly, as has been seen elsewhere, the abbot had originally slept either in the dormitory or in a small room adjoining it: at Battle* he had only abandoned this practice in the late twelfth century and at Westminster traces of an abbot's bedchamber have been found near the junction of transept and dorter.[1]

This, therefore, was the general practice immediately after the Conquest, when abbots were still primarily the spiritual fathers of their monks, and guests were relatively few and moderate in their needs: the abbot when at home lived with his monks, and the guests had a modicum of accommodation in the western range; this took the form, when fully developed, of hall, parlour and chapel on the two floors of the range in the part nearest to the church. When, in

[1] Lanfranc in his *Constitutions* (ed. Knowles [Edinburgh, 1951], p. 73) presupposes that the abbot is sleeping in the common dormitory, and Abbot Odo of Battle, who had been prior of Christ Church, Canterbury, did so in the last quarter of the twelfth century (see *Mon. Order*, p. 406). The abbot's house, however, at a considerable distance from the cloister, appears in the St Gall plan of *c.* 820.

more settled conditions and an expanding society, guests multiplied, while the abbot, for his part, became more and more of a feudal magnate, especially after the separation of his revenues from those of the convent, he felt the need of a room or rooms near the guests and the outer world, and it became common for him to have a chamber near the guest-hall, and to use as his own the chapel there. This change took place in the late twelfth or early thirteenth century, and almost simultaneously there came in a division among the guests, the most distinguished being allotted to the abbot, and the rest to the community, who became responsible on the one hand for visiting monks, and on the other for the poorer sort of pilgrims and travellers. This led to the erection of new and larger guest-quarters further away from the cloister, usually to the west, where a complete guest-house, including hall, kitchen, parlour and chapel, was constructed. The next stage was for the abbot, under the influence of the universal change in social habits, to enlarge his own accommodation by building a lodging of private rooms, using the existing guest-hall in the western range, now vacated by the poorer guests, as a state apartment.[1] This change was usually made in the early part of the fourteenth century, when the standards alike of comfort and of domestic architecture were everywhere rising. Later in the same century the whole establishment was often rebuilt on a still more elaborate scale, and the abbot's lodging attained perfection as an architectural form. Additions and enlargements, however, still continued to the end, and magnificent abbots' halls and houses were being put up in the opulent and fully domesticated style of the early Tudors.[2]

As has been said, the abbot's quarters were normally in the western range, and the fully developed abbot's house often formed a complex extending from or abutting upon the claustral building; sometimes it even formed a small court or cloister of which one side coincided with the western range. The whole process of develop-

<hr>

[1] The *loci classici* for the development of the abbot's house are J. A. Robinson, *The Abbot's House at Westminster* (Cambridge, 1911) and H. Brakspear, 'The Abbot's House at Battle', in *Archaeologia*, vol. LXXXIII (1933), pp. 139–66.

[2] For example the abbot's house at Muchelney, and the prior's lodging at Montacute and Castle Acre*.

ment can be traced clearly at a number of houses, the first abbot's chamber and guest-hall usually dating from the mid-twelfth century, to be superseded by a complete abbot's house in the reign of Henry III, which was again rebuilt in a richer and more comfortable way towards the end of the fourteenth century, to receive its final complement of panelled hall and parlour under the early Tudors. Though the site in the western range may be described as the norm, in houses where the whole layout was irregular or where (as at some of the cathedral monasteries) the prior's lodging had originated near the dorter, other positions were chosen for development. Thus at Christ Church, Canterbury, at Durham, Worcester and Winchester the prior's house was to the east of the dorter, while at Ely, where the whole plan had been dislocated, the prior's lodging, rebuilt by Prior Crauden early in the fourteenth century, lay due south of the cloister and south of the prior's great guest-hall, and the abbot's house had a similar position at Malmesbury. The last sentences will have indicated that a parallel evolution to that of the abbot's house was taking place at the cathedral priories in the accommodation of the prior, whose social position in the later Middle Ages was indistinguishable from that of an abbot.

While normally the guest-hall adjoined the lodging of abbot or prior, the course taken by building schemes might prevent this. Thus at Much Wenlock, a Cluniac house which perhaps was late in attaining social position and affluence, the large and unusually beautiful prior's house of the late fifteenth century lay in what must have been the primitive position of the prior's lodging, adjoining the infirmary to the south-east of the cloister. When no new building was erected earlier, the existing lodging was often reconditioned in the interests of comfort and privacy in the fifteenth or early sixteenth century, as at Castle Acre, where the relatively small prior's lodging in the western range was remodelled and decorated in a most skilful and attractive fashion. In general, the lodging of the superior of a house of any size must have been, both in grace and comfort, among the finest examples of small-scale domestic architecture of their age in the country. The rooms were of convenient size, well lighted with oriel windows, and provided with fireplaces, garderobes and even wash-basins in the wall fed by taps from a cistern. They were wainscotted or hung with arras, and the latest had often carved overmantels and ceilings, while some of the great halls of the abbots could vie in size and beauty not only with the neighbouring monastic frater, but with the halls of the new colleges of Oxford and Cambridge, and those of all except the largest palaces of the early Tudor age.

Comfortable provision for the superior was not confined to large or moderately sized houses but was a feature at all, even the smallest, as may be seen at such an insignificant priory as that of Ewenny* in Glamorgan, or in still greater elaboration at Finchale*, a cell of Durham. Finally, it was characteristic of the later medieval centuries that the second in command also should acquire a lodging; at the abbeys, as at Gloucester, the prior would sometimes move into the original abbot's house when the latter erected his last and most elaborate lodging, while at the cathedral monasteries the subprior would take over the chambers similarly vacated by the prior. At the greatest houses even the third in rank had a modest chamber, as at Westminster, where the site of the subprior's lodging is known.

A similar process of elaboration may be seen in the development of accommodation for the daily work of reading, writing, illumination and theological study. All this, in the early days of Norman monasticism, was carried on in the alleys of the cloister. The senior monks worked alongside the church, where the cloister was presumably furnished with tables and benches, as it was also with a book cupboard, though as we know that books were 'issued' to individuals it is probable that they were carried away and kept by them near their beds in the dorter. The disadvantages of the damp and draughty cloister as a place for reading and study, and still more for writing and illumination, are obvious, but it is almost a century after the Conquest before we hear of an apartment, the scriptorium, being provided for the precentor and his assistants, though from other sources we gather that it was permitted to scribes and illuminators to have access to the fire of the warming house or kitchen when preparing their materials, and perhaps to the chapter house for their work.[1] Probably, although definite information is wanting, the warming house was in frequent use by workers in the winter, and from the early thirteenth century a scriptorium was provided at many houses, though it was normally a small room of which the very site is unknown. When, at the end of the thirteenth century, a new class, that of the student and doctor in divinity, made its appearance, there was a fresh need, which was met in time at some of the greater abbeys by the erection of a lecture-room and a row of studies. At about the same time the cloister, which had not originally been glazed, received panes of the fine clear glass now being made, and was equipped with small individual wainscotted studies or carrels, complete with desk and bookshelf.[2] Last of all, and strangely so to modern thinking, a special room was provided for the books in the late fourteenth or early fifteenth century. The library, even so, was never an architectural feature; arriving too late to find space for itself on the ground floor near the cloister, it was usually built at first-floor level, either over the alley of the cloister backing on the nave of the church, or over one of the galleries leading from the cloister to the infirmary.[3] Thus a single alley of the cloister had, so to say, proliferated into scriptorium, studies, lecture-room and library, while remaining the normal working place for many of the community. Proliferation of another kind had meanwhile taken place in regard to another alley, that in which the children of the cloister had in Lanfranc's day received elementary instruction. They had disappeared as a class in the twelfth century in England, and

---

[1] This was certainly allowed in Cistercian houses: see Marcel Aubert, *L'architecture cistercienne en France* (Paris, 1947), vol. I, p. 118. Here again the Carolingian abbey was well equipped; the St Gall plan shows a *scriptorium* over the library adjoining the choir of the church on its northern side.

[2] *Rel. Orders*, vol. I, p. 289.

[3] J. W. Clark, *The Care of Books* (Cambridge, 1901), pp. 100 ff. The library at Christ Church, Canterbury, dates from 1414–43 and lies above the prior's chapel: F. Godwin, *De Praesulibus Angliae*, ed. W. Richardson (Cambridge, 1743), p. 126, and H. Wharton, *Anglia Sacra* (London, 1691), vol. I, p. 145. That at Durham, built by Wessington *c.* 1430, lay between the chapter house and the south transept: *Rites of Durham* (Surtees Soc., 107; Durham, 1903), p. 26, and *Historiae Dunelmensis Scriptores Tres* (Surtees Soc., 9; London and Edinburgh, 1839), p. cclxxiii. Those at Gloucester and Winchester were in the same position; that at St Albans dates from 1452 (*Registra S. Albani* [RS, London, 1872–73], vol. I, p. 423); that at Worcester was over the south aisle of the nave; that at Bury dated from 1425–45.

had never been replaced, but during the two last medieval centuries most large monasteries supported both a song school and an almonry school, and buildings for these formed customary additions to the offices of the great court, the almonry finding its most convenient site adjacent to the great gateway.[1]

Meanwhile the infirmary had also grown and changed its character. It was at several houses the last of the conventual buildings to take shape towards the middle of the twelfth century, when it took the usual form of a large rectangular aisled hall, its roof supported by columns of wood or stone, and having curtained beds in the side aisles and an altar at the eastern end. In the first rebuilding it acquired a chapel projecting to the east, and often also wooden cubicles, together with more elaborate kitchen accommodation, where special food, including meat, could be prepared. Rooms were built for the infirmarian, and additional accommodation was soon added for those partaking of special food at seasons of blood-letting. Finally, from the mid-fourteenth century onwards, the neighbouring site was replanned as an infirmary cloister, and either in the old hall or in a new range a number of small private chambers were built for the sick and aged, with fireplaces and garderobes. Near this cloister also were found the apartments in which ex-superiors and retired officials who had deserved well of the house were allowed to end their days.[2]

Finally, a series of changes took place in and around the frater. This, one of the first parts of the monastery to be built, was usually rebuilt on a grander scale either in the thirteenth or fourteenth century. If in the latter, it often acquired a lobby with 'screens' such as still survive in college halls at Oxford and Cambridge, and sometimes it was of set purpose raised above ground level, with an undercroft for storage, and approached by a wide flight of steps ascending within the range from a door in the cloister. In this way

[1] As, for example, at Durham. Magnificent gateways abound: Battle, Bury, Chester, Ely, Gloucester, St Albans, Much Wenlock and St Mary's, York.

[2] The development of the infirmary may be seen particularly clearly at Westminster (first infirmary, early in twelfth century; restored early in fourteenth century; infirmary cloister, 1364–93) and St Albans (first in eleventh century under Paul of Caen, rebuilt with chapel under Geoffrey of Gorham, 1114–46; infirmary cloister built by 1214; new infirmary, 1260–90; separate cubicles under Whethamstede [first abbacy, 1420–41]).

13-2

the frater attained its maximum size, which was often greater than that of the original room. In the later centuries, however, there was something of a contraction. Already in the thirteenth century it had become customary for the monks, either by selection or in batches, to eat meat at periods of recreation in a room other than the frater; this, as has been noted above, was often a chamber in or near the infirmary, whence the food could be served without violating the regularity either of the frater or its kitchen. When, however, in 1336 Benedict XII regularized the practice of meat eating on certain days each week for the whole community, a larger room was usually needed, and this was found either by constructing one between the cloister and the buildings of the infirmary, or by using the under-croft of the frater, or by cutting the frater in half or even by inserting a floor to create a dining-hall of two storeys. In any case the original frater was often by this time too large for the shrunken numbers and, when not structurally altered, it was sometimes, as at Durham, abandoned altogether save on great feast days,[1] and the community dined in two sections (save in times of fasting) in rooms constructed or adapted in the vicinity.

To these 'proliferations' of the essential community rooms there were added, as the centuries passed, numerous other apartments at the greater abbeys. Thus St Albans, besides the accommodation for guests of the abbot and of the convent, had separate provision for black monks and white monks, while it was not unusual for a number of flats and maisonettes to exist within the precinct, as at Christ Church, Canterbury, where corrodians or confraters of distinction were allowed to live.

The buildings of a Cistercian abbey and the phases of their development present more than one point of contrast to those of the black monk houses.[2] The Cistercians, as planners, had two great

---

[1] *Rites of Durham*, pp. 79–82.

[2] The foundations of the critical study of the early Cistercian plan were laid in three elaborate monographs: W. H. St John Hope, 'Fountains Abbey', in *Yorkshire Archaeological Journal*, vol. XV (1900), pp. 269–402; Hope and J. Bilson, *Kirkstall Abbey* (Thoresby Soc., 16; Leeds, 1907); and J. Bilson, 'The Architecture of the Cistercians', in *Archaeological Journal*, vol. LXVI, N.S. XVI (1909), pp. 185–280. As the reader can perceive, the paper on Kirkstall represents an advance in knowledge beyond that on Fountains*, parti-

advantages over their predecessors: they had a detailed code of observance, to which all were bound under penalties to conform; and they could set out their monastery upon a virgin site. As a result, the Cistercian abbeys over the whole of western Europe present a compact subject of study which is unique among the many manifestations of medieval construction and design; they resemble a single botanical or ornithological species which, recognizable at once wherever it occurs and sharply differentiated from all others, has nevertheless small regional peculiarities that are equally recognizable.[1] What is perhaps most remarkable in this great family of abbeys is, that the abbeys, let us say, of Germany or of Provence show similar deviations from the type-abbeys of Burgundy, and similar evolutions of detail to those visible in the houses of Spain or of the British Isles. For while the family resemblance of all Cistercian monasteries is more striking than any individual variations, the remark that has been made, to the effect that a blind Cistercian, transferred from Burgundy to Scotland or Italy, would find himself able to move round his new home without difficulty, is not absolutely true. While he would certainly be far less at sea than a black monk in similar plight there were, as will be noted, a few points of difference that frequently occurred, besides occasional eccentricities that distinguished one abbey from its sisters.

The Cistercians, as has been said, almost invariably started with a virgin site. This circumstance helps to account for a feature in their history, as noteworthy on the continent as in the British Isles. The transference of an abbey in its early years from one site to another is

cularly in respect of the frater. The information and conclusions contained in the first two of these works have been developed in many subsequent monographs and histories. Still more recently, all the medieval Cistercian abbeys of France have been described, photographed and measured in all their component parts by the eminent director of the Soc. Française d'Archéologie, M. Aubert, in his monumental *Architecture cistercienne* (p. 194, n. 1 above). A similar task, on a slightly smaller scale, has been excellently accomplished for Germany by H.-P. Eydoux, *L'architecture des églises cisterciennes d'Allemagne* (Paris, 1952). See also M.-A. Dimier, *Recueil de plans d'églises cisterciennes* (Grignan–Paris, 1949).

[1] Strictly speaking, there are three kinds of *differentiae* in the Cistercian order's buildings. Two are specific, *viz.* the characteristics deriving either from a region or from the mother-house of a filiation; the third affects abbeys all over Europe and is social: the introduction of new elements of convenience or comfort.

extremely frequent.[1] Sometimes this transference took place almost at once; elsewhere after two or three, or even after ten or twenty years. Sometimes the new site was less than a mile from the old, sometimes one or five or twenty miles separated them. At first sight these frequent changes might seem to argue both an excessive care for material advantages and an inefficiency in recognizing or exploiting the character of a site, but actually the explanation would seem to be very simple. The white monks were usually presented with a wide tract of waste land and a general mandate to choose a site. Almost by hypothesis both they and others were ignorant of local conditions and potentialities in a district that had never been inhabited or cultivated; they could not tell whether the soil could be made fruitful or whether it was exposed to excessive saturation or drought or cold wind. It was essential that vegetables, fruit and some grain should be produced in the near neighbourhood of the abbey, and sometimes it was only by the experience of several years that they found all this to be impossible. The first buildings, which, in spite of decrees to the contrary, seem often to have been of a temporary character, were then abandoned, and a fresh start made.

From a study of a number of Cistercian sites and ruins it is possible to ascertain what the planners sought. One rule was almost universal, one commodity was essential, and one circumstance decisive. The church stood upon the highest point of the site, a fair-sized stream of water was needed for drainage and power, and the drainage must be available at particular points of the monastic buildings.[2] In addition, a sheltered site was desirable. The ideal terrain was therefore a level space of land, sloping almost imperceptibly from north to south towards a stream forming its southern

---

[1] Some twenty-eight such moves in England and Wales alone are noted in Knowles and Hadcock, *Medieval Religious Houses*, pp. 104–18 and map. Aubert, vol. I, p. 80, gives numerous instances in France.

[2] As Aubert, vol. I, p. 112, remarks: 'L'église est toujours au point le plus haut de l'emplacement.' This rule was followed by all orders when untrammelled by other buildings, e.g. at Kirkstead (Cist.) and Barlings (Prem.), where the surviving fragments of the church are visible at a surprisingly great distance in a low-lying situation. For drainage as a decisive factor, see Aubert, vol. I, p. 116, where the abbey of Sénanque (Vaucluse) is instanced: the church lies on a north–south axis owing to the direction taken by the stream; no doubt a similar reason determined the eccentric orientation of Rievaulx* (Yorks.).

limit or, failing a stream, facilities for leading over the site an artificial current of water. When the abbey (as at Tintern* and Buildwas*) could not easily be placed to the north of the stream the planners did not hesitate to set the cloister to the north of the church, while in exceptional cases they were prepared, as at Rievaulx, to swing the church and the whole complex out of the traditional orientation in order to get water for their drains. The Cistercians, indeed, were almost from the beginning skilled water engineers. In addition to the network of channels and drains of running water that flowed beneath all the offices of the monastery, pure spring water was piped to the house, sometimes from a distance of a mile or more, and distributed throughout the buildings with a complexity and lavishness rarely if ever exceeded by even the wealthiest abbeys of black monks.[1]

Strange as it may seem, although physical continuity was preserved in so many abbeys from the beginning till the French Revolution, and in Austria and elsewhere later still, while in the case of the reformed Cistercians the spiritual succession was all but unbroken, the traditional layout of the basic parts of a Cistercian abbey faded from memory and record, half-buried beneath the accretions of a later age or obscured by the débris of ruins, and was only recovered, largely by English antiquaries, some fifty years ago.[2] It has often been described, but must necessarily be repeated as a preface to any historical account of Cistercian developments.

The church was cruciform, with a short square-ended presbytery, north and south transepts, and a nave of moderate length, which in almost all the primitive abbeys, and in smaller ones of later date, was without aisles. To the east of each transept was an aisle containing one, two or three chapels; in addition, the nave of all larger abbeys was aisled, and the transepts sometimes had aisles to the south. The presbytery and transepts were often rebuilt on a somewhat larger scale when the community grew, but it was rare for the eastern limb

---

[1] The skill with which water was harnessed for every domestic and industrial purpose at Clairvaux, even in St Bernard's lifetime, is commended in a remarkable passage in the contemporary *S. Bernardi Abbatis Vita Prima*, lib. II, ch. V, no. 31. E. Vacandard, *Vie de Saint Bernard* (4th ed., Paris, 1910), vol. I, pp. 421 ff., expatiates upon it.

[2] See above, p. 196, n. 2.

of the church to attain the length and amplitude found at Fountains and Rievaulx. Occasionally, as at Beaulieu* and its daughters Netley* and Hailes* (all late foundations) and rarely elsewhere as at Croxden, the east end terminated in an apse with apsidal chapels as at the rebuilt Pontigny and Clairvaux. There was normally a squat tower[1] at the crossing; all else was forbidden and the bell that summoned to offices was originally hung at the gable of the south transept. When, as at Fountains and Kirkstall and Cymmer*, towers large or small remain or can be traced, they are later additions.

The Cistercians needed the same community apartments as the black monks, but they had other needs besides. The distinguishing feature of their version of the monastic complex was the provision of what amounted to a second monastery for the lay brethren or converses, who often in the twelfth and thirteenth centuries far exceeded in numbers the monks of the choir.

The order of the buildings, as occurring in the normal house with cloister south of the church, was as follows. Next to the south end of the southern transept, on the ground floor, came a narrow space, divided by a party-wall into an eastern sacristy and a western book-room; then came, in order, the chapter house, parlour, day-stairs to dorter, and passage to the buildings east of the cloister. Over all at first-floor level ran the dorter,[2] which was almost invariably prolonged beyond the cloister to the south, having underneath its southern extension a spacious undercroft used originally in its northern bays as a warming house (as with the black monks) and in its southern part as noviciate. At the southern end of the dorter, and at right angles to it, stood the rere-dorter over the great drain. The southern range of the claustral square was formed by the frater, which originally lay, as with the black monks, parallel to the walk of the cloister, having the kitchen at its western end. In the western range, given over to the lay brethren, there was a long building of two storeys, corresponding to the dorter range of the monks to the

---

[1] This was a peculiarly English feature; the French abbeys had a *clocheton*.

[2] Waverley, the first Cistercian foundation in England, appears to have had its dorter on ground level, next to the chapter house: H. Brakspear, *Waverley Abbey* (Surrey Archaeological Soc.; London, 1905), pp. 43–5; but the excavator may have been mistaken and the ruins are now under grass.

east. On the ground floor, running from the church southwards, lay the outer parlour, with an exit to the outer court; cellarage of several bays; a passage with doors opening on the cloister to the east and the great court to the west; and the lay brothers' frater. Sometimes, but by no means universally, a long passage within the range, parallel to the west walk of the cloister and known as the 'lane', served as an adit to the church from the frater and other rooms of the lay brethren; they were thus given access to their choir in the nave of the church by a door at the west end of the southern aisle without having to pass along the monks' cloister. This 'lane', an exclusively Cistercian feature, is, somewhat unexpectedly, far from universal in France as also in England.[1] Over all the western ground-floor rooms ran the dorter of the lay brothers, with their rere-dorter at right angles over the drain at its southern end. To the south-west of the lay brothers' rere-dorter lay their infirmary, corresponding to that of the monks to the east. Thus the stream or great drain, running from west to east, passed under both rere-dorters and infirmaries, and ran near enough to the kitchen to take thence refuse also.

Such was the typical plan of the claustral buildings, but even before the changes shortly to be mentioned there were always houses with minor eccentricities. Thus the chapter house, normally a small rectangular room either wholly within the range or pro-jecting slightly to the east, might extend eastwards in an apse, as at Rievaulx, or stand free of the range as a polygon as at Margam* and Dore, while the infirmary might lie in an unusual position to the south of the dorter range, as at Byland*, Furness* and Netley. In addition, there are the fairly numerous cases where the cloister lay to the north of the church; Rievaulx is perhaps unique among English abbeys in being entirely disorientated.

This primitive Cistercian plan underwent normally an important modification within fifty years of its inception. Many of the com-munities grew rapidly to a size equalling or even exceeding even

---

[1] Aubert, vol. II, pp. 122–3, holds that the 'lane' was originally all but universal, but disappeared when the cloister was rebuilt or enlarged. It may be so, and in many cases ocular verification is impossible, but it is not clear why such a seemingly useful feature should have been discarded, where it already existed, so early.

the largest black monk houses. This led to the serious inconvenience of overcrowding in the frater. The expedient was therefore almost universally adopted of rebuilding the frater on a larger scale with its axis perpendicular to the middle point of the southern alley of the cloister, thus admitting both of still further enlargements to the south (as at Furness) and of greater space to east and west.[1] The space to the east was now used as the warming house, thus freeing the dorter undercroft either for the scribes and illuminators, or for the novices. As often an almost simultaneous extension southwards of the dorter had taken place, the opportunity was taken to clear floor-space for beds and give a more central access to the dorter by constructing a new day-stair between the dorter and the warming house. It is noteworthy that abbeys built *de novo* after *c.* 1160 have the frater in the new position (e.g. Byland, Netley, Beaulieu, Hailes), while those which never prospered (e.g. Cymmer) retained the original site, to which those founded or rebuilt in the fifteenth century (e.g. Whalley* and Cleeve*) reverted. Among minor eccentricities in this part of the monastery may be noted the rere-dorter of Furness, approached by a bridge running east from the middle of the dorter, and the fraters of Byland and Basingwerk*, which lie respectively near and adjacent to the dorter range, thus necessitating special treatment for the warming house, which at Byland was of two storeys and at Basingwerk lay south of the dorter range.

The Cistercians, owing partly to advantages of site and partly to the technical advances in design and construction made between 1050 and 1130, neither needed nor desired to be perpetually rebuilding. The early houses often passed through two stages. The original monastery, executed by the labour of lay brothers, was supposed to be in existence when the founding community and its abbot arrived, and architectural evidence is often forthcoming, as at Byland and Jervaulx*, that the lay brothers' range was the first to be built, showing sometimes, by its lack of a bonding junction, or

---

[1] The same change occurred in France, with exceptions of a similar type. Another advantage of this position was the easier service of monks and converses from a single kitchen.

even of physical connexion, with the church, that it was in existence before the latter was built or planned. More often, perhaps, the colony of builders lived in wooden huts. In any case, an early start was made upon the eastern portion of the church, comprising transepts and presbytery, followed by the eastern range of the cloister and so forward round the cloister in a clockwise sense. These early buildings were usually modest in scale and without finish in detail; when the community prospered and grew a general rebuilding took place, either in the latter decades of the twelfth or in the early years of the thirteenth century. This rebuilding, which usually included an enlargement of the eastern part of the church, and a refashioning of the main parts of the eastern and southern ranges of the cloister, was accomplished in the purest architectural style and the most finished building technique of the age. Sometimes, as at Fountains after the destructive raid of 1147, this reconstruction took place relatively early; elsewhere, as at Rievaulx, it was *c.* 1230 or even later. In contrast to the black monks, the Cistercians rarely rebuilt the claustral ranges and the cloister itself in the later styles of Gothic; their days of expansion ended in the first part of the thirteenth century and few of the houses in later times were as wealthy or populous as even the moderately large Benedictine abbeys. Moreover, the termination of the grange-and-lay-brother economy in the early fourteenth century greatly diminished the total population and labour force of the houses.

Two important parts of the abbey, however, usually underwent a succession of changes: these were the infirmary and the abbot's lodging. The infirmary seems often to have been the last essential part of the complex to be given permanent form. The founding monks were presumably as a rule young and vigorous; early Cistercian traditions had little respect for the physician, and it was long before the elderly monks retired to the infirmary for their declining years as did their black brethren. Even when built, the first infirmaries were often of wood and were not replaced by stone erections for thirty or forty years; the twelfth-century infirmary hall resembled that of the black monks in being a building of three aisles, its roof supported by two rows of posts or columns, and containing a fireplace. This was often rebuilt *c.* 1300 on a larger scale, with an adjacent chapel and a second fireplace. The next stage was for the aisles to receive partitions and become a row of cubicles. Finally, in the early part of the fifteenth century at latest, the hall was broken up internally into rows of private chambers in two storeys, often each having its own fire. The Cistercian infirmary rarely developed into a cloister, but of all the components of the white monk plan this shows the least fixity in its siting.

The second member of the complex to show constant evolution was the abbot's lodging. The constitutions prescribed that the abbot should sleep in the dorter, and in early days he certainly did so. The first move was to a small sleeping chamber at the northern or transept end of the room;[1] this was abandoned, in the second half of the twelfth century, for a larger room, adequate for use in interviewing as well as for sleep, on the east side of the dorter near its southern end. This, as opening upon the dorter or rere-dorter, might be held still to fulfil the letter of the law. The accommodation in this position developed rapidly. At Kirkstall, one of the earliest known examples in England, a lodging of three storeys was erected east of the rere-dorter *c.* 1230, complete with hall and solar.[2] This building, adjoining the chapel of the infirmary which the abbot could use, was connected to the main infirmary block by a set of chambers that could be used by the abbot of the mother-house when on his visitation, and by other visiting abbots. Finally, in the late fourteenth century, the whole building was reconditioned and fitted out with fireplaces and garderobes. At other houses a similar process took place somewhat later. Thus at Croxden the abbot's camera was constructed *c.* 1269–74;[3] at Meaux between 1286 and 1310;[4] the Croxden lodging was rebuilt on a larger scale in 1335;[5] while at

[1] For examples see Aubert, vol. II, pp. 90–1.

[2] See the elaborate account by Hope in his *Kirkstall Abbey* (p. 196, n. 2 above), pp. 34–8.

[3] According to the unpublished chronicle (Brit. Mus. MS. Cott. Faustina B 6, fo. 75v) cited by Hope, *Kirkstall Abbey*, p. 35, n. 1, Abbot William of Howden 'edificavit egregie cameram abbatis superiorem et inferiorem'.

[4] *Chronica de Melsa* (RS, London, 1866–68), vol. II, p. 238: 'in orientali parte infirmatorii monachorum.'

[5] In the Croxden chronicle quoted, n. 3 above, Abbot Richard is said to have begun to build 'novam cameram suam inter coquinam infirmitorii et dormitorium'.

Fountains and Jervaulx the abbot's chambers were constructed in the fourteenth century.[1] Finally, in the last phase of all, many abbots brought their lodgings up to date on the lines of the abbatial houses of the black monks and canons. Thus Abbot Huby of Fountains reconditioned his suite at the end of the fifteenth century, while Abbots Paslew of Whalley and Chard of Forde* constructed lodgings which, in their different ways, reflected the developments of taste and comfort of their age.

The Cistercians, like the black monks, were accorded certain dispensations from the meatless diet of the Rule by the Cistercian pope, Benedict XII, in 1336. Unlike the black monks, however, the Cistercians had no tradition of previous semi-official relaxations, and therefore had no room in existence to serve as a meat-eating refectory. They accordingly constructed a 'misericord', usually a square room of moderate size, near the infirmary, whither service could come from the infirmary kitchen. Occasionally, as at Basingwerk, this is on an eccentric site, with a kitchen of its own.

The white monks, in common with all the religious, experienced a marked contraction of numbers in the fourteenth century, and as in many cases their income also contracted they often avoided the expense of upkeep or transformation by frank destruction. Thus at Rievaulx the size of the chapter house was reduced by filling in the arcading of the aisles, while the south end of the long dorter, always a trouble to maintain in repair owing to the steep fall of the ground, was removed altogether. At Furness the refectory was shorn of its southern half, at Kirkstall, Jervaulx and Forde it was divided by a floor into two storeys, the upper being the frater proper, and the lower the misericord, while at Cleeve it was rebuilt altogether, parallel to the southern walk. At Cleeve, indeed, where funds were apparently available for large operations, the whole abbey was reconditioned to suit changing times, and the rebuilt frater was on the pattern of a fifteenth-century black monk frater or college hall, with screens and a great fireplace. In addition to the normal contraction of numbers, the Cistercians were, from the latter part of the

[1] For Fountains see Hope's monograph (p. 196, n. 2 above), pp. 335-9. For Jervaulx see Hope, *Kirkstall Abbey*, p. 35, n. 1.

fourteenth century onwards, faced with a problem of their own through the virtual extinction of the class of lay brothers who in primitive times had filled to overflowing the spacious western range with its appurtenances. No real solution was found—perhaps none was ever consciously sought—for the disposal of the void thus created in the buildings. At some of the greatest houses, such as Fountains and Furness, the long dorter and frater remained unchanged and presumably empty save for occasional stores. Sometimes the part south of the cloister was demolished or allowed to fall into ruin; more frequently the range along the western walk was converted, probably in direct imitation of the black monks and canons, into accommodation for the abbot and distinguished guests, and the detached guest-house may sometimes have been allowed to disappear. Such seems to have been the treatment at Beaulieu, Cleeve, Hailes,[1] Sawley* and elsewhere, while at Forde[2] a similar use of the western range took an unusual shape in the late splendours of the abbot's hall and entrance tower. In general, the Cistercians seem to have done as much, if not more than, the black monks in adapting themselves to the new age and its amenities. In addition to the private rooms of the infirmary, individual chambers with fireplaces were often constructed in the southern part of the undercroft of the dorter range, presumably for the older monks, while the abbots and ex-abbots had comfortable apartments in the heart of the abbey.

The buildings of the black and white canons, though often of an elaboration that gives them an antiquarian interest equal to those of the monks, are less susceptible to historical examination owing to the very numerous idiosyncrasies which almost all the large houses display. These departures from normality do not follow any discoverable principle, and the individual buildings themselves are often irregular to a degree, the cloister being trapezoid or rhomboid in shape, and the various ranges standing at unusual angles to the

[1] At Hailes the abbot's lodging is described in a Dissolution document printed by Hope, 'Fountains Abbey', p. 337, note, as 'extending from the church to the frayter southward with payntre buttre kitchen larder sellers and the lodgings over the same'.
[2] For Forde see RCHM, *West Dorset*.

cloister and to each other.[1] In general, the houses of the canons resemble those of the black monks in the arrangement of their parts and the uses made of the buildings, with the important exception of the western claustral range. For some reason, connected perhaps with the relative mediocrity of so many of their houses, the canons did not make this an essential or even a normal element of their plan, though they invariably retained the cloister with its four alleys. Sometimes, as at the Augustinian Haughmond or the Scotch Premonstratensian abbey of Dryburgh*, the west walk was backed only by a curtain wall. Elsewhere, parts of a range existed as cellarage, while occasionally in the later centuries the example of the black monks was followed, and the range used as lodging for the prior and guests; there were also houses, such as Thornton and Easby*, where the dorter or other rooms stood in the western range. Another characteristic of the canons' planning was the meagre size of the nave of their churches. Since they had no need of a long and aisled nave either for ritual processions or for a lay brothers' choir, and often lacked the funds and ambitions necessary for the construction of a great church, they were content with a short and often aisleless nave—so short, indeed, that the western range, where it existed, not infrequently lay west of the end of the nave and even overlapped it as at Bolton. With the Austin canons in particular a nave with a single aisle—that to the north—is characteristic; the original cloister had been built against a nave originally without aisles, and in later enlargements only a north aisle could therefore be added.

The Austin canons, like the black monks, made a great display with their gatehouses in the later Middle Ages. The fourteenth-century fashion of great crenellated towers was followed on the grand scale at Thornton; the gateway there is perhaps unique among extant remains since it embodies the abbot's living rooms and

[1] For example Kirkham* (Yorks.) and Haughmond* (Salop), where plans and air photographs show the irregularities very clearly. The variety obtaining among the black canons may be seen in the following sites for the abbot's or prior's lodging: Kirkham, east of dorter; Bolton*, (first) in the west range near the church, (second) south of dorter; Thornton*, in the gateway; Newstead*, in west range; Haughmond, south of infirmary cloister; Ulverscroft*, in western range; St Osyth*, north-east of cloister; Michelham*, south-west angle of cloister. It is noteworthy that even in the very small houses, such as Shulbrede*, the prior had special accommodation.

state apartments, though lying some two hundred yards west of the main buildings. Of a very different type was the smaller gatehouse of Butley*, with its celebrated armorial frieze; the magnificent erection at St Osyth's is one of the East Anglian family of master-pieces in brick and flint to which the church of Ingatestone and the entrance tower of Layer Marney belong.

The developments in construction and adaptation in the friaries are scarcely susceptible of analysis. With very few exceptions, the friars' buildings lay near the centre of what are now, and were even in the Middle Ages, closely built-up areas; they had often grown from humble beginnings in a few tenements and had never emerged fully from their cramped quarters. The few examples that survive of friaries in open country, such as the houses of the Minors at Walsingham* and Llanfaes, and those of the Carmelites at Hulne* and Aylesford*, show that, with certain characteristic modifications, the main lines of the traditional monastic plan were followed. Scarcely anything remains of the domestic buildings of the largest friaries—those of Oxford, Cambridge and London—and it is to be regretted that the most important friary to be erected to order on an open site, that of the Dominican royal foundation of King's Langley, has wholly disappeared.

In general the friars had small cloisters in the normal monastic position, save that there was normally a narrow open space between the south wall of the church and the north wall of the cloister; the north alley thus stood free. The other alleys usually ran within the range, thus becoming architecturally a passage or corridor, and the entrance from the outside world was obtained, not through a door in the western range, but through the door into the church and thence by way of a passage, known as the 'walking-place', across the church to the north door. The reason for the arrangement is nowhere explicitly given, but it may well have been the only way of safeguarding the domestic privacy of a popular community.

The friars of the first generation often repaired to an existing parish church for their Masses, and when first they had oratories of their own these were small and purely domestic, but when they became popular preachers and confessors, and relations with the secular clergy became strained, it was natural that they should build churches of their own. These had from the first an individual architectural character; they were in fact large preaching halls with choir stalls and an altar at the eastern end. The great age of building seems to have begun in the decade 1270–80, and thenceforward all the four orders built and rebuilt large churches in the cities and towns which created a new species of Gothic church planning and decorating.

Within the friary the cloister was rarely if ever used as a place for work or assembly, and lecture-rooms for the friars and their extern pupils formed part of the complex. A library was essential, and as the academic position of the doctors grew in dignity, special provision was made for the bachelors and masters in divinity by allowing them rooms or cubicles of their own; the preachers in particular seem to have made a practice of cutting part of the common dormitory into cells or cubicles with a reading desk and bookcase near the window. Nevertheless, the shift towards a more comfortable and elaborate career never greatly affected the architectural style or furnishings of the friaries. The letters and surveys and inventories of the commissioners at the Dissolution make it clear that the friars had few costly fittings, and that the buildings were on the whole modest in scale and style.

A word may be added as to the furnishing of the monasteries, in so far as it reflected a change in the life of the monks. The brethren not in office spent the greater part of the day in one of three places— cloister, dormitory and choir—and in each of these considerable changes took place. The cloister in the Anglo-Norman monasteries was a cheerless place on all save warm and sunny days: its unglazed arcading admitted the cold and the damp; it had no fixtures save a book-cupboard, though benches and tables must have been available. Conditions in the darker and colder seasons would have been extremely rigorous and, as has been seen, more tolerable accommodation was provided for some at least of the scribes and illuminators. The cloister, however, remained the common working and reading room, and when it was rebuilt in the thirteenth century or later windows took the place of open arcading, and the windows were glazed. Almost at the same time wainscotted carrels were introduced, containing a seat and a reading desk, and usually lighted by a half-window; these were now the private studies of the monks.

In the choir the original furniture would seem to have been merely a bench, with a low movable form in front over which the monks prostrated for certain prayers; from the first there was probably a wooden screen behind the benches. Wooden 'stalls' for the individual monks may have existed in the late twelfth century, but the earliest known examples from Rochester (1207) and Westminster (*c.* 1240) are later. These already have canopies, to give protection from down draughts, but the desk in front was still low, and could not be used as a book-rest. In the next century desks as we know them came in, and whenever possible enough stalls were provided in what is now the rear and higher row to accommodate all the monks.

Finally the dormitory, in which the beds had originally been pallets to which only a low side-curtain gave privacy, was equipped with oaken beds and later divided into cubicles. These were equipped with a chest, seat and book-case, and often, as at Durham, with a small window, and thus became small private rooms, in which the monks slept, took their siesta and read at certain times.

This brief survey will perhaps have served to indicate two of the chief conclusions that the historian is able to draw from the existing remains. The first is that the construction, embellishment and adaptation of buildings went on unceasingly from the Conquest to the Dissolution. When once the initial Norman spring-time had passed, almost all medieval building was extremely leisurely, and it was no uncommon thing for a single piece of work, such as the alley of a cloister or the transept of a church, to be in building for a decade or more. There can have been few monks during the whole existence of a great house such as St Albans or Bury who succeeded in spending their whole monastic lives free from the necessity of avoiding masons' scaffolding in the cloister or of watching the sailing cloud through gaps in the unfinished vaulting, while discomfort, often amounting to real hardship and lasting over a whole monastic generation, must have inevitably followed not only such major catastrophes as the fall of the central tower at Ely in 1322 or the burning of the minster at Bury in 1469, but such deliberately planned upheavals as the reconditioning of the choir of Gloucester and the rebuilding of the naves at Canterbury and Westminster. What is, however, of more interest to the historian is the realization that building was almost the only visible growth that continued ceaselessly throughout the centuries, and those who pause to contemplate that slow and ever-flowing stream will be less ready to speak of sudden declines and great changes and utter torpor within the monasteries, and will see instead the monastic story as it really was: the enduring for ages of a living, moving organism, tending ever towards a greater complexity of detail and a more advanced degree of material convenience and comfort.

One who has spent hours and days among the records and the ruins of monastic houses, great and small, is aware at last of a sense of direct contact with the material life of the past. The rounded stairs and thresholds, the cracked hearths, the stone worn smooth by hand or bell-rope, the socket of the towel's holdfast by the frater door, the maze of passages, the personal names given by a succession of inhabitants to this or that part of the buildings—Traill at Bury, Le Spendiment at Durham, The Gallery at Ely, Bell Harry at Canterbury—all these recall a life that continued for five centuries or more, and which must have seemed to those who lived it as enduring and changeless as the natural life of the woods and fields. How many generations of monks or canons gazed upon the Tor at Glastonbury, or the hurrying Wharfe at Bolton, or the unharvested waves at Whitby. How many, in the cool morning of life, when the beauty of the external world strikes so suddenly and deeply into the mind as a revelation and an anguish, must have paused in the cloister to regard the silence and glory of the December stars, or have met there the breeze of a spring morning, laden with the scent of may blossom or bean flower. These emotions and experiences are indeed common to all; they are not for monks alone and have nothing to do with the deeper life of the spirit; but we are men, and it is in a building where a succession of men have passed from youth to age among the same towers and trees that we seem for a moment to cross the abyss of time and to be upon the point of seeing with their eyes these lichened walls, once harbouring such a busy world of life and reverberating to the sound of footsteps and the music of bells, and now standing in silent fragments in the mown lawn or framing the byres of a farmyard.

10

JEAN MABILLON[1]

The absence of any adequate modern biography of Mabillon has long left a deplorable gap in the history of French scholarship. Almost immediately after his death his intimate disciple, Dom Thierry Ruinart, wrote a short life[2] which must always remain essential for any estimate of its subject's character, and a more formal notice found its place in Dom Tassin's history of the Maurists.[3] After that, no work of any originality or insight appeared until 1879, when a well-documented study of Mabillon's early life and some of his work was published in a most inaccessible fashion by H. Jadart,[4] who continued his patient investigations for another thirty years. Then, in 1888, Emmanuel de Broglie[5] produced his classical picture of the society of St Germain-des-Prés and the journeys of Mabillon which, though a work of genuine scholarship and high literary charm, was extremely selective and made no attempt to cover the whole of Mabillon's life and work. De Broglie's volumes, however, soon followed by a similar work on Montfaucon,[6] by their very excellence deterred would-be biographers until in the early years of the present century Dom P. Denis began to make preparatory soundings among the mass of Maurist documents with

[1] [First published in *The Journal of Ecclesiastical History*, vol. x (1959), pp. 153-73.]
[2] T. Ruinart, *Abrégé de la vie de Dom Jean Mabillon* (Paris, 1709). This book, now very rare, was translated by Dom Claude de Vic into Latin as *Vita Joannis Mabillonii* (Padua, 1714). A reprint of the French original, with the title *Mabillon*, appeared in 1933 (Maredsous: collection Pax, xxxv).
[3] *Histoire littéraire de la Congrégation de Saint-Maur* (Brussels, 1770), pp. 205-69. Mention may also be made of the *Histoire de la Congrégation de Saint-Maur*, by Dom E. Martène, which remained unpublished till the edition of Dom G. Charvin in 9 vols., Ligugé, 1928-43. For a short account of the Maurists, see an article 'The Maurists' by the present writer in *TRHS*, 5 ser., vol. ix (1959), pp. 169-87.
[4] *Dom Jean Mabillon*, Reims, 1879; a reprint of 300 copies from *Travaux de l'Académie nationale de Reims*, vol. LXIV (1877-78), pp. 49-324.
[5] *Mabillon* [*et la Société de l'abbaye de Saint-Germain des Prés à la fin du dix-septième siècle*], 2 vols. (Paris, 1888).
[6] *Bernard de Montfaucon et les Bernardines*, 2 vols. (Paris, 1891).

a view to writing a formal history, which must have contained a long account of Mabillon. His labours issued in a number of valuable articles in the *Revue Mabillon*, but he died with his main task unaccomplished. Meanwhile Dom Henri Leclercq contributed to the *Dictionnaire d'archéologie chrétienne et de liturgie* an article,[1] as long as a short book, on Mabillon, as well as numerous other articles on topics connected with his works, but it was not generally known that during the last years of his life, in what time that indefatigable worker could steal from compiling single-handed the last volumes of his great *Dictionnaire*, he had written what was at least the first draft of a full-scale biography. He succeeded, as is well known, in finishing his encyclopedia a few months before his death, and he also dispatched the manuscript on Mabillon to his Paris publisher, but, for an unexplained reason, publication was long delayed and it was only a year ago that the second volume appeared. It is nowhere stated what editorial changes have been made, though it is implied that there has been some abbreviation.[2]

These volumes will undoubtedly rank for very many years as the standard life. Dom Leclercq, as his other writings and the foreword to the present work show, had always felt a great attraction, amounting indeed to a personal devotion, to the greatest of the Maurists, and he can have had no rival in his combined knowledge both of Maurist scholarship and of the many subjects of historical and archaeological interest with which Mabillon was concerned. Those who knew Leclercq's writings, and especially some of his work outside the *Dictionnaire*, might reasonably have feared that a certain fluidity and facility of writing, not to say a superficiality of judgement, based on a wide and rapid rather than on a deep and pondered reading, might have neutralized the qualifications just mentioned. It is, indeed, true that these lengthy volumes lack the ultimate

---

[1] *DACL*, vol. x, pp. 427 ff. Mention should also be made of the bicentenary volume *Mélanges* [*et documents*, etc.], in *Archives de la France monastique* (Paris and Ligugé, 1908). This contains fourteen articles, many of them of unusual merit, by scholars of the calibre of Besse, Cabrol, Delisle, Jadart, Levillain, Omont, etc.

[2] *Mabillon*, 2 vols. (paged consecutively) (Paris, 1953, 1957). The publishers, in a prefatory note, say that they are publishing 'les meilleures pages de son étude'; the phrase is ambiguous, but it is difficult to believe that they have jettisoned very much. There are a few, but only a few, traces of editorial work.

cohesion and inspiration of the greatest biographies. The reader receives the impression that every chapter was written apart from the rest *in vacuo*, and that either the author's temperament or his realization that his time was short prevented the attainment of a final fusion and synthesis.[1] Moreover, no attempt is made to show the development of Mabillon's mind and character, and almost all the pages dealing with the monk and the man take the form of long extracts from Ruinart or Martène. Nevertheless, the book is so wide in its scope, and the documentation is so extensive and complete that the specialist and the historian alike will probably find, over the years, that these advantages counterbalance any literary or biographical limitations, and the careful reader will certainly be able to extract for himself a vivid picture of 'le doux Mabillon', the most learned and the most humble of the subjects of Louis XIV.

Those unfamiliar with the history of the Maurists, or those who have read only the pages devoted to them by Henri Bremond, might well suppose that Mabillon's life would make monotonous reading and be devoid of incident. He was indeed an exemplary monk and delighted to refer to himself as a 'solitaire'. Nevertheless, the close relations between the Maurists and all the learning and much of the grandeur of Paris and France at the height of *le grand siècle*, the journeys and contacts made by Mabillon throughout his life, and the numerous controversies in which he was engaged, combine to make the story of his life a varied and vivid one, while the distinction of his mind and character illuminates and elevates every theme of his work and every phase of his activity. It is with the hope of conveying something of this variety and distinction to those who lack the opportunity of reading the full story of his life that the pages that follow have been written.

Jean Mabillon was born in 1632 at the upland village of Saint-Pierremont, on the borders of Champagne and the Argonne.[2] His

---

[1] Particularly in the later chapters, where sub-editing has left references to an intended treatment of a subject 'later' when in fact it has been dealt with on a previous page.

[2] Saint-Pierremont is in the modern department of les Ardennes. The fullest account of Mabillon's early years, based on the work of H. Jadart, especially his 'L'Origine de Dom Mabillon à Saint-Pierremont' in *Mélanges*, pp. 1–47, is by Dom Leclercq in *DACL*, vol. x, pp. 427 ff.

parents were in modest but not necessitous circumstances, and occupied a house of three or four rooms, which still exists, near the village church, where the child was baptized and in due course served at the altar. His mother died young, but his father, whose own father had lived to be 116, reached the respectable age of 108, leaving his second wife to equal exactly the tale of years of her father-in-law. Mabillon himself, for all his capacity for spare living and hard work, was constitutionally delicate and his life and activities were punctuated by serious illnesses. He remained to the end of his days a countryman, thriving on the open air, walking long distances and welcoming withdrawals from Paris, and he repeatedly visited his home when his travels took him to Rheims, traversing the familiar fields and woods to the oak that long bore his name. Distinguished from childhood by his intelligence, he was educated first by a priest-uncle of unedifying conversation, and then at the Collège des Bons-Enfants at Rheims, whence he passed to the diocesan seminary, but before ordination he felt the call to the monastic life at the celebrated abbey of St Remy de Reims, which had become a Maurist house twenty-five years earlier through the influence of its titular abbot, the English Benedictine archbishop of Rheims, William Gifford. Mabillon always retained his affection for St Remy, though his stay there was short, and several of his closest associates in later life, among them his biographer Thierry Ruinart, were in origin monks of the house. Members of the congregation of St Maur could be moved, like friars or Jesuits, from house to house, and Frère Jean, whose health broke down seriously, was soon sent to Nogent, a country priory on a famous site inhabited by a few old men, where, we are told, he wept at the remembrance of past happiness and was put in charge of the poultry, though he soon showed where his tastes lay by excavating the abbey church in the hope of finding the tomb of the celebrated Abbot Guibert. From Nogent, now a priest, he was sent to another home with a famous name, Corbie, where his health remained poor and he was appointed cellarer. Throughout these years his sole desire was for monastic solitude, and for the first and last time in his life he begged for a change of occupation; his request was granted, and he was sent to

St Denis, the royal abbey on the outskirts of Paris, where he was appointed keeper and showman of the abbey's treasures.

In spite of his bad health, the young monk had managed to do a great deal of reading in the Fathers and monastic writers and chroniclers, and his intellectual distinction at the age of thirty-two must have been obvious to any reasonably intelligent acquaintance. It is not surprising, therefore, that when the invalid Luc d'Achery was looking about for a new assistant his choice should have fallen on Mabillon, who crossed Paris on foot and entered the abbey of St Germain-des-Prés in July 1664. Four months later Dom Claude Chantelou, d'Achery's lieutenant, died, and the new arrival took his place.

Admiration has often been expressed at the immediate burst of literary blossom that took place, beginning with the first volume of the *Acta Sanctorum O.S.B.*, little more than three years after Mabillon's arrival (1668), and continuing with the *Opera omnia Bernardi*, copiously annotated, in 1669. It was indeed a notable achievement, but we must not lose sight of the surroundings and the circumstances. D'Achery, a scholar of genius, had been for years accumulating material, assisted by others as well as by the meritorious Dom Chantelou, who had himself produced an excellent collection of miscellaneous texts in 1661 and had published a volume of St Bernard's sermons in 1662. Moreover, it was not the edition of 1669 that became and still remains standard, but the revised version of 1690, for which Mabillon used a number of additional and excellent manuscripts. In this, its final form, the edition was indeed an achievement, and it is difficult to think of another edition of a celebrated and widely read author which has remained standard for nearly three centuries. Yet, even so, the science of textual criticism has advanced since the seventeenth century, and the edition of Bernard by Dom Jean Leclercq and his colleagues will present a text differing considerably from that of Mabillon. When all these reservations have been made, however, the edition of St Bernard is in its final form a masterpiece of permanent value. Of all the many historians, Cistercian and Benedictine, catholic and non-catholic, clerical and lay, who have written of St Bernard,

Mabillon still stands supreme for the justice and ripeness of his judgements.

Two years after the appearance of Bernard came the works of Pierre de la Celle, friend and patron of John of Salisbury. Mabillon's share in the edition, which neither the title-page nor older bibliographies disclose, was made clear fifty years ago by Léopold Delisle.[1] Among other contributions, Mabillon provided an account of the life and work of Abbot Peter. As printed, however, this is shorter by two-thirds than Mabillon's original composition, which has survived. The missing sections describe Peter's character and virtues, and it appears from a letter of Mabillon that his superiors refused permission for one of the sixteen sections to be printed, that in which Peter's denunciation of contemporary evils in the monastic order was retailed. The authorities feared a scandal; Mabillon bowed to their command, but cut out also all the other sections dealing with Peter's character and in a dignified letter made it clear that the historian must tell all or none of the story.[2]

Meanwhile the *Acta Sanctorum* were steadily passing into print. Vol. I had come in 1668 (to A.D. 600), vol. II (600–700) in 1669, vols. III and IV (700–800) in 1672, vol. V in 1677 and vol. VI in 1680 (800–900).[3] This undertaking, planned before Mabillon's arrival at St Germain, may have been suggested by the work of the Bollandists but it was in no sense a rival. The Bollandists followed the calendar, and after three centuries have not come to the end of the year. The Maurists' volumes were chronological and confined to monastic saints. No doubt there were a few overlappings, but they were not significant. Besides printing the lives, many of which had been lying ready in d'Achery's cupboards, Mabillon made the volumes memorable by adding numerous appendices on points of history, liturgy and monastic custom, and by supplying general prefaces giving a survey of each century. In these, as in the similar prefaces to the later *Annals*, he displayed more clearly than in any other of his works his gifts as an historian. While in the appendices he dealt

---

[1] 'Dom Jean Mabillon, sa probité d'historien', in *Mélanges*, pp. 93–103.

[2] Dom P. Denis, 'Dom Mabillon et sa méthode historique', in *Revue Mabillon*, vol. VI (1910), pp. 1–64.

[3] Leclercq, *Mabillon*, pp. 78 ff.

critically, fully and magisterially with a series of historical problems, such as the diffusion of the Rule of St Benedict, the discipline of the last anointing, and the practice of Communion under both kinds, in the prefaces he displayed the characteristics and trends of the age in a broad sweep, not hesitating to express a firm judgement on men and events. Mabillon commanded a Latin prose style of exceptional purity and clarity. Contemporaries did not hesitate to compare his mastery of Latin with the genius of M. de Meaux in the vernacular, and they could give no higher praise. Medievalists of today would be none the worse for taking a course of the prefaces of Mabillon.

Besides lives of saints d'Achery and his team had assembled texts of every kind; of these they had printed twelve volumes with the title of *Spicilegium*. These are the principal monument to d'Achery's name today, for in them are found what were until recently, or are still, the standard texts of numerous works such as the monastic constitutions of Lanfranc; several were reprinted by Migne. When Mabillon was convalescing from one of his recurrent attacks of illness he spent the time in preparing a similar volume from his *trouvailles*; it was the first volume of *Vetera Analecta*, and was followed by three others (1675, 1676, 1682, 1685).[1] The pieces printed had either been found by Mabillon or sent to him by friends and copyists, and nowadays most of them would have been printed in a learned periodical with a short introduction. Those who have wished to trace the various documents printed by a scholar such as Dom Wilmart or Dom Morin may well think that the older fashion was the more convenient.

The notes and acknowledgements in the *Vetera Analecta* show clearly for the first time two of the great sources of material that made Mabillon's wide range of work a possibility: learned correspondence and foreign travel. These features of his life, so characteristic of his age and country, have received fuller treatment and wider recognition in the past than has any other aspect of his life; it will therefore suffice to give them only brief mention here.[2] Behind both lay the basic advantages of St Germain's, which are

---

[1] Leclercq, *Mabillon*, pp. 234 ff.
[2] De Broglie (followed by Leclercq) deals fully and well with these.

assumed as known to the readers of these pages: the magnificent library, the groups of workers and the meetings each week of the most eminent scholars of the capital in d'Achery's room; with Baluze and Du Cange 'on tap', so to say, one could dispense with a row of encyclopedias.

As for Mabillon's correspondents, there were, first in time and in importance, the innumerable Maurists throughout France who had been alerted by the prospectuses of d'Achery and Mabillon, and who poured in a vast and steady stream of documents, memorials and notes; but as Mabillon's fame grew and his journeys multiplied personal contacts, almost all the historians, antiquaries and *virtuosi* of France, Italy and South Germany became his correspondents and potential assistants. The 1856 letters calendared by Dom Leclercq represent only a fraction of the correspondence that passed between Mabillon and his friends and helpers, and it is one of the many wonders of his life that the great scholar, unassisted by shorthand-typists, should have managed to find any time for his own work after acknowledging the gifts and answering the queries that streamed in on him for almost forty years.

As for his journeys, they are still more characteristic of the age.[1] In the days before national, municipal and academic libraries were available for scholars the Maurists were at a very great advantage in having in Paris not only an excellent library of their own, but the *entrée* to the royal library[2] and that of Colbert, and to the cabinets of such men as Baluze; all these contained manuscripts, inscriptions and coins as well as printed books. Even so, the number of essential manuscripts and original documents *in situ* in religious houses, in family archives, or in foreign countries, was overwhelmingly great; moreover, many still awaited discovery or identification at the hands of a competent scholar. The Bollandists in 1660 had realized the necessity and reaped the harvest of an extended *voyage littéraire*; Mabillon's first journey, a modest tour in Flanders, came in 1667. This was followed by a visit to Louvain (1680), a tour of Burgundy

---

[1] For these again see de Broglie.

[2] Mabillon's journey to Italy was financed by the king, and he travelled ostensibly as 'buyer' for the royal library. Compare H. Omont, 'Mabillon et la bibliothèque du Roi', in *Mélanges*, pp. 107–23.

(1682), a long journey in Germany, Switzerland and Austria (1683), a visit to Normandy (1684), the long and celebrated fifteen months' sojourn in Italy (1685–86), a long tour in Lorraine and Alsace (1696) and a final visit to Champagne and Burgundy in 1703.[1] Apart from these there were many lesser journeys, some of them scarcely recorded, and visits to such friends as Bossuet at Meaux and Archbishop Le Tellier at Rheims, with journeys to meetings of general chapters thrown in. Mabillon even projected, but unfortunately never executed, a visit to the England of Hickes and Archbishop Wake. On all these tours he was accompanied by one of his assistants, almost invariably one of the three intimate friends and distinguished scholars who succeeded one another at his side, Dom Claude Estiennot, Dom Michel Germain and Dom Thierry Ruinart. Mabillon wrote an account of the German tour[2] and later wrote and published the well-known *Iter Italicum*; for the rest we depend upon the voluminous correspondence of the travellers, the letters of those they left behind at St Germain, and the later accounts of Ruinart and Martène.

Meanwhile the fame which Mabillon had won with Bernard and the *Acta Sanctorum* became universal with the work, usually held to be his masterpiece, that appeared in 1681.[3] Like many another great work, including at least one other of his own, it was a *livre d'occasion* originating in a learned controversy. In the seventeenth century historians and antiquaries began for the first time to use and to criticize the charters and diplomas of the early Middle Ages. It was soon common knowledge that many of them were wholly or in part unreliable; some were falsifications of the medieval centuries, others were copies, more or less inaccurate and interpolated, of genuine originals now lost, while some *soi-disant* medieval pieces were in fact forgeries of the modern world. The last class owed its origin to the use made of medieval documents in disputes over property and still

[1] Leclercq deals with all these; de Broglie gives full accounts only of the German and Italian tours.

[2] 'Iter Germanicum' in *Vetera Analecta*, vol. IV (1685), pp. 3 ff. Colbert arranged the German tour, which was paid for by the royal treasury. Archbishop Le Tellier of Rheims organized the Italian expedition.

[3] The best analysis of *De Re Diplomatica* is that of L. Levillain, 'Le "De Re Diplomatica"', in *Mélanges*, pp. 195–252. Compare also Leclercq, *Mabillon*, pp. 154–80.

more to the efforts of noble families in France, and ancient abbeys in Germany, to establish the precedence and prestige and rights that were due to extreme antiquity. In default of adequate training and wide experience critics of these documents were quite at sea, or at best dependent upon subjective impressions or guesswork, and while many interested parties were lax in their criteria, others tended towards an excessive and unwarranted scepticism that reached the extremes of nihilism in the vagaries of Hardouin, or, with Sir John Marsham in England, denied that charters had been composed before the tenth century and resisted ocular proof that papyrus could have survived so long, and in consequence denied authenticity to all documents earlier than the particular date they chose as a baseline. The first attempt to formulate rules of criticism was made by the great Bollandist Daniel Papebroch who devoted part of the introduction to vol. II of the April *Acta* (1675) to a discussion of the subject.[1] Papebroch, following the German Conring, had grasped the fact that theoretical principles were useless, and that the first touchstone for a questionable charter must be an authentic one of like date and provenance, but he was unlucky in his choice of examples. He had moreover impugned the authenticity of some earlier charters of the abbey of St Denis. Mabillon, with all his fairness of mind, never wholly lost his monastic *esprit de famille*, and it is probably to this that we owe his treatise *De Re Diplomatica* (1681). When once roused he worked rapidly in a vast field, and as he worked he saw the necessity and the possibility of constructing a new discipline, if not a new science. In the sequel the *De Re Diplomatica* provided at once a description, a critique and a text-book of the new expertise. Mabillon frankly admitted that the authenticity of a charter could not be proved by any metaphysical or *a priori* argument; a decision could be reached only after the expert had examined a whole series of different indications—the material used, the seal, the signature, the grammar and orthography, the modes of address, the plausibility of the dating, the intrinsic consistency of the whole document. In consequence, the certainty attainable in a favourable case could

---

[1] Leclercq, *Mabillon*, pp. 161–3; A. Poncelet, 'Mabillon et Papebroch', in *Mélanges*, pp. 170–5; de Broglie, *Mabillon*, vol. I, pp. 116–18.

be no more than a moral certainty, but this was very different from doubt or complete scepticism. To round off his treatise he printed a series of facsimiles of charters to serve as demonstrations of the art.

The *De Re Diplomatica* made the name of Mabillon famous throughout Europe. It was the occasion of the most familiar incident of Mabillon's life. Papebroch and his methods had been treated very courteously in the book, but he had been hit hard. He felt the blow, and retired to his corner for more than a year. Then, at last, he replied with a frankness worthy of the scholar who came nearest to being the rival of Mabillon:

I was indeed at first pained by your book, where I saw myself refuted beyond hope of reply, but in the end the value and the beauty of such a precious work overcame my weakness, and I was filled with delight at seeing the truth presented in its most attractive shape....Count me as your friend, I beg of you. I am not a learned man, but I desire to be taught.

Mabillon replied in a letter in which his style and his character were seen to full advantage: 'Pray for me that God may grant that I, who seek to imitate you in the scientific excellence of the *Acta Sanctorum*, may imitate you also in the paths of Christian humility.' Mabillon never forgot a friend, and it is pleasant to remember that when Papebroch was in trouble at Rome for his forthright attack on legend, at a time when no love was being lost between Maurists and Jesuits, Mabillon wrote repeatedly and insistently, both to the Maurist procurator and to friends in the Curia, in support of the Bollandist.

It was probably also about this time that Mabillon was summoned to Versailles to receive the recognition due to one who had, as a back-room boy, done his duty as a subject of the Grand Monarque. He was presented by Le Tellier, the haughty archbishop of Rheims, and the great Bossuet, regarded by all as the most learned divine of the Gallican Church. Le Tellier introduced Mabillon to the king as 'the most learned man in your kingdom'. M. de Meaux, suspecting an insult in the precise superlative, rejoined: 'His Grace should have added "and the most humble".'[1]

---

[1] De Broglie, *Mabillon*, vol. I, pp. 126–7, gives the words of the two prelates as follows. Le Tellier: 'Sire, j'ai l'honneur de présenter à Votre Majesté le plus savant homme de votre royaume.' Bossuet: 'M. l'archevêque de Reims devrait ajouter: "et le plus humble".'

Four years after the publication of the *De Re Diplomatica* Mabillon showed himself a pioneer and a master in yet another field, that of liturgical study. In the course of his journey through Burgundy in 1683 he had visited the monastery of Luxeuil and there had 'leapt with joy' at the discovery of the so-called 'Luxeuil lectionary', now generally regarded as having originated at Langres, which he recognized at once as a monument without peer of the ancient Gallican liturgy. In his study of the subject in *De liturgia gallica* he once more produced what was both a pioneer and a definitive work. His account of the pre-Carolingian Mass and Office, though naturally requiring revision in detail, remains in essentials a classic. Four years later again, after his Italian journey, which he celebrated in his *Iter Italicum* (1687), he re-entered the field of liturgy with his *Museum Italicum* (also 1687), two volumes of texts and studies based on manuscripts copied in Italy. The first volume was rendered notable by the publication of the so-called Bobbio Missal, which he had discovered in the monastery of that name, the second by the collection of fifteen *Ordines Romani* (some of which had been previously published) in which he traced the development of the liturgy at Rome from the age of Gelasius I to the fifteenth century.[1]

Alongside of his major publications and his critical and historical works, great and small, more than one controversial issue in which he took a leading part drew Mabillon into the public eye and into the treacherous waters of ecclesiastical politics. If the emergence of a series of intellectual or spiritual disputes, conducted by men of high mental attainments and followed passionately by a great part of the educated public of the day, is an indication of a great era in a nation's life, the age of Louis XIV in France must be pronounced to have been an exceptionally great age. During more than sixty years a series of intellectual *causes célèbres* succeeded one another—the battle of the great Arnauld's *Fréquente Communion* merging into the first and most brilliant phase of the Jansenist controversy, the disputes on morality which produced the *Lettres Provinciales*, the Gallican

---

[1] Leclercq, *Mabillon*, pp. 288–93, 465–71; F. Cabrol, 'Mabillon et les études liturgiques', in *Mélanges*, pp. 147–67.

issue illuminated by the genius of Bossuet, the *affaire Guyon* with Bossuet again and Fénelon as principals, and the eternal literary debate between ancient and modern are all controversies that are part of the heritage of Europe, and they did not stand alone. Among the controversies that had a less universal theme, but which nevertheless captured the imagination of the educated world, was that over the lawfulness of study for monks initiated by Armand de Rancé, abbot of La Trappe, and taken up by Mabillon on behalf of the other monks of France. The debate has been repeatedly recounted, and needs no more than a mention here.[1] Rancé, greatly gifted as he had always been, and admirable as he was after his spectacular conversion, was by temperament authoritarian, limited in vision and abounding in his own sense; he was withal a publicist and propagandist of the highest skill, without a vestige of diffidence or self-knowledge. He had published in 1683 a large work *De la sainteté et les devoirs de la vie monastique*, a *réchauffé* of conferences delivered to his monks, in which he presented the Trappist practice of extreme austerity, perpetual silence and mute, unlearned docility as the only defensible version of the Benedictine ideal. The book, warmly approved by Bossuet and other authorities, not unnaturally fluttered all the monastic dovecotes of the land, and Mabillon, urged on by his superiors, proposed a few gentle and well-deserved criticisms, which Rancé brushed impatiently aside. In 1685 M. de la Trappe followed up his previous success with another weighty volume which by its title professed to enlighten those who had found difficulties in the earlier work. This was in essence a polemic against any kind of intellectual occupation for monks. It drew from Dom Mège, Mabillon's ancient adversary, a lively riposte which was censured at the instance of Bossuet by the Maurist authorities. Nevertheless, Rancé once more overcame his loudly expressed reluctance to break silence and dislike of publicity by putting out a translation of the Rule of St Benedict (1689) with a commentary directed towards exposing its true spirit, in which the Maurist ideal

---

[1] Compare Sainte-Beuve, *Port Royal*, IV, vi (ed. 1848, vol. III, pp. 555–61); H. Didio, 'La querelle de Mabillon et de l'abbé de Rancé', in *Revue des sciences ecclésiastiques*, vols. LXIII–LXVI (1891–92) and separately, Amiens, 1892; and H. Bremond, *L'Abbé tempête*, Paris, 1929; English trans., *The Thundering Abbot*, London, 1933.

was once more violently attacked. Meanwhile Mabillon had been slowly maturing a reply to Rancé's main contention; this appeared in 1691 as a *Traité des études monastiques*. It was a long and sober account of the place learning had always held in the monastic life, and a weighty defence of this practice; it ended with a long reading-list for young monks. Studiously temperate in language and tone, it was addressed professedly to his own brethren, to confirm them in their own interpretation of the Rule. Though written in Latin, it had all the comprehensive sweep and clarity that marked Mabillon's best work, and it was hailed with delight not only in monastic circles but throughout cultivated French society and even in Rome, where Rancé's extravagances were not appreciated. As for the abbot, he did not lose a moment, and, in March 1692, he was ready with his *Réponse aux Etudes*, a direct attack on Mabillon's arguments in which he did not hesitate to hint that Mabillon was too learned to believe all he had said. The dispute had now caught the attention of Europe; cardinals in Rome and Leibniz in Germany were following its phases, and in France every feeling of passion or amusement was engaged. Bossuet, the friend and admirer of both champions, was finding the fence upon which he had seated himself more and more uncomfortable, and did his best to persuade Mabillon not to play the ball that Rancé had volleyed into his court. Mabillon, however, had been provoked both by Rancé's unwillingness to see reason and by his hint of Mabillon's lack of candour, and had his answer out by June of the same year. This time he wrote in French, addressed Rancé directly and threw back his points in order with a brilliant mixture of erudition and urbanity. Readers throughout Europe had no doubt that he had won game and set. The great Arnauld and the prudent Nicole agreed that the abbot had ventured too far out on the branch. Nevertheless, Rancé would not be beaten, and soon had another large book ready for the printer, with the title 'Examination of the Reflections of Mabillon upon the Answer to the Treatise'. There seemed no reason why the controversy should ever end. End it did, however, somewhat unexpectedly. Among the friends and admirers of Rancé was Princess Elizabeth, daughter of Gaston d'Orléans and now dowager duchess de Guise. She had tried before, but without success, to end the controversy by bringing the combatants to a meeting. Now, it so happened that in May 1693 Mabillon was passing not far from La Trappe on his way back from a meeting of the chapter-general at Marmoutier, and he accepted an invitation to visit the abbey. His simplicity, courtesy, piety and transparent sincerity completely won the tempestuous abbot, and the two embraced on their knees with expressions of mutual esteem. Rancé decided not to publish his latest book, though he carefully put it on ice for the benefit of posterity, and though he never publicly withdrew from any of his positions, the controversy came to an edifying end. Rancé was always incalculable, but with all his obstinacy he was a good man and not unintelligent, and he may well have felt that he was making himself ridiculous by his attacks on the most learned man in France, who was in addition an estimable and a peaceable monk.

Mabillon's *Reflexions* had won him a position in the cultured world equal to that he already held among the learned; he was now acclaimed also as the champion of his order. Henceforward he was the obvious 'trouble-shooter' to whom superiors turned in need, and it was not long before another and a still more acrimonious controversy broke out.[1] The Maurists had recently all but completed what was perhaps the most notable single enterprise in their history, the edition of St Augustine. It had been accomplished principally by three eminent scholars, Doms Blampin, Constant and Guesnié, but they had been helped by a small team of assistants, and Mabillon had more than once lent a hand. The explosive nature of the material had been recognized from the start. The climate of opinion that ultimately resolved itself into Jansenism had from the beginning a strong Augustinian character, and the storm had been polarized by the *Augustinus* of Antoine Arnauld. In the endless theological debates that ensued, and that had rekindled the smothered fires of earlier contests, St Augustine had been cited and annotated *à l'envi*. The inveterate opponents of Jansenism, the Jesuits, had a theology

---

[1] Leclercq, *Mabillon*, pp. 628–58; A. M. P. Ingold, *Histoire de l'édition bénédictine de S. Augustin* (Paris, 1903); Leclercq, *DACL*, vol. x, pp. 619 ff. Mabillon wrote the dedicatory epistle to Louis XIV 'du soir au matin'; it is a sober but glowing tribute to the king's statesmanship.

of grace which made a more sparing use of Augustine; they were therefore ready to brand as crypto-Jansenists (as they had a century before branded as crypto-Calvinists) all who based their opinions on St Augustine as interpreted in the traditional sense of St Thomas and the great Spanish Thomists of the sixteenth century. Though the Maurists as a body were by no means full-blooded Thomists, they were decisively anti-Molinist, and might conceivably, if not reasonably, be represented as followers of the Port Royal interpretation of the Doctor of Grace. St Augustine, therefore, was a living force, and a pure text of all his works greatly desirable, but his works were a dangerous minefield in which to become engaged. The Maurists were not Jansenists in 1690, but their way of life, austere and sombre, gave them a sympathy for the spirituality of Port Royal, and in the event, after Mabillon's death, there was a strong Jansenist contingent among the monks. As party feeling hardened, they found themselves in the opposite camp to the Jesuits, and each body was prepared to believe the worst of the other. Nevertheless, the publication of Augustine had proceeded from 1679 to 1690, and had reached the tenth volume; it only remained to produce a final volume of indices. There had been incidents, but no explosion. Now, at the very end of 1698, an anonymous letter appeared, attacking the latest volume as favouring Jansenism. There was an immediate flare-up. The Jesuits supported the letter while officially denying (as the monks thought, deceitfully) that a Jesuit was its author, and despite the efforts of Maurist superiors, assisted by Mabillon, a bitter war of letters and pamphlets began, while at Rome a long series of intrigues developed, the Jesuits hoping to secure the condemnation of the edition, while the monks hoped for a similar fate for the letters written against it. The two main charges against the Maurist editors were of having adopted readings that favoured a Jansenist interpretation of a few crucial passages,[1] and of having added marginal commentaries in a similar sense. Feeling ran high; the editor-in-chief, Dom Blampin, was immunized by appoint-

---

[1] Such, for example, as the celebrated sentence in the *Enchiridion*, c. 95 (M. J. Rouët de Journel, *Enchiridion Patristicum*, no. 1925): 'Nec utique Deus iniuste noluit salvos fieri, cum possent salvi esse, si vellent [*var. lect.* vellet].'

ment to an administrative post, and the monks did all they could to secure Bossuet as an advocate to offset Père de la Chaise at court. Finally, in August 1699, the superiors of the congregation decided to entrust the defence of their cause to Mabillon. He went to work rapidly, and in ten days had produced a draft of forty pages to form the basis of a general introduction to the edition. He was not by training or temperament a speculative theologian, but he had an old familiarity with the works of Augustine, and once again his judicious moderation and clarity of thought and expression produced a short masterpiece in which the teaching of Augustine on grace was set out with lapidary precision and in which principles were established for its technical expression. Endless discussions took place, and Mabillon was requested to lengthen his preface considerably and to re-write it again and again till he wept with frustration and fatigue. Finally, in 1700 a decree of the Holy Office appeared, impartially condemning the whole dossier of pamphlets on both sides; this in effect quashed the attack on the Maurist editors, and the eleventh volume appeared with Mabillon's preface. Six years later the matter was clinched by a brief of Clement XI praising the Maurist editions of the Fathers and bestowing a medal on Mabillon.

Meanwhile Mabillon himself had been responsible for a third episode of controversy.[1] When in Rome he had visited the catacombs and remarked on the traffic in relics obtained from the new groups of galleries that had been discovered less than a century previously, and that had since been undergoing a systematic excavation under the direction of the papal officials who were endeavouring to meet the many requests for relics of the martyrs from all over the Catholic world. It was assumed by those concerned that the remains in all these galleries were those of Christians of the pre-Constantinian era, and that the persecutions had enriched the Roman church with an inexhaustible store of martyrs' bones. These, it was currently thought, could be identified either by the palm-leaf, often inscribed on gravestones in the galleries, or still more surely by the small *ampullae* with a red-stained sediment often found in niches in the tombs, but it was far from certain that the relics dispatched from

---

[1] Leclercq, *Mabillon*, pp. 132–8.

Rome had even these degrees of authentification. Mabillon and his *confrère* were themselves presented with a skeleton apiece in the catacombs, and were expected to complete the process of excavation and cleansing the moist remains for themselves.[1] The Maurist historian was well aware that as early as the eighth century the bones of acknowledged martyrs in the catacombs had been removed to shrines within the city and that in the ninth century popes had transferred the bodies of the Christians *en masse* from the neglected catacombs to graves within the walls. He was therefore justified in doubting whether any relics of martyrs remained in the original tombs, and was convinced that in any case no dependable criteria were used in the selection of relics for export. Nevertheless, he let the matter rest for several years, and was only stirred to action when he heard that a Paris church had received from Rome and duly honoured the reputed head of a martyr which had proved on examination to be nothing of the kind.[2] He felt he could be silent no longer, and wrote a dissertation on the subject in 1691 which he passed to a few friends but did not publish. In 1696 he made the further move of sending it, in the form of a letter, to his friend Cardinal Colloredo in Rome. He had used all his familiar moderation of language, and the authorities in Rome and the Congregation of Rites were treated with the utmost deference, but even so the cardinal counselled silence. Mabillon yielded for the moment, but it seems that his hand was forced by the threat of a pirated edition, and in 1698 he printed the letter in Paris with the title *Eusebii Romani ad Theophilum Gallum Epistola de cultu sanctorum ignotorum.* The book had an immediate vogue; five printings were called for and two French translations appeared. At Rome enlightened opinion was sympathetic, but it was the very moment when Papebroch was being silenced by the obscurantists, and a strenuous effort was made by interested persons and the enemies of the Maurists to get the book on the Index. Mabillon's guiding principle, that historical truth

[1] Dom Germain (cited by Leclercq, *Mabillon*, p. 712): 'J'ai eu toutes les peines du monde à le tirer de terre, parce qu'elle étoit toute humide.... Je suis encore tout rompu de cette fatigue.'
[2] Mabillon to Cardinal Colloredo in *Ouvrages posthumes*, vol. I (1724), p. 359. The printed text omits the offending phrases.

could never in the last resort be prejudicial to the Church, was not appreciated; even the pope drew attention to the acts of piety evoked by relics accepted in good faith, and was apprehensive that earlier recipients might be plunged into a state of doubt by Mabillon's arguments. In the event, the *Epistola* was put into the hands of the Holy Office and would probably have been condemned but for the intervention of Pope Clement XI, Mabillon's friend, who rescued it with the proviso that a new edition must be produced in which certain points were presented less directly. Mabillon was by nature firm, but never difficult; he made the requested changes with singular adroitness and without conceding a principle, and the new edition was duly approved by the pope. Time has wholly vindicated Mabillon in this affair, but his contentions were not finally accepted till the conclusions of De Buck and de Rossi settled the matter in the nineteenth century.

Meanwhile Mabillon had been hard at work on his last great achievement, the Annals of the Benedictine Order.[1] As early as 1670 or thereabouts he had planned these as the crown of his work upon the Benedictine centuries, and Dom Estiennot and Dom Germain had expended much time and labour in collecting materials, some of which were used in the proposed, but long delayed, *Monasticum Gallicanum* (1687–1871), but Mabillon did not actually begin composition till July 1693; thenceforward he proceeded steadily with a satisfaction that surprised him. The first volume was not published till ten years later (July 1703), but thenceforward the march was steady and the volumes appeared as follows: I (down to A.D. 700) 1703; II (to 849) 1704; III (to 980) 1705; IV (to 1066) 1707. The last-named appeared six months before the death of the writer, who had left the material in an advanced state of preparation down to the death of St Bernard. The work was carried on by the faithful Ruinart; he died in 1709, but he had left vol. V all but ready (to 1116), though it did not appear till 1713. His successors, who had a harder task before them, fell off in one way or another, and it was left to Mabillon's protégé of other years, the distinguished liturgist Dom

[1] Leclercq, *Mabillon*, pp. 751–9; M. Lecomte, 'La publication des Annales O.S.B.', in *Mélanges*, pp. 255–78.

231

Edmond Martène, to complete the sixth volume (to 1167), though he died some weeks before its appearance in 1739.

The *Annals* must take rank along with the *Acta*, the *De Re Diplomatica*, and the two pieces of the Rancé controversy among Mabillon's masterpieces, and, as a work of 'straight' history, it is perhaps the finest fruit of his genius. It still remains today the only full and connected survey of the history of the monastic order in Europe from the earliest time to the death of St Bernard, and at first or second remove it has lain behind all subsequent accounts. The prefaces in particular are exemplary specimens of critical and judicial assessment which every medievalist may read and ponder with profit; they are composed in Mabillon's dignified Latin. Had they been written in French they might have been among the classics of the language alongside the funeral orations of Bossuet.[1] Mabillon had prayed that he might carry the story down to the death of St Bernard, ever his patron next only to St Benedict, and his prayer was granted. His *diadochi* had hoped to carry the story down the centuries to their own day, but though the Maurists were accustomed both to plan and to execute in the grand manner, this task was beyond them. They divided Mabillon's empire into many parts, some of which they surveyed in print, while for others all that remains is a quarry of material which others from their day to our own have gratefully used.

Mabillon has been acclaimed by an eminent scholar of our own time as the greatest of monastic historians,[2] and proud though the claim is, it would be hard to defend a rival. Wherein, then, does his greatness lie? To the casual acquaintance, the first impression is one of immense industry; the tale of folios is truly overwhelming. Beyond this, there is the weight of learning. Never before, and perhaps never since, has a single mind mastered and retained such a vast array of sources, literary and diplomatic, in so many fields of

[1] The present writer remembers that his first appearance in print, now forty years since, was as a translator of Mabillon; cf. 'A preface of Mabillon', in *DR*, vol. XXXVIII (1919), pp. 53–7.
[2] G. G. Coulton, *Five Centuries of Religion* (Cambridge, 1923), vol. I, p. 3: 'There is no monastic historian who for learning and impartiality comes even into the same class as Mabillon.'

Church history and medieval society between the age of Augustine and that of St Bernard, and retained them so as to be able to survey any topic from above, with a wealth of illustration. Yet there were many industrious and erudite scholars in the Europe of his day who remain names only, if indeed so much as names, to historians of today. Mabillon stands out from his contemporaries as one of the world's greatest scholar-historians by reason of the vision, the intuition, the creative quality of his mind, by reason of his critical powers, and by reason of his intimate sense of the dignity and obligations of his calling. His creative quality, by which he was able to impose order upon chaos and shed light in dark places, shows at its brightest in his work on diplomatic and liturgy. In both these fields, then practically virgin, he created a method and established principles which were, in their own sphere, as valid and as fruitful as the principles established by his contemporaries in mathematics and natural sciences. After this, his critical power is his most obvious excellence. It is apparent in almost every piece of work, and in this he is eminently a 'modern' historian. When he takes up a problem, great or small, he shakes it out and holds it up, and then applies to it tests of every kind from every angle. Whether it is Augustine's teaching on grace, the meaning of a word in the Rule, the Eucharistic practice of the early Church, the order of succession of bishops and abbots, or the date of a charter, Mabillon brings to bear upon it the same acuteness of observation, the same wealth of information, the same sanity of judgement, the same lucidity of exposition. When he has done with it, the matter is, in four cases out of five, settled for good. Finally, there is the higher wisdom of the great historian, the seeker after truth who believes that truth can be attained and that the historian, in his particular field and trade, is autonomous. Mabillon is unique among those of his age in giving us more than once a manifesto of his cause and a statement of his *credo* in the demonstrative value of history.[1] One example may suffice; it is from

[1] Mabillon has no 'philosophy of history'. He shows no trace of the Augustinian concept of world-history, and never moves into the realm of a Vico, a Hegel, a Marx or a Croce, though he was not without a philosophy in general—that of Descartes, as modified by Malebranche. His concept of history was that of the common man, *viz.* that it was the discovery and presentation of what had happened in the past, and there-

the *apologia* written at the command of his superiors when he was attacked early in his career by some of his *confrères*; it is scarcely doubtful that it, or some similar passages, served as food, two hundred years later, for the meditations of Lord Acton.

> A judge [Mabillon wrote] is a public functionary appointed to give everyone his due....Such is also the function of the historian, to whom, on behalf of the rest of the world, is committed the examination of past actions. For since all cannot make this inquest for themselves, the rest must accept his judgement; he is therefore guilty of deception unless he has a candour of mind which prompts him to say frankly and openly what he knows to be true....If he is honest, therefore, he must present as certain things certain, as false things false, and as doubtful, things doubtful; he must not seek to hide facts that tell for or against either party to an issue. Piety and truth must never be considered as separable, for honest and genuine piety will never come into conflict with truth.[1]

Twenty years later Rancé's hint that Mabillon had written some passages with diplomatic insincerity drew from him the only retort in his reply: 'I may fall into error, like other men; I may even fall into inconsistency; but that I should write against my conviction—that, I trust, by the grace of God shall never happen to me.'[2]

We may believe the man who writes thus, and his life and works are a standing proof of his high resolve and honesty. But Mabillon, as he says, was fallible like the rest of us, and a glance at some of his mistakes may serve at once as a warning and a consolation to lesser folk.[3]

Vast and meritorious as were his labours as an editor, he was capable of the occasional misjudgement or omission; he could transcribe an inscription faultily, and miscalculate a date. He could even—not write against his conviction, but—allow his affection for his order to temper the severity of his approach, as in the matter of

fore a pursuit comparable to that of a judge summing up a case for the jury, though Mabillon laid the accent on the revelation of the past, while Acton emphasized the moral judgement pronounced on the criminal.

[1] Cited by L. Delisle in *Mélanges*, pp. 93–4. Compare Dom P. Denis in *Revue Mabillon*, vol. VI (1910), pp. 1–64. The last sentence quoted above reads in Latin: 'Non debet a veritate sejungi pietas: neque haec, si vera ac sincera sit, veritati unquam adversari.'

[2] Cited by Leclercq, *Mabillon*, p. 562.

[3] For Mabillon's errors see especially Leclercq, *Mabillon*, pp. 237–48, 826–7.

the antiquity of the abbey of St Denis, and in the still more regret-table affair of the Holy Tear of Vendôme. He could, as in the curious controversy as to the author of the *Imitation of Christ*, come heavily down in favour of what recent scholarship has shown to be, not only the wrong side, but a mare's nest.[1] He was not infallible even in his own speciality: he had propounded correct principles in the *De Re Diplomatica*, but the technique of the subject was still in its infancy, and he could mistake a manuscript of the late fifteenth century, written in an archaic hand, for one three centuries older. Finally, he came a resounding cropper in the matter of the origins of the house of La Tour d'Auvergne.[2] There is more than a touch of irony in the affair. He had already, in 1703, exposed the fabricated charters of the Carmelite Father Andrew, in a model memorandum which later fell into the forger's hand, and was taken by him to heart with such good effect that he was able with a subsequent fabrication to have his revenge by planting one of his forgeries on the editors of the *Gallia Christiana* and another on Mabillon himself. This, how-ever, was nothing when compared to the master's strange com-placency in the great genealogical case of the house of La Tour, when Baluze, Ruinart and himself, solemnly called in as referees, gave a certificate of authenticity to a charter skilfully forged by a sub-librarian who ended his days in the Bastille. The episode is a curious one, and it is difficult not to suppose that for once deference to the reputation of Baluze and a certain loyalty of friendship swayed his judgement, but he held to his opinion even after the accused had confessed. It is indeed possible that on the point of historical fact Mabillon (and the forger) were in the right, and that the fabrication was sufficiently skilful to deceive one who considered principally the matter and the script.

Baluze paid for the mistake by exile, as did Cardinal de Bouillon, but Mabillon's endorsement did nothing to obscure his fame, and he was shortly afterwards admitted, at the king's order and with an

[1] *Ibid.* pp. 119–31.
[2] *Ibid.* pp. 680–711; J. Depoin, 'Une expertise de Mabillon: La filiation des La Tour d'Auvergne', in *Mélanges*, pp. 126–43, and A. de Boislisle, 'Le cardinal de Bouillon, Baluze et le procès des faussaires', editorial note to Saint-Simon, *Mémoires*, vol. xiv (1899), pp. 533–58.

unexpected colleague, Père de la Chaise, into the newly created Académie des Inscriptions. Nor did this and his other mistakes do anything to lessen the respect and admiration that all who knew him had for his character. He appears, indeed, even to those who know him only from the written record, as a very admirable and a very lovable man. Gentleness and humility, qualities not always associated with the tribe of scholars, seemed to his contemporaries to be eminently his. Throughout his life he behaved as the simplest monk of the house, refusing all privileged treatment, whether of diet or of accommodation, as he refused the pension offered him by Colbert or the dignified abbacy that could have been his in later life. His intimate companions tell us that when on a journey he kept the strict monastic abstinence from meat, and observed as far as possible the liturgical hours of recitation of the Office. Yet he was never a guest who made others feel ill at ease. He accepted the invitations of the great at Rome, and we hear even of his dining out in Paris and making frequent visits to the country priory of Faron for rest or convalescence. His letters show a mind that is sober, indeed, but also keenly aware of natural beauty (saving only for mountain scenery, which had to wait for the Romantics and the Goths for appreciation) and caught all the associations of the past; he had a vein of amused irony in the cross-currents of controversy. Above all, he was a very warm-hearted man. From first to last Mabillon's life at St Germain was full of friendships. He was the friend of innumerable scholars and great ecclesiastics, as well as of the multitude of others, great and small, who had come to know him, but there were always a few in his life with a deeper intimacy, those who were among the inner group of scholars, the 'petit dortoir', those who were 'du dedans'. He had entered St Germain as the protégé of d'Achery, and ever regarded him as a father, deferring to him in their common work and nursing him in his illnesses. When he, in his turn, chose his assistants the bond of affection was quickly formed. A whole group counted themselves as his disciples, among them Edmond Martène—'le bon Emond', 'le saint homme Emond'— and Bernard de Montfaucon. But there was an inner succession of three whom we know well from their letters, Claude Estiennot,

Michel Germain and Thierry Ruinart, who were his constant companions at home and on his journeys. Claude Estiennot, 'Stephano-
tius noster', of Varennes (1639–94), his first travelling companion,
historian of the Vexin and indefatigable collector of documents, spent
twelve years in sweeping the monastic archives of France. He was a
man of tact, judgement and energy, and was taken from his researches to fill the post of procurator in the Curia; there he died
relatively early.[1] Michel Germain (1645–94), a Picard and professed
monk of Rheims, large of habit, vivacious, impulsive and outspoken,
was his companion in the German tour and on the long journey to
Italy. The historian of the abbey of Soissons, he was also largely
responsible for the fourth book of *De Re Diplomatica*. His letters are
a primary source during his years of close association with Mabillon.
He died suddenly in January 1694, and Mabillon mourned him long
and deeply.[2] The third and most intimately linked of all was Thierry
Ruinart (1657–1709), another Remois, by birth as well as by profession. Ruinart, whose *Acta sincera martyrum* is one of the most
precious jewels in the Maurist crown, was in every way a contrast to
Dom Germain.[3] Sober, a little serious—'tâchez de vous tenir gay',
wrote Mabillon more than once—ready to give and ready to receive
affection, he became the beloved disciple of Mabillon. He survived
his master by only two years; it was time enough for him to write,
but not to see in print, the *Life* that is the most authentic source of
our knowledge of Mabillon's character, and is likewise one of the
most fragrant flowers of French biography, recalling our own Izaak
Walton's life of Herbert. There was yet another, of whom Mabillon
might have written 'tu Marcellus eris'. Brother Denys de la
Campagne was the relative of an old friend, and Mabillon had
marked him out and begun to train him as a future companion and
assistant.[4] Nowhere else does Mabillon appear as a bad judge of
character, but something serious went wrong with brother Denys;

[1] For Dom Estiennot see Leclercq, *Mabillon*, pp. 262–6, and A. Vidier, 'Un ami de
Mabillon, Dom Claude Estiennot', in *Mélanges*, pp. 281–312.

[2] Leclercq, *Mabillon*, pp. 267–9; E. de Broglie should also be consulted.

[3] Leclercq, *Mabillon*, pp. 269–75; H. Jadart, 'Dom Thierry Ruinart', in *Travaux de
l'Académie nationale de Reims*, vol. LXXVII (1884–85), pt. 2, pp. 1–190.

[4] Leclercq, *Mabillon*, pp. 578–605.

he may have been treated harshly or stupidly; in any case, he threw his habit off and reappeared in Paris a few months later in poverty and debt. Whatever we may think of Mabillon's judgement in the matter, his heart and his loyalty were never seen more clearly than in what followed. He raised money to pay the truant's debts, welcomed him back to St Germain, obtained the gentlest possible treatment for him and took him on one of his short journeys. All was in vain. Brother Denys, frail or neurotic or both, once more borrowed the key of the garden gate[1] and left his habit among the nettles. This time there was no indulgence; he was arrested and sent for fifteen years' solitary imprisonment in the redoubtable cells of Mont St Michel, that 'Bastille super Mare'. Mabillon, profoundly shocked as he was by this second fall, might well have bidden the errant brother good riddance. Instead, he moved heaven and earth —superior-general and cardinals—to obtain at least a mitigation of the sentence. The whole affair cost him, as he wrote, more anguish than any other event of his life, but the anguish was all at the thought that one whom he had supposed to be destined to a life given wholly to God's service should now be driven to despair or insanity by cruel treatment. Meanwhile, Brother Denys, who would seem to have been more able to take care of himself than Mabillon realized, succeeded in breaking prison;[2] he was retaken and put in irons, which his faithful advocate duly persuaded the authorities to remove, only to be rewarded by a second and more successful escape of the slippery brother, who this time disappeared from Maurist history to the great relief, as we gather, of the superior-general. Mabillon, however, never forgot him, and we owe to Brother Denys his *Réflexions sur les prisons des ordres religieux*, in which, after a masterly survey of monastic punishment and imprisonment throughout the ages, he denounced in dignified but scathing language the

---

[1] Leclercq, *Mabillon*, p. 583. 'Parmi ses confrères...d'autres chansonnèrent:

> Frère Denis de La Campagne
> A donc pris la clef des champs.'

The play on the family name defies translation.

[2] Mabillon's comment was: 'Je ne conte pas cela pour une faute, n'y ayant rien de plus naturel à un misérable que de tascher à sortir de sa misère' (Leclercq, *Mabillon*, p. 584).

folly, futility and lack of Christian charity that were revealed by the harsh and cruel punishments still current in his days among religious, and gave an outline of remedial and rehabilitating treatment for delinquents which any reformer of the nineteenth century would have been proud to claim as his own. That was not quite the end. Mabillon, who had, perhaps for the first time in his life, made something of a nuisance of himself to those in authority, was taken severely to task by the unsympathetic prior of the day, a worldly man who actually endeavoured to remove both Mabillon and Montfaucon from the house; he was damaging discipline by his over-indulgence. He fell ill about this time, and while ill, asked pardon and did penance for what he conceived to have been his fault. The whole episode, which must draw from many a reader a smile that is near neighbour to tears, brings us perhaps more closely than any other to the essential simplicity of Mabillon's character.

There is one last occasional piece that only Mabillon could have written. This is *La Mort chrétienne*, a collection, made for his own reading, of accounts of the last days of saints and others that he had collected from his medieval sources. It is a worthy pendant to the more celebrated relations by the abbot of La Trappe of the edifying deaths of his religious. Mabillon dedicated his booklet to the ex-queen of England, who had recently lost her husband. Shortly after the appearance of the book, the writer himself gave an example of a monk's last days as moving as any that he had extracted from the records of the past. Dom Ruinart, who was at his side during the last weeks, devoted a book of his Life to a detailed account which should be read in its entirety, with all its record of physical pain and mental serenity, by all those who admire Mabillon. He died on the feast of his patron, St John the Evangelist, 27 December 1707.

11

CARDINAL GASQUET AS AN HISTORIAN[1]

Many of those present today may have felt, when they first read the title of this lecture, that the subject was an insignificant one; they would agree with the latest historian of the Tudor age that Gasquet's work 'is best ignored'.[2] By way of dialectic, let me remind you that H. A. L. Fisher pronounced his book on the monasteries 'far the best modern treatise on the subject...a very learned and careful work';[3] that T. F. Tout could write of his *Henry III* as 'in many ways a well-informed, painstaking, and important book';[4] that J. Willis Clark, the historian of Cambridge architecture and of medieval libraries, dedicated one of his principal works to Gasquet with the words *magistro discipulus*;[5] and that Lord Acton not only invited him to write a chapter for the *Cambridge Modern History*, but mentioned Gasquet, along with Bishop Stubbs and Felix Liebermann, as a representative historian in his celebrated letter to his contributors.[6] I have often been asked for an opinion on Gasquet's work; what follows is an attempt to present it.

Francis Neil Gasquet was born in London in 1846. His father, a naturalized Englishman, was the son of a distinguished French *émigré* naval officer, who had been taken off by the British fleet when Toulon was abandoned in 1792. His mother was a Yorkshire woman, and it may be said at once that in character, tastes, looks, prejudices and failings Gasquet was typically English. His father

---

[1] [The Creighton Lecture in History, University of London, 1956. (Athlone Press, London, 1957.)]

[2] G. R. Elton, *England under the Tudors* (London, 1955), p. 484.

[3] *The Political History of England*, vol. v (ed. 1934), p. 495.

[4] *EHR*, vol. XXI (1906), p. 782.

[5] *The Care of Books* (Cambridge, 1901). The dedication runs: Francisco Aidano Gasquet/Monacho Benedictino/ D.D./ Magistro Discipulus. The writer was for long Registrary of the University and Fellow of Trinity College.

[6] This letter, dated 1898, is printed in *Lectures on Modern History*, ed. Figgis and Laurence (1912); see p. 318.

was a successful London physician, and as a small boy Frank acted as train-bearer to Cardinal Wiseman and served the Mass of the convert Dr Manning at Bayswater. In 1862 he was sent to school at Downside. The school and monastery were very different from what they have become within the past sixty years. Catholics were until 1871 banned by a religious test from entering Oxford or Cambridge, and *de facto* prevented till the mid-nineties from going there by Archbishop Manning. In the Catholic educational system and curriculum there was as yet not a breath of influence from the public schools or public examinations. Downside was a small and stagnant school of some sixty boys of all ages from twelve to nineteen, who existed from October to July without holidays at home; it was staffed entirely by nine or ten monks, all under thirty years of age. The boys came mostly from the upper middle-class homes, with a fair sprinkling of the old Catholic county families—Stourtons, Petres, Smythes, Throckmortons, Berkeleys, Vaughans, Fitzherberts—and a seasoning from the Irish landowning class; the monks themselves had almost without exception passed through the school, and there was consequently a family solidarity throughout school and monastery. The teaching was poor, and by contemporary standards at Winchester or Shrewsbury the scholarship was rudimentary and the intellectual attainment contemptible, but a long tradition from the past and a succession of notable men, together with the possession of a library fairly strong in patristics and church history, gave an atmosphere of culture and breeding of a peculiar cast but of very real power, and for some years at that time a young aristocrat of means, the newly ordained Father Petre, acted as guide and philosopher to the senior boys and as a fairy godmother to the community.[1] The outlook was still that of a proud people aloof, and on the defensive. Downside had educated many a Catholic squire and bishop; Ullathorne, the apostle of Australia and later Newman's bishop in Birmingham, was one of them, and shortly before Gasquet's time Roger Vaughan, later archbishop of Sydney, and Herbert

---

[1] Father (later Lord) Petre (1847–93) was in residence at Downside 1874–77; a brief account of his influence and benefactions, by Abbot Cuthbert Butler, is in *DR*, vol. XXXIII (1914), p. 60 [see also p. 266].

Vaughan, later cardinal archbishop of Westminster, had been at the school. While still at school Gasquet decided to try his monastic vocation; he passed successfully through the noviciate at Belmont, and in 1867 returned to Downside and began almost at once to teach in the school.

At that time, as also for the two previous centuries, the English Benedictines were principally occupied in parish work all over England. The monasteries were not autonomous, and the monks were at the disposal of the common president, who drew his parish priests from the priories at the age of thirty or so. It should be added, and remembered, that Gasquet, once he had returned from Belmont, neither then nor at any other time had any experience of full monastic life in its traditional form. The régime at Downside in the early seventies was physically austere, unworldly and laborious, but there was a minimum of solitude and liturgical observance, monks and boys were very much on top of each other in their narrow quarters, and the life, if hard, had neither the difficulties nor the spiritual advantages of the unchanging conventual round of observance, silence and personal solitude. Gasquet took the life as he found it, and threw himself into it with zest. We hear of him as 'revelling in work' and as 'eaten up with activity'. After ten years he was elected prior of Downside. It was the first of many strokes of fortune that were to determine his career. Normally, the prior was appointed by General Chapter, with a preference for a 'safe' man, but if the prior died in office or resigned the community elected, and this happened in 1878.[1]

The period that followed was in some ways the most fruitful in his life. The prior in those days had many of the duties of bursar and headmaster. Though he had under him only a dozen able-bodied men, they were in many ways a remarkable group. Besides Gasquet himself, there were Edmund Ford, later first abbot of Downside and the inspiring leader of a generation, the young Cuthbert Butler, scholar and second abbot, and Gilbert Dolan, whom all his con-

---

[1] The prior who resigned was Dom Bernard Murphy, to whose initiative and foresight the lay-out of church and monastery at Downside was primarily due; Gasquet, here as elsewhere, came in on the flood. [On the history of Downside and the English Benedictine Congregation, see pp. 271 ff.]

temporaries ranked high.[1] The last survivor of that age, the distinguished antiquary Ethelbert Horne, died a nonagenarian in 1952. To him the reign of Prior Gasquet was always the golden age. The prior was vigorous, versatile, ever planning, building and teaching. It was in those years that the church and monastery of Downside took the shape that can still be recognized. It was then, also, that an event of a very different kind took place, the meeting of Gasquet and Edmund Bishop.[2]

Bishop, who had recently become a Catholic, was already a scholar of note. As a young man he had acted as private secretary to Thomas Carlyle, and had then obtained a post in the Education Office which left him a fair margin of leisure for his own work.[3] He was a born scholar, a self-taught polymath of the family of Muratori or Leopold Delisle. With wide sympathies, a prodigious memory, a passion for accuracy and truth, he had ranged far and wide among the great works of scholarship of the past and among the medieval manuscripts in the British Museum. His forte was early medieval church history, with a bias, which later became a passion, towards liturgy, but liturgy widely understood so as to become almost Christian social history. He had a genius for finding and noting the significant manuscript or out-of-the-way text, and had already been used by Mommsen as an editor for the *Monumenta*. Felix Liebermann and the French Comte Riant were his friends and admirers, and later Duchesne, Batiffol and André Wilmart. At the same time he was physically frail, highly strung, fastidious, sensitive and lonely, both as a freelance scholar and as a recent convert. He came to visit Downside and was greeted by the young prior in the parlour of the old manor-house. The attraction was mutual. Gasquet, self-taught in another way, recognized at once the wide learning and intellectual stimulus of Bishop, while the recent convert found a young superior of congenial tastes, who had been bred and had lived in the traditions of Catholic religious life, and who had all the vigour, boldness and

---

[1] He was the anonymous editor of Bennet Weldon's *Chronological Notes [on] the English Congregation of the Order of St Benedict* (Stanbrook, 1881).

[2] [On Edmund Bishop see now N. Abercrombie, *The Life and Work of Edmund Bishop* (London, 1959).]

[3] For Bishop's own account of his early years see *DR*, vol. LI (1933), pp. 97–113.

drive that he himself lacked. Thenceforward, Bishop was a regular visitor at Downside for almost forty years, and the associate of Gasquet in much of his early work.

For the moment, however, this could not have been foreseen. Normally, in a few years' time, Gasquet would have been posted to parish work. It was now that a second unforeseeable event took place. In 1884 Gasquet fell seriously ill, partly from strain and over-work. His heart, already damaged by a previous illness, showed signs of failing compensation, and it was thought that he had not many months to live. He resigned, and retired as an invalid for care and medical attention to his mother and home in London.[1] Here, as he slowly mended, he began a course of reading on Tudor history, and, as his health improved, began to visit the British Museum, and conceived the idea of a work of research on Tudor monasticism. In this he was certainly inspired by Bishop, who remarked years later, 'I pulled Gasquet out of his coffin'. He was, however, in the position of a mouse closely observed by a cat. The abbot-president, who had a poor opinion of historical studies, was only waiting for a certificate of fitness in order to send Father Gasquet out to a parish—one had even been selected as a quiet spot for an invalid, the chaplaincy to the Smythe family and their tenants at Acton Burnell in the depths of Shropshire. Gasquet, however, had a friend at court. Cardinal Manning was in general little enamoured of religious; it was, indeed, profanely said that in his priority of dislikes they followed close on the heels of his especial *bête noire*, the brewers. He had, however, known Gasquet well as a boy, and more recently Gasquet's brother had married his niece. It was, moreover, only two years since Leo XIII had thrown open the Vatican archives and addressed his celebrated letter on historical studies to Cardinal Hergenröther.[2] Manning therefore offered to write a strongly worded letter to the pope begging him to protect Gasquet from the fate that threatened. Leo responded with alacrity; the president was

[1] Gasquet himself, many years later, wrote: 'It seemed at the time that I was at the end of all things and that my life's work was over' (S. Leslie, *Cardinal Gasquet* (London, 1953), p. 32).
[2] *Acta Sanctae Sedis*, vol. XVI (1883), pp. 49–57. The brief *Saepenumero*, of 18 August 1883, was addressed to Cardinals de Luca, Pitra and Hergenröther.

bidden to hold his hand, and Gasquet was given leave to reside and work in London. In the event, he was never again to live the monastic life as a member of a community. After spending a few years with his mother he settled first in Great Ormond Street and later in Harpur Street, where he was joined by Edmund Bishop.

During the next half-dozen years Gasquet, now restored to health, threw himself into his new work with all his old energy. The future in 1886 must have seemed dark indeed. His successful work at Downside was ended and could never be resumed. His present work was temporary and if he failed to make a success of it the only future would be Acton Burnell or its equivalent. Between him and achievement of any kind lay an uncertain number of years at the British Museum or the Record Office. Those who have lived laborious days at either of those great workshops, even when surrounded with the present amenities and a *décor* superior to that enjoyed by the Victorians, will know what moments and days of doubt and heart-searching inevitably occur. And Gasquet was a man of forty when he began his work. Those years indeed claim our respect.

Let us recall for a moment the historical landscape of the mid-eighties. In the academic world Stubbs at Oxford had inaugurated with brilliance the epoch of the historian trained upon chronicles and charters; Gairdner, succeeding Brewer, was working steadily through the Tudor papers, and Gasquet at the Record Office may have sat next to Maitland or S. R. Gardiner, but the shift from the prize essay to the seminar, from the literary text to the record, from the Reading Room to the Public Record Office, was still a thing of the future, and the vanguard of the academic historians was still absorbed in constitutional history. We can only dimly imagine an investigation of the Tudors unassisted by Pollard and the complete *Letters and Papers*, but when Gasquet began his work Pollard was a schoolboy and Gairdner had only reached 1535. Gasquet was in fact the first to explore methodically not only the whole of the relevant Cromwell papers, but also the accounts and particulars and pensions of the Court of Augmentations, and the pension list of Cardinal Pole. How much he was helped by Bishop, and how much by Gairdner, who respected his early work, we have no means of knowing, but

Gasquet, then as later, had a real gift both for hard work and for discovering and appreciating the value of documents. He did not confine himself to the British Museum and P.R.O. He visited Oxford, Lambeth, Peterborough, Wells, Hereford and other libraries, and solicited access to private collections, such as that of the difficult Lord Ashburnham. He did not shrink from a day of seven or eight hours with the records, and living as he did in Bloomsbury he wasted no time in travel. The result, after less than three years' work, was the first volume of *Henry VIII and the English Monasteries*.[1] The success of the book was immediate and lasting; it became at once, and remained for more than a decade, an historical best-seller. Less than two years later the second volume appeared, to be greeted with equal or even greater applause.

This success won for Gasquet immediate recognition both among his own co-religionists and among the wide reading public. Seventy years ago history was not the academic preserve it has since become, or perhaps we should say that the various currents that now have merged still ran apart. In those days the Society of Antiquaries, the Camden Society, the P.R.O. and the British Museum were all in a measure learned, without being academic. Gasquet, not altogether through his own fault, always remained a stranger to the world of Oxford and Cambridge, with great loss to himself, but the other foci of learning welcomed him from the start. He got to know James Gairdner, S. R. Gardiner, W. H. Hunt, Dr Jessopp and Dr J. C. Cox. His value was recognized in the small but enlightened Catholic educated world; there was now no longer any danger of a call to Acton Burnell. Leo XIII commissioned Manning to bestow the Roman doctorate of Divinity on him. He was always a hard worker, and he followed up his first success by two other books of considerable value—*Edward VI and the Book of Common Prayer*[2] and *The Eve of the Reformation*.[3] The former, largely the work of Bishop, was a pioneer study of lasting value which can still be read with profit; in

[1] Two vols. (London, 1888, 1889).
[2] *Edward VI and the Book of Common Prayer* (London, 1890). In this Gasquet did little more than assemble Bishop's notes and overlook some slips and misprints. But he doubtless had taken part in the discussion of the arguments to be used.
[3] *The Eve of the Reformation* (London, 1900).

the latter he was able to collect and publish a multitude of facts from his researches.

The work on the Book of Common Prayer was another instance of Gasquet's good fortune. When, two or three years later, the question of Anglican orders came up in the Roman Curia, Gasquet seemed the obvious choice as one of the representative Catholic historians from England—and if by Gasquet we understand the partnership Gasquet-Bishop the choice was undoubtedly reasonable. We are not concerned with that controversial issue, save to note that it took Gasquet to Rome, where he made the acquaintance of Leo XIII, and won the friendship of the brilliant young Monsignor Merry del Val. One thing led inevitably to another. A domestic controversy among the English Benedictines, in which Gasquet had taken little part, was now settled by Rome in the way which he and his old colleagues at Downside had desired. The priories became independent abbeys, and when the pope needed a generally respected figure to pilot the new constitutions and serve as abbot-president, Gasquet was to hand and was duly appointed; his re-election was a normal piece of routine till 1914. The wheel had come full circle: the quasi-rebel of 1885, who had held the abbot-president off with a papal brief, was now himself president and wielded authority from Harpur Street.

The early years of the century were in many ways Gasquet's apogee. He was president of the English Benedictines, his books were still selling and his reputation as a scholar stood high. His name had been mentioned as that of a future cardinal, and the papal choice had been anticipated (if that is the right word) by the committee of The Athenaeum, who in 1903 brought forward his name for election under Rule II. In that same year he came within an inch of a still higher distinction.[1] On the death of Cardinal Vaughan the Westminster chapter, in forwarding the customary three names to Rome, chose those of Merry del Val, an English-born Spanish aristocrat, Gasquet and Hedley, the Benedictine bishop of Newport, in that order. When the names passed to the meeting of the English bishops

---

[1] For this episode, see the letters and Gasquet's contemporary memorandum in Leslie, pp. 80–9. Vaughan died 19 June, Leo XIII 20 July, 1903.

there was some demur at Merry as a foreigner and the name of Francis Bourne, the young bishop of Southwark, was added by a single vote at the last minute. All this was an open secret, and for some weeks it seemed to all, and to Gasquet himself, that he would shortly become the fourth archbishop of Westminster; Hedley was infirm, and the death of Leo XIII a few weeks after that of Vaughan called Merry del Val to a higher sphere of work. The committee of Propaganda would indeed probably have endorsed the English choice but for an unpredictable occurrence. When the discussion came on at Rome, it so happened that Cardinal Moran of Sydney was in Rome on his election visit. Moran, who like his fellow countryman and successor, Archbishop Mannix, was a redoubtable fighter, had succeeded at Sydney the English Benedictine and Downside monk, Roger Bede Vaughan, brother of the late cardinal; he was himself no friend of monks—Gasquet somewhat ungallantly described him as an aged cuckoo in a Benedictine nest—and he intervened with great warmth in the Roman debate.[1] Persuaded or exhausted, the cardinals by the majority of a single vote, it was said, voted for Bourne, and the recently elected Pius X who knew not Gasquet confirmed their choice. The story ran that when Gasquet next visited Rome, the pope alluded to his narrow escape from the purple. 'Yes, Your Holiness,' Gasquet is said to have replied, 'the Holy Spirit decided otherwise.' 'The Holy Spirit?' remarked St Pius, 'I thought it was Cardinal Moran.'

Though disappointed at Westminster Gasquet's star did not set. Rightly or wrongly, Rome had the idea that he was a scholar, and when Pius X decided to set up a pontifical commission of Benedictine monks to revise the text of the Vulgate his name presented itself as that of a suitable head. In 1912 he was appointed to the post and left Harpur Street for good. In April 1914 he received the red hat that he had long been expecting, not so much a token of his achievement as a scholar as a recognition of services rendered to the Holy See and of the importance of his new post, for which, indeed, many of his qualities served him well. With the remainder of his life, and his

---

[1] For Vaughan and Moran, see *Dictionary of National Biography*. Gasquet's *mot* is in Leslie, p. 83.

valiant activities at Rome on behalf of the allied cause in World War I, we are not here concerned.

It will have been seen that from 1888 onwards Gasquet's progress from one success to another and one distinguished position to another had taken him further and further from the interests and leisure of his few years of research. It may be added that in 1901 he had lost the companionship of Edmund Bishop. These circumstances, and the positions of authority and respect in which he found himself, undoubtedly affected his work and his character. He was, in the three different fields of scholarship, the monastic life, and the wider affairs of the Church, advancing steadily from one office to another in which his expertise did not correspond either to his eminence or to his reputation. To appreciate this we must return a little to consider his historical work.

Why, may we ask, did Gasquet's early work, and in particular *Henry VIII*, enjoy such great and lasting success? Though well written it is not a literary masterpiece. Nor, as Creighton in his first review pointed out,[1] and as recent critics have repeated, was it an epoch-making revision of a verdict of history. A very long tradition in English scholarship and English sentiment, stretching from Spelman and Selden, through Fuller, Dugdale and Burnet to Hallam and the editors of the *Monasticon*, had provided severe critics of Henry VIII and Cromwell, and had more than suggested that the Dissolution was a mere pillage. The contemporary Anglo-Catholic historian, Canon Dixon, was reaching and expressing conclusions almost identical with those of Gasquet. Moreover, the Romantic and Tractarian movements had combined to give a large section of cultured England nostalgia for the medieval world. Anyone who reads a succession of the articles on monastic remains published in

---

[1] *EHR*, vol. III (1888), pp. 376–9. Creighton remarked that 'there is nothing new in Father Gasquet's first volume', and 'Father Gasquet's book is more distinguished by good intentions than by erudition'. As, however, he made no attempt at a thorough-going criticism, his notice must be considered ungenerous. Gasquet, perhaps rightly, considered that Creighton was reacting against his account of the religious revolution. An unsigned notice (presumably also by Creighton) of the second volume, in *EHR*, vol. V (1890), p. 811, is more favourable: 'The second volume of Father Gasquet's book shows a marked advance upon the first...his book is likely to be the standard authority on the subject for some time to come.'

the national and regional journals of the day will be impressed by the almost universally favourable tone adopted towards the monastic life. Dr Augustus Jessopp and Dr J. C. Cox and the more scholarly W. Hunt were typical of their class.

All this is true, but it is not the whole truth. When Gasquet began to write, the Tudor historian for the wide reading public was Froude, and Froude was an eloquent, powerful and radically unfair critic of the traditional religion of the Middle Ages. Moreover, the quantity of fierce and irrational prejudice against all Catholic institutions, and against monasticism in particular, was still very great. There was, therefore, a live issue for readers, and a 'Cause' for Gasquet to champion.[1]

At the same time, the door was not shut against him. Gasquet, himself a monk—and English critics have ever been indulgent to Benedictines—had many of the qualities and foibles of the normal Englishman; he was good-humoured, moderate, patriotic, and had more than a dash of both sentimentality and philistinism. Even as a historical writer he had strong points. He had not only gone to the original records, but he had woven them into his narrative, and cited their racy phrases. He had a genuine appreciation of the power of words to transmit atmosphere and character. Compared with his pages, Dixon's careful distillations and even Froude's sophisticated cadences seem frigid. Moreover, he touched a whole series of topics, social, economic and artistic, which the academic historian still eschewed.

Many of Gasquet's good qualities appeared also, if to a less degree, in several of his other books written between 1890 and 1900, such as his booklet on the Great Pestilence and his two volumes of collected studies, *The Eve of the Reformation* (1899) and *The Old English Bible* (1897). The first of these was in its original form submitted to Lord Acton in response to an invitation to contribute a chapter to Vol. I of what Gasquet characteristically referred to as '*The Modern History of Cambridge*'.[2] Acton returned it for revision, and we can comprehend his reasons; between his ideas of impartial history and Gas-

---

[1] Compare Gasquet to Bishop, 29 February 1888 (Leslie, p. 145): 'It's the Cause, not me.'   [2] In an autobiographical note printed by Leslie, p. 112.

quet's there was a gulf, and neither was prepared to bridge it, but in the event the gap was never adequately filled, and Gasquet's essay has ever since been used as a quarry. He was among the first to see the value of wills, library catalogues, inventories, and guild records as evidence for religious history.

In addition to his real gifts as an interpreter and a historical antiquary, Gasquet had a flair for discovery. He was the first to emphasize the importance of the medieval bishops' registers, even though their contents did in fact aid in his undoing. He had read and transcribed the Norwich visitations before they were printed. He was the first to make consistent use of the Augmentations accounts and Pole's pension book, to appreciate the value of surviving medieval books as evidence of the tastes and interests of their scribes and owners and to indicate the riches of medieval sermon literature. Again and again during his career he was able to throw a crucial new document into the arena. He found a bundle of the commissioners' reports of 1536 which Gairdner had missed and which did not appear in the relevant volume of *Letters and Papers*.[1] In the matter of Anglican orders he unearthed the brief and bull of Paul IV and part of Cardinal Pole's Register, and he printed in his sole contribution to *The English Historical Review* an important letter of Roger Bacon, and drew attention to his significance as a critic of the text of the Vulgate.[2] He disposed of one of Froude's worse mistakes by a reference to a Hereford register, and went a long way towards settling the Wallingford problem by his discoveries at the British Museum and in the Vatican library.[3] He printed the earliest life of Gregory the Great.[4] He discovered and published an important pre-Conquest psalter.[5] He noted in his *Henry III* a large number of unpublished papal bulls.

Yet in any appraisal of Gasquet's work one unknown factor, one x,

---

[1] Printed in *DubR*, vol. CXIV (1894), pp. 245–77.

[2] *EHR*, vol. XII (1897), pp. 494–517. Gasquet identified the piece as the introduction to the *Opus Maius*.

[3] For the literature of the Wallingford affair see M. D. Knowles, 'The Case of St Albans Abbey in 1490' in *JEH*, vol. III (1952), pp. 144–58; for the Hereford register, the same writer's 'The Last Abbot of Wigmore', above, pp. 171–8.

[4] *A Life of Pope St Gregory the Great* (Westminster, 1904), from MS. Sangallen, 567.

[5] *The Bosworth Psalter* (London, 1908) (with Edmund Bishop).

remains to perplex the calculator. How much did he owe to Edmund Bishop? That the debt was great was common knowledge to all who knew the two men personally, and Gasquet both in print and in private letters acknowledged it. It was, however, felt, even at the time, that this acknowledgement was less explicit and less generous than might have been expected. Gasquet was not a humble man, nor was he in personal relationship a notably generous man. We know from his letters that the manuscript of *Henry VIII* was submitted piece by piece to Bishop and ruthlessly criticized. What we do not know is how much the book owed to Bishop's own transcripts and notes, and how far Bishop saved Gasquet from endless delays by naming or suggesting documents that should be consulted, or even by time spent at the Museum on Gasquet's behalf. It seems certain that the introduction to the English translation of Montalembert's *Monks of the West*, one of the earliest and most successful of Gasquet's productions and one which, translated into Italian, had a considerable influence over Leo XIII and others during the recasting of the English Benedictine constitutions, was almost entirely the work of two 'ghosts', Edmund Bishop and Dom Elphege Cody.[1] It is also arguable—and it has been argued—that after Gasquet and Bishop ceased to live together in 1901 Gasquet's work never again reached its earlier standard. There were those, also, forty years ago, who thought that Gasquet had taken advantage of Bishop's good nature and had not acknowledged his help in sufficient detail. They had not, perhaps, read the dedication of one of his books to 'My old and tried friend Edmund Bishop, to whom I owe more than mere words can express'.[2] All that can be said for certain is that Bishop never voiced and probably never felt any grievance. His was a mind of the type that can amass knowledge more easily than write books; his health was never robust and his mind worked inwards. He gave freely what he would never have used himself. Nor was the giving all on his side. Gasquet provided companionship, a home, affec-

---

[1] So at least the present writer was more than once told by Abbot Cuthbert Butler, who weighed his words. Gasquet's account (in Leslie, p. 33), especially when all allowances are made for his constitutional inaccuracy, does not seem altogether incompatible. See also below, p. 309, n. 1.

[2] This is the dedication of *Henry III and the Church* (London, 1905).

tionate care and, in the event, a share in vivid enterprise; he was also the occasion of many lasting friendships and a second home at Downside. When all is said and done, it is certain that, from first to last, Bishop admired Gasquet and loved him. When he was dying, he dictated a letter to the Cardinal. 'He says,' wrote the amanuensis, 'that you have had his love so long that he isn't going to send it any more.' Gasquet replied to the dead man's niece: 'What I owe to him no one can tell except myself, and you may be sure that he will not be forgotten for a single day as long as I live.'[1]

Thus far I have tried to put before you the positive and admirable qualities of Gasquet's work. We have also to consider its defects.

In the first place, he was handicapped from the start through no fault of his own. He had never passed through an exacting mental discipline of any kind. He was tolerably well read in some parts of English history, but had no academic training in medieval history, or in constitutional or economic history, still less in critical method. He taught himself to read late medieval manuscripts and Tudor court hand, but he was not a trained palaeographer and a transcription by him was rarely immune from error. He had a good working knowledge of Latin, assisted by his daily acquaintance with the missal and breviary, but he had not the solid, instinctive foundation given by the Tripos or Classical Moderations, or even by a good classical fifth form, and he could and did make egregious mistakes with notable frequency. Moreover, he made no effort to make himself familiar with contemporary scholarship. It may be doubted whether he was at all aware of the significance, for example, of Pollard or Maitland. All this was his misfortune, and was in part due to the existing deficiencies of Catholic education. Unfortunately Gasquet had other failings, both technical and psychological.

He was in the first place unusually inaccurate. Lack of training may help to explain his constant failure to adopt an adequate and consistent system of references, but it does not excuse his inveterate habit of giving no reference at all, or the wrong one, on crucial points. His inaccuracy in details can only be appreciated by one who has had frequent occasion to use his books. Only the other day

---

[1] Leslie, p. 51. See also Gasquet's tribute to Bishop in *DR*, vol. XXXVI (1917), pp. 2–11.

I noticed that throughout his account of Abbot Hobbes of Woburn he gives him a wrong Christian name, though he had the original documents and Froude's printed page before him. Nor had the mistake been corrected twenty years after it had been made.[1] A few days later a still more curious error turned up. Sir John St Clair or Seynclere, a well-known Suffolk magnate, figures in the case of Abbot Marshall of Colchester. Gasquet printed the name as 'John Seyn, clerk',[2] and continued to do so through all the many subsequent editions, though both *Letters and Papers* and the *V. C. H. Suffolk* had printed correct transcripts in the meanwhile.

We all make slips from human frailty, and most of us also from real carelessness, and we expect indulgence within reason. Gasquet's inaccuracies in his early books were many, but they could be numbered. But from *c.* 1900 Gasquet's pages crawl with errors and slips. His three-volume edition of Premonstratensian documents for the Royal Historical Society must be one of the worst-edited contributions to the Camden Series. The plan and execution of the edition are alike faulty. When the volumes first appeared, more than fifty years ago, Mr Charles Johnson, who was then younger than he is now, ventured to put readers on their guard.[3] Some years later, Coulton printed a list of mistakes in the work, and later deposited a revised list in the Library of the University of Chicago. More recently still, Mr Colvin has deposited *his* list in the Bodleian.[4] I have grave doubts whether the consolidated total has achieved a full enumeration. Towards the end of his life, indeed, Gasquet's capacity for carelessness amounted almost to genius. He could refer, in a tribute to Edmund Bishop (of all places), to Gibbon's *Rise and Fall*,[5] and he could print a stanza of *In Memoriam* in five or six lines of type without any ascertainable metre or rhyme.[6]

[1] 'Richard' for 'Robert', *Henry VIII*, vol. II, p. 192; still thus in ed. 1906, p. 289, and so in all edd.

[2] *Henry VIII*, vol. I, p. 398, 'John Seyn, a clerk'; vol. II, p. 383, 'a cleric, John Seyn'. The same mistake is repeated in *The Last Abbot of Glastonbury* (London, 1895), p. 172.

[3] *EHR*, vol. XIX (1904), pp. 770–2. [Mr Johnson died in 1961, aged 91.]

[4] Colvin also prints a select list of errors in *The White Canons in England* (Oxford, 1951), pp. 389 ff. Coulton's first draft is printed in *Medieval Studies* (First Series, 2nd ed., London, 1915, pp. 92–7).

[5] This was in the tribute referred to above, p. 253, n. 1.

[6] In the privately printed booklet *Religio Religiosi*.

In many cases this was just deplorable inertia. We all know that few tasks are more tiresome than reading proofs or than keeping notes of every correction that is sent to us and then, on the sudden demand of a publisher, going through a big book to correct errors and supply omissions without altering the pagination. In justice to Gasquet it should be remembered that many of his mistakes were not pointed out until years after the books first appeared. If J. H. Round or Mr H. G. Richardson had tackled his first volume in *The English Historical Review* Gasquet might have become a far better scholar—or he might have retired to Acton Burnell. In any case, Gasquet never revised. Not till years after *Letters and Papers* had reached 1540 did he consent to adapt to the printed text his own often inadequate references to the original documents. He never wove into his original narrative his own remarkable discovery of the additional reports of the 1536 commissioners. He never changed the wording of his appeal to unpublished bishops' visitations even after many of them had been printed and had provided evidence against his thesis. He never took any notice of articles and monographs which his own work had inspired; he never, for example, gave any hints, even in the latest editions of *Henry VIII*, that Mary Bateson had printed Robert Aske's examination in full, or that Savine had dealt with the *Valor Ecclesiasticus*.

More serious was his inability to grip a problem or argument and to shed light on dark places. Gasquet had inherited from his Provençal ancestors little of the Gallic lucidity of thought. One or two of his later compositions give one the mental impression of being lost in a maze or engulfed in a nightmare. If anyone thinks these expressions too strong, let him read slowly and carefully the little book on Abbot Wallingford, which incidentally furnishes specimens of almost every kind of technical error.[1] Yet in spite of that, the booklet settles from documentary sources problems of identity and chronology that had led astray the editors of Dugdale, Froude and James Gairdner himself. You have in it an epitome of the splendours and distresses of Gasquet's achievement. More serious still,

---

[1] *Abbot Wallingford; an inquiry into the charges made against him and his monks* (London, no date; actually 1912).

perhaps, was a lack of fidelity as an editor, shown particularly in his transcription of the Acton correspondence in *Lord Acton and his Circle*.[1] Besides technical inaccuracies of many kinds, Gasquet consistently omitted or even altered without indication passages or phrases which might, he felt, cause personal offence or exhibit Acton's critical or petulant attitude towards venerable ecclesiastics. Thus he would print 'Newman' where Acton had written 'old Noggs', and the forthright remark that 'Pius IV was an ass' appears in the anodyne form 'Pius IV was no good'.

Beyond all this, there was a root of something in Gasquet which led him to ignore even the most cogent evidence against anything he had written. It was this that led Coulton to his most serious charge of intellectual dishonesty. The affair of the *Old English Bible* is of course the palmary instance. There is no need to repeat the facts of that case; they have been repeated again and again by Coulton, and accepted, at least tacitly, by all subsequent writers on the subject. I may be allowed, however, to mention a similar instance which escaped the vigilant eye of Coulton. In *Henry VIII* Gasquet presented the last abbot of Colchester as a martyr to the faith for opposing the Royal Supremacy. In this he followed both the chronicler Hall and an old Catholic tradition, which seemed to derive support from the evidence given against the abbot which Gasquet turned up, and there is no reason to doubt his good faith when he wrote in 1889, after giving this evidence: 'Nothing more is known of Abbot Marshall's last days but the fact of his execution.'[2] He repeated this sentence verbally in his chapter on Abbot Marshall in *The Last Abbot of Glastonbury*.[3] When, however, Gairdner's volume of *Letters and Papers* covering the latter part of 1539 appeared in 1895, it contained a long document in the abbot's handwriting in which he denied his opposition to the Royal Supremacy, revoked anything he might have said in support of papal claims, and begged for pardon.[4]

---

[1] *Lord Acton and his Circle*, London, 1906. For Gasquet's treatment of Acton's text see H. Butterfield and A. Watkin, in *Cambridge Historical Journal*, vol. x, i (1950), 'Gasquet and the Acton–Simpson Correspondence', pp. 75–105.
[2] *Henry VIII*, vol. ii, p. 384.
[3] First ed. 1895, p. 173; cf. ed. 1908, p. 105.
[4] *Letters and Papers of the reign of Henry VIII*, vol. xiv, ii, no. 459.

This has naturally been accepted by subsequent writers, including the Catholic martyrologist, Dom Bede Camm,[1] as rendering Abbot Marshall's claim to the title of martyr unprovable, if not positively disproved. Yet Gasquet continued to allow his chapter in *The Last Abbot* to be reprinted unchanged, and the sentence quoted above duly appeared in the posthumous edition of 1934. As for the parallel passage in *Henry VIII*, this also remained unchanged until 1906, when Gasquet substituted the following paragraph without any reference to *Letters and Papers*: 'Under the stress of imprisonment in the Tower...Abbot Marshall's courage appears somewhat to have failed him for a time....His excuses, however, as we know, were made in vain, and in the end he...laid down his life for conscience sake.'[2] The point is more important than it appears. Gasquet's book on the three abbots was part of a process of historical examination which issued in a petition to Rome for a recognition of an ancient cultus of these men as martyrs for the Catholic faith. In 1897 the Congregation of Rites accepted the petition and confirmed the cultus. An equipollent beatification (as it is called) of this kind lacks the solemnity and finality of a canonization, and further inquiry would be necessary before the case could be carried further. Meanwhile however, largely as a result of Gasquet's work, the abbot of Colchester is venerated as a martyr. Gasquet was at the time the one man in England qualified to enter a firm caveat for the sake of historical truth, and to warn his readers of his earlier ignorance. Instead, he persisted to the end in a *suppressio veri* which in the circumstances carried with it more than a trace of *suggestio falsi*.

Lord Acton may have been mistaken in asserting that the historian always has the last word in judging his fellow-men, but it is undoubtedly true that no historian can be false to his calling and escape down the ages without a whipping. Sooner or later the slip, the suppression, the incautious statement will come home to roost. Thucydides, after twenty-three centuries, has been convicted of bias against Cleon, and Bury noted that Gibbon tripped over the name of the city from which Gregory Nazianzen took his name. In

[1] Dom B. Camm, *Lives of the English Martyrs* (1904), vol. I, pp. xviii–xx, 396 ff., 409.
[2] *Henry VIII*, ed. 1906, p. 395.

257

Gasquet's case the triumphal car had a good start, but Vengeance came limping after in the person of George Gordon Coulton.

In the first years of the twentieth century, as we have seen, Gasquet's reputation both as an historian and as a churchman stood at its height. Even the long-hostile academic world had at last capitulated. In 1906 the brilliant Tudor volume of H. A. L. Fisher appeared; it was clearly influenced by Gasquet, as were the earlier works of Gairdner on the same period. At almost the same moment, however, the sharpshooting that was to shake his reputation had begun. The first telling shot had been fired in 1900-1 by Mr Arthur Ogle in the matter of the *Old English Bible*,[1] and in the same year the then obscure Mr Coulton wrote his first and most polite letter to Gasquet, who was ill-advised first to ignore, then to evade, and finally to slight his formidable critic.[2] With the details and fortunes of the relentless guerrilla warfare of the next forty years we are not concerned. The academic victory lay certainly with Coulton. Obscure he may have been in 1901, but when he died in 1947, a Fellow of St John's and of the British Academy, recognized by all as one of the most learned medievalists of the day, Gasquet's writings had been blown upon and all but driven into oblivion.

Coulton had, very deeply engrained, two atavistic prejudices which ever since the days of Wyclif have possessed a large section of his countrymen, the one a fear and distrust of ecclesiastical potentates in general and of Romans in particular, the other a conviction that monasticism is an unnatural institution which of itself always leads inevitably to disaster.[3] To these he added an almost emotional

---

[1] *Church Quarterly Review*, vol. LI (October 1900, January 1901), pp. 138 ff., 265 ff.

[2] Gasquet returned no answer to Coulton's first letter; he refused the moderately worded and reasonable request of his second with the excuse that doctor's orders forbade him to undertake extra work. A few years later in the preface to a cheap edition of *Henry VIII* (1906), p. viii, he used the words 'any would-be literary *chiffonnier*'. Coulton (perhaps rightly) saw a personal allusion, and it rankled.

[3] Coulton on more than one occasion implied that modern religious were only respectable because they were closely observed by the Press and the police, e.g. *Medieval Studies* (First Series, 2nd ed., 1915), p. 63: 'These [monks and nuns] whom we see in modern England are a small minority [*sc.* of the population], living amid a healthy public opinion, and under a system of law and police such as no man even dreamt of in the Middle Ages.' He goes on, however, to express his fears 'lest the convents should become sweating-houses of cheap and insanitary labour, in the absence of such proper supervision as our law enforces in the case of other workshops'.

attachment to a particular point of historical accuracy, *viz.* the ability to support one's assertions by exact references to authorities, accompanied by a readiness to alter or withdraw publicly from any error once it had been indicated. No one would wish to deny the desirability of such behaviour; Coulton's idiosyncrasy lay in making of this particular manifestation of honesty in this particular field of accuracy the touchstone of the whole man. To this it should be added that Coulton had in full measure the distinctive qualities of the controversialist: persistence, love of the reiterated question, the ability to focus attention on a single tree in the forest, a desire for printed acknowledgement, and great self-assurance. But it should in fairness be remarked that, unlike many controversialists, he was courteous and generous in personal intercourse; he had, moreover, immense learning and was, at least on the surface of his own chosen field, almost always right.

On the wider view he was unfair to Gasquet. He ignored altogether —as controversialists often do—the real merits of some of his books and, still more, the numerous discoveries which he had made; he also ignored the judgements of values and institutions with which he did not agree, but which were none the less defensible. Many, indeed, will feel still that Gasquet's judgements on the later Middle Ages and Tudor characters were truer and more humane than Coulton's. But in the particular points of factual accuracy which he selected for criticism Coulton was almost invariably right. His long catalogue of Gasquet's errors is substantially correct—indeed, the only criticism that might be made against it is that it is unconscionably short. His mistake lay, I believe, in attributing these errors, and an unwillingness to correct them, to a studied policy of ecclesiastical discipline and apologetics, and to a callous, even cynical, disregard of the demonstrated truth. The Gasquet he attacked—the suave, polished, successful hierocrat, lying for the sake of his Church and rewarded for so doing—was to that extent so much a caricature of the real Gasquet—patriotic, 'broad-brow', often indiscreet, often critical of persons and policies within the Church—that it diverted many of Gasquet's friends and apologists from meeting or admitting the detailed charges.

Having said so much, however, it must be frankly confessed that for many of Gasquet's mistakes, and still more for his failure to admit and correct them, no defence can be offered. They may be explained, but they cannot be excused. His apologists repeated, and with truth, that he was a busy man, who had been called from his historical work to a succession of administrative offices, and who had therefore lost touch with his old trade and with the advances made by younger scholars. They added, what was also in part true, that Coulton was inspired by an anti-Roman bias that had an element of the irrational in it; if you gave him an inch, 'the old idiot' (as Gasquet called him) would take an ell. They might have added that Coulton did not show the same passion for outraged truth when writing of historians such as Froude, whose *Short Studies* and *Henry VIII* were still in print in cheap editions fifty years after they had been shown to be erroneous and biased on many important points. All this may have been true, but it was beside the point.

How then shall we explain Gasquet's behaviour?

First, we must realize that Gasquet had never passed through the gymnastics of a training in critical method. Like all other disciplines, the object of such a training is to render a course of action more secure and more easy by means of correct habits and a mental awareness which prevent or detect errors. Had Gasquet employed as a matter of course the automatic signalling system of a scientific and critical method he would have avoided not only his inaccuracies, but also many of his failures to attain the truth.

Next, we must say that he rarely approached an historical topic with an open mind; in other words he rarely approached it as an historian. Either he wrote to convince others of what he believed to be the truth, or he set out a discovery which he held to be significant. In other words, he started with a conviction or a fact, and went to other documents to find confirmation. He had little or no sense of history as a stream of eddying currents or a web of many threads, nor did he think of his craft as an exercise of patient and passionless mental discipline.

Thirdly, his mind was not naturally clear enough to compensate for his lack of training. He felt no inclination to get at the roots and difficulties of a problem; he never shook it out, so to say; instead he tended to tangle the skein beyond hope of unravelling. Evidence, whether old or fresh, did not impinge upon his consciousness with the cogency which it in fact possessed. In his later writings he sometimes dismissed a critic with rotund avuncular platitudes which exasperated those who had pointed to undoubted mistakes.

Finally, behind all this, there was a further reason. Gasquet was not an intellectually humble man and he showed little insight into his own limitations of knowledge and training. His successes and offices had done nothing to help him in these ways. The circles in which he moved accepted him for what he appeared to be; no criticism of equals or superiors troubled his equanimity. He lacked that passion for absolute intellectual chastity, which is desirable in any man, but in an historian is as much an occupational requirement as is absolute integrity in a judge. He did not primarily seek for truth without fear or favour. He held obstinately to what he had thought and when he should have recognized the force of fresh evidence he ignored it, probably quite unaware that a great issue was at stake.

It was here, I think, that Coulton was in error. He simplified the matter even to crudity. Gasquet was a liar (as he did not hesitate to imply),[1] and he was a liar because he was an ecclesiastic. Gasquet's fault (if we are to use the word) was, I would submit, on another level altogether. It had nothing to do with his being a Catholic or a cardinal; he might just as well have been a Non-conformist or an agnostic. It did not differ in kind from the conduct of a politician or a diplomat who defends all his past actions and remains silent about his failures of judgement or policy in spite of quotations and challenges in debate—as it might be Asquith upholding his conduct of Irish affairs or Bethmann-Hollweg justifying his tenure of office. It was the fault of a man who saw only one side—his own side—and who was blind to all else. It was not without reason that Pope Benedict XV, harassed by Gasquet about some alleged German misdemeanour, exclaimed: 'Audi alteram partem.'

In the course of this lecture some severe things have been said

---

[1] See *The Scandal of Cardinal Gasquet* (Taunton, 1937) and *A Premium upon Falsehood* (Taunton, 1939).

about Gasquet. Let me end by endeavouring to assess his place in historiography.

It must be said at once that he initiated no new discipline and founded no school. It is a glory of academic scholarship that it lives on in assured knowledge, in germinal ideas, and in the living mind of the disciple. Gasquet had few germinal ideas and formed no school. In the strict sense of the word, indeed, he was not a scholar at all. He did not use the tools, or pursue the ends, of an accomplished scholar. Abbot Cuthbert Butler once remarked, when Gasquet was still living, that Downside had produced only two scholars, Dom Hugh Connolly and himself, and the judgement was both characteristic and true.[1] Nevertheless, Gasquet's influence on others was not inconsiderable. Even if he did not, in James Gairdner's oft-quoted words, 'dispel the charges against the monks for ever', he certainly put the Tudor monasteries boldly on the map, and killed what was certainly the popular opinion that they were merely abodes of vice and rich living. It is largely due to him that so much research has been undertaken upon a relatively small topic. But for Gasquet, we should not have much of the work of Savine, Mary Bateson, Archbold, Hibbert and a whole group of recent young scholars, while if the merit of an action can be seen in the reaction it provokes, we must add Baskerville to our list. In other fields, also, J. W. Clark, M. R. James, Professor Owst and many other scholars and antiquaries have received from Gasquet an impulse of one kind or another. Over and beyond this, Gasquet, as we have seen, discovered and in part exploited more original documents than many a faultless academic historian.

These are not small achievements, and they cannot be cancelled out or reduced to zero by an enumeration of his numerous errors and failings. If it is perilous to accept Gasquet uncritically, it is foolish utterly to neglect or despise him.

In the letter of Leo XIII, to which reference was made earlier in this lecture, and which helped to found Gasquet's fortunes, there

[1] I remember as a boy asking Abbot Butler, shortly after Gasquet had been created Cardinal, whom he considered to be the greatest Old Gregorian. The answer was unhesitating: 'Ullathorne. Cardinal Gasquet is the most distinguished, but Ullathorne was the greatest.'

occur the following words, which I am not aware that Coulton ever quoted in his flight of pamphlets. They might well have served as a text for this lecture—a text by which to judge both Gasquet, his critics and his apologists. 'Above all,' wrote the pope, 'the historian should ever bear in mind that the first law of history is that he should never dare to write what is false and that the second is that he should never lack courage to say what is true. The third law is that he should never write to win favour or to satisfy his spleen.'[1]

Gasquet, at least in middle life, was an unusually handsome man. To one who looks on his portrait, after reading a page of Coulton, the well-known words of Macaulay upon the portrait of Warren Hastings seem to haunt the mind. 'He looked like a great man, and he did not look like a bad man.' Gasquet was not a great man; he had neither the power nor the depth of greatness. But to those who knew him he was not, in any normal sense of the words, a bad man.

---

[1] *Acta Sanctae Sedis*, vol. XVI, p. 54 [see p. 244, n. 2, above]: 'Illud in primis scribentium obversetur animo primam esse historiae legem ne quid falsi dicere audeat; deinde ne quid veri non audeat; ne qua suspicio gratiae sit in scribendo, ne qua simultatis.' The pope made his own the words of Cicero, *de Oratore*, II, 15, 62.

12

EDWARD CUTHBERT BUTLER:
1858-1934[1]

I. Abbot Butler: a Memoir

No apology, surely, need be made for the number of pages in this Review devoted to the memory of Abbot Butler. The place he will always hold in Downside history, and that which he held in the estimation of many unconnected with Downside, alike make it a duty to leave on record some considerable account of his life and personality. For just sixty-five years his life had been connected with St Gregory's; for some fifty of them he had had a part, great or small, in all events affecting the destiny of the house, and for sixteen he was its superior. During almost the whole of his monastic life he was occupied with literary work of some kind; thus both by personal contact and by the medium of the written word his influence on his brethren and sons in religion was constant and great; a sense of piety, therefore, would seem to demand that some memorial of words should be erected to him.

In the pages which follow Abbot Butler and his personal outlook fill a large place in a narrative of events in which many besides himself were concerned. A historian would be under an obligation to fill in the canvas, and to set the figures in perspective. The scope of a memoir is somewhat different; there, its subject must occupy the foreground; *ex hypothesi* he is a figure of importance, and events are considered rather as seen by him and moulded by him; *ex hypothesi*, too, the subject of a memoir is recently dead, and the latest events of his life are not yet matter for the historian. In any case, be the picture true or false, those who owed much to Abbot Butler will wish it to have been drawn. *Valeat quantum.*

---

[1] [*Downside Review*, vol. LII (1934), pp. 347–465 (followed by 'Abbot Butler: A Bibliography', pp. 466–72, omitted from this reprint).]

Edward Joseph Aloysius Butler was born in Dublin on 6 May 1858, the only son of Edward Butler and his wife Mary. His father's name appears on the original list (1854) as Professor of Mathematics in the university which Newman organized in Dublin;[1] his mother was a sister of Sir Francis Cruise, an eminent consulting physician who in later life published a valuable discussion on the authorship of the *Imitation of Christ*. Although he always regarded himself as an Irishman, and was regarded by others as possessing many characteristics of the Irish, Edward Butler had very little Celtic blood in his veins. Of his eight great-grandparents, only one (a great-grandmother) was Irish by race. Similarly, through neither mother nor father had he completely Catholic ancestry: the family of Butlers, indeed, were of northern Protestant stock, and his grandfather was a convert to the Church.

The intellectual atmosphere of his early home must have influenced him unconsciously, and he had a sincere affection for his mother, but he did not owe directly to home influence any of the abiding interests and pursuits of his life nor, so far as those who knew him could ever ascertain, did any friendships or local associations remain deeply in his memory from the days before he came to Downside. He recently remarked that the first public event he remembered was the funeral of Cardinal Wiseman, in February 1865, when he would have been rising seven, and this of itself suggests that his mind did not dwell on his childhood. He entered the school at Downside in September 1869 and remained till June 1875. His gifts of mind naturally singled him out for notice, and though he was without much capacity or attraction for organized games, he was never unduly sensitive or diffident of himself, and entered fully into the ordinary life of the school, which still retained the characteristics of an earlier generation, in particular the Christmas holidays spent at Downside with the King's Court and the frequent theatricals. In his last year, Christmas 1874, Edward Butler was head of the school and King.

[1] He held this position during the whole of Newman's residence, and during the first months was acting Vice-Rector. So Abbot Butler in *Life of Ullathorne*, vol. II, p. 312 n. [see below, p. 352].

Although the opportunities for study and the teaching provided must have left very much to be desired, he nevertheless laid during his last years at school the foundations of that sound and accurate knowledge of Latin and Greek which he came to possess. Though never in any sense a specialized classical scholar, and though he rarely, if ever, in later life read Latin or Greek literature for pleasure, he had read and taught the outstanding masterpieces, and was never at a loss in translating either language.

During his last years at Downside he came greatly under the influence of Father (later Lord) Petre,[1] who was then living there in 'a somewhat anomalous position which gave him a great influence among the elder boys, and who at that time was [his] guide, philosopher and friend'.[2] It was to Father Petre, as well as to the prior, Dom Bernard Murphy, that he turned for advice as to his vocation. He did not, however, proceed at once into the noviciate at Belmont: it was the wish of his parents that he should have time away from Downside to consider. Accordingly, he spent a few months as a member of Cardinal Manning's ill-fated Catholic university college in Kensington, where he met Mivart and Paley, and in travelling fairly widely on the Continent. While in London in 1875–76 he was a not infrequent theatre-goer, and heard *Faust* and other operas; he also witnessed the Boat Race of that year.

His entry into religion may be described in his own words:

I went to Belmont towards the end of August, 1876, being just past 18. I had no notion whatever, not even the most rudimentary, of the nature

---

[1] [See also p. 241.]

[2] I have made use, in the account of these early years, of two manuscripts of Abbot Butler's which came into my hands after his death. Both are accounts, largely auto-biographical in character, of the movement at Downside associated with the names of Gasquet, Ford and himself. The one, by far the shorter, was begun 1 October 1891, and apparently written in entirety at least within six months; it carries the story only as far as the summer of 1881. It is lively, even exuberant, in tone. I refer to this as MS. A. The second, five or six times as long, was also apparently written all at one time; it was completed on 18 February 1905. It presupposes the earlier narrative (which it occasionally supplements) as far as the summer of 1881, and then carries the story down to the election of Abbot Ford in 1900. It is somewhat more soberly written, and marginal notes show that it had been carefully read by Edmund Bishop and others. I refer to it as MS. B. Neither document contains any private matter of any description, and both were clearly written to be read by others, if not ultimately published, so I have felt no diffidence in making these extracts.

of the religious state or the monastic life. I acted on a perfectly blind impulse; I felt a strong call to be a monk, but I had no clear idea of what was meant by being a monk.[1]...I had no great attraction for church services or prayer; I was not drawn by affection for any of the monks; I was not flying from the dangers of the world—I knew nothing of them. ...I entered the noviciate, my mind, as has been said, a perfect blank as to the mode of life I was embarking on. I remember shortly after my entrance saying to an old school friend among the juniors that I should not have been surprised at anything I found at Belmont—not even at perpetual abstinence or silence, or midnight office.[2]

Belmont, at that time the common house of studies and noviciate for the Congregation, and the pro-cathedral and chapter-church of the diocese of Newport and Menevia, was under the rule of Prior Wilfrid Raynal, a monk of St Gregory's and a man of powerful mind and character who throughout his long period of office left a strong impress of straightforward simplicity and severity on the generations trained under him. He was, however, by nature a man who governed rather than taught or inspired, and his influence on the development of Br. Cuthbert's mind does not seem to have been marked. The novice-master was Dom Cuthbert Doyle, a monk of St Edmund's, a man of ability beyond the average and of a most lovable character. The Junior Master for part of his time at Belmont, Dom Augustine O'Neill, later president and ultimately bishop of the Mauritius, was also a man of distinction, spiritual, clear-sighted and amiable. He had a great influence over Brother Cuthbert, and some of his doctrine on the monastic life remained with Abbot Butler to the end. Life at Belmont was severe, almost Spartan, in character; the house was without central heating; the food was plain and all the manual house-work was done by the young monks. A tradition of summary and (to our eyes) artificial penances was still maintained in the noviciate; there was much healthy out-of-door exercise and work, but almost no contact with the life 'of the world'. Abbot Butler always looked back upon his noviciate with pleasure as a year of enthusiasm, and to his novice-master (who lived to extreme old age,

[1] So MS. A (1891). MS. B (1905) has: 'I had no clear ideas about the life, or what I wanted, or why I became a monk. I acted under a sort of blind impulse.'
[2] MS. A.

dying only in 1932) with affection and gratitude, but he owed the decisive force of his year's noviciate to another source.

In the spring of 1876 Dom Norbert Sweeney had re-edited the neglected spiritual classic *Sancta Sophia* of Fr. Augustine Baker. Bishop Hedley, in a long article of great power and eloquence in the October *Dublin Review*, had drawn the attention of Catholic England to its importance, and, naturally, the bishop's commendation in public and private had great influence at Belmont. The book was taken up by Dom Doyle in the November of 1876 as the public spiritual reading of the noviciate and its teaching adopted as normal. Bishop Hedley, who had known Edward Butler as a boy, inquired of him during the noviciate what books he was reading. 'I answered "*Sancta Sophia*". "I am glad to hear that," he replied, "it is a noviciate in itself."' After profession, Brother Cuthbert found the Junior Master, Dom R. Riley, taking *Sancta Sophia* for public spiritual reading, and shortly afterwards Prior Raynal approved of Brother Cuthbert's reading it as a 'Lent book'. Unquestionably, this early meeting with Father Baker marked an epoch in his life, and determined his spiritual outlook and doctrine once and for all. He writes:

I have said that before Christmas of the noviciate *Sancta Sophia* had been put into our hands; it formed the staple of our spiritual reading for the rest of the noviciate; our Novice Master exhorted us to study it in private and analyse it.... It became in the fullest sense our text book of the spiritual life; we did not see even a page of the traditional Rodriguez. From the first I felt a strong attraction for *Sancta Sophia*—its logical order, its philosophical sweep of the spiritual life, its lofty ideal, its piety in tone, its eloquence in language, all combined to influence my fervour and enthusiasm. It came to us also recommended by the highest authority. ...Under these circumstances it is not surprising that I and two of my fellow-novices became ardent 'Bakerites'. By this I do not wish to make any absurd claim to high spirituality; I mean that we took Fr. Baker's theory as the orthodox theory of Benedictine life, and tried to walk along the earlier stages of his system, hoping that, as he says, when we came to 'almost a declining age' we might be found worthy to enter on some of the higher paths.[1]

[1] MS. A.

And he adds, in a characteristic and illuminating passage:

In after years I modified Fr. Baker's theory in a few points, especially his views as to the relative positions of mental prayer and the Divine Office in Benedictine life; but substantially I have ever been faithful to my first love, and to this day [1891] I regard my early acquaintance with and admiration for *Sancta Sophia* as one of the chief graces of my life. It gave me a definite theory of the spiritual and monastic lives, and a high ideal to aim at. A high ideal is a great thing; it is to a man's life what a sound philosophy is to his intellect. With a high ideal a man *may* do something; without it he certainly cannot.

We can without difficulty see the development in these years at Belmont of the two dominant interests, spiritual and intellectual, of his whole life.

From *Sancta Sophia* I got a firm grip of the great and fundamental principle that the Benedictine Order is contemplative....After my profession I began to read some of the books most recommended by Fr. Baker; thus I read all of St Theresa's works I could lay my hands upon; and soon I turned to Cassian and the *Lives of the Fathers of the Desert*.[1] Other writings that influenced me a good deal were Cardinal Newman's two essays on the Benedictines and Bishop Ullathorne's Sermon[2] on All Monks.[3]

There was an immediate practical issue to the reading of Cassian which, like his love for Fr. Baker, remained a life-long force: 'I took to manual labour of a serious and heavy kind, and spent a great deal of time digging, &c., in the garden. This I did on principle, for I thought manual labour of that kind was the right thing for monks.'[4] But the reading of Cassian had also another consequence:

[I became] much attracted to the study of early monachism; I also read the 'Contestation' between Mabillon and de Rancé on monastic studies; I also compiled a lengthy essay on the question 'Was St Augustine of Canterbury a Benedictine?'[5] which made me read the Bollandists and

---

[1] MS. A.
[2] A reader of this sermon of Ullathorne's (delivered in 1875) will not fail to notice at once the penetrating insight of that great man, and the extent of Abbot Butler's debt to him.   [3] MS. B.   [4] MS. A.
[5] The essay was printed in *The Downside Review* in 1884. It is a solid, able piece of work, especially in its section referring to St Gregory, and shows that even at the age of 21 Dom Butler, without anyone to teach him, had seized (or found innate in himself) the principles of criticism and accuracy.

Mabillon and many other writers on English ecclesiastical and monastic history. Thus I acquired a great liking for the historic studies and a desire that this side of Benedictine life should be revived among us.[1]

The work for the essay was done chiefly in the Lent of 1879. During Lent Vespers are recited before the mid-day meal, thus leaving a clearer evening in the monastic time-table. He thus describes his work:

I always look back on that Lent of 1879 as one of the happiest periods of my life. We used to have long afternoons from 2 till 7, and I used regularly to have a couple of hours digging by myself in the garden, then half an hour at Cassian, and the rest of the evening with Mabillon and the Bollandists.[2]

The absence of any reference to philosophy and theology during these years at Belmont is noteworthy and significant. In truth Dom Butler, though naturally passing through at least part of the regular course of studies at Belmont (for he returned to Downside early in 1880, and never thenceforward had time to devote much attention to his ecclesiastical studies), and acquiring a working knowledge of theology, never studied theology as he then and later studied ecclesiastical and monastic history. He was, in truth, no theologian, and was not disinclined to emphasize the fact. This want of full training is partly, doubtless, to be explained by the demand for men which drew many of the young monks away from Belmont to join the teaching staffs of the schools, leaving them to complete their theology as best they might in their own time, or in private classes. Partly also it was due to the circumstances of the time. Speculative, scholastic theology was then but slowly recovering from the all but complete extinction of the schools during the period of the French Revolution and the Napoleonic Wars. When, as the Catholic revival began to gain ground, theology began again to flourish, it was for long kept occupied with fighting a defensive war against liberalism, positivism and the so-called higher criticism in all its forms. Thus positive theology, Christian origins and scripture studies were, during the period of Dom Butler's youth and young manhood, absorbing the energies of the most distinguished Catholic scholars

[1] MS. B. [2] MS. A.

and teachers. The epoch-making recall to St Thomas, in the encyclicals of Leo XIII, was about to be heard, but the theologians and text-books then in vogue were either eclectic or at best represented only formalized scholasticism, which seemed, above all in England, to have no connexion with and shed no light upon the burning questions raised by Mill, Huxley, Darwin, and the agnostic, idealist or materialist schools in general. Dom Butler, so far as can be ascertained, had no familiarity whatever with the *Summa* in his early life, and till the very end his excursions into the realm of pure theology were tinged with a certain diffidence and agnosticism regarding any conclusion for which a definition of the Church could not be quoted.

In the downright, austere, secluded atmosphere of Belmont he had, then, found influences which directed and satisfied his soul and his mind. He himself tells us of his aspirations:

After my [simple] profession an ever growing hope took possession of my mind that I should spend all my life in the monastery....I renewed my study of Greek, with a view to making myself useful as a teacher...my pet hope was that I might become some day a professor at Belmont, and live on there like some of the canons.[1]

He returned to Downside on the eve of the Assumption, 14 August 1880, to find the community of St Gregory's at one of the turning points of its history. The prior, at that moment half way through his *quadriennium* of office, was the young Dom Aidan Gasquet, and he had at his command a very remarkable group of men.[2] Indeed, when the size of the resident community is taken into account, the number of those who in character or ability were far above the average becomes striking to a marked degree. Since it was the norm for all to pass from the jurisdiction of the superior of the house and to go upon the mission at or even before the age of thirty, for many years the resident community had been extremely slender in numbers. In the sixties the number had sometimes fallen below twelve; in 1869 there were fifteen choir monks and one lay brother; in 1875 only thirteen, including two disabled from age; at the moment of Dom Butler's return from Belmont there were sixteen

[1] MS. A.   [2] Dom Gasquet was 32 in 1880.

able-bodied monks and two disabled. Moreover, this small group of sixteen were all young; the prior (Gasquet) was thirty-two, the sub-prior forty, all the rest under twenty-nine. But among them were, besides the future cardinal, two future abbots of Downside—Edmund Ford and Cuthbert Butler—a future cathedral prior of Belmont (Clement Fowler), and men of such varied gifts as Wilfrid Corney, Gilbert Dolan, Aidan Howlett and Bede Cox, and within a few years other names of note—Wilfrid New, Aelred Kindersley, Edmund Kendal, Norbert Birt and Ethelbert Horne—were added to them, and Edward Bishop was often there. The years of Prior Gasquet's rule left a deep and permanent impression in the memory of all who lived through them.

It was a time of vigorous life in the community. There was a general sense that a strenuous effort must be made to work up the school; lay masters had just been imported; the young monks were sent in for the London University examinations, and Dom Edmund Ford, the prefect of studies, was carrying [out] a radical change in the whole system of studies and school management.[1]

Inspiring all was the prior. All his contemporaries bear witness to the charm and enthusiastic energy that were his at this time. Dom Cuthbert's characterization of him and others may be given, not as necessarily the final word, but as an almost contemporary view of a clear-sighted and remarkable man looking out upon his fellows who were equally remarkable.

A man in those days eaten up with activity, revelling in work, entering with enthusiasm into every phase and department of our life, Prior Gasquet was keenly alive to the shortcomings of the system then in vogue, and did not conceal his desire for great changes. He more than anyone else embodied the then spirit of St Gregory's in its many sided phases; he was the most representative Downside man of the day.[2]

Here is his judgement upon another great figure:

In connection with studies and school politics I was brought into close connection with Dom Ford, and from the first became one of his warmest supporters. I saw him to be a man of extraordinary ability, with clear

---

[1] MS. B.   [2] MS. A.

head, cool judgment, great determination, and much tact in dealing with men and pushing his own views....He was much distrusted in many quarters; but I became greatly attached to him and used warmly to defend him.[1]

The life at Downside at this period was one of considerable physical severity: 'Up to 1878 this handful of young men had carried on the school without external assistance, and lived a life of great hardship—without fires or heating of any kind in the cells, meat only once a day and only bread and butter and tea at breakfast and supper.'[2] But, as the writer goes on to add, this life was only in prospect for a few years. After that, it was normal to pass out upon the mission.

Such, then, was the life and such the circle of companions in which Brother Cuthbert found himself on his return to Downside in 1880. He remained there for fifteen years, teaching, reading, and in the last few years of the fifteen seriously studying with a view to a work of scholarship. But the real interest of his mind and the centre of his energies during this time lay in the long struggle to obtain a return to a more normal form of Benedictine government for the monasteries of the Congregation. It was this that called forth the resources of his mind, which led him through many anxieties and days of tension, and which has influenced, at least to some degree, the lives of all who have come to Downside since his day.

The history of those years has yet to be published. Abundant material exists and neither the theme nor the actors are unworthy of presentation. In a memoir of one recently taken from us no such task shall be attempted, but in order that the story of Abbot Butler's life may not lack all coherence, the briefest sketch must be given. As he himself wrote:

Just as during the Arian controversies we are told that the theological points in dispute used to form the staple of conversation in the squares and taverns of Constantinople and Alexandria, so in those days used the affairs of the Congregation and the proposed changes to form a frequent topic of public conversation in the calefactory at Downside.[3]

[1] MS. A. [2] MS. B. [3] MS. B.

In order, therefore, to have any understanding of the interests and controversies which occupied so much of his energies in the following ten years, it is essential to grasp, at least in outline, the constitution of the English Benedictine Congregation as it then was.

The English Benedictine Congregation as renewed in the early years of the seventeenth century naturally took its form of government and general polity from the Congregational type then dominant among Benedictines in the Latin countries, and especially from the Spanish Congregation, in which the vast majority of the English monks had made their profession; indeed, the early constitutions in regard to government were little more than an adaptation of those of the Congregation of Valladolid, and these features were handed on intact through the successive revisions of the [constitutions of the] English Congregation, up to and including that of 1888.[1]

The chief of these features was what Dom Butler goes on to characterize as the 'oligarchic' form of government. All power and jurisdiction lay radically with the general chapter, which met every four years. During the interval between chapters the supreme power was vested in the president and three councillors, called Definitores Regiminis; these latter were (as was the president) elected by chapter, and on appeals could sit in judgement on him. The superiors of the monasteries were likewise elected *ad quadriennium* by the chapter, and between chapters were subordinated to the president whom the constitutions defined to be 'omnium superiorum superior'.[2] The president was indeed forbidden to exercise any jurisdiction in the monasteries, but his power of translation was absolute, without appeal. He could move any monk from one monastery to another, or from monastery to mission, or vice versa, at discretion. Moreover, the chapter was not representative; by a system of co-optation every chapter had been in one way or another constituted by the previous chapter; and the only occasion for a free election in the monasteries was when a house superior died or resigned during the *quadriennium*. Instead, therefore, of the houses being each a unit, loosely knit into a Congregation, as was in

---

[1] MS. B.

[2] Obedience at profession was vowed not to the prior of the monastery, but to the president.

the main the case in England before the Reformation and is again the case today, the Congregation, governed by chapter and president, was the unit, and the houses mere component parts.

This oligarchical form of government had been at one time not uncommon among Benedictines, and although under any circumstances it was a departure from the traditional Benedictine patriarchal government it had not, in the Latin countries of its origin, affected the monastic character of the houses concerned. The wholesale destruction of the religious life consequent upon the French Revolution and the Napoleonic wars had however brought to an end all such Congregations save the English, and the nineteenth-century revivals had for the most part followed more traditional lines. But there was a characteristic of the English Congregation which profoundly altered the aspect of all exercise of authority.

At the restoration of the Congregation one of the objects proposed was apostolic work upon the English mission, and every monk at profession bound himself by oath to undertake and desist from this work at the command of the president. As, from its origin until the French Revolution, the Congregation possessed no monastery in England, it was necessary for some superior on the spot to be responsible for the missioners, and the expedient, unique in Benedictine government, had been adopted of providing two provincials in England (of Canterbury and York, south and north) under whose jurisdiction the monks passed upon leaving their monastery for the mission. As the missions pertained to the Congregation in common, not to the houses in particular, the monks upon the mission had little more than a connexion of origin with their monasteries; the mission-field was filled by the president at the request of the provincials from the material accumulating in the monasteries, and, whatever was the case in the early days of the Congregation, in the nineteenth century a monk rarely returned from the mission save in the isolated case of an invalid. The state of things in the second half of the nineteenth century may be given in Abbot Butler's own words:

In the monasteries lived twelve or fifteen quite young men...the call came to most within a few years of ordination to go out of the monastery, and to pass from the jurisdiction of the prior to that of the provincial, and to spend their lives doing the work of the secular clergy on the mission and under conditions undistinguishable from those of other [*sic*] secular clergy; sometimes a quite old man came back to die in his monastery, but it was the exception: in most cases when a man went on the mission...he had finished for life with the externals of the monastic life...the exceptions were so few as to be negligible....In 1880 the priors of B[elmont] and D[ouai] were the only men of fifty in the whole Congregation who had lived in the monastery uninterruptedly; and those of forty could be counted on the fingers of one hand.[1]

Such a state of affairs had had its inevitable influence on the composition of the general chapter:

Out of some thirty chapter men only the four priors, and sometimes one or two old men who had retired from the mission emeriti, were conventuals, the rest were missioners. The president and Definitors of the Regimen all lived on the mission....The recognised ideal was that after a few years of teaching in the school...everyone, soon after thirty, should go on the mission.[2]

And upon the composition of the monastic communities:

Under the combination of the quadriennial system [of appointment of superiors] and the provincial system it was impossible that the communities could ever develop or grow either in numbers or in age. A new prior as a rule, quite naturally, desired to appoint his own sub-prior and procurator and school officials, and there was a natural tendency for those older than the prior to pass out to the mission.[3]

And in consequence there was no possibility of any other work being accomplished save the educational work in the schools and the pastoral work of the mission. Higher studies, or literary work of any description, were non-existent and had been non-existent in the Congregation since the days of Weldon. Such was the aspect of things when Brother Cuthbert was passing through his first years after profession.

Of his frame of mind on leaving Belmont he wrote after ten years:

I had got hold of the following principles which I have never lost:—
  1. Fr. Baker's view of the mission.
  2. The truth that we are contemplatives.

[1] MS. B.   [2] MS. B.   [3] MS. B.

3. A love of an early type of monasticism.
4. A desire for better observance.
5. An interest in monastic studies.
6. A belief that the Congregation was in a 'transitional stage'. As yet...I acquiesced without question in the provincial system, the common noviciate and tyrocinium, the quadriennial term of office and the centralised modern [i.e. post-Renaissance] Congregational form of government.[1]

Shortly after his return from Belmont Brother Cuthbert attended the community retreat, preached that year by Mgr. Weld, an old Downside boy. A man of real piety, impulsive and perhaps somewhat emotional, he was a frequent visitor at Downside, and made no secret of his hopes that the monastic, conventual life might be greatly developed. To these views he gave public pronouncement during this retreat; Dom Butler speaks of one conference in particular, where his words 'found a welcome echo in my heart and in the hearts of others that heard them. But this I believe was the first time [such views] had been formally and publicly uttered, and so that night of Mgr. Weld's retreat deserves to be marked as an epoch.'[2]

In all the years of stress that were to follow the practical leader of the young community was Dom Edmund Ford, for Prior Gasquet retired, to all appearances broken in health and spirits, in 1885. As those who knew him well remember, he was a born leader of men who could, in a way never granted to Abbot Butler, charm and powerfully attract hearts and minds. *Homo inter homines*, he never repelled by any suspicion of the doctrinaire, and he had something, in those years, of the gaiety which takes reverses with a laugh and welcomes difficulties in an earnest matter as other men might welcome them in a game. His clear, realist mind worked most happily with men and events; he was an excellent judge of character and of situation. That he and Dom Cuthbert had for each other a real affection and respect goes without saying. In later years Abbot Ford assumed it as natural that Dom Butler would succeed him in office, and the latter, when abbot, constantly appointed his predecessor to a seat in his council, and more than once travelled up to Ealing for

---

[1] MS. A. [2] MS. A.

the express purpose of taking his advice before an important decision. At the time of Abbot Ford's death, indeed, Abbot Butler went so far as to declare that this friendship 'was during just fifty years the closest and fastest friendship' of his monastic life.[1] This was, no doubt, the pardonable exaggeration of one writing with the memories of the past in the presence of death. The two men were never close personal friends in the most intimate sense of the word, nor did the younger stand wholly in the relation of follower to the other's leadership. For friendship, indeed, Dom Butler had no genius; and Dom Edmund Ford, for his part, could most readily influence those much younger than himself. The closest alliance between the two came some years after Brother Cuthbert's return from Belmont.

Thus if we would follow the development of his mind it is not to Dom Edmund Ford that we must look.

The one from whom I got most at this time was Dom Dolan. He was the first of us to get hold of sound principles on Benedictine life and government. He was the only one among us who had read monastic history or had visited monasteries of other Congregations. He was the first among us to cultivate historical and archaeological tastes, and studies of the type identified with the Benedictine name....Dom Dolan thus had ideas very much in advance of the rest of us, and he lost no opportunity of spreading the light.[2]

From him Dom Cuthbert acknowledges that he first received the idea that the natural place for a Benedictine noviciate is the house of profession, and that the quadriennial system or even a longer period of office could only be regarded as in some sense a departure from Benedictine tradition. 'These and similar statements staggered and even shocked me at first; but the seed thus broadcast struck root, and by the end of the year [1880–81] I came to see that our polity was unique [and that] Dom Dolan's principles were right.'[3]

The two others with whom he came into most intimate contact at this time were Dom Wilfrid Corney and Dom Ildephonsus Campbell—the former, by his gentle, lovable character and (we may add) by his holiness of life cannot but have appealed to Dom Cuthbert;

---

[1] In the memoir in *DR*, vol. XLIX (1931), p. 21.
[2] MS. A.   [3] MS. A.

the latter, though he dropped early out of his life, seems to have been more nearly a personal friend than any other contemporary.

An event of great importance in the growth of his mind may be given in his own words:

> During the Lent of 1882...took place the community retreat at Downside, given by Dom Laurence Shepherd, for many years the chaplain at Stanbrook, and probably at the time the most forward man in the Congregation in the way of monastic policy....As a young monk he and Fr. Bury had been sent to Italy, the former to study asceticism and monasticism in the Italian monasteries, the latter to study theology....Fr. Shepherd visited Solesmes in the early days and became a close friend of Dom Guéranger, and for many years he spent his summer holiday at Solesmes and became saturated through and through with Dom Guéranger's spirit and views on the monastic life. This was what he set before us at the retreat. Especially did he emphasize the fine doctrine of the *Préface Générale* to the *Année Liturgique*, in my judgment by far the best piece of all Guéranger's writings I have ever read; according to this teaching he urged upon us the view that the choral celebration of the office is not only our great and first corporate duty and public act of divine worship as a Benedictine community—this of course we held—but also as individual monks it is our chief means of personal sanctification and of progress in the spiritual life.[1]

This served to correct or supplement for Dom Cuthbert and some others of the audience the emphasis which is laid on private prayer in *Sancta Sophia*, and the apparent minimizing of the value of the divine office as prayer.

> Another point insisted on by Fr. Shepherd was the place held in Benedictine life by higher ecclesiastical studies—the Bible, the liturgy, the Fathers, the theologians, the canonists, the councils, the commentators, the church historians—'If I went round your cells', he said, 'and found on the table of one a volume of your own St Gregory, and on another Cassian, on another a volume of the Bollandists, or of Cornelius a Lapide or Thomassinus, and so on, I should say that here is a community which, in spite of the busy life it leads, has its heart steadfastly fixed on its Benedictine life.' After more than twenty years [1882–1905] I remember

---

[1] MS. B.

279

the words well, for this making of ecclesiastical studies an integral part of Benedictine life not only was altogether congenial to my own bent, but

helped once again to supplement and correct what he had always felt to be lacking or distorted in the picture drawn in *Sancta Sophia*. 'The retreat made a great impression: nearly all were pleased... I must say, for myself, that I learned more of what has proved to me permanent theory of Benedictine life from Fr. Shepherd in this retreat than from anyone else in all my life.'[1] This is an avowal quite without parallel in Abbot Butler's autobiographical notes or conversations. Such a statement, and the living witness of Stanbrook, are testimony enough to the work and life of one who is only a name—if so much—to those of today.[2]

During that summer of 1882 took place the opening of the new church—that is, the transept (if so it can be called) of the present abbey church. The preacher and chief guest was Bishop Ullathorne, and both he and the diocesan, Bishop Clifford, spoke of the future that lay before St Gregory's.

That autumn we moved into the new church. It had been common talk for some time before that that event would mark a new departure in the way of increased solemnity in the celebration of the liturgy, and now the wishes of the community were consulted as to whether Vespers should be sung daily.[3]

In the event, it was decided to sing Vespers only on Doubles of the Second Class.

In this sketch of the growth of Dom Cuthbert's mind we have anticipated a little; we must now resume the story of external events.

All unknown to him, and indeed even to the highest superiors of the Congregation, forces quite outside the monastic body were at work making for a change. As early as 1870 Propaganda had proposed to revise the constitutions of the English Benedictines, and had called upon Bishop Ullathorne, then in Rome for the Vatican

---

[1] MS. B.

[2] Dom James Laurence Shepherd (1826–85), educated at Ampleforth and professed there in 1844, was chaplain at Stanbrook 1863–85. He was the grand-nephew of two abbesses of the Community of Our Lady of Consolation. He translated the *Année Liturgique*.   [3] MS. B.

Council, to express his views on the subject. This he did, and a similar request was made of Bishop Brown of Newport. For a time there was even a question of either Ullathorne or Brown acting as Apostolic Visitor. The whole matter, however, after dragging on for several years, was held up by the controversy in which the bishops of England, under the leadership of Cardinal Manning, were involved with the regulars, and in particular with the Benedictines and Jesuits. Nevertheless, shortly before the bull *Romanos Pontifices* put an end to this dispute, Manning, Ullathorne and Clifford (the diocesan of Downside) were working in Rome to bring about a Visitation of the Congregation. Of all this Brother Cuthbert and the others at Downside were at the time, and for many years after, unaware.[1]

Thus two almost unconnected tendencies of thought and action were converging upon the superiors of the Congregation during the first years of Brother Cuthbert's monastic life. There was the movement, largely directed by those outside, towards an examination and rejuvenation of their way of life and government; there was the spontaneous spiritual and intellectual movement within, expressing itself in various ways, of which Dom Laurence Shepherd, the disciple of Guéranger, was one representative, and the group at Belmont, rejoicing in the newly discovered *Sancta Sophia*, another.[2] The course of events may be briefly narrated. In the summer of 1881 Leo XIII appointed Fr. Krug, the claustral prior of Monte Cassino, Apostolic Visitor of the Congregation. So unexpected was the final decision in Rome that all concerned received their first notification in a telegram which appeared in *The Tablet*. At Downside the news was a complete surprise. Dom Edmund Ford, meeting Brother Cuthbert on the turret stairs of the monastery on the morning of Saturday, 11 June 1881, remarked: 'So a Visitor is

[1] Abbot Butler was apparently unaware that any agency except that of Bishop Clifford and Mgr. Weld had been at work as late as 1905, when the second recension of his *Recollections* was written. An account of Ullathorne's share will be found in the *Life*, vol. II, pp. 207–13.

[2] It is not suggested that these were the absolutely original sowers of seed; there had been others before. Abbot Butler mentions Prior Barber (prior 1818–30), and DD. Hodgson, Blount, A. Bulbeck, B. Bulbeck, Guy, de Paiva and G. Kendal. Of these D. Benedict Blount had been novice-master at Downside 1851–54, and DD. B. Bulbeck, Guy and Bede Vaughan had passed through his hands.

coming.' 'I did not understand the remark, and said in a puzzled way: "Who? Anybody special?"'[1]

Fr. Krug in due time arrived at Downside. We need not concern ourselves with the details of his stay in England, but it is interesting to read the draft of the paper which the young Brother Cuthbert (he was just twenty-three) handed in to the Visitor and discussed with him. It was in essentials, he tells us, identical in sentiment with the views and desires of several of his contemporaries, including of course Dom Edmund Ford:

I advocated:

1. That a definition of our monastic and contemplative character should be given; that it should be made clear that the monasteries exist for their own sake and are not seminaries for the missions or staffs of professors for the schools.

2. That missions and missioners should be put under the monastic superiors.

3. That the monasteries should be erected into abbeys, and the abbots eventually chosen for life.

4. That as soon as the monasteries were ready for it, they should each have their own noviciate.

5. That general chapter should be reformed, so as to lessen the missionary and strengthen the house element.

6. That the individual monks should be given some kind of fixity of tenure in the monastery; so that they might look forward, during good behaviour, to remaining in their monastery if they felt that such was their vocation.

7. The reorganization of the studies.

8. An improvement in the discipline in the monasteries.

9. The appointment of a rector to work the school.[2]

10. A change in the vacation system.[3]

As soon as Fr. Krug left England there 'was circulated throughout the Congregation, high and low, the first of a series of pamphlets that formed for some months a prominent and lively episode in the

[1] MS. A.

[2] At this period the prior filled, to a certain extent, the position of Headmaster, though he did not teach or organize in the school. Under him a Prefect of Studies and a Prefect of Discipline (at the moment Doms Ford and Fowler) exercised ill-defined powers, neither subordinated to the other.

[3] MS. A.

course of events'.[1] Dom Benedict Snow, after Fr. Bury the most stalwart champion of the *status quo*, led off. His pamphlet was translated into Italian, and was followed by another in Italian by Fr. Bury, entitled *Funeste Consequenze* (sc. of any change in the polity of the Congregation), which went so far as to declare 'that the proposed changes would do greater injury to the English Benedictines than had been [done] by Henry VIII or the French Revolution'.[2] Replies to these naturally followed, including an ill-judged attempt on the part of Mgr. Weld to give expression to the views of his friends at Downside by publishing (against their wishes) a strongly worded pamphlet in Italian entitled *La loro voce*, and a more temperate one written by Dom Elphege Cody, a man of great gifts and originally a Gregorian, who became affiliated to Fort Augustus. It was in the midst of this pamphlet warfare that the retreat, preached by Dom Laurence Shepherd, took place as mentioned above. Meanwhile instructions came from Rome that the general chapter of 1882 was to be postponed; thus Prior Gasquet remained in office beyond his *quadriennium*.

The Roman decision, when it came, reflected the strong conflict of opinion which had made itself felt. The rescript *Cliftoniensis* of 1883 confirmed in effect—and especially as it was interpreted—the *status quo*. It was decreed that the clauses of the bull *Plantata* of 1633 which had set up the provinces and the machinery of government should not be derogated, and that Belmont should remain the common noviciate and tyrocinium. The composition of general chapter was altered slightly, and a revision of the constitutions was ordered, though with the proviso, *salva indole*, that their general character should remain unchanged. One decree, that the monks should abstain from gambling ('a ludis aleatoribus sc abstineant'), 'created much wonderment, and what it aimed at never transpired, whether it referred to card-playing, or to risky speculations in stock-jobbing'.

This pronouncement of Rome was not unnaturally taken as a victory for those of conservative views. The protagonist in the

[1] MSS. A and B.
[2] MS. B. All further quotations come from this MS. unless otherwise noted.

maintenance of the *status quo* had been Dom Austin Bury,[1] then Provincial of York, 'a man of extraordinary ability and learning, of strong will and great determination of character'.[2] Shortly after the arrival of the Rescript he

started on a lecturing tour round the missions of the North Province exposing his views on the Rescript, and the whole situation. Prior Gasquet invited him to come and give it at Downside, and to the surprise of all he accepted the invitation. The purport of the lecture was to apply to our life the principles on the religious state laid down by St Thomas.

Dom Butler adds that 'the lecture did not impress me much'. The lecturer himself, however, did; and it may be of interest to quote a description of Abbot Bury as he appeared at this time:

I was a young man reading the classics in those days, and Fr. Bury was a very good Greek scholar with a wonderful memory; he could recite Homer by the yard, also the Greek tragedies. He had a fine massive countenance and splendid eyes, and to hear him declaiming with enthusiasm and gesture fine pieces of Homer and Aeschylus was very inspiring. We became quite friends and I saw a lot of him. He told me how when a young man in the Italian monasteries he had studied St Thomas *De Ente et Essentia* through the night, shivering with cold and with only a dip candle. . . . He told me that of all the things he had done in his life what he had enjoyed most was teaching theology at Ampleforth. . . . I take it he was the ablest theologian and metaphysician the Congregation has produced in modern times.

For a brief space at the end of 1883 attention was diverted from constitutional issues by an energetic attempt, directed by Dom Edmund Ford with the approval of Prior Gasquet and the support of Dom Butler and others, to improve beyond recognition the studies of the Congregation. The matter came before general chapter, where the proposals received sympathetic attention, but no radical changes were made; the movement is of interest to us only as directing Dom Butler's attention to educational questions, which

[1] Dom Austin Bury (1827–1904), a Laurentian, who had studied theology in Italy as a young monk. He was Provincial of York 1878–83; in the latter year he was given the dignity of Abbot *sine titulo*.
[2] MS. A.

issued in a series of articles in *The Downside Review*. Another field of interest was opened by Dom Edmund Ford. This was:

A great scheme for the study of Benedictine traditions and history in England....It was divided into periods and [the] subject-matter was carefully mapped out under heads, and a list of all the documents of period I (570–850) was drawn out by the aid of Mr Edmund Bishop.... I read nearly all the documents proposed.

Again and again, when reading of this epoch at Downside, one is struck with admiration at the variety of intellectual life displayed. Doubtless the frequent presence of Edmund Bishop, mature but still comparatively youthful, was of great influence, but when we recollect that in the ten years from 1878 to 1888—the years of the keenest controversy on the politics of the Congregation—not only did the school recover from an epoch of stagnation, not only did the buildings grow, but both Gasquet and Butler laid, in different ways, the foundation of their literary achievement, *The Downside Review* was founded, and a serious study of the early history of the Congregation undertaken for the first time. 'Those were great days', Abbot Butler exclaimed within a few weeks of his death, and no historian of St Gregory's will be forward to dispute his verdict.

For the moment however, in 1885, the future did not seem bright to those who wished for new things at Downside. The Rescript *Cliftoniensis* of 1883 had seemed to consolidate the *ancien régime*. The chapter at the end of that year had been a trying experience for Prior Gasquet, who was held responsible for the activities in his community, and although reappointed in office his health and spirits seriously declined. Dom Gilbert Dolan had passed to the mission; Dom Edmund Ford had gone to Rome to complete his theological studies; his return to the house seemed problematic.

Events, however, took a sudden turn of great importance. In the summer of 1885 Prior Gasquet's health became seriously affected, and medical advice insisted on his relinquishing office. He was not yet forty years of age, but for him it seemed an end, and a prophecy of his future career would have seemed unbelievable. His withdrawal during the *quadriennium* gave a free election, and the almost unanimous voice of the young community chose Dom Edmund Ford. Immediately after his election he directed Dom Cuthbert's attention once again to a piece of work he had begun before and then cast aside—a research into the early documents of the Congregation with a view to discovering the opinions as to its nature and end held by the early superiors and chapters. Meanwhile, Prior Ford and others, largely because they were impelled by a series of practical problems connected with the future of Downside, were using every effort to attain, within the limits laid down by *Cliftoniensis*, some degree of autonomy for the monasteries and possibility of residence within them for the individual monks. Writing almost twenty years later, Dom Butler thus summed up these objects:

1. The assertion of the principle that the Congregation is not essentially missionary, but in the full sense a normal Benedictine Congregation, like any others; which has received a commission to carry out missionary work and for that purpose is empowered to dispense individual monks from the obligations of claustral life.

2. The securing of the fundamental Benedictine conception that a monk may spend his life in his monastery and an enlarging of the ideas current as to the kinds of work suitable for our own monks, so that biblical and historical studies and the other traditional forms of Benedictine work should be recognized as being lawful and suitable objects of the life work of any of our monks suited for it [*sic*].

3. The raising of the monasteries from the abject estate in which they lay, and the winning for them that power of controlling their own destinies, and that autonomy which is the birthright of a Benedictine monastery, that they might take their due place in the Order and in English Catholic life.

Despite his full time-table of work in the school, Dom Cuthbert proceeded eagerly with his task of research in congregational records. It took him eighteen months of work in spare hours, but his discoveries exceeded his expectations: the resulting pamphlet, *Notes on the Origin and Early Development of the Restored English Benedictine Congregation*, privately printed and circulated, appeared in May 1887. Dom Bernard Murphy, sometime Prior of Downside and now a chapter man in residence there, contributed an able preface. This tractate produced a considerable impression among all shades of opinion; the appeal to the past was now recognized as at best a double-edged weapon, for the movement of which Prior Ford was leader was now (if centuries and not decades were to be counted) seen to be conservative, not revolutionary in tendency.

This serious and weighty appeal to the past was shortly after followed by a pamphlet setting forth the normal constitution of a Benedictine Congregation as expounded in a certain bull *Behemoth*, unearthed by Prior Ford. Shortly afterwards Dom Butler, in the spring of 1888, was elected a member of the house council.

The historical and constitutional light thrown by the *Notes* and *Behemoth* emboldened those who desired changes to put forward once again thorough-going political reforms, such as the abolition of the 'quadriennial system' and the institution of house elections for superiors. Dom Wilfrid Corney, who was in Rome as economo of the new Benedictine College of Sant'Anselmo (not yet on the Aventine), assisted in making these views known in influential quarters. But any hopes of radical change were to all appearances shattered once and for all by the long delayed approval of the revised constitutions. These were promulgated at the chapter of July, 1888, and contained no changes of any moment in the system of government of the Congregation: in the same chapter Dom Clement Fowler was appointed prior of St Gregory's in place of Dom Edmund Ford. These two events, the one of constitutional, the other of practical significance, implied once more the maintenance of the *status quo*, and a group at Downside, among whom was Dom Butler, resolved upon an appeal to the Holy See to send Mgr. Persico, who at that moment had just completed his historic mission as Apostolic Delegate to Ireland, as Visitor to Downside. Technically, the appeal rested on a small irregularity in the composition of the body of electors at the recent chapter; actually, of course, the intention was to bring the whole question of Congregational government once more to the notice of Rome. Monsignor Persico duly came as Visitor, and after a lapse of some months, at the beginning of November, the Congregation of Bishops and Regulars gave its decision, approving all the acts of the chapter, including the elections.

To all appearances this ended the controversy, and for some weeks those who had for the past years set all their hopes upon obtaining for Downside the full status of an autonomous monastic house, holding out to its members the prospect of living their lives under conditions of monastic observance, felt that they must look elsewhere, even, if necessary, outside the Congregation, for their fulfilment. Meanwhile, Dom Edmund Ford left the house, as all thought in permanence, and Dom Clement Fowler was installed as prior towards the end of December, 1888. Of him Abbot Butler wrote almost twenty years later:

The [new] prior had been prefect [of discipline] in the school for several years...and he was deservedly most popular and most beloved by the boys...not even then, and much less later, was there any break in the cordial personal relations of mutual respect and esteem between Prior Fowler and myself, or in the personal kindness and consideration which I have uniformly through life experienced at his hands.[1]

To those, however, who loved and admired Dom Edmund Ford, and who had regarded him as the one to lead Downside for many years to come, the change of superior, and the traditional celebrations with which it was accompanied, were a trying experience; Abbot Butler, indeed, characterized it as 'the worst day I have ever gone through'. Shortly before the arrival of Prior Fowler occurred an incident, trivial in the extreme, yet exquisitely opportune:

Dom Fowler had been prefect of the boys, and because of his thin wiry build, he was familiarly called 'Bones' by them.

It so happened that the chapter of scripture that had to be read at dinner shortly before his arrival was Ezechiel's prophecy about the resurrection of the dry bones, and the whole community gave vent to their amusement.

The period of extreme depression did not, however, last long. The president elected at the chapter of 1888 was the Edmundian Dom Augustine O'Neill, formerly subprior of Douai, later Dom Cuthbert's junior master at Belmont and afterwards bishop of Port Maurice. He is referred to in the autobiographical notes so often quoted in these pages as 'my guide, philosopher and friend' and 'an

[1] MS. B.

intimate friend', and even if such expressions must not be pressed, there is no question but that he was acquainted with, and largely in sympathy with, the ideals which Prior Ford and Dom Butler and others had so much at heart. As president, he had considered it his duty to obtain full ratification for the acts of chapter, but when he found that high Roman authority regarded with a certain dissatisfaction the conservative revision of the constitutions, he was prepared to take all steps necessary to meet their wishes, and wrote in this sense to all officials of the Congregation. An immediate practical result was to lessen the sense of tension at Downside, and when, shortly after Christmas 1888, Prior Fowler proceeded to appoint his officials, he continued Dom Cuthbert in the responsible position of Prefect of Studies in the school, which office he held till the autumn of 1892.[1] It must be said that his gifts were not such as to make him a conspicuous success in the position. He lacked in great part the capacity of organization and maintenance of discipline, and lacked altogether that rapid, summary grasp of a situation, just in general if often unjust in detail, which is necessary in one who is to deal immediately and successfully with boys. Conceivably he could have filled the more aloof position of headmaster as it has in the past been conceived at some public schools; he was less fitted for the more intimate, rough and ready work required of him at Downside in 1888.

One who was a boy in the school at the time writes:

What I could see was a tall man, somewhat ungainly in his carriage and prematurely bald, but with a shapely head and good features—decidedly a fine-looking man, but not so as to strike one at first sight (in the way that Prior Ford did) as being positively handsome. In 1888 he was barely thirty years of age, yet I never seem to have thought of him as a young man. As to the man himself, I can realise now that some of my early impressions were quite beside the mark; but others—not of course consciously formulated at the time, but still impressions that have remained— were, I think, on the whole true. He was not, I should now say, one who could discern subtle differences of character, but was content to class boys and others under large categories, such as intelligent and stupid, or

[1] For some time previous to December 1888 he had been both Prefect of Studies and First Prefect (of discipline).

reasonable and, to use his own word, 'unconscionable'. His interest also in the boys he had to deal with seemed to be engaged more with their mental capabilities than with themselves as individuals. Nor had he the qualities which go to make a disciplinarian. His natural downrightness and simplicity hindered him from understanding, and a certain impulsiveness and lack of *sang-froid* prevented him from dealing effectively with the impish genius that some boys have—often without malice or hostility—for detecting and penetrating weak points in the armour of authority. I feel sure that he had no enemies, but there were some who entertained themselves with trying to 'draw' him, and a good many more who found amusement in looking on and discussing the results. He had, moreover, and this throughout his life, certain mannerisms and fixed methodical habits which lent themselves to parody and were a temptation to mimics. But to those who really knew him these things appeared as the merest accidentals, and served only as foils to throw the real quality of the man into stronger relief.

To complete the picture we may perhaps be allowed to transcribe Dom Butler's account of an incident in the following summer:

Shortly after the chapter [of 1889] an amusing incident occurred. It was during the summer vacation, and those of the young Downside party had not had a reunion since the break-up at Christmas. We wanted to hear from Dom Bernard Murphy what had happened at chapter, and to talk over the situation, and the hopes and prospects...and above all to see one another again. Dom Gilbert Dolan was in command at St Alban's, Warrington, the head priest being on his vacation; Dom Bernard Murphy was on his way to Whitehaven; I was returning from Ireland; Dom Ildephonsus Campbell came down from Cleator....So we arranged to congregate at Warrington....It was a very pleasant meeting, and we talked much of old times, and were in very good spirits over the change in our prospects. At dinner Dom Gilbert produced champagne from the cellars, and while the merriment was at its height, it so chanced that the head priest, Dom A[rthur Richard] O'H[are], found himself at Warrington and thought he would lunch at home. The door opened and he entered. It was a tableau. It was hard to say whether he or we were the more taken aback...and the good story soon circulated in all directions, how the reformers had been surprised in secret conclave, drinking champagne.

Before following the career that opened to him in a wider sphere we must briefly indicate the further and final stages of the controversy with which he had become so identified. With the president's declaration of December 1888 a new phase in the constitutional movement began, in which all the priors and many others throughout the Congregation worked towards the abolition of the provincial system and the establishment of house autonomy. This, however, though an integral and essential part—or rather basis—of the programme of Dom Ford and those with him, was chiefly important in their eyes as making possible the further restoration of permanent residence in claustral life as a normal, or at least probable, consequence of monastic profession.

The outcome of the activities of President O'Neill was the bull *Religiosus Ordo* of 12 November 1890. This was a highly important document; indeed, the first clear pronouncement that Rome had made. It declared the essentially 'monastic' character of the Congregation—that is, as against the extreme view that held the working of the English mission to be its *raison d'être*—and declared that apostolic, educational and literary work came equally within its scope. The provinces were abolished and the monks working on the missions put under the jurisdiction of the priors of their houses of origin. A commission was to be set up to divide the missions and (within three years) to revise the constitutions once again. For the latter purpose the president erected a number of subcommittees to prepare reports; on one of these, that appointed to consider the question of studies, Dom Cuthbert served, and spent some pleasant days at Ampleforth in 1891 on its business: 'We drew up a programme which would have made the studies in the English congregation probably quite the best in the Order.'[1] He adds: 'But nothing came of the subcommittees', although all members of the Congregation had been invited to communicate their views on any or every subject to any or every subcommittee, in compliance with which invitation 'I myself sent in something to each subcommittee'.[2] And in the event the papal commission itself, after dividing the missions, lapsed, without proceeding to revise the constitutions, in

[1] MS. B.
[2] Some of his proposals were indeed drastic and austere in the extreme; thus, e.g., he advocated a great deal of fasting, on the lines of some other Benedictine Congregations, etc.

the latter months of 1891. Before it lapsed, and in an attempt to give effect to suggestions, rather than commands, of *Religiosus Ordo*, Dom Cuthbert

drew up a series of proposals...concerned with the celebration of the Divine Office; the chief thing was that Vespers should be sung every day; besides this it was proposed to sing Tierce on feast days and Sundays, and Lauds on some of the great festivals. A daily [sung] Missa Conventualis was held out as something that might hereafter be aimed at when the Communities increased in number.

Owing to the lapse of the commission nothing ever came of these proposals, though the seed remained, to fructify during Abbot Butler's abbacy twenty years later, but criticisms at the time led him to examine the observance at St Gregory's, Douai, in the first half of the seventeenth century, and to print the results of his research in an article entitled 'Daily Life at old St Gregory's' in *The Downside Review* of March 1892.

Meanwhile Rome, in answer to applications from various quarters, by a Rescript in the spring of 1892 tacitly abrogated the commission and decreed the convocation of an extraordinary general chapter to decide on the method of revision of the constitutions and elect three commissioners. The chapter was duly held; its composition was conservative, not to say reactionary, and its decision was to confine the revision of the constitutions to a bare excision of those passages which dealt with the provincial system, which had been explicitly abrogated by *Religiosus Ordo*. The three commissioners chosen naturally reflected the sense of the majority; President O'Neill was not among them. These events produced a most painful impression on Dom Cuthbert. There now seemed nothing more to hope for or to wait for in the Congregation: 'When the results of the chapter were published, I thought the thing over carefully, and then... I wrote to President O'Neill to ask his permission to initiate the necessary steps for translation to Fort Augustus.'

The president refused to entertain such a proposal. Rome, he wrote, had not yet finally spoken, and he would continue to do all in his power to give effect to what he knew to be the wishes of the Holy See; he therefore refused to send in to Rome the constitutions as revised by the three commissioners. This produced a deadlock. Meanwhile the state of affairs at Downside underwent a great change. Prior Fowler had been appointed by general chapter of 1888 as a representative of the old Congregational system; and his period of office had been extended *sine die* by Rome, pending a final settlement. The old system having been largely modified by *Religiosus Ordo*, he now found himself in a situation which neither he, nor those who appointed him in 1888, had ever anticipated; he was superior for an indefinite period of a community which now included all the monks working on the missions and embraced a wide variety of responsibilities and interests. Moreover he was well aware that a large number, if not the majority, of his subjects looked, and had for many years looked, to Dom Edmund Ford, still in exile at Beccles, as their natural leader, not only in the field of monastic polity, but in every department of practical and intellectual expansion. Under these circumstances Prior Fowler, with the good sense and personal self-effacement which had always distinguished him, resigned his office, and at an election in July, 1894, Dom Edmund Ford became prior.[1]

But in congregational politics the end was not yet. Before the matter of the constitutions could be settled President O'Neill was appointed bishop of Port Louis in the Mauritius (June 1895) and was automatically succeeded by Abbot O'Gorman, who had previously as president been responsible for the proceedings of the reactionary chapter of 1888. The Holy See thereupon, to end the deadlock, commissioned the recently appointed Abbot Primate (Abbot de Hemptinne) to visit the English Congregation.

We were again invited, for the fifth or sixth time, to put our views on paper, so once again I wrote out my ideas and wishes on all the questions in controversy: I look back with complacency on the fact that on such occasions I never spared myself any trouble but wrote out at great length all I had to say.

---

[1] This election was conducted *per modum compromissi*, and Dom Cuthbert was one of the 12 electors chosen. The election was of the greatest importance for the future of St Gregory's; it was protracted and the tension was great; he describes it as 'the most trying ordeal I have ever gone through'.

Even then there was a delay before the Primate's report went in and another before the papal document giving a decision and appointing a commission to produce new constitutions was signed. At last, on 29 June 1899, the bull *Diu quidem* was promulgated, which, among its other provisions, raised the three existing houses to the rank of abbeys. Dom Aidan Gasquet was named president of the commission, and speedily performed his work. The constitutions were presented to the pope on 1 July 1900, and promulgated four days later; Dom Gasquet had already been elected president *ad interim*; at the first general chapter under the new constitutions he was elected first abbot president, and in the autumn of 1900 Prior Ford was elected first abbot of Downside. Thus with the summer of 1900 the movement in which Dom Cuthbert's interests and energies had been so deeply engaged came to a conclusion with the triumph of many at least of the principles for which he had fought. Of the significance of *Diu quidem* he writes:

The full autonomy of the houses has been won; the communities have the management of their own affairs in their own hands, the president's powers of interference (out of Visitation) being reduced almost to a vanishing point; the community elects its own abbot; and the abbot has the control of the monks, to employ them all on whatever works are considered for the good of the house. Thus the houses have become the predominant factors in the Congregation, and thanks to the decentralization of authority, the old bonds are so far untied that each house is, within broad limits, free to go its own way and work out its own destinies along its own lines.

This brief narrative, treating as it does of

> old, unhappy, far-off things,
> and battles long ago,

has a twofold appropriateness in an account of the life of Abbot Butler. In the first place, it is necessary in order to assess his importance in the history of Downside. All who lived through that period of stress, or who have studied it from afar, will readily admit that had the struggle not been waged—or had it proved unsuccessful—the Downside that we have known in the last thirty years could never have been.[1] Neither community nor school could have attained the size which they have maintained for a quarter of a century [1934]; neither liturgy nor literary work of any kind could have flourished as they have; and the dependent centres of activity—Ealing, Worth, Benet House—could not have been thought of. Few Gregorians will deny that the great changes of the last half-century have been in the main due to four great men—Gasquet, Ford, Butler and Ramsay; history must decide to which of the four Downside owes most, but in the matter we have just been considering there is little doubt that the greatest debt is due to Edmund Ford, and, after him, to Cuthbert Butler.

But the twenty years of controversy have another significance in Dom Butler's life. They forced him, from the noviciate upwards, to study the records, near and remote, of monastic history and polity, to bring the existent state of things to trial at the bar of history, and to endeavour to restore the traditional in place of an accidental development. It was this harsh preparation, added to his later experience as superior, that gave to his writings their reality, their practical judgement, and that helped to fit him to pronounce with authority on the most vital questions of Benedictine life.

The amount of time and energy absorbed by these controversies was doubtless very large; we must not, however, allow ourselves to obtain a distorted picture of life at Downside in the 'eighties. The year's traditional round went on, and many other interests besides those of monastic politics found their place. Dom Cuthbert had much work in the school which kept his classical knowledge alive; there were the Christmas and other holidays, with the family spirit— half Benedictine, half English—which is always so much in evidence in our houses at that time; there were the visits to Sir John's, the school theatricals and debates, the summer visits to Longleat or Wells. There was the burning question of a reorganization of the studies, both in school and monastery; there was the intercourse with a growing number of friends who came to look on Downside,

---

[1] We speak of Downside only, but the statement is equally true, *mutatis mutandis*, of the other two original houses.

the home of Dom Gasquet and Dom Dolan and the chosen residence of Edmund Bishop, as a place to visit at Holy Week and during the year. Among such visitors were the two most distinguished English Benedictines—Bishop Ullathorne and Bishop Hedley, both of whom had much sympathy with the aims and aspirations, spiritual and intellectual, of the young community. The diocesan, Bishop Clifford, a man of great ability and breadth of view, was another; and, till circumstances broke the intercourse for a time, Monsignor Weld.

Among the notable events of Prior Gasquet's tenure of office had been the foundation of *The Downside Review*, and although at first it was edited from London by Alfred Maskell and circulated almost entirely among Old Gregorians, it supplied a sounding-board to every development of doctrine and a stimulus to every interest—literary, archaeological and historical—that came to birth among an exceptionally talented group of men. Gradually, too, the contributions of Edmund Bishop and Dom Gasquet imposed themselves upon the notice of a wider public, and those whom *Henry VIII and the English Monasteries* attracted to Benedictine history found a school for its study in being in a Benedictine priory in the west.

Abbot Butler throughout his life had a remarkable capacity for concentration and perseverance; he had also a natural gift of clearness of perception. But it remains a remarkable thing that, in the laborious and yet disturbed atmosphere of Downside, he should have been able to acquire for himself the grasp of essentials in early Christian history that is shown in his first important essay, 'Bishop Lightfoot and the Early Roman See', published in 1893 in *The Dublin Review*. The essay, indeed, shows no trace of original work, and, save for the lucidity of exposition, would attract little notice at the present day, but at the time, when the study of Christian origins was still a new thing, and when the greatest works of Batiffol and Duchesne had not yet appeared, it shows very great insight that a student at Downside, himself unacquainted with English university circles, should have so unerringly assessed the value of the work of Lightfoot and Westcott, and while appreciating its significance, should have been capable of re-assembling the evidence provided by their scholarship and of interpreting it in another sense. The essay, and its fellows which appeared at intervals within the next half-dozen years, showed little sign of the wasting influence of time when it was republished in 1930; indeed it does not a little to remind us that there is a danger, in the field of Christian origins, of neglecting to hold the territory which has been incontestably vindicated for the Church by orthodox scholarship.

During the first half of the last decade of the century, then, Dom Cuthbert was, in such time as he could command, acquiring a solid groundwork of knowledge in monastic history and in Christian origins. We have seen that for eighteen months (1885–86) he was absorbed in the seventeenth-century history of the Congregation; a little before this, he had read many of the sources for English monastic history in its first period (600–800). Shortly before the decisive change in his life came, he and some others, in consultation with Edmund Bishop, had considered the possibility of dividing early and medieval monastic history into a series of periods, each of which would be allotted to a single worker, with a view to producing a complete account. To Dom Cuthbert fell the origins in Egypt; as in all such cases, the horizon, which at first seemed limited, opened out more and more, and he was confronted with the uncertain basis upon which all knowledge of the earliest monastic history rested, since there were serious doubts as to the trustworthiness of the chief authority, the *Lausiac History* of Palladius.

He was at this time living at the house in Great Ormond Street occupied by Dom Gasquet, whither he had been sent by Prior Ford soon after the latter's election in 1894; Edmund Bishop also was there. The story of his first contact with Cambridge may be told in his own words:

I had collected and roughed out into shape a great mass of material, and the question arose, how to get it printed. Bishop said, *The* place would be 'Texts and Studies'! Write to the editor [J. Armitage Robinson, then Norrisian Professor] and see if he would consider it. I did, not without trepidation at approaching a Cambridge Divinity Professor, explaining the nature and purpose of the work.

Robinson having seen the MS. replied with an invitation to stay for some days at Christ's:

So in May 1895 I went to Cambridge and we met. Straightway, I may say, we were good, even intimate friends....He had congenial friends to meet me in his rooms, brought me to dine in Hall at Christ's; and so on this visit were sown the seeds of some of the best friendships of my life.[1]

The sequel will be related in due course; meanwhile the growth of another friendship must be indicated. This was with a man very different in tastes and temper from those whom Dom Butler had met in English Benedictine circles or in the wider ambit of Catholic clerical life; different, also, from Edmund Bishop, to whom theology and philosophy had little appeal. But Baron Friedrich von Hügel appealed very deeply to another side of Dom Butler's nature—to a real capacity, never developed in the course of his studies, for abstract thought, and to an interest, existing since his Belmont days, in the spiritual, even the mystical, life. Now that the study of mysticism has been popularized, and perhaps vulgarized, it is hard to recapture the atmosphere of forty years ago, when few even among catholics had read the great mystical classics of the Middle Ages and Counter-Reformation, and still fewer knew of any mystical theology save in such works as those of Schram or Görres. It is not then surprising that those who first turned the current of thought from matter to spirit should have turned to the great mystics primarily as witnesses to religious experience, in order to draw from their testimony a further proof of the existence of a spiritual order, and should have tended to sever unduly mysticism from theology—should even have regarded the 'mystical element' in religion as something distinct from, and even opposed to, the strictly intellectual or formally dogmatic.

All these tendencies—and others besides—were present in the mind of Friedrich von Hügel in the 'nineties, and Abbot Butler undoubtedly owed to him, not only the creation of new interests and the re-awakening of old, but a cast of thought which remained with him to the end and which more than any other intellectual consideration hindered him from making a fully satisfactory theological synthesis of the spiritual life. But the immediate gain was unquestionably greater than any limitations; Dom Cuthbert found in the baron one

[1] Memoir of J. A. Robinson in *DR*, vol. LI (1933), pp. 392–3.

who joined to a wide and deep religious knowledge a taste for the greatest that rarely failed him and a lofty enthusiasm that in later years was so often to fire others. When Dom Cuthbert was in London, and later when he passed through town so often on his way to and from Cambridge, he saw much of the baron, and the presence of his brother Anatole at Cambridge was another link:

For some twelve years, from 1894 to about 1906, while he lived at Hampstead, I used frequently to stay with him for three or four days. In the afternoon we every day went for a walk over the heath; it was while the *Saint Catherine* [i.e. *The Mystical Element in Religion*] was in the making, and he used to discourse of how the work was shaping itself in his mind, and develop the proposed treatment of the various parts, following up any train that emerged—often Fénelon, Bossuet, Père Grou, St Teresa, or other favourites. Such talks were as walks over the mountains in the fresh keen breeze, in the light and warmth of the sun, in view of a panorama of wild scenery or spreading landscape—exhilarating, bracing, deepening, broadening, uplifting: I have never experienced quite the same with any other man. And we always returned home by the way of the little Catholic church in Holly Place—it was his daily practice— and went in for a long, long visit to the Blessed Sacrament; and there I would watch him sitting, the great deep eyes fixed on the Tabernacle, the whole being wrapt in an absorption of prayer, devotion, contemplation. Those who have not seen him so know only half the man.[1]

In 1895 Prior Ford decided to open a Downside house of studies at Cambridge, and in October 1896 the move was made. The restrictions on Catholics attending the universities had lately been removed and it was felt that no step would be more likely to give a greater impetus to the cultivation of those higher studies which Dom Gasquet, Dom Gilbert Dolan and Dom Butler himself had always hoped to see an integral part of Downside activity. New-found friends at Cambridge existed who, seeing in all Benedictines a kinship with the great Maurists, smoothed the way for the venture, above all Armitage Robinson, and John Peile, Master of Christ's. Thus it was that the connexion with Christ's College began which still happily endures; the original Benet House, an old-fashioned building, was actually a part of the college property in Hobson

---

[1] Memoir of F. von Hügel in *Tablet*, 14 February 1925.

Street. And it was natural that Dom Butler should be chosen as its first head, that he might edit Palladius as what was then called an 'advanced' student, and qualify for a research degree. But before passing to speak of his years at Cambridge, another event of great significance for the future must be mentioned. It was in 1896 that the brilliant young Vice-Principal of Wells Theological College, Henry Havelock Ramsay, decided upon becoming a Catholic. He was directed by Dom Gasquet, upon whom he called in London, to Downside, and there, in the crypt, he was received into the Church by Dom Cuthbert Butler. His future successor was the only convert Abbot Butler ever received into the Church; he was characteristically proud alike of this reception and of its unique character.

The eight years at Cambridge from 1896 to 1904 were years of steady work and very great happiness. Constantly in the last years of his life Abbot Butler would remark that the years at Cambridge were the happiest of his life. To those whose only acquaintance with him was in the years of his abbacy, or to those who knew him only as the editor of the Rule and the author of *Benedictine Monachism*, it may seem strange that one who devoted such a large part of his life's work to a vindication of claustral life should have regarded as most happy those years—the only ones in his life—in which he lived almost entirely outside monastic life. The admission, surely, was as sincere as it was revealing. Strange as the assertion may seem to those who knew only other aspects of his character, it would seem true that Abbot Butler was at heart a scholar, a student. In his earliest years his hopes turned to a professor's life at Belmont; later, the great Maurists appeared to him as the *beau idéal* of the Benedictine; and to the very last day of his life he found happiness in the steady, unchanging work of a scholar. It was at Cambridge in 1896 that the possibility of living a scholar's life first became real, in surroundings which left nothing to be desired. He was for the first time at a great centre of intellectual life; interests such as his needed no defence, for they were shared by some of the most brilliant members of the academic society in which he found himself; there were ample hours for work, and all the facilities of a great library and numerous private collections; moreover, there were friendships and opportunities for social intercourse of precisely the kind that he most appreciated. Abbot Butler, however he might seem to some apathetic towards social comfort and pleasure, was not really so. He savoured to the full the calm, dignified, but none the less substantial hospitality of hall, combination room and private gatherings. The gracious setting of this life, the view from windows over green courts, college gardens and grey towers, the combination—peculiar to the ancient universities—of immemorial existence and the ceaseless flux of young, eager life; above all, the presence in this social intercourse of a reverence for the things of the mind—all this was in the highest degree sympathetic to his nature. It had, too, the added charm of being at once his life and not his life. He could look out upon it and in a measure share in it with the abiding knowledge that for him it was only one part of life, and that behind it lay a background of other duties and interests, in which he might eventually be called to play an important part.

Meanwhile, Cambridge brought out all that was most amiable in his character. Those who lived with him or who met him constantly in those years agree that there was none of that constraint of manner which was felt later, that there was a geniality, almost an expansiveness, in his daily life. Gradually, he found himself on relations of easy friendship with men of distinction. Armitage Robinson and Baron Anatole von Hügel introduced him to their circles, and more than one eminent scholar was found to be predisposed to sympathy with a Benedictine, and delighted to find, in the first Benedictine he had met, so many qualities which he could assess and appreciate, and which seemed to embody his conception of a Mabillon or a Montfaucon. At Christ's the Master, John Peile, was an early friend; still more, through community of tastes and interests, the present Master [1934], Dr Norman McLean. Henry Jackson, not yet Regius Professor of Greek, was another whose rooms he could often visit, and, among younger men, two who soon rose into eminence in the divinity school, Dr F. C. Burkitt and Dr Bethune Baker. Acton, too, was in residence for some of the years, and there were others whose names are less familiar to the present generation.

These were years of solid achievement for him in the realm of patient scholarship. He always loved, and throve upon, a regular, laborious life; at Cambridge it was enlivened by unpretentious hospitality, by not infrequent calls and visits, and by contact not only with the academic society but with those who for this reason or that pay a visit of a few days or a week-end to such a place. For some of the time too, his father, who lived beyond the age of ninety, was at Benet House, and Professor Burkitt has recently recalled the zest with which the old man attacked the study of Coptic, with a view to reading the Old Testament in that language, only a few months before his death.

The first volume of Palladian matter, containing historical and critical studies, and an important essay on the origins of monasticism, appeared in 1898, and on 11 June of that year Dom Butler, along with his first companion Dom Benedict Kuypers, editor of the *Book of Cerne*, took degrees as Bachelors of Arts—the first occasion on which a Catholic priest gained and received a degree at one of the ancient universities since the days of Queen Mary. The publication of a second volume containing the critical text had already been decided upon, and it therefore became necessary to visit a number of foreign libraries for the purpose of examining and collating MSS. Accordingly in the late spring of 1898 he travelled to Venice where he stayed for three weeks with the Benedictines of St Giorgio Maggiore; his own description of a typical day is characteristic in the extreme:

My life at Venice soon fell into a routine. By nine each morning I was at the library; at twelve I went to the Piazza of St Marco for a cup of coffee and a roll; by half-past twelve I was back in the library, and I worked away at my MSS. till the hour of closing at four. I then returned to the Piazza and dined at Quadri's. After dinner till eight (the supper hour at St Giorgio in the summer months) I sometimes wandered about the narrow streets...or I would go on the Grand Canal....More frequently I went out by steamer to the Lido....On the far side of the Lido there is excellent sea bathing, with deep water forty or fifty yards out. Sea bathing at seventy-five degrees, when one could stay in at pleasure without the least chill, was a new and delightful experience. Then after the bathe to have for twopence as much delicious fruit as one cared for;

and then to say the Office sitting out on the bank that overlooks the Adriatic...and then to return home while the sun was setting behind the campaniles and cupolas of Venice, and lighting up the distant Paduan [*sic*] mountains: all this will explain how...I never felt the mere joy of existence so keenly as during my three weeks' stay at Venice.

It was in the course of this voyage littéraire that he paid the first of many visits to Rome; he was there for four days only, and I accordingly laid down for myself the following rules:—

1. that I would not attempt to see any galleries of paintings or sculptures, any museums or collections of any kind;
2. that what I would lay myself out to do was to make the pilgrimage of the Seven Basilicas;
3. that I would see what else I could.[1]

During these four days he sustained a painful injury to his knee, while ascending the Scala Santa. There was an old weakness in the joint, arising originally from an accident while playing the bat-and-ball game at Downside; this was now seriously aggravated and kept him in bed for ten days at Sant'Anselmo. He was then able to proceed to Monte Cassino, where he met two old acquaintances, Abbot Krug and the prior Dom Amelli, but the knee still gave trouble, and, indeed, confined him to his room and again sent him to bed for a fortnight in Rome on his return journey; the trouble, indeed, remained chronic with him for many years and never entirely departed.

The Greek text of Palladius was published in 1904, and to mark the occasion Dom Butler gave what he afterwards referred to as a 'garden-party' in the diminutive precincts of Benet House. Melons were provided for the guests, among whom were most of the friends he had made at Cambridge, and the gathering thus accepting Benedictine hospitality, and numbering Presbyterian, Anglican, Jewish and agnostic scholars, caused no little astonishment to a distinguished French prelate who happened to be staying at Benet House.

The happy life at Cambridge came to an end in 1904. For the moment, however, he did not come into residence at Downside, but

---

[1] 'Notes of a Voyage Littéraire', *DR*, vol. XVII (1898), pp. 205–17.

went to pass some time in the abbey of Maria Laach, with a view to perfecting his German for studies in early Church history and the New Testament. It was there that he met the young abbot, Fidelis von Stotzingen, who later succeeded Abbot de Hemptinne as Primate, and who remained on terms of affectionate friendship with Dom Butler for the rest of his life. His stay at Laach had other consequences, for he persuaded the abbot to send some of his young monks to Bonn, and thus originated the present great literary activity of the house. In particular he inspired Dom Cunibert Mohlberg, his tutor in German, with an enthusiasm for literary work.

If the years of controversy had driven Dom Butler, at the very outset of his monastic life, to discover and maintain, under the fire of the enemy, the traditional lines of Benedictine polity, and had sent him to the study of early congregational history—the rock from whence St Gregory's was hewn—the years at Cambridge gave him a knowledge, unrivalled among Benedictines, of monastic origins, and of the extent to which St Benedict made use of or modified the ideals and practices of earlier monachism. It was thus with a mind accustomed to dwell both upon the remote past and the urgent present that he became acquainted with some of the most celebrated contemporary Benedictine houses of the Continent.

On his return to Downside, he found himself the witness of an energetic growth in every direction. Dom Leander Ramsay had for more than two years been headmaster, and the school was launched upon that period of expansion which was to continue without a break for all the years of Abbot Butler's time of office. The magnificent choir of the church had been slowly rising, and now was on the point of completion, with all the prospect that it held of richer liturgical life. The community was growing in strength, and among the youngest in the habit were a number (of whom Dom Leander Ramsay was one) who were converts to the Church or who had not passed through the school at Downside, and thus were able to open new vistas in every direction. The distinction attained by Gasquet and Butler, under the encouraging influence of Prior Ford and Edmund Bishop, had stimulated intellectual and artistic interests of every kind. Besides *The Downside Review*, whose pages in these years bear witness to the variety of interest and high level of achievement of so many of the community, a numerous group were engaged upon historical work for the forthcoming *Catholic Encyclopedia*. Probably, indeed, the literary output of Gregorians, at Downside or elsewhere, for the decade 1900–10, exceeded in quantity that of any ten years before or since. Dom Butler himself spent many months of 1905 writing an important series of articles on monastic and religious history for the *Encyclopaedia Britannica*.

Before the next great change in his life a short episode took place which he always regarded as a pleasant memory. He had always maintained his connexion with Ireland, and when in 1905 a relative of one of the community made possible a small foundation in County Wexford, Dom Cuthbert was its warmest advocate. In view of his interest, he was sent for three months in the summer of 1906 as one of the pioneers of the house, originally at Enniscorthy, and later at Mount St Benedict's, Gorey. Here again there emerged a trait so apparently foreign to the precise, regular habits of mind which all associated with the name of Abbot Butler. Underlying all was a strain—whether Irish or not, who shall say?—of the half adventurous, half haphazard, which delighted in the experiences of making a beginning in the Irish countryside, travelling on errands in a jaunting-car, taking little thought as to the hour of the day or the day of the week.

This, however, was a phase of very short duration. He was recalled to fill the office of subprior left vacant on the departure of Fr. Wilfrid Corney for Rome as procurator in Curia early in 1906, and to himself and to most of the resident community this seemed an indication that Abbot Ford considered him as the one most fitted to succeed him. Dom Ford's health had long been impaired, and he let it be known in August 1906 that he wished to resign office; the election of his successor took place on 6 November. Abbot Butler was solemnly blessed by the diocesan, Bishop Burton, on 12 March 1907.

The new abbot, in his forty-eighth year, had been chosen by a large majority of his brethren and could count on the willing support of the resident community of Downside. He entered on his term of

diate and lasting effects, and must always be regarded as opening a new epoch in the history of Downside. Equally prompt was his action in developing the liturgical life of the house. The circumstances mentioned in the early pages of this memoir had made anything like an elaborate liturgical activity quite impossible, but the growth in numbers and the opening of the new choir removed past handicaps. Gradually, Abbot Butler initiated the observance which has remained with little alteration or addition since his day. The daily singing of Vespers was followed by the introduction of sung Tierce on Sundays and greater feasts; the daily sung mass came later, as will be noted. Along with the solemnization of the Office came a great change in the chant. Downside had hitherto retained the Mechlin version, together with certain other compositions entirely outside plain chant tradition; Abbot Butler, in accordance with the desires of Pius X and the decisions of those most competent to pronounce in musical matters, decided to make the change to the version of the chant established on critical principles by the school of Solesmes. The day chosen for the inauguration was the feast of St Gregory, 1909. Here again the change was made gradually, and not without conservative criticism; it was as wise as it was inevitable.

During all the years immediately preceding the war a succession of benefactions, great and small, made it possible to add continually to the fabric and ornament of the church. Chief in bulk among these additions was the new sacristy, completed in 1913, which freed the north cloister and added greatly to the amenities of all great functions.

In spite of all the administrative work connected with such a large establishment as Downside was becoming, Abbot Butler found time to keep abreast with the literature in the subjects of his study, and to prepare his critical edition of the Rule. We have already seen that he himself regarded his years at Cambridge as the happiest of his life; if varied and beneficent activity and the employment of many talents be a source of happiness, few periods, one would think, can have been happier than those early years as superior. Responsibility, and responsibility for souls, and especially for souls as yet unformed in the religious life, undoubtedly deepened his character greatly. He now found himself with a duty upon him to teach—*proferre nova et vetera*—and his conferences to his community and novices were often true lessons. He remarked more than once that the one office he had coveted was that of novice-master; it was never given to him to hold that position, but when the noviciate was opened at Downside he took a large share of the formation into his own hands. For many years he was in the habit of giving the novices a second daily conference during the periods of school holidays; he thus introduced them to those books which had deeply influenced his own spiritual and monastic life or which seemed best fitted to express his ideals—the *Confessions* of St Augustine, the Fathers of the Desert, Cardinal Gasquet's introduction[1] to the English translation of Montalembert's *Monks of the West*, Newman's Essays on the Benedictines, one or two of his own addresses and pamphlets and—most important of all—Father Baker's *Sancta Sophia*, which he usually reserved for reading in the summer holidays, at the end of the year's noviciate.

With all these occupations, he was a model of regularity and punctuality at all conventual duties, including the weekly choir practice, and he never omitted his two periods of private prayer—half an hour in morning and evening—and his daily recitation of five decades of the Rosary.[2] Normally, he never took the weekly rest (entailing absence on one day from Matins, Lauds and Prime) which he introduced for others, and he always rose before the caller began his rounds. After Lauds, he said his mass, and before breakfast spent half an hour in mental prayer. He invariably attended the sung conventual mass when it was introduced, and as invariably held his gradual and followed every word—it would be scarcely true to write 'note', since musical notation conveyed little to him. The rest of the morning he devoted to his correspondence and inter-

---

[1] Perhaps it is worth recording that Abbot Butler told me more than once that this introduction was half the work of Edmund Bishop and half of Dom Elphege Cody, the constitutional section being Bishop's, and that on the monastic life by Dom Cody. He had himself seen the latter's MS. at Great Ormond Street. [See p. 252.]

[2] This daily recitation of the Rosary can, I believe, be traced to the advice given by the celebrated Abbé Huvelin to the young Friedrich von Hügel.

views, save when he gave the noviciate a conference at midday. In the afternoon, after a walk or work in the garden, he said his Rosary walking out of doors if fine, or in the cloister if wet; then he gave time to his own studies till Vespers. Before supper he devoted another half-hour to prayer in the church, and after recreation following supper returned to his work again till Compline; after Compline he retired immediately to bed, after a few minutes' prayer before the statue of Our Lady.

Such an enumeration of his daily occupations is not without significance in a sketch of his life, since the regularity, the simplicity—we might almost add the austerity—of such a life reflect a trait of his character which his years in office emphasized. Undoubtedly those who knew him—even those who knew him intimately—during his abbacy felt that there was about him an atmosphere of aloofness and austerity; they were at the time somewhat incredulous of what was told of his geniality at Cambridge and, when the time came, surprised at the greater flexibility he showed in his last years. Socially somewhat aloof he always was, and the reasons for this will be suggested in their place, but he was not by temperament or resolve austere, and even repudiated any such suggestion. Rather, it was his sense of the responsibility of a superior that led him—often, no doubt, unconsciously—to adopt the simplicity, even severity, of life which avoided self-indulgence of any kind.

In those years, too, with all his occupations and all his regularity, he never failed in the duty of a superior and the head of a great establishment to give countenance to every kind of activity. He was present at every school concert or dramatic presentation or important match; he called regularly upon the parents of his young monks when they visited Downside, and upon friends of the abbey living in the neighbourhood; he was indefatigable in visiting the Downside missions—then more numerous than at present—and in pontificating on all great occasions of opening or jubilee celebrations at Whitehaven, Liverpool, Swansea and elsewhere. His position in the world of learning was universally acknowledged, and few events during these years gave him more pleasure than the reception, in the summer of 1908, of the D.Litt., *honoris causa*, at Trinity College,

Dublin—the first occasion in the history of that body on which a Catholic ecclesiastic had been the recipient of such an honour.

But it must not be supposed that, even in the 'honeymoon' period, he was without serious difficulties of one kind or another. His health, indeed, was excellent, and, save for periods of inactivity due to his injured knee, he spent scarcely a day in bed during the whole of his monastic life. But there was, first, this trouble of his knee, which hampered his movements and from time to time grew more serious and necessitated rest. Finally, in 1903, he decided to make a pilgrimage to Lourdes. Characteristically, he asked for no complete cure, but for such an amelioration as would allow him for the rest of his life to accomplish his work without interruption. In the event, after his return from Lourdes his knee, though remaining stiff, never again caused him to lie up. 'A grace, not a miracle', were his invariable words when recalling his pilgrimage. Then there was a strange, though small, nervous affliction which affected the steadiness of his hands. This in part was responsible for the enormous size of his handwriting, and it necessitated his using both hands when drinking from cup or glass; at one time, during his first period of office, it became so troublesome as to make the holding of the chalice and the fraction of the Host at mass well-nigh impossible, and for a long period he had to abandon saying mass, and then, for a time, made use of the services of an assistant priest. To the end of his life he found it impossible to distribute Communion to a large number.

Finally, though his domestic changes and developments not only gave a lead to, but reflected the deepest aspirations of the vast majority of the resident community, another aspect of his policy, which aimed at carrying out the programme which he and others had set before themselves twenty years before, did not command such universal support. Among the chief aims, as we have seen, of the movement towards realizing the autonomy of the houses *vis-à-vis* the president and general chapter had been to secure for the monasteries a larger community and for the individual monk at least a possibility of permanent residence under the conditions of claustral life. The first of these aims—the growth of the community—had been largely secured by the transference of all monks to the jurisdiction of their domestic superior; but the second question had been left untouched by any legislation. Writing in 1905, with the future still hidden, Dom Butler had said:

The restrictions placed by *Religiosus Ordo* and the constitutions on the abbot's power of sending his monks on the mission as of old are in practice ineffective for securing that element of fixity of tenure which was one of the chief objects in the minds [of many during the long debates]....As a fact, all that has in this matter been done has been to transfer to the abbots the full powers in translation of monks to and from the mission formerly wielded by the president....No doubt this question will have at some future time to be faced again.[1]

He now found himself as abbot in a position of some difficulty. Twenty years before, it had always been assumed that no difficulty would ever be found in filling vacancies on the mission from a growing community. In his own words:

In view of the facts of actual [i.e. previous to 1894] experience, there could be no likelihood of any dearth of men in Downside whose vocation would be for the mission, and who would be willing and happy after some years in the monastery to pass out of the claustral life to the missionary.[2]

At best, such a view, though most comprehensible under the circumstances of the time, was liable to be challenged by the facts of subsequent experience. Actually, by 1906, the position at Downside had become complicated by unforeseen developments. In the first place, the growth of the school and of the whole establishment, together with the increase of liturgical observance, demanded a resident community of a size far in excess of that imagined twenty years before. Besides this, there were the new developments at Ealing and Gorey demanding men. On the other hand, developments scarcely imagined twenty years before demanded an increase of staff and churches on several of the important missions. Finally, a succession of invitations, many of them in themselves both flattering and attractive, were made to the abbot and community of Downside to open monasteries and schools in various parts of the British Isles, and even so far afield as Australia, Canada and India.

[1] MS. B.   [2] MS. B.

In these circumstances, Abbot Butler conceived it to be his duty to outline some kind of programme to serve as a guide for the future. He did so in two propositions, present in germ in a document composed as early as 1907, and finally enunciated in 1910:

1. That it be accepted as a principle that our first aim should be to increase the resident working community, until the monastery attains to the full stature of an adequately manned and completely organized Benedictine Abbey.

2. That it be recognized that the time has come to begin lessening our sphere of missionary activity.

It is unnecessary to follow in any detail the stages of his endeavour to carry out this programme; still less is it fitting to discuss in such a place as this the wisdom of the course upon which he embarked. But no sketch of his life would be adequate which did not hint at this undertone of controversy which was present during all his period of office.

For all this, let us turn to some of its happier periods. Abbot Butler had a true paternal spirit, and it was an abiding joy to him to watch a numerous group of young monks growing up beneath his eyes. In the summer of 1911 he travelled out to central Europe where a number of Downside juniors were spending part of the Roman vacation, for the express purpose of taking them with him on a visit to a number of the great Austrian and Hungarian monasteries, still in the heyday of prosperity. Everywhere welcomed as one of the most distinguished of Benedictines, he enjoyed to the full the opportunity of seeing unfamiliar centres of monastic life and of showing to others the glories of Melk, Kremsmünster, Pannonhalma and the Danube. In the summer of 1914 it fell to him as abbot to organize and preside over the celebrations commemorating the centenary of residence at Downside. By a happy coincidence, the year was distinguished by Abbot Gasquet's elevation to the cardinalate, and the ceremonies of his formal reception in England were combined with those of the centenary in the middle of July. As first assistant to the abbot president, Abbot Butler automatically succeeded to the office of president left vacant by Cardinal Gasquet, so it was as head of the English Benedictine Congregation that he was able to welcome Downside's cardinal returning to his old home, now completing her hundred years of existence.

Those July days of celebration were to end an epoch in the life of Downside, and were, in a sense, a kind of culminating point in the life of Abbot Butler. The years before the war—careless years, as they were so soon to seem in retrospect—had been marked by a succession of great occasions at Downside; there had been the opening of the choir in 1905, the laying of the foundation stone of the new school buildings in 1910, their solemn blessing by Cardinal Bourne in 1912, and now, attracting a still more brilliant and distinguished company, including most of the hierarchy and almost all monastic superiors and heads of religious orders in England, the reception of Cardinal Gasquet. A fortnight later came the first declarations of war.

The war, with all its problems and legacy of problems, could not but affect the development of Downside and the life of its abbot. Externally, indeed, there was little change save in accidentals, but the strain of those years on all those with work and responsibility, and the cessation for half a dozen years of the normal influx of novices, had its effect in ways which all agree in feeling though they might differ in expressing.

For the moment there was little change. Abbot Butler's first term of office would have come to an end in November 1914; to avoid an election in term time, it had been arranged to hold it at the beginning of August. Under the provisions then still in force of *Diu quidem*, all elections subsequent to the original ones of 1900 were to be for life-abbots. Actually, whenever an election had occurred in the Congregation, the Holy See had been petitioned to fix a term of years for the tenure of office. As we saw on an earlier page, Dom Butler in his early years had always defended the system of life abbacies which is indeed implied by the Rule, was traditional all over England for a thousand years, and is the norm in most Benedictine Congregations. Consequently, he was desirous that the matter should be fully considered by the Downside conventus, and a discussion took place at which, naturally, he was not present. The sense of the community, however, was clearly against departing from the practice hitherto customary, but the period assigned by the Holy See was one of twelve years. Abbot Butler was re-elected without serious division of opinion, and could therefore look forward to a period of office lasting till 1926.

He undoubtedly took this re-election (which, indeed, he had confidently expected) as a ratification of the main lines of his government and as a mandate for introducing still further changes along those lines. His steadying influence was of great value in the early weeks of the war when, as all who lived through that period will remember, a spirit of adventure and hasty decision was abroad; he was just as resolute then in refusing to allow essential members of the school staff to volunteer as chaplains as he was later in allowing a number to go at considerable sacrifice. In the course of the autumn he proposed to the community that a sung conventual mass should become part of the daily observance, and it was duly initiated at the end of the Christmas vacation in January 1915. This unquestionably, after the return of the noviciate, was the most important act of Abbot Butler's period of office; it was the second of the three actions upon which he looked back with the greatest complacency. The third dated from the same winter. As Abbot President it fell to him to conduct a visitation at Belmont, in the course of which he decided that the time was ripe for Belmont to become a completely autonomous house on a level with the other houses of the Congregation. The step was duly taken and he was not without influence in the selection of Dom Aelred Kindersley, then prior and procurator of Downside, for the post of superior. Some years later, in 1920, when he was still president, he was responsible for the negotiations leading to the bull *Cambria* which created the archdiocese of Cardiff and deprived Belmont of its unique ecclesiastical status as cathedral priory, while raising it to abbatial dignity.

At the departure of Dom Aelred for Belmont Abbot Butler appointed as his procurator Dom Bruno Hicks, and as sacristan *vice* Dom Bruno, Dom Anselm Rutherford. Dom Anselm had already had a share in designing several new sets of vestments; he now embarked upon a scheme of complete replacement in every department of the sacristy, and in the course of some three years, with the help of several generous benefactors, provided the bulk of the vestments, altar frontals and hangings with which all who know Downside are familiar. The encouragement and interest shown by Abbot Butler in this work—in which, by natural bent, he had little interest or competence—is typical of his policy throughout his tenure of office to support and encourage every movement that could enrich in any way the many-sided life of Downside.

In spite of the war, the years 1915–17 marked something of a summit in the artistic and liturgical life of Downside. The observance was now, for the first time since the migration from France, that of a typical large Benedictine monastery. The liturgical ceremonies, which especially since the opening of the choir in 1905 had attained full stature, now received additional lustre from the new vestments which were brought into use at regular intervals. The practice of celebrating Vespers on second class feasts with a priest in cope was introduced; Prime was separated from Lauds and a number of other small musical and ceremonial changes were made. For a short time the experiment was tried of singing Lauds on the greater feasts, and Abbot Butler could reflect that all had come to pass of which he and others had dreamed at the dawn of their monastic life.

Though the war brought its difficulties, demanded its sacrifices, and left its legacy of problems at Downside as elsewhere, its effect was not wholly one of making Abbot Butler's task harder. The spirit of willing self-sacrifice was abroad, and the restrictions of all kinds, and the difficulty of communications, did much to postpone for some half-dozen years what those who knew Downside thirty years ago would call the invasion of its privacy by the modern world. And in spite of the added calls of the office of president, in which he was confirmed by election in 1917, and which necessitated, besides Visitations, a number of visits to the convents of the Congregation, Abbot Butler found time to compose the series of studies on every aspect of Benedictine life which were published in 1919 with the title *Benedictine Monachism*.

This is perhaps the fittest point to mention the place held in his interests by the many communities of nuns with whom he came into contact. Throughout his life he had always had a very deep affection for all the English houses of religious women that had been founded abroad during the time of persecution. He considered their history one of the most heroic episodes in the Catholic life of England and wished to see the story of all these houses published, so that English Catholics might realize their spiritual indebtedness to the saintly and intrepid women of the seventeenth century, and English girls of today might be drawn to enter their communities. As time went on, he came to have personal relations with almost all these houses. At Taunton, he had a near relative among the Franciscans whom he used regularly to visit every year; after leaving Downside he gave retreats to the communities of Old English Carmelites at Chichester and Lanherne, and was this very spring to have visited Darlington; he had the most friendly relations with the Austin canonesses at Ealing, and his latest published literary work was undertaken at the request of the Sisters of the Visitation at Harrow.

But naturally the link was closest with Benedictine nuns, and East Bergholt, Princethorpe and others could doubtless all bear witness to acts of friendly care. But it is without question true to say that at Stanbrook he was better known, and felt himself more at home, than at any other house. As early as 1885, shortly after his ordination, he had spent some days there, attracted primarily by the memory of Dom Laurence Shepherd, who had died early in that year, and whom, as we have seen, he greatly reverenced. The young Dom Cuthbert immediately made friends with Abbess Dubois for whom he retained throughout his life the greatest veneration; the same intimacy was continued with Abbess Heywood, a woman of rare spiritual gifts, and with the present abbess,[1] with whose wide intellectual interests he had long been familiar and who looked to him as a personal friend and a wise counsellor. But he did not confine his interest to the superiors of Stanbrook; first as extraordinary confessor, later as president and last as friend, he was acquainted in greater or less degree with all the community. Almost every summer, in the fifty that elapsed since his first visit, he spent some days there, and often read to the nuns from the manuscript of his as yet

[1] [Dame Laurentia McLachlan, 1866–1953. For her see *In a great tradition. A tribute to Dame Laurentia McLachlan, Abbess of Stanbrook*, by the Benedictines of Stanbrook (London, 1956).]

unpublished books and articles. One best qualified to judge thus describes the impression which he has left behind him:

While we recognized in Abbot Butler a brilliant and powerful intellect which compelled admiration and respect, we were much more impressed by his spiritual gifts, his love of prayer, his supernatural outlook, his genuine humility, and what I should like to call the clarity of his soul. A great man in heart and mind, he carried throughout life the heart of a child, and of him one says naturally: *talium est regnum cœlorum*.

A serious blow came in 1918. As early as the summer of 1913 Dom Leander Ramsay had felt the strain of his work in the school where, since the departure of Dom Wulstan Pearson in 1912, he was all but wholly responsible for both organization and administration, but there seemed no reason to suppose that his health was seriously affected. Suddenly in the Lent term of 1918 an illness declared itself which proved to be an advanced malignant growth. The news was a great shock to Abbot Butler; and its effect was increased when the surgeons after performing a small operation declared that the disease had run its course too far for a major operation to be possible and that only a few months of life remained for the patient. To the present writer, Abbot Butler's immediate reaction to this news has always seemed among the nobler actions of his life, especially as any kind of public appeal for prayers was foreign to his taste. He announced that he would not accept the verdict of the doctors as the final word, and within a few days sent to all Downside parishes and the majority of religious houses in England an appeal, worded in dignified language, for co-operation in a novena for the preservation of a life so calculated to aid the advance of the kingdom of God. This appeal was received with much sympathy; in particular, public prayers were offered at a number of the Catholic schools and by the children of many elementary schools. In the event, as we know, Dom Leander had no recurrence of the malady and suffered no further bad effects up till the day of his death, from pneumonia, eleven years later.[1]

[1] Some four years after his illness, so he told the present writer, he was carefully examined (though without X-ray) by a doctor, who could discover no trace of the growth remaining.

318

Meanwhile it was assumed that Dom Leander's life was near its end. Abbot Butler, on his advice, appointed as his successor Dom Sigebert Trafford, and on Dom Leander's return to residence in the monastery he was given a number of the young monks as assistants in an endeavour to make sufficient advance in assembling the manuscript material for the edition of St Cyprian's works (long in contemplation) to be produced after his death. When, after some months, his health remained normal, he was appointed novice-master.

Early in 1917, while the war was still in progress, Dom Leander had suggested that the memorial to the Downside fallen should take the form of an addition to the abbey church, as an assertion of spiritual values in an age which attached so much weight to the material order. Abbot Butler welcomed and adopted the proposal, and thus was responsible for the completion of the nave; he himself cut the first sod in the spring of 1922. It is only fitting that for this great work, as for the 1912 school block, he should receive the credit which must always be due to the authority ultimately responsible alike for success as for disaster in all under his charge.

No one in 1920 would have supposed that Abbot Butler's period of office was drawing towards its close. It will be for some future historian of Downside (if indeed such things are not better left untold) to narrate the questions of policy which he brought forward; we are too near that time to make it possible or desirable to write its history. Many, however, both at the time and since have sought for some explanation of the remarkable fact that while, only a year or two previously, the prospect of change seemed alike remote and most undesirable, in 1922 there was scarcely a member of the community but felt that Abbot Butler, in signifying his desire to resign office, had acted wisely. The writer of such a memoir as this, which has endeavoured to set in some perspective all the events of Abbot Butler's life, cannot avoid expressing a personal judgement on an event of such importance. To him, as to many at the time, it seemed that Abbot Butler had lost his power of initiative owing to a mixture of compromise in deliberation and irresolution in action. In any case, an impasse was reached in which he found himself alone. At the general chapter of 1921 he was not re-elected abbot president; in the early summer of 1922 he signified his intention of resigning office as from the following September.

The decision was unquestionably a relief to him, and though all who knew him were aware that he suffered keenly at this time, yet it was not his deep piety alone that kept him from any long brooding or depression. He was by nature buoyant; besides, as has been hinted already, the realm of thought was always at root more attractive to him than the realm of action, and his sixteen years of office—which included the physically and mentally wearing war years—had left him in a sense tired and sated with the flux of action. He was already in the summer of 1922 putting the finishing touches to *Western Mysticism*, and though the work may have been in part an anodyne, there can be little doubt that satisfaction at the prospect of leisure for study and writing all but outweighed the inevitable distress at relinquishing high office at an age when such retirement must be final.

On leaving Downside he took up his residence at Ealing which he had in 1916 erected into a conventual priory. It was the natural place for an ex-superior to choose for a residence, at least for a time; there was further reason for the choice in its proximity to the British Museum and other London libraries. Abbot Butler had no intention of being idle—'I've got books in me', he was wont to pronounce at this time—and he had long hoped to be able to write a biography of the great Gregorian, Archbishop Ullathorne. This work, and the research necessary for it, occupied him for some years, and a succession of books kept him engaged till the day of his death.[1]

That Abbot Butler would after his retirement produce, one by one, a series of weighty studies was naturally to be expected, but few would have prophesied the growing popularity which his work came to enjoy, or the zest with which he entered into new and to him supposedly uncongenial activities. Indeed, the last eleven years of his life were in no sense a declension from the years that had gone

---

[1] Only those who realized how much the reading of books meant to him could fully appreciate the quiet courage with which in 1929 he faced the prospect of the loss of his sight and underwent an operation on both eyes for glaucoma.

before; they served not only to extend the circle of his spiritual influence, but to give scope to faculties and talents hitherto only half realized. The most striking of these new manifestations was the eagerness and success with which he threw himself into the open-air preaching work of the Catholic Evidence Guild. To those who had known him only as abbot he had often seemed intellectually aristocratic and by temperament a lover of retirement and silence. To imagine him preaching alongside of the Marble Arch in competition with communists and Seventh Day Adventists would have seemed outside the realm not only of the possible, but of the fitting. Such an experiment, it would have been said, could only result in a failure painful to those who admired his great qualities in other fields. In the event, his success was complete, and he speedily became one of the most successful Sunday afternoon speakers. Not only did he succeed in adapting his clear and forcible expositions to the mentality of his hearers, but he showed himself perfectly capable of dealing with interruptions and questions, whether intelligent, imbecile or merely obstructive, without losing the sympathy of his audience. It was strange that one who as a young man had not been found a successful teacher, and who as abbot had often failed to impress or interest when addressing his community, should have secured the attention of an audience so unacquainted with the subjects and ways of thought familiar to him. It may be that the very lack of perception and sympathy, which frequently prevented him from gauging the temper of a sophisticated audience, saved him from undue sensitiveness and from any mistaken endeavour to descend to the level of his hearers. But however it be explained, his success was undeniable, and he continued in the work till, some years before his death, its physical strain was pronounced harmful to him.

Besides speaking in the Park, Abbot Butler was a frequent preacher, either for single sermons or for a course, at various London churches from Westminster Cathedral downwards, and not infrequently he gave retreats to nuns or communities of men. He also spent many hours each week as confessor to a number of convents, so that his days and years were full of activity, in which he gave with unfailing patience, often to those quite undistinguished in the eyes of the world, the resources, intellectual and spiritual, of a most distinguished personality.

But his chief labour was literary, and here he had the satisfaction of finding his work appreciated by an ever-growing circle of readers. As late as 1919, the date of publication of *Benedictine Monachism*, when he was over sixty, an exceptionally well-read friend had expressed surprise that Abbot Butler could write a book which was, at least in parts, thoroughly readable. No one could accuse his later books of pedantry or dullness, and gradually—almost, one would say, by a process of 'suggestion'—his name came to stand to educated readers, Catholic and non-Catholic alike, as a guarantee for sound scholarship and robust common-sense. One would hear him mentioned, or see his name quoted, in the most unexpected quarters, as a final authority, and many of his judgements, historical and spiritual, can be traced in their progress from hand to hand till they have become axiomatic in current religious literature.

Relief from responsibility seemed to bring a mellowness into the last years of Abbot Butler's life. Those who, during his long term of office, had been disconcerted and even rebuffed by his apparent lack of personal sympathy, were all but astonished to find him, at Ealing or elsewhere, eager to take a genial interest in all round him and expansive without a trace of condescension. Above all, no one who saw him in the daily life of the small community of his new home could fail to be deeply—overwhelmingly—impressed by the simplicity with which he took his part in the recurring duties, reading lessons in choir, saying or singing the parish masses, preaching short discourses at an early mass and hearing the confessions of the people. He loved giving, and giving readily, and how many were his benefactions of advice, of encouragement and of prayer, done by his right hand without knowledge of his left, can be known only to God. But the present writer may be allowed to say that as a priest, after Abbot Butler's death, he came into contact with one such case, among the humblest, where the gratitude and grief were so profound and so spontaneous as to leave an impression far more lasting than any formal tribute to his memory.

In his last years Abbot Butler received some marks of esteem at the hands of his brethren which caused him great satisfaction. Only a few years after his resignation he was elected as delegate to general chapter by the community of St Gregory's, and he retained the position till his death; and at the chapter of 1933 he was given the Doctorate of Divinity *honoris causa.* For some time after ceasing to be abbot he was unwilling to assume, as is customary, a titular abbacy, and steadfastly refused to pontificate or, except on the rarest occasions, to wear ring and pectoral cross; at last, he was persuaded to take the titular abbacy of St Augustine's, Canterbury, and, sub-sequent to the death of Cardinal Gasquet, that of St Albans. He celebrated the golden jubilee of his clothing at Downside in the autumn of 1926 and looked forward with pleasure to the jubilee of his priesthood in the autumn of the present year. Until some four or five years ago his health had appeared so robust that there was every expectation of his rivalling the longevity of his father. His heart then gave trouble on a few isolated occasions, but although this caused him to relinquish his preaching in the Park it did not curtail his activities any further. A further attack took place on St Benedict's day in March 1933, when he lost consciousness in an omnibus, but although he fully realized the significance of such warnings he con-tinued his normal life, never failing to appear in church for the early Office, and fulfilling preaching engagements when called on. So he remained, equable, regular, laborious till the end. He assisted as usual at all the Offices of Holy Week, including those of Easter Day, and at the midday meal was in the best of spirits. He then went, as was his invariable Sunday custom, to call upon and take tea with a friend in Clapham. When still in the underground he felt unwell, but proceeded to his destination and then was forced to take to bed. A doctor was summoned, and at first there seemed no cause for immediate alarm, but his heart gradually failed and a priest was summoned who absolved and anointed him. His strength con-tinued to fail and at last, about eight o'clock in the evening, having retained full consciousness to the end, he died peacefully and without pain. On several occasions during the last years of his life the question had been mooted of his returning to Downside; for various reasons the day had been repeatedly postponed, but he had always hoped to spend the years of decline, should they come, in the place which he loved so dearly, and it would have been singularly fitting that he should have ended his days there. But it was not to be.

His body was brought to Ealing on the day following his death, Monday, 2 April, where it lay till the solemn Requiem on Wednesday, which was attended by Bishop Butt and many of his friends among the clergy and laity. It was then conveyed to Downside where on Thursday, after a Requiem at which the abbot of Downside pontificated, it was committed to the grave by the bishop of Clifton, and lies beside that of Abbot Chapman, in a grave to the east of the sacristy, under the shadow of the Lady Chapel.

In the foregoing pages only passing reference has been made to the outstanding qualities of Abbot Butler's mind and character. It would seem only fitting that an attempt should be made to portray, while his memory is fresh in our minds, one so long familiar to all at Downside, who influenced the lives of so many around him and who is an honoured name to a wide circle who have never seen his face.

Twenty years ago it was often remarked that no one who saw the superior and ex-superiors of Downside for however short a time could fail to recognize that they were men of distinction. Cardinal Gasquet, Abbot Ford, Abbot Butler, and, we may add, Abbot Ramsay were indeed all men of striking personal appearance. Abbot Butler was tall of stature with regular features, a somewhat aquiline nose and a high forehead; his countenance was no unfaithful indication of his open nature and his mental power. The first impression of dignity was, however, marred when he walked; partly owing to his weak knee, partly to his whole build, his movements were ungainly, at times positively awkward; he bowed abruptly and descended steps heavily. He had a powerful voice, without modulation; originally, he was quite incapable of even the remotest approximation to the notes of the chant, and when he was first abbot, a pontifical mass sung by him was almost barbaric in character. Later, by unremitting industry, he achieved some command of his voice.

Undoubtedly what distinguished Abbot Butler most in the natural order was his powerful and essentially masculine mind. He had all a scholar's qualities—that is, an appreciation of absolute accuracy, a capacity for attaining it and an instinctive distrust of all assertions whose authority and source he could not control; he had besides, at least in the matters in which he was most competent, that virtue which Friedrich von Hügel loved to call 'intellectual chastity' —a repugnance, that is, to anything short of pure, white truth, so far as it can be known; and where it cannot, a preference for silence. He had, besides, a nobler quality which not all scholars possess— a grasp, a penetration of the essential, of the central. He never wasted the instrument of his mind in the production of a useless or trifling or perverse conclusion. When Abbot Butler pronounced judgement on a matter in which he had real competence, that judgement was almost invariably just, clear and of abiding value.

As has been related, he never enjoyed the benefits of a complete university training such as is given by Greats at Oxford or the classical tripos at Cambridge. There is little doubt that he would have passed brilliantly through such a course and would have had little difficulty in qualifying for a fellowship, had he so desired. Humanly speaking such a discipline would have broadened his interests, by bringing him into contact over a series of years with pure literature and abstract thought, though it is conceivable that a merely academic life would have proved on the whole far more mentally narrowing to one not naturally myriad-minded. As it was, it would be equally untrue to say *tout court* that Abbot Butler's intellectual interests were few or many. He certainly had the capacity —essential in some degree to every scholar—of limiting severely the field of his survey. And beyond this, he undoubtedly was unsympathetic, almost unresponsive, to a whole range of aesthetic and intellectual interests generally accounted part of the possession of all educated men. Thus he had no comprehensive knowledge at all of art, architecture or music; scarcely any of several of the most vital periods of English history; little of many of the great masterpieces of literature, ancient or modern. Thus it is probable that such names as Cotman, Cézanne, Stravinsky, Blake, Sir James Barrie (to take them at hazard) would have conveyed nothing to him; that he would not have been able to date into a hundred years a medieval building or into fifty an Italian painting. When abbot he not infrequently seemed so unmoved by the enthusiasms of those round him and so unwilling to take sympathetic interest that many held the opinion that all forms of pure literature and art were a closed book to him, and that he was utterly incapable of being absorbed or transported by any work of the imagination. Two small incidents will show that this was not the case. When living at Cambridge he happened one evening to embark upon *Bleak House*, which he had never read as a boy. The plot of the story so roused his excitement that he read all through the night, and finished the book at about four o'clock in the morning. The other incident dates from his last years as abbot. He was paying a visit of some length to Benet House and his stay happened to coincide with the performance of a Greek play—on this occasion, an abbreviation of the *Oresteia* trilogy. Abbot Butler went to an afternoon performance with others, and afterwards learnt that one of these, on returning, had immediately entered the chapel to pray. 'I could not have done that,' he said, 'my mind was in such a turmoil that I had to walk round Parker's Piece to quiet it.'

Indeed, those who lived with him in his last years at Ealing soon became aware that unsuspected memories remained in his mind. As a young man, and even later, he had read widely in English and French classical literature, and would show a surprising recollection of Victorian writers of the second class, such as Bulwer Lytton, Wilkie Collins and Sir Walter Besant, besides complete familiarity with the giants. In fact, just as there was no saying what he had read, so there was no certainty in predicting what he had *not*, and his memory rarely lost what it had once received. Still, it is probably true to say that for all this the masterpieces of art and literature, and even the beauty of nature, counted for comparatively little in his mind's life. He once remarked, speaking of architecture: 'I like something great, huge, vast, *big*!' The sublime, therefore, appealed to him; it is doubtful whether the beautiful as such did so at all, and the present writer, in many years of acquaintance with him, never heard him quote or allude to a single passage of lyric poetry in any language.

Nor was Abbot Butler an abstract thinker. As we have seen, he had as a young man no thorough-going philosophical formation, either in ancient, scholastic, or modern philosophy. Indeed, he had something of that distaste for abstract thought which Edmund Bishop, who himself was perhaps influenced by Acton, seems to have impressed on all his friends—something, but not all, for he had a more speculative mind than Bishop, had been influenced by von Hügel and had absorbed a certain knowledge of German philosophy. But he had grown to maturity untouched by the Thomist revival and remained curiously eclectic and agnostic, even on many of the deepest questions of philosophy and speculative theology. Although without feeling any attraction towards the specific opinions of the opponents of Thomism, he undoubtedly, especially in his latter years, became less receptive to Thomist ideas and doctrines, and was in the habit of saying that in these deep questions a healthy agnosticism was the best course, and that one should recognize that they were too profound for our inspection.

His forte was unquestionably the critical elucidation and presentation of historical and literary questions regarded in their positive aspect. In assessing the value of the internal and external evidence for a document's genuineness, in making the meaning of an author clear by analysis of his thought and comparison of many texts; in fixing the significance of a phrase, and in tracing the history of an idea—in all this Abbot Butler was supremely competent. The careful reader of *Benedictine Monachism*, for example, will notice again and again that many problems, great and small, are thus decided in its pages— and few of the points thus decided will ever need to be re-opened. It was only when he trespassed upon questions not susceptible of 'positive' treatment—where eternal truth and falsehood, right and wrong, were at stake, and the weighing of evidence and massing of authorities counted for nothing—it was here that Abbot Butler's mind was seen to less advantage.

We have remarked on his relative lack of appreciation of the beautiful. Many of those who first came to know him when he was abbot formed the opinion that the exclusion of so many interests and appreciations from his mind was the outcome of asceticism of some kind. This would seem, at least to the present writer, to be an incorrect view. Doubtless he always had in a high degree the power of dispensing at need with much that to many seems indispensable; one secret of his industry and success was his power of concentration, and it is probable that when abbot he consciously made a selection from the many matters and interests which attracted him and closed his eyes to some to avoid useless dissipation of time and energy. But there was a fundamental characteristic which was not due to any religious or practical motive, and which accounted for not a little in the story of his life. It is hard to describe in one word; perhaps self-sufficiency, rightly understood, comes nearest. There was in Abbot Butler a certain inability to give and to receive—and to perceive.[1] He often spoke and wrote of his intimate friendships with others, but he understood by friendship and intimacy less than is properly their meaning. In many ways affectionate and emotional by nature, it may be doubted whether he had that capacity of giving which is of the essence of deep friendship, or the correlative capacity of receiving the impress of another's personality. Besides this, he was not a good judge of character, either natural or spiritual. More than once during his years of office his judgement was proved utterly wrong in this respect, and even when his main judgement of character was correct, it was correct, so to say, only *in grosso*, and the various potentialities, flaws and excellencies were lost on him altogether. Conversely, for all his transparent kindness, Abbot Butler was never one to whom to turn at a crisis of doubt or difficulty. Although as abbot he encouraged all, and especially his young monks, to come to him if ever they needed help, and although his kindliness was taken for granted by all, it may be doubted whether many approached him in those periods of hesitancy and anxiety which do not fail to come, especially in the early years of religious life. Certainly, more than one made the experiment, only to retire disappointed, for he was almost entirely without intuition, both in

---

[1] I have written above that 'he loved giving'. So he did; he loved giving help, advice, money where he could. But he did not, could not, give *himself* to another.

great matters and in small. In such things, a miss is as good as a mile; by some moral law of reaction, one who fails to understand almost always creates an atmosphere of misunderstanding. Certain it is that few, if any, felt that sense of sympathy and understanding which, even if it be but tacit, has such power to win affection and inspire devotion. No one could fail, if not to admire deeply, at least to respect Abbot Butler sincerely, but between respect and admiration, on the one hand, and ardent affection and devotion on the other, there is a gulf hard to bridge. The contrast here between him and his predecessor was great, and goes far to explain why it was that on more than one crucial occasion Abbot Butler found himself without the support on which he had counted.

He was not by nature a strong or masterful character. It would indeed be absurd to a degree to attribute radical weakness of will to one who throughout his life was an example of self-control and ordered regularity, and who had throughout so great an influence upon others. Yet it is certain that when no clear principle was at stake, that is, on all the numberless occasions of daily life when purposes cross, he readily gave way to any masterful or self-confident temperament. This was the more noticeable since Dom Leander Ramsay, his headmaster, was a man of great natural self-confidence; Abbot Butler, indeed, used to speak of Dom Leander's 'iron will', and the very phrase by its exaggeration shows the influence a dominant personality could exercise over him. Yet even here his natural lack of complexity was apparent, for he was not weak or hesitant, like many of great mental ability, because he could see clearly various conflicting points of view; he could not. Rather, he lacked the qualities of force and initiative and self-assertion in the face of determined opposition. Also, like many minds of a scholarly type, he was easily impressed by one who either really or apparently possessed the power of immediate and efficient practical action; he was thus led not infrequently to ignore the solid practical ability of others not naturally self-assertive, and, by a kind of subconscious revenge, to be abrupt and instant in his commands to them. Though never sensitive or intuitive to public opinion, he felt very deeply— sometimes more deeply than the facts warranted—any direct or out-

329

spoken opposition. Indeed, his inability to withstand or break down a determined resistance, together with his inability to sympathize with and understand others at all deeply, were undoubtedly his two greatest natural disabilities, and were responsible for any element of failure there may have been in his life as superior.

Abbot Butler was on the whole an extremely ineffective public speaker and preacher. The deepest cause of his failure was probably once more that lack of intuition and sympathy which prevented him from making the personal contact with his audience without which the spark cannot pass. A contributory cause was, however, a curious negligence in preparing what he was about to say. As a result, he would on occasion enter the calefactory at Downside, to give a conference to an exceedingly alert audience, with no kind of preparation whatsoever, relying on a passage from the Rule to provide a text and inspiration. As his whole genius was singularly unadapted to extemporary exposition, the result was sometimes quite ludicrous, and he would spend several minutes translating simple Latin into faulty English.[1] At other times he would read chapters of his forthcoming books, and here again many of his hearers were left quite unmoved and uninterested by pages which later, when printed, seemed full of vigour. On the other hand, when some domestic event or spiritual issue touched him deeply, he would trenchantly and familiarly (and often with real insight and humour) deliver a pronouncement or an exhortation which could hardly be bettered. But he rarely shone when preaching to a mixed audience. It came, therefore, as a genuine surprise to all who knew him, when he so successfully captured the attention of Hyde Park audiences. Doubtless the serious preparation he made and his transparent sincerity had much to do with his success.[2]

The word self-sufficiency has been used on a previous page; not to imply that Abbot Butler was in any serious way self-centred, but that through all his dealings with others there ran that strain of un-

---

[1] A celebrated utterance of his in a conference on the vexed question of the precise meaning of Benedictine stability may be instanced: 'A stable monk—well—is a monk—well—who is stable.'

[2] Professor F. C. Burkitt, in *The Cambridge Review* (27 April 1934), speaks of this 'success due rather to obvious sincerity and enthusiasm than to oratorical power'.

perceptiveness which occasionally amounted to something very near stolidity. It was a common experience with those who lived in close contact with him that he would on occasion pass them by on the stairs or in the cloister, looking directly at them but without the slightest smile, nod or sign of recognition. This experience, indeed, was so common and so trying, that I have known more than one in the habit of going a considerable distance out of his way to avoid passing the abbot. Indeed, in many small ways he completely lacked the social tact that sets others at their ease. He lacked entirely the gift of taking the colour or atmosphere of a conversation; he lacked also the capacity for 'making' conversation or drawing out the best in another, yet apparently he was quite unconscious of his disability in this respect. Often I have seen him, when abbot, approach a group and stand perfectly silent on its fringe; it was as if an iceberg had drifted up; the conversation flagged, members of the group dropped off, and as likely as not the abbot would be left standing alone, apparently oblivious of what had happened, exactly where he had first halted. Another kind of incident was equally common. He was, when abbot, exceedingly careful, indeed punctilious, in calling upon parents of boys he knew well or of young monks, when they were staying at Stratton, and taking tea with them; but, having announced himself, would make no attempt whatsoever to break down the feeling of constraint caused by the presence of a prelate who was known also to be extremely learned. Long pauses would take place in the conversation, during which he drank tea, lifting the cup slowly with both hands to his lips, and when the allotted time had passed, he consulted his watch and departed. At times his discouragement of conversation was not merely negative, but positive. He would receive a statement with a cold 'Oh', or an expression of enthusiasm with a still more emphatic 'It doesn't appeal to me' It was not to be wondered at that many thought that this lack of interest was due to the intolerance of a man of learning or an ascetic for every-day trifles. This was, however, certainly not the case. Often he was simply pre-occupied with other thoughts. But even when this was not so there was something in his mental composition which made him insensitive to any topic of conversation which did not evoke memories in his own mind. Even in his last years at Ealing, when his geniality was more in evidence, he would automatically fall out of any conversation which became desultory or trivial—not from any ethical or spiritual principle, but simply because it meant nothing to him, and he had none of that sympathetic tact which takes and enjoys all that comes, the small with the great.

It was often thought and said that he had no sense of humour. This was not so, yet it would be equally untrue to say that his sense of humour was normal. Here, as elsewhere, it was not that he lacked the humanity, the kindly feeling, the tolerance that lie behind humour; rather, he lacked the tact, the flexibility, the grasp of the subtleties of character or situation that lie behind the daily wit and humour of a body of men. Topical allusions, slang, plays upon words, catch phrases—to all such he was stone deaf; and whereas most men, from whatever varied motives, conceal their lack of appreciation, Abbot Butler would ask, point blank, 'What does that mean?' and, having been informed, would assert roundly, 'If that is a joke, I don't see it'. This inability to catch the point of a story was so notorious that on one occasion two young men, one of whom was the brilliant and lamented Stephen Hewett, then an undergraduate at Balliol, engaged in a competition of telling anecdotes to Abbot Butler—the winner being he who told the greater number of proved excellence which were not appreciated. In particular he was entirely unperceptive of the type of humour which Mr P. G. Wodehouse has made his own, and it is not surprising that on more than one occasion the mention of Mr Wodehouse's name provoked the question: 'And who is he?' Needless to say, he would have fallen a ready victim to a hoax of any kind. When on one occasion a bogus letter, purporting to come from the bishop of the diocese, but actually concocted by two of his community, accused a third member of modernistic tendencies, Abbot Butler was completely deceived. Yet to say that he had no sense of humour would be quite untrue. It was, it may be granted, often of a somewhat primitive kind. Only a few weeks before his death he was heard to give a life-like imitation of the pulpit voice of a Benedictine prelate, long since dead, whose mourn-

332

ful cadences in a dim Liverpool church were indistinguishable from the sirens of the shipping groping its way down the Mersey. But he could appreciate subtler things, and some of his anecdotes of past worthies of the Church and Congregation were exquisitely amusing. And although, as has been said, witty allusions were completely lost on him, he certainly had, as abbot, the saving quality of being able, on occasion, to laugh heartily at the vagaries of individuals, where heavy-handed treatment would have failed altogether.[1] Nor is the phrase 'to laugh heartily' a *façon de parler* when applied to him. One who knew him well writes:

He could break St Benedict's rule as to *risus multus aut excussus* as well as anyone.[2] When he was abbot and occupied the large south-east room on the second floor, it was no unusual thing to hear his loud guffaws ringing along the gallery; and in my experience his laughter was not that of dull good humour: when he gave vent there was usually something to laugh at. Artificial jokes he could not do with, but incongruities arising in real life tickled him—his laughter, loud and long, is one of the recollections that are fixed in my mind.

His complete inability to appreciate any kind of allusive humour was most apparent when there was a question of his own words bearing a second meaning. Indeed, his capacity for verbal tactlessness in this respect on public occasions amounted to something very near genius, and his speeches of welcome or congratulation were often heard by an audience divided between dismay and irreverent delight; it was once suggested that a ceremony of inauguration in which he took part should change its description from 'laying the first stone' to 'dropping the first brick'—a suggestion, it may be remarked, of which the point would have been entirely lost on Abbot Butler himself. Equally tactless was his habit of addressing to unsuspecting guests, on rising from the breakfast table, some such

[1] An example may be given which will perhaps appeal only to those familiar with the daily round of the religious life. Many years ago a certain junior monk frequently, when 'antiphoner', omitted to ring the prescribed bells. Abbot Butler often supplied the omissions himself. One day he left in the junior's room a note to this effect: 'Shall be away today. Please get another to ring Angelus. E.C.B.' Then espying on the table a heap of small coins, which should have been given back to the procurator, he weighted his note down with it, and so departed.

[2] *Reg. S. Ben.* c. 4: 'Risum multum aut excussum non amare.'

sentence as: 'Well, I'll say good-bye as I expect you'll be gone by midday.' Those unacquainted with him may be pardoned for having taken this as a broad hint; actually, it was merely the spontaneous expression of his thoughts: he judged the visit had come to an end, and did not wish to miss the formality of leave-taking.

This trait of lack of sensitiveness and tact was shown in yet another way. His appreciative references to his own writings in conversation were frequent—'It's a good piece of work—it's interesting—it's *grippy*'—and an observant reader of his later work can easily detect a whole series of cross-references to his own opinions and actions as to some final criterion. This was certainly not vanity, in the ordinary sense of the word; yet it was not exactly, as some supposed, simple candour. Direct and unreflective it certainly was; it sprang from what has already been called his self-sufficiency, and Abbot Butler had not that social sense which instinctively realizes what impression words will produce upon others, and that self-commendation, even when justified, rarely escapes remark.

He was, as has been said, exceedingly—some would say excessively—regular in all his habits. One could safely have set one's watch by his appearance in choir before Matins. This regularity extended to the smallest detail. All will remember his progress round the cricket field at Downside when a match was going forward. He felt it his duty to be there and to speak to any visitors; accordingly at a precise moment he appeared, in an uncovered habit if the weather were settled, in an Inverness cape if it were chilly, with an umbrella carried on his shoulder like a rifle if there were fear of rain; he always appeared at the north-west corner and disappeared beneath the bank to the north-east, having all but completed the circuit; he was never known either to take a seat or make a single step in the reverse direction.

With an equal regularity, extending throughout the year, he took his bath at a quarter before five on Saturday afternoons. Should the bathroom he affected be occupied he would inquire at the door who was within and beg him to make haste. Nothing was allowed to displace this bath hour. On one occasion it so happened that Dr Armitage Robinson, then dean of Wells, brought over his friend

Dr Davidson, archbishop of Canterbury, to visit Downside. Abbot Butler showed the distinguished visitor round till the appointed hour arrived, when he duly excused himself and proceeded to the bathroom.[1]

If this regularity, which could not escape notice in a superior, served occasionally to raise a smile or to start a legend, it was altogether admirable in its wider effects. It enabled Abbot Butler, as has been said, to accomplish a great deal without any parade at all. Not uncommonly those in important offices in a great establishment such as Downside betray their lack of leisure and absorption in work by the irregularity of their hours and appearances; Abbot Butler's regularity was such, even in the midst of anxieties, that he doubtless lost some of that sympathy and consideration which is given to those who show symptoms of anxiety and fatigue. He never wasted the time of himself and others in aimless conversation; he never lost time by indecisive pondering. Others naturally came to respect his regularity. They knew that whatever the matter under discussion (short of the rarest extremity) the abbot would break off to make his half-hour's prayer before supper; they knew also that at the sound of the bell for Office he would immediately rise; and all this served as a most salutary tonic.

Abbot Butler was careless of external appearances, and here again there was room for legend to grow. Owing to his hand's shaking and to the fact that he never used a safety razor, his morning's shave always left much to be desired; his face often showed clearly enough both where the razor had cut too deep and where it had not cut deep enough. He was equally careless about his dress, and although when abbot he had his habit perforce regularly brushed and repaired, he rarely was measured for a new suit of clothes. Besides this, just as some men can look well dressed in borrowed or ready-made clothes, so upon Abbot Butler the best clothes seemed ill-fitting, and hung loosely or fell into creases. During the greater part of his abbacy he was in the habit of digging in the garden for an hour or so on two or three days in the week; the spectacle was then to be seen of the

---

[1] This story is often told with the addition that he gave the reason for his departure to the archbishop. This was not the case; but the incident is otherwise quite historical.

abbot president of the English Benedictine Congregation, who was also a scholar of European reputation, issuing from the door of his abbey carrying a spade over his shoulder, rifle fashion, and wearing mud-encrusted boots, ancient trousers and tail coat green with age, with a shapeless green cap on his head, worn back to front. It says much for the mental power and distinction that was present in every line of Abbot Butler's countenance that even when so clad he would never have passed for an ordinary man. Indeed he recalled nothing so much as one's conception of an impoverished nobleman.

So regular was Abbot Butler's life that the memory can easily recall his habits. He rarely remained working in his room all the afternoon. When he did not work in the garden or walk to the cricket field two alternatives remained. On wet or threatening afternoons he would walk in the grounds—never in the long shrubberies—and on these days he always came to tea without a hood, having taken it off when putting on his cape. The other alternative was a walk. Despite his weak knee he was an energetic walker, and wisely used his walks as a means of contact with the younger members of his community. Generally, to be asked to walk with the abbot meant that some pronouncement was pending affecting one's conduct or one's future. Such a prospect became well-nigh a certainty if the direction taken was along the Wells Road. The conversation, never brisk, would flag perceptibly as the railway bridge and the 'Thousand-pound House' were reached. Here, if at all, the pronouncement would be made; if that buoy were rounded without incident nothing further was to be anticipated. Besides these semi-official walks, Abbot Butler would not infrequently lead the novices out on 'month-days' for a longer excursion, which included tea. The present writer well remembers one such occasion when, with a single companion, he was so taken. The going was heavy; at tea-time we found ourselves at Oakhill; Abbot Butler entered a wayside public house and ordered tea. The meal was long coming, and as we sat in the frigid surroundings of an inn parlour conversation ceased altogether and the abbot fell asleep, leaving us in ludicrous silence on each side of his chair. This delay upset all calculations; when we reached the far end of the Mile Road it was clear that we should be late for Vespers; Abbot Butler therefore instructed us to run, and passers-by had the satisfaction of seeing two young clerics running down the main road followed by an older companion, in a long coat, walking fast and awkwardly behind.

The memory runs back to many such incidents, all of which recall at once the simplicity and the formality of his tastes. There were the long walks each Easter vacation along the ridge of the Mendips, with a picnic lunch at the Waggon and Horses. The ritual each year was invariable, even down to the formula employed on the postcard sent to the inn on the day before, and the spot in the lane leading to Stoke House where Abbot Butler took off his coat and handed it to the senior novice to carry. There were the open-air bathes in the summer (for Abbot Butler loved bathing) when he sat on the end of the diving board and crossed himself before tumbling into the water. Such recollections may seem to some trivial in the extreme; they are certainly only concerned with small strokes of character; but only by a mass of such small strokes can a picture take shape. To a long generation at Downside Abbot Butler was an institution, and as such scrutinized under every aspect. Had he not been essentially massive such trifles would never have clung to the memory; as it is, they, and the recollection of his mental power, will alike be long in fading from the mind.

Of set purpose, nothing has hitherto been said of the deepest and most essential aspect of Abbot Butler's character—the spiritual, supernatural life of the soul, in so far as it is traceable in its external manifestations. Here, necessarily, we touch on ground which is sacred and which cannot be explored without hesitation. But to leave unsaid or unsuggested what alone gave Abbot Butler his supreme significance to many would seem unfitting in such a memoir as this.

We may, then, say at once and without the slightest fear of contradiction that the greatest debt that Downside owes to him is a spiritual one. His teaching and his writing did much, but the example of his life—of a man *simplex et rectus ac timens Deum*—and above all of his love of prayer, did far more. If a spirit of prayer, the direct love and adoration of God, be the most priceless possession of a religious community, the debt of St Gregory's to Abbot Butler will only be known when the secrets of all hearts are revealed and that tremendous judgement, of which St Benedict so repeatedly warns his abbot in his Rule, shows to all the value of his works.

Abbot Butler was often, when alive, referred to as a typical Benedictine; and I have heard at least one of those who came under his care say that he seemed to realize in himself the picture that the imagination paints of St Benedict himself. Certainly in his years as abbot he gave to his sons an almost perfect model of a monk's life. In all his tastes he was simple—and even, as has been said, severe. He never smoked, and drank water only; he made it a strict rule never to possess more than a hundred books for his private use—and at the time of his death had less than this. He never failed his hour's mental prayer, wherever he might find himself. The present writer has seen him making this prayer on the platform of Mangotsfield Junction and walking round Parker's Piece at Cambridge; when visiting Dulwich, when it was a Downside parish, he used for this purpose the half-hour he spent on the top of an omnibus. He took from Father Baker the practice of a morning and evening half-hour of private prayer. The former is binding on all English Benedictines by their constitutions; the latter, called in distinction the 'second half-hour', was warmly recommended to his young monks. Often he would advise them to take it up as a Lenten exercise, and often, when once adopted, it became a life-long practice.

He loved the liturgy, and welcomed the reforms of calendar, breviary and chant which were effected during his life-time. It needed no small courage, no small belief in supernatural values, to initiate the daily sung conventual mass at Downside, for it was instituted, not merely from a love of dignified external forms of worship, but from a conviction that the presence of the monastic family at prayer during the Holy Sacrifice was the best employment of time that could be made. All, whether at Downside or at Ealing, will remember his visits to the Lady Statue after mass or in the evening; and for many years he was in the habit of burning seven candles before the statue of St Benedict at Downside as a petition to our Holy Father for seven novices.

Indeed, to those who knew him as abbot, his whole life seemed bound up with religious duties, and it was impossible to imagine him acting in a merely worldly manner. His spirituality, like the whole of his character, was simple and straightforward; the present writer would hazard the opinion that at no period was there a great interior struggle or crisis, and this may have made him the less sensitive to the needs of others. He himself repeatedly referred to one book, and one alone, as the chief formative influence upon him—Father Baker's *Sancta Sophia*. This he re-read every Lent for many years, perhaps more than thirty, besides going through the greater part each year with his novices. No other book, no other writer—not the *Imitation*, not St Teresa, not St Francis of Sales, not St John of the Cross—ever challenged the place held by Fr. Baker. When first visiting Cambridge in 1895 Dom Butler, along with others in Armitage Robinson's rooms, was asked what single author he would choose to take with him if marooned on a desert island. He chose St Augustine, and twenty-five years later he wrote in words which are very revealing:

Augustine is for me the Prince of Mystics, uniting in himself, in a manner I do not find in any other, the two elements of mystical experience, *viz.* the most penetrating intellectual vision into things divine, and a love of God that was a consuming passion. He shines as a sun in the firmament, shedding forth at once light and heat in the lustre of his intellect and the warmth of his religious emotion.[1]

But St Augustine did not mould Abbot Butler's mind as did Father Baker.

This memoir then would have failed entirely of its purpose had it not done something to show that Abbot Butler's chief work for Downside and for all whom he helped to mould was a spiritual, supernatural work. What priest, what monk but would wish such an epitaph could be his! But there is a gulf between virtuous excellence of life and sanctity, and although perhaps none of those who lived in daily intercourse with Abbot Butler could call to their remembrance any occasion when he had acted or spoken against charity or truth, or had uttered any seriously unworthy or lowering word, however

[1] *Western Mysticism* (2nd ed., London, 1927), p. 24.

unpremeditated, perhaps they would feel that there was something too 'sensible', too natural in him, that there was nothing in his life of that folly of the saints, that sharing of the Cross, that loss of everything to gain Christ which, rare though it be, is the only hall-mark of sanctity. And, weighty as his words and example doubtless were, they did not come with that ultimate sanction, that *quod scio loquor* of the saints, nor did they possess that rare power of wrenching a life from its set course and turning it to God. Another great Gregorian, his successor, had something of this power. In the years that have passed since his death more than one of those who knew Dom Leander Ramsay well has recalled that to serve his mass or to speak a few words with him was an experience unique of its kind; that there was there the impact of something akin to holiness.[1] Be this as it may, there was something measured, a *ne quid nimis*, about Abbot Butler which, we feel, the saints cannot have. Nor, when we read his utterances on the contemplative life, can we fail to realize that he is as it were speaking *ab extra*. Indeed, he frankly and characteristically disclaimed any kind of mystical experience, and the manner of his disclaimer conveys far more than the mere words. Abbot Butler wrote more about mysticism than did those great elder brethren in religion, Ullathorne and Hedley, but they both reach a depth he does not touch. Hard as it may be to express in words, yet in some strange, inexplicable way many must have felt that Abbot Butler thought in terms of mind rather than of soul, of the natural rather than of the supernatural.

Yet, when all is said, the memory of him that will remain as long as life to those who knew him best is the memory of his simplicity of life, his charity and dignity of thought, and his unfailing regularity of adoration. He loved Downside dearly, very dearly; and

---

[1] There is always a strong temptation to assess the various qualities of the three great Gregorians—Ford, Butler and Ramsay—and compare one with another. To the present writer, Ford appears the ablest administrator and the wisest leader of men, and the one who (apart from health) was least handicapped by disabilities of one kind or another; Butler, unquestionably the ablest scholar, appears also as the most masculine intellect and diffuser of ideas; Ramsay, with more limitations than either of the others, appears most to realize in himself what we mean by the word 'great', when applied to character: he appears also, as has been suggested in the text, as the most near to supernatural holiness of the three. *Alii aliter judicent.*

Downside owes much to him. He won for St Gregory's a recognition in the realm of scholarship which was never accorded to the more widely known work of Gasquet; he helped to win the position which the house has as a fully autonomous abbey; he gave to it when abbot the full liturgical life; but above all this, he lifted up the minds of his sons to God. Those who remember reading *Sancta Sophia* with him in their noviciate will doubtless recollect the emotion with which his voice was filled as he read the eloquent last lines:

If God, by the means of our prayers, give us the grace and courage to proceed *de virtute in virtutem*, according to these steps and directions we shall, without doubt, sooner or later arrive unto the top of the mountain, where God is seen: a mountain, to us that stand below, environed with clouds and darkness, but to them that have their dwelling there, it is peace and serenity and light. It is an intellectual heaven, where there is no sun or moon, but God and the Lamb are the light thereof.

With such memories in our minds we can recommend his soul to the mercy of God, confident that he, *ipse memor suae gentis*, will not forget us when he stands in eternal light, before the Throne.

II. THE WORKS AND THOUGHT OF ABBOT BUTLER[1]

In his last years, when looking back over his life, Abbot Butler, as has already been remarked, was heard more than once to say that his happiest years had been those spent at Benet House, Cambridge. He was, in fact, by inclination and capability a scholar; he moved more easily in the world of books and of ideas than of men and events; he enjoyed above all the society and conversation of scholars. He himself habitually wrote of the Venerable Bede and Mabillon as the 'type for all time' of the Benedictine student and scholar; he may be allowed to speak on in words which many would have applied to the writer himself:

Benedictine history has not produced many Bedes...who, 'amidst the observance of regular discipline and the daily care of singing in the church, always took delight in learning, teaching and writing'....At no

[1] [The original article was followed by a Bibliography of Abbot Butler (*DR*, vol. LII, pp. 466–72), here omitted.]

time have the general mass of Benedictines been learned. But they have tended to produce at all times individuals re-incarnating the type of Ven. Bede. And when monks of this type do appear they are recognized as no chance product, no extraneous growth or grafting; but the natural fruits of certain elements of Benedictine life and the character and temper of mind it fosters.[1]

The period of his early manhood at Downside was in many ways favourable to him. It is true that the level of teaching and achievement in the school could not for a moment bear comparison with the standards of contemporary public schools, and the ecclesiastical prohibition against Catholics attending the universities was still in force. But there was the presence of Edmund Bishop, who at that time was a stimulating and helping force of great power, and whose own tastes had led him along the lines of ecclesiastical and monastic history—indeed, in the latter field, as in that of liturgy, he probably had a sweep of accurate knowledge, based on a wide reading of the sources, unsurpassed by any contemporary Englishman. Bishop, also, had helped to develop the natural gifts and tastes of Prior Gasquet, Dom Gilbert Dolan, and others. The Downside with which all have been familiar for more than a quarter of a century—extensive buildings housing a great public school—was then quite in the unseen future, and although Prior Gasquet and Prior Ford turned much of their attention to the school, they had no conception of the developments they were to live to witness, and it was possible, under the inspiration of Bishop, for the most gifted of the young monks to suppose that the chief work of Downside for the Church in England—apart from the mission—might well be in the realm of letters, thus reviving some of the Maurist glories.

What they hoped for was indeed realized in large measure far more speedily than any could have foreseen, for the talents and industry of Dom Gasquet, who was singularly fortunate in the choice of subject for his first considerable work, were rewarded with a wide and instantaneous recognition which must have been both reassuring and stimulating. Dom Cuthbert, for his part, had, as we have seen, many of the essential qualities of a scholar and developed them him-

[1] *Benedictine Monachism* (2nd ed.), pp. 336-7.

self without aid; when the comparative insufficiency of his actual training is remembered, the mastery he achieved, not only in the realm of history, but in that of Greek and Latin textual criticism, is as remarkable as it is admirable.

He had of his own accord, when at Belmont, turned to the early history of English monasticism. The first piece of work which really showed his gifts was the outcome of this, and appeared in two long articles in *The Downside Review*, then in its infancy, with the title 'Was St Augustine of Canterbury a Benedictine?'. The first of these, devoted to proving that St Gregory the Great was a Benedictine monk, is typical alike in its exact method, careful citation of authorities and clear style of all that was to come after. Significantly enough, it appeared in a number of the *Review* of great strength, which included amongst its contributors Bishop Hedley, Doms Gasquet, Dolan and Almond, Edmund Bishop, St George Mivart and Alfred Maskell. No other work by him of any weight appeared for more than ten years, with the important exception of the *Notes* on the origin and early history of the Congregation which have been referred to on an earlier page. Although he continued to contribute from time to time to the *Review*, the total list of his articles in the twenty-five years (1880–1905) before his abbacy is not large, though the titles serve to show the direction his studies took, e.g. 'Daily Life at Old St Gregory's' (1892), 'Mabillon' (1893), 'The Apostles' Creed' (1894), 'The Text of St Benedict's Rule' (1899). Early in the 'nineties he began to turn his attention to the history of Christian origins which had recently been illustrated by the work of Lightfoot and was at the moment being exploited in an anti-Catholic sense by Harnack and other German historians, to whom Duchesne and Batiffol were replying in France. These studies issued in a remarkable quintet of articles in *The Dublin Review*—'Bishop Lightfoot and the early Roman See' (1893), 'Early Christian Literature' (1896), 'The Apostolic Age' (1897), 'The Modern Critical School' (1898) and 'Harnack's Chronology' (1899).[1]

These two groups of articles show his capability in two very

[1] [Reprinted in *Religions of Authority and the Religion of the Spirit* (London, 1930).]

different directions—that of exact, methodical, critical scholarship, and that of lucid, if more superficial, exposition. They thus foreshadow the two classes into which the more important works of his maturity fall. On the one hand are the *Lausiac History* of Palladius, the critical edition of the Rule and the basis, at least, of *Western Mysticism*; on the other, the encyclopedia articles and the historical and spiritual writings of his later years. The *Lausiac History*, which secured his reputation and is undoubtedly his most important work of pure scholarship, originated as we have seen at Downside, and was taken to Cambridge when Dom Cuthbert went thither as head of Benet House in 1896. It appeared in two parts as one of the series of Texts and Studies, then appearing under the general editorship of Armitage Robinson. The first part was published in 1898 and consisted of essays on points of textual and historical criticism. A twofold problem had awaited the editor. Until some twenty-five years previously the *Lausiac History* had been accepted by all as being reliable history and the work of Palladius *c*. 420 A.D., but recently it had been attacked on grounds both textual and historical; Dom Butler had therefore first to decide whether a genuine text of the *Lausiac History* existed, and then to judge what, if any, authority belonged to it and other documents dealing with Egyptian monachism. The textual question was solved as follows: 'Palladius' work exists in two different forms or redactions, a long recension and a short recension... the thesis is enunciated that in spite of the current and universal acceptance of the long recension by historians..., the short recension is in reality the true *Lausiac History*.' And as regards the authorship: 'The Greek *Lausiac History* is accepted as the authentic and original work of Palladius, there being no ground for suspecting that he used earlier written materials.' As regards its historical authority: 'It is found to possess the ordinary marks of an authentic and veracious document.' Finally, the general result of this twofold inquiry was: 'To determine canons of sound historical criticism for the employment of the documents relating to monastic origins; and...to restore confidence in this whole circle of literature.' This, it may be said, Dom Butler's work triumphantly succeeded in achieving, and since the appearance of these two volumes his conclusions have been treated as solidly established by all historians of the period and by all students of monastic origins.[1]

At the end of the first volume was inserted a survey of monastic history from the earliest beginnings to the days of St Benedict; the work necessary for this and the general conclusions arrived at stabilized, so to say, for the remainder of his life all Dom Butler's outlook on the relation of the Rule to previous monastic and eremitical theory and practice.

His general conclusion was enunciated as follows: 'This twofold break with the past, in the elimination of austerity and in the sinking of the individual in the community, made St Benedict's Rule less a development than a revolution in monachism. It may be almost called a new creation.'[2] These critical studies served at once to justify and to prepare for an edition of the Greek text, and Dom Butler was already engaged on this work when the first part appeared.

All familiar with his handwriting and literary methods, and with the meticulous care and neatness employed on his collation-slips by Dom Leander Ramsay, who for part of the same period was engaged in similar work on St Cyprian at Munich and elsewhere, will not be surprised that the latter was horrified at the rough-and-ready appearance of the Palladius collations; but Palladius was printed and accepted as a definitive edition, while the collation sheets of Cyprian are still gathering dust in cupboards at Downside. The text of the *Lausiac History* duly appeared in 1904, and, as we have seen, its publication marked the end of Dom Butler's residence at Cambridge.

Between the work on Palladius and the completion of the edition of the Rule came a steady output of articles, chiefly of a critical and learned nature. Several of these appeared in *The Journal of Theological Studies*, and its pages contained many careful reviews of important books by Dom Butler; to it, also, he contributed for several years (1900–06) the Chronicle of Hagiographica.

---

[1] [Since this was written Abbot Butler's edition of the *Lausiac History* has been severely criticized by Prof. R. Draguet in *Muséon*, vol. LXIII (1950), pp. 205–30, and defended by Mr D. J. Chitty in *Journal of Theological Studies*, N.S., vol. VI (1955), pp. 102–10.]

[2] All the above quotations are from a kind of précis which Dom Butler made of his book in *The Downside Review*, vol. XVII (1898), pp. 261–78.

To *The Hibbert Journal* in 1906 he contributed what is perhaps his most able essay on a general subject—'Religions of Authority and the Religion of the Spirit'[1]—an essay which reveals an understanding of currents of thought and an ability to grasp and enunciate wide principles. Undoubtedly, for a short time immediately before and after leaving Cambridge, Dom Butler cherished the hope of entering actively into some of the philosophico-theological discussions then arousing so much interest in Europe and which had their ending, so far as the Church was concerned, with the papal pronouncements on modernism. For a variety of reasons the hope was never realized, and this essay in the *Hibbert* is almost its sole memorial.

The *Lausiac History*, despite the fact that the number of those who read even the English Prolegomena must have always been small, created for Dom Butler a reputation which travelled far outside Cambridge or Catholic circles, and for the following decade his pen was in request whenever the services of Catholic scholarship were enlisted by those outside the Church. Thus the editors of the first volume of the Cambridge Medieval History and those responsible for the eleventh edition of the *Encyclopaedia Britannica* recognized him as the most eminent Catholic scholar to whom they could turn for the history of the monastic and religious orders; for the Cambridge History he wrote the chapter on monasticism; for the *Encyclopaedia* some sixty articles on the founders and history of almost all the monastic and mendicant orders, including the important and necessarily somewhat controversial ones on St Francis and the Franciscans. Naturally, these articles varied much in value according to the measure in which they covered fields where Dom Butler was a specialist; but some, and especially the monastic ones, are careful pieces of work, and it is unfortunate that in the remodelling consequent upon the more popular aim of the latest (twelfth) edition many have been considerably cut down and therefore do not present to the reader the original design of the author.

Meanwhile the material was gradually being amassed for his second serious piece of critical work, which was completed during

---

[1] [Reprinted in the book of that title (1930).]

Abbot Butler's first term of office at Downside (1912) and took the form, appropriately enough, of a critical edition of the Rule of St Benedict. Here again, though he was aided by the work of Wölfflin, Plenkers and Morin, this edition was the first text that could fairly be called critically satisfactory, and this, together with the extremely valuable collection of 'sources' printed at the foot of each page and the elaborate indices, made it at once, what it still remains, the only edition which satisfies students of St Benedict's word and thought. On the title-page the edition was called *critico-practica*, as the intention was to produce a book which could be used with comfort by individual monks (not necessarily interested in textual criticism) and for reading in chapter, choir and refectory; no attempt, therefore, was made at an archaeological reproduction of the orthography and small grammatical solecisms of St Benedict's day, and the *apparatus criticus* of variant readings at the foot of the page was restricted to those really significant, *cruces* being relegated to an appendix; but these minor concessions in no way affected the critical nature of the edition. It may be worth recording that the preface was done into Latin by the then Bishop of Clifton, Dr Burton.

The value of the book was greatly enhanced by the addition of a kind of catechism of the doctrine of St Benedict, compiled for the first novices at Downside. The idea and method of execution of this were alike happy in the extreme; the thing, indeed, could scarcely have been better done; the reader can see, almost at a glance, the *Leitmotive* of the Rule and isolate the key-words. With this *medulla* before him, together with the full *index rerum*, he needs no commentator to come between him and the Master.

The *Rule* was printed with Herder at Freiburg, so as to facilitate its sale in the central European countries. With it Abbot Butler's name first began to penetrate outside England and a narrow circle of scholars, and although the penetration was slow, it was sure, and the *editio critico-practica* gradually found its place in Benedictine monasteries throughout Europe. Fifteen years after its publication a second edition was called for; no changes were found necessary save a few corrections and additions to the *fontes*, and later students have accepted Dom Butler's text. A larger choir edition has within recent years been printed at Stanbrook.[1]

Naturally, this work, added to his routine occupations as abbot, fully occupied his time, and for a few years immediately before and after the outbreak of the war he wrote very little, save a series of pamphlets, privately printed and issued to his community, many of which showed to an eminent degree his grasp of principles and his gift of lucid and compelling exposition. Mention must, however, be made in passing of his contributions to the summer centenary number of *The Downside Review* (1914), which he edited *pro hac vice*. For this he wrote several articles, in particular a sketch of the history of the house from its origins, which included an exceptionally judicious and vividly written account of the conflict with Bishop Baines. This, like all Abbot Butler's serious work, represented the fruit of much reading, and its judgements and conclusions remain as valid today as when they first appeared.

Towards the end of the war, he began composing the series of studies—for they are studies rather than chapters—on St Benedict and the Benedictines which ultimately made up *Benedictine Monachism* (London, 1919). This, in spite of the criticisms of which it has been the object and which could scarcely have failed to find a target on a subject of so wide a scope and such debatable issues, is probably Abbot Butler's greatest single achievement in the realm of original work, for the book combines the critical acumen of a scholar with judgements on spiritual and constitutional questions which derive their value from both the mental and the moral qualities of the writer, and from his long experience in responsible office. Moreover with this book he reached immediately two audiences to whom he had never before spoken *in propria persona*—the cultivated Englishman interested in religious matters, and Benedictine monks scattered throughout the world. Among the former many, not themselves specialists, who had hitherto saluted Abbot Butler's learning from afar, now acknowledged, with something akin to sur-

---

[1] [Abbot Butler's edition has now been superseded as a critical text by B. Linderbauer, *S. Benedicti Regula Monasteriorum* (Bonn, 1928), and R. Hanslik, *Benedicti Regula*, in *Corpus SS. Ecclesiasticorum Latinorum* (Vienna, 1960), but retains its value for the additional matter mentioned above.]

prise, his ability to write a book which could be read with pleasure and interest by the general reader, while among the latter the writer's judgements and doctrine gradually acquired an almost world-wide, if necessarily restricted, influence, especially when translations appeared in French and German. With *Benedictine Monachism*, in fact, began Abbot Butler's influence as a writer on religious and spiritual matters which grew steadily in extent during the fifteen years of life that remained. *Benedictine Monachism* is indeed a remarkably original book, both in matter and form, and we cannot help feeling that alike in its objectivity and its subjectivity—alike in its appeal to history and to personal experience—it is itself typically Benedictine. Many histories and sketches of the Benedictines, as of other religious orders, have been written before and since, and many essays and appreciations of the Benedictine spirit, but never before had there appeared any book treating so fully all the topics—historical, constitutional, ascetical, spiritual—of vital interest to all black monks. Almost every chapter lives and has been lived; it is not written for the occasion or after an academic research; it is the considered judgement of one who has sought and believes himself to have found an answer to a question affecting his whole life and life's interests. *Benedictine Monachism*, in fact, *is* Abbot Butler; therein we may find,

veluti descripta tabella,
vita senis.

In after years he would quote verbatim from it in conversation, and even refer to chapters by their number as to a *locus classicus*. And such indeed more than one of them is.

Benedictine Monachism, besides its historical and constitutional chapters, contained several dealing with prayer and the spiritual life, which revealed an aspect of Abbot Butler's mind hitherto scarcely known to his readers, though familiar to many of his own community.

We have seen on a previous page that from his noviciate upwards Fr. Baker's *Sancta Sophia* had been his spiritual guide, and that contact with Baron Friedrich von Hügel had helped to develop an interest in what is loosely called 'mysticism'. Many years before the appearance of *Western Mysticism* he had copied passages out of

349

THE HISTORIAN AND CHARACTER AND OTHER ESSAYS

St John of the Cross[1] and St Augustine, and the necessity which he always felt of having a theory behind his practice led him often to consider the nature of contemplation and the contemplative life. In *Benedictine Monachism* this element of his thought is seen chiefly in the valuable discussion of Cassian's Conference on Prayer, and in the chapter entitled: 'Is Benedictine Life contemplative?' His next work, *Western Mysticism* (London, 1922), is, as its title implies, consecrated entirely to the subject.

This book, wide as is the popularity which it has enjoyed—a popularity due partly to the subject, and partly to the reputation of the author for a sane outlook and enlightened criticism[2]—cannot be considered an entirely satisfactory piece of work. What may be called its core, the collection, juxtaposition and analysis of a number of passages from SS. Augustine, Gregory and Bernard, is a piece of original work of great interest and provides the reader with a mass of material on which to exercise his judgement; in the realm of mystical theology it resembles the studies in positive theology of the early centuries by such scholars as Tixeront and Batiffol. But the very title shows that Abbot Butler meant to go further than this, and to oppose the 'mysticism' of his three doctors to other forms of mysticism—and this thesis tacitly assumes that 'mysticism' is in some way fluid or changing, unlike the deposit of the Faith. Abbot Butler, in fact, saw, as he supposed, a type of mystical experience in the 'Benedictine centuries' different from others, and in particular from both the Dionysian and the Juanine, and still more from what he took to be the Teresan, and he stated this thesis at some length. Not content with this, he passed on to discuss the reality and the apologetic value of the mystical experience, and to compare Christian with 'nature' mysticism. Finally he added some remarks on the nature of contemplation, and practical instructions for contemplative prayer.

[1] He read St John and copied these passages in preparation for a retreat given at Stanbrook early in the present century. Strange as it may seem, he never again read St John—all his subsequent judgements and citations depend upon these extracts.

[2] In the Preface Abbot Butler quotes a writer in the *Nation* as saying: 'One could read a book on the subject [Mysticism], say, by Abbot Butler of Downside, in complete mental comfort....One would know where one was, what one started from, what had to be taken for granted.'

In all these questions, though many of his judgements and reflexions are of the greatest value, he was venturing upon very deep waters. He was, in fact, attempting to deal *ab extra*, by an eclectic, almost empirical method, with subjects that demand great theological and spiritual precision. He even would appear to have been unaware that these and kindred subjects had been for many years debated by some of the ablest theologians and psychologists in Europe. During the very months in which *Western Mysticism* was going through the press, Père Garrigou-Lagrange was preparing the epoch-making lectures on mystical theology which have given an orientation to so much subsequent work.

For all these reasons the book, though suggestive in the highest degree, left a sense of dissatisfaction, of *malaise*, in the mind of almost every careful reader—a dissatisfaction which not a few critics voiced in reviews or letters. It is significant that Abbot Butler admitted in the second edition that there was a 'serious structural flaw' in the original work; but in truth the flaw was not structural only, and could not be remedied by shifting the component parts, as was done for the new edition. Abbot Butler himself tacitly recognized this by prefacing the second (1927) edition with a theological essay eighty pages long in which he endeavoured to make a synthesis of the conclusions of modern Catholic theologians regarding the mystical life. This preface, which he named 'Afterthoughts', and which represented a year's study, was a gallant attempt, and the author characteristically regarded it as successful and final. But probably few readers have found it so, for once more, as in the original book, it attempts an impossible task—that of arriving at a commonsense, 'practical', eclectic solution of problems not susceptible of such treatment. The 'Afterthoughts', like all Abbot Butler's work, contains many luminous pages, and not infrequently in his search for the true solution he becomes so 'warm' (to use the phrase of the children's game) that the reader fancies that all is about to fall into place,[1] but invariably his curious dislike of

---

[1] Thus on pp. xxx–xxxii he cites with high approval a long passage of Bishop Hedley which leaves nothing to be desired—yet in the pages which follow all is once more set *sub judice*.

351

scientific theology gains the day,[1] and the search ends on a note of uncertainty. Truth, like the ghost in the play, eludes our grasp: ''Tis here! 'Tis here! 'Tis gone!'

Western Mysticism was, in its original form, the work of the two last years of office at Downside. The external record of Abbot Butler's 'last phase', and the unexpected and unfamiliar energies and interests which it revealed, have been described elsewhere. A corresponding descent into the plains took place in his literary labour; he never again produced a work of pure scholarship while, on the other hand, his reputation with the general reading public undoubtedly grew till the day of his death. On arrival at Ealing he began at once the course of reading necessary for a book which he had long desired to write. In his years at Downside, whenever he was asked whom he considered the greatest son of St Gregory's, he always replied without hesitation 'Ullathorne' and had always wished for his life to be written. As it happened, no one had hitherto attempted the task, though many lesser men of that time found their biographers, and although Ullathorne figured as an actor of the first importance in the lives of Wiseman, Newman and Manning. The field was thus clear, and it was appropriate that the work should be done by one of Ullathorne's own monastic family and one, more-over, not wholly unlike him in temper of mind and character, who had been a life-long admirer of his spirit. The book when it appeared, *The Life and Times of Bishop Ullathorne*, 2 vols. (London, 1926) —always referred to by its author as 'the Ullathorne'—was un-questionably a success. Its sales exceeded the publishers' expec-tations, and the main aim of the writer, to vindicate for Ullathorne a secure position among the half-dozen greatest Catholic ecclesiastics of the nineteenth century, has, to judge from all subsequent esti-mates of him, been completely achieved. The book, indeed, was recognized at once as a worthy companion and necessary supple-

---

[1] On p. lxxxii he writes: 'I hope it may not be deemed over venturesome for one not pledged by profession to any particular Catholic theological school to wonder if the rigid methods of speculative theology...really are helpful towards explaining the nature...of mystical theology.' Speculative theology, of course, cannot adequately *explain* what is essentially incommunicable; but it can define mysticism, and say what it is not.

ment to that noble *corpus*—the work of Burton, Bernard and Wilfrid Ward, Purcell and Snead-Cox—which presents so vividly and so adequately the whole of Catholic history from the birth of Challoner to the death of Cardinal Vaughan.

It must, however, be said that it is rather a 'Life and Times' than a biography. Apart from the early chapters, compiled almost entirely from Ullathorne's own autobiographical sketch, the reader is conscious throughout that the outlook is that of a critic and a historian rather than of a biographer *tout court*. The book does little to preserve the strong and original personality of Ullathorne, which impressed itself so vividly on his contemporaries and survived in legend through the next generation. Nor does it throw new light on the inner life and wisdom which helped to develop and were themselves developed by the sanctity of Mother Margaret and her first companions, and which, in the eyes of one admirer at least, give Ullathorne a claim to a place not below but above the three great cardinals with whose lives he was connected. But, within its limits, the Life achieved success and will undoubtedly live, along with the others mentioned above, as long as the figures of that great period continue to fascinate and to challenge.

The Life of Ullathorne showed to a still wider circle than had read *Benedictine Monachism* that Abbot Butler could write vivid, if not always elegant, English, and pronounce sane and incisive judgements on men and movements. It opened the way naturally to his next book. Ullathorne had been present at the Vatican council, and had written from Rome voluminous letters, hitherto unpublished, chiefly to his great friend Mother Imelda Poole at Stone. These had been put at Abbot Butler's disposal, and, unable to make anything like full use of them in the Life, he considered that they would form a basis, or give a character, to a new account of the Vatican council, which had been for the most part neglected, if not shunned, by historians since the first years of polemics immediately after its prorogation.

The *History of the Vatican Council* in two volumes duly appeared in 1930, received on the whole excellent notices in all quarters, and has recently been translated into German, but although the subject might have been expected to have a far wider appeal, the sales were

353

less than in the case of Ullathorne's Life, and the general impression upon the reader's mind is not so satisfactory. This was perhaps largely due to two causes, the one accidental, the latter more essential. The accidental cause was the genesis of the book from Ullathorne's letters. These cannot be said to be of the first importance, however interesting they may be as throwing light here and there on a familiar story. Ullathorne's very real greatness was not of a kind to manifest itself in either the theological or the diplomatic warfare which preceded and accompanied the council, and though his judgement was ever sound and shrewd, his ear was not receptive of the subtler undertones and overtones of that stormy symphony. Nor was he of the innermost circles where the decisive movements were evolved. But there was a deeper cause than this. In his previous books Abbot Butler had indeed dealt with periods of history, but with limited departments which he could control from his knowledge of the sources and personal experience. In the *Vatican Council* he cut across all the great political and intellectual currents of the mid-nineteenth century (to say nothing of earlier discussions), and he was not by training a historian of that period, or indeed of the intellectual and political life of any period. He could, and did, read a dozen or two standard works and sources, but he had only the educated English Catholic's knowledge of the great and manifold movements of thought and policy which were the background and the nursery of all the great European events, and, in consequence, his surveys and narratives however lucid seem thin and superficial to those who have gone deeper. But for all this the *Vatican Council* is by no means a negligible book. It is, and will probably long remain, the only satisfactory history of the council in English; it helped to dispel for non-Catholic Englishmen much of the legend which, originating with Döllinger and fostered in varying measure by Acton, Gladstone and Purcell, had so obscured the true theological issue, and it contains a very great number of shrewd and captivating reflexions on the chief actors and their motives.

As it happened, it was Abbot Butler's last 'substantive' work, to use a favourite adjective of his own. Circumstances, and the problems and questionings to which *Western Mysticism* had given rise, directed his attention once more to the spiritual life, and he undertook a popular exposition of the spiritual teaching of a number of saints and spiritual masters, giving especial attention to St Teresa and St Francis of Sales, and once more wrestling with the problems of applied mystical theology. *Ways of Christian Life* (1932) has all the qualities and defects which characterized Abbot Butler's other writings on spiritual subjects. It is eminently sane, straightforward and helpful, and has probably given encouragement to many to persevere in the devout life. At the same time it has the defects of the 'Afterthoughts'; its theology is professedly eclectic and his interpretation of St Teresa and St John of the Cross is not always in agreement with that commonly put forward by those who have made a special study of the subject.

Meanwhile, besides writing a number of memoirs for *The Downside Review*, he had collected a number of his own essays under the title *Religions of Authority and the Religion of the Spirit*,[1] and had written a long biographical preface to a similar collection of Bishop Hedley's, besides contributing introductions to the volumes of selections from the writings of their founder compiled by the Visitation nuns of Harrow.

Two pieces of work remain unpublished. The first was written in 1932, and was intended to form part of a history of European civilization, to be published by the Oxford University Press. It is in the form of a long article, called 'The Catholic Church and Modern Civilization', and was designed to appear in vol. VI of the history.[2] As it was duly completed and dispatched to the editor, it will doubtless appear in due course. The second was also a long article, to be one of a collection, with the title 'The Pageant of the Popes', and aimed at presenting the most significant figures and periods of the papacy, from the earliest to our own times. Abbot Butler was engaged upon this at the time of his death; as it was far from complete it will presumably never be printed. In any case it may be said that he left behind him nothing that would materially

[1] London, 1930.
[2] [Abbot Butler's contribution was printed in *European Civilisation, its Origin and Development*, ed. E. Eyre, vol. VI (Oxford, 1937), pp. 1333–1510.]

23-2

add to his reputation, and few unused materials. Methodical in all things, he wasted no time or energy in gathering superfluous matter. A word must be said on the form of his literary output. To many —at least till within a few years ago—to speak of Abbot Butler's style would have appeared ludicrous. The formal beauty of language, whether in prose or verse, seemed to mean so little to him, and never at any time of his life does he appear to have felt the need of using words for any purpose save a purely utilitarian one. If he wished to prove, to argue, to demonstrate he would write, but he never wrote from any desire to express himself, his experiences or his emotions in words.[1] A man's letters reveal his character, and it is significant of much that he wrote few letters that were not of a coldly practical character; rarely, I imagine, did anyone experience pleasure in receiving them or feel an inclination to treasure them. What is in so many lives an occasion of self-revelation and bestowal was never so to him. Most will remember his letters (and still more his post-cards) for their characteristic brevity, often telegraphic in form, with the omission of all definite and indefinite articles and auxiliary verbs. Certainly they were not the letters of a stylist.

One reason for this, and for similar peculiarities of style in his books, would seem to have been purely physical. Writing was never easy to him, owing to the nervous malady affecting his hands. He wrote slowly and noisily, with a steel nib (never a fountain pen) which often blotted and scratched the paper, and his writing was enormous in size. Naturally he tended to abbreviate so as to shorten labour and economize space. But apart from this he had little sense of style. As a preacher and speaker he had absolutely none, and his familiar conferences would often be bald enough even to the edge of the comical. Yet in his serious writings there was always a clarity and power; there was nothing cloudy or redundant. The *Dublin* essays showed this well enough, but in his years at Downside carelessness seemed to grow. The constant use of particular words and phrases, not in themselves unusual, became a mannerism; all will remember examples: 'definitive' was one, 'substantive' another,

---

[1] Such apparent exceptions as the 'purple patch' with which *Benedictine Monachism* opens only prove the rule. Abbot Butler felt the book should open with a piece of fine writing.

a 'contribution to the work of the world' a third. To those on the watch the recurrence of these was noticeable even in *Benedictine Monachism*; there was besides always a tendency to coin words— 'grippy' (i.e. showing a grip of the subject) was one such—or to use unusual ones (e.g. 'pullulate') in a neutral, commonplace context. In the very latest years he adopted colloquial words (e.g. 'blurb'), and his chapter headings and characterizations caught some distant echo of film 'captions'.[1] But his straightforwardness of mind always prevented affectation, and on occasion, when the subject called it forth, a real eloquence of language made itself felt, especially in the later books. An extract may be given, typical both as language and for the judgement it embodies:[2]

After reading again and again, and maturely pondering over the materials collected for the Lives of the four great churchmen, Wiseman, Manning, Newman, Ullathorne, the impression finally and clearly graven on my mind is that, taken all in all, Wiseman stands out as the greatest. He was not the deep acute thinker that Newman was; nor the masterful resource-ful man of affairs that Manning was; nor had he the sound practical grip of men and things that Ullathorne had: but in the combination of richly endowed nature, and attractive lovable personality, and well-balanced all-round character, and many-sided intellectual attainments, and successful achievement of a great life-work—in short, as a complete man, he surpassed them all.[3]

Such language as this, if lacking in some of the qualities of the greatest English prose, is nevertheless a serviceable, masculine instrument of thought. One other passage deserves quotation. It is his last tribute to his friend and master, Edmund Bishop, in the *Liber Benefactorum* at Downside, and many will remember his emotion each November when, in reading the list, he came to this name:

EDMUND BISHOP. On 19 February 1917, died at Barnstaple, in his 71st year, Edmund Bishop. He came as a postulant to the monastery in 1886, but was unable to take the monastic habit owing to the delicate state of his health. From that time onward he was constantly staying with us, and for

---

[1] This was not because Abbot Butler was a film fan. So little was he familiar with the language of the screen that he always spoke of 'the mōhvies', 'a mōhvie star'.

[2] I venture to direct the reader's careful attention to this extract; it reveals much of the writer's own character.

[3] *Life and Times of Bishop Ullathorne*, vol. II, pp. 299–300.

357

many years before his death he spent the summer months in our midst. During those years he gave freely to all who sought his aid of the riches of his immense learning, and strove at great pains to impart those true methods of study which he himself had so thoroughly mastered. For his thus fostering amongst us a love of study we shall be for ever grateful, no less than for the valuable advice, founded on his unique knowledge of the constitution and history of the black monks of St Benedict, that he was able to give at a critical moment in the history of our house. His wonderful library,—his most dearly loved possession,—which he had brought together with great pains and sacrifice, he allowed us to inherit on conditions which made it practically a donation, thus enriching the community to a degree which it is difficult to estimate. For these gifts, for his unchanging devotion to Downside, and for the example of his simple and humble life, it will ever be our duty to look upon Edmund Bishop as one of the great benefactors of our monastery.

Abbot Butler, both as teacher and writer, was so essentially a man of thought that any sketch of his life and work would be incomplete without a summary, however brief, of the main lines of his doctrine. As the religious life was, in one way or another, the theme of all his works, we may consider its various aspects, interior and exterior. And first, what may be called its constitutional, political aspect.

Here, by his study of monastic history, he, along with Bishop, Gasquet, Ford and others, early arrived at a conception of Benedictine polity which he never abandoned or modified. This was to regard alike as the norm and the ideal a maintenance of the autonomous abbey of the Rule, associated with others of the same locality or nationality in the congregational bond first imposed by the Lateran council of 1215. In other words, he consistently vindicated for Benedictines direct and ultimate government by the abbot; no intermediate superior should normally come between monk and abbot, nor any higher superior (other than the Holy Father) be above. He also assumed as axiomatic that a monk's life should in normal circumstances be passed wholly in his monastery. All more articulated constitutional organization among black monks, he would say, has in the course of history proved in the long run to be inimical to one or other of the essential notes and virtues of their institute. Few acquainted with monastic history will wish to question this judgement, which Abbot Butler, more than any other writer in modern times, has made acceptable far and wide.

In his early years he had on occasion advocated a life of considerable external severity. Later, partly no doubt owing to the influence of Edmund Bishop and others, and partly as a reaction from certain contemporary movements which he justly regarded as aberrations, he came to see things somewhat differently. We have seen that in his work for the *Lausiac History* he stressed the moderation of St Benedict's Rule, and in all his subsequent writings he reacted very strongly against any note of austerity. For this, and for the thesis current in his books that all modern Benedictine houses may claim to be, even on the purely material side of things, a fair equivalent in the modern world of St Benedict's Cassino, he was attacked by many critics both within and without the Benedictine body. His replies—for Abbot Butler never let a critic have the last word—may be read in the second edition of *Benedictine Monachism*. Few will deny the justice of his comments on the material moderation of St Benedict's Rule when compared with what had gone before; not all would be prepared to go as far as Abbot Butler in concessions to the claims of the world of today. But the real stone of stumbling, as it appeared in varying forms to many readers, does not lie so near the surface. The most damaging criticism that can be made of Abbot Butler's theoretical presentation of monastic life is that it remains concerned with phenomena and fails to grip the reality beneath. This criticism takes the form of a doubt whether the writer has always seized the just distinction between the exterior and material, and the interior and spiritual; between nature and grace; between a human, ethical ideal and a fully supernatural one—whether, in short, he always appreciates the real meaning of the words he uses. The following extract, which is only one of many possible examples,[1] may be presented for the reader's reflexion without comment:

It will have been noticed that the renunciation St Benedict calls for always comes back, one way or another, to the renunciation of the will; it is

---

[1] Another may be seen in his discussion of the influence of 'things of the world' upon modern monks. (*Benedictine Monachism* (London, 1919), pp. 308-9.)

always 'one's own will'...that has to be renounced. Nothing is said of renunciation of the affections....When we examine the Rule we find no exhortation to renunciation of the affections....St Bernard [in his lament on the death of his brother] clearly does not come up to the standard of detachment required by St John of the Cross....This shows that the kind of detachment called for by St John of the Cross...is at any rate not necessary for sanctity: at most it is only one kind of holiness; there is another to be attained without it, which lies not in the suppression but in the due regulation and sanctification of the affections....Both views [*sic*] can find support in the gospels. There are utterances of our Lord that seem to call for detachment even the most rigorous; on the other hand, we are allowed to see that He had His human friendships and gave scope to His human affections.[1]

A similar hesitation, as we have already noted, makes itself felt in the mind of many readers when Abbot Butler is discussing contemplation and the interior life of the soul. When he was satisfied with the careful selection and presentation of the words of others, his characteristic gifts had full scope—his critical judgement, his honesty, his sanity. His extracts from Cassian, from the three Western doctors, from St John of the Cross, from St Francis of Sales are of the utmost value. But in his comments, and in the pages where he develops his own views, the reader is not infrequently left with a feeling of discomfort and uncertainty.

When Abbot Butler was young, what Bremond has named *ascétisme* was still in the ascendant; during his early manhood the tide turned; the first stirrings of the *invasion mystique* made themselves felt, and with it he felt a certain kinship and sympathy. This new movement, like all great movements of religious thought and sentiment, has embraced a number of elements far from homogeneous. An almost natural reaction from method towards simplicity in the life of devotion, an equally inevitable recoil of thought from materialism, a noteworthy theological and doctrinal renaissance which has substituted St Thomas and St John of the Cross for the theologians of second and third rank of the eighteenth and early nineteenth centuries, and, highest and deepest of all, a great spiritual renewal within the Church—all these are manifestations, on different

[1] *Benedictine Monachism*, pp. 53-7.

planes, of a movement (as we call it) that has been in progress for some fifty years. Poulain, Bremond, Friedrich von Hügel, Gardeil, Père Garrigou-Lagrange, M. Maritain, Dr Karl Adam—and, higher, St Teresa of Lisieux, *Laudem Gloriae*, *Consummata* and many another—all these would not unreasonably be classed together by a historian who took account only of what appeared on the surface; and among this *turba magna*, in his place and measure, was Abbot Butler. Alike in spirit and intellect he felt the attraction and followed the gleam. Yet we may perhaps think that alike spiritually and intellectually he compromised. Intellectually, he remained unsympathetic to scientific theology;[1] he loved to say that he belonged to no school and could therefore choose for himself without *parti pris* between opposing opinions. In the event, this could not but result—and did in fact result—in a failure to share in the new life that was springing up, and in a blurring of the outlines of his own thought. In particular, the theology of grace and of the infused virtues and gifts, and the distinction between natural and supernatural, interested him not at all. Yet here, if anywhere, were to be found the answers—so far as the human mind can attain to them and express them in words—to the profound questions round which so much of his thought turned.

Spiritually, also, he was hesitant and eclectic in temper. It may be doubted whether he ever came into direct contact with a soul living the fully mystical life he so often attempted to describe. Certainly his competence, in so far as it was not derived from reading, gives every appearance of being limited to the experience common to all devout souls; he never builds the road from the valley to the heights. We have seen, in a quotation from the notes he made as a young man, that in early life he lifted up his eyes to the hills;[2] in his latest years he appeared to many almost wayward in his love of the valley, or, rather, in identifying valley with hill. Shortly before his death, he gave to the present writer two letters—one from

---

[1] To avoid the slightest possibility of misconception, I would emphasize that Abbot Butler had the profoundest love of all the dogmas of the Church and all pronouncements of authority; but he was unsympathetic to what he called 'theological systems', and this had the effect, in practice, of making him something of a minimist.

[2] See above, p. 269.

M. Saudreau, the other from Père Garrigou-Lagrange—acknowledging the receipt of proofs of his doctrinal introduction to the letters of St Francis of Sales. Both correspondents, the one a past master in directing souls, the other a theologian of the first order, took exception to important points. The one regretted a lack of ascetical firmness, the other an absence of theological precision; and they were surely justified.

Space has been given to this discussion of certain apparent weaknesses in the fabric of Abbot Butler's thought because they have made themselves felt to many readers. Even if the criticisms expressed are justified, his work nevertheless remains an achievement of great and permanent value. There can be little doubt that he will be long remembered as the most remarkable English Benedictine scholar and historian of his time. Equally is it certain that no other English Benedictine of his day had so powerful an influence in moulding the ideas of others upon the monastic and spiritual life, and it will be long before this influence ceases to be a most potent force upon all those who immediately or at second hand may come within the influence of his personality and his writings.

A BIBLIOGRAPHY OF THE WRITINGS
OF DOM DAVID KNOWLES:
1919–1962

This bibliography is designed to include all of Professor Knowles's published writings, with the exception of book reviews, etc., of less than one page in length. For the abbreviations used, see above, p. xxix; articles marked with an asterisk are reprinted in this volume.

1919
'A Preface of Mabillon', *DR*, vol. xxxviii, pp. 53–7.

1924
'The Religion of the Pastons', *DR*, vol. xlii, pp. 143–63.
'Italian Scenes and Scenery', *DR*, vol. xlii, pp. 196–208.

Reviews
Cicero: the Speeches, tr. N. H. Watts, in *DR*, vol. xlii, pp. 97–9.
Harold Stannard, *Rome and Her Monuments*, in *DR*, vol. xlii, pp. 230–1.

1925
Review
Stephen Gaselee, *An Anthology of Mediaeval Latin*, in *DR*, vol. xliii, pp. 151–2.

1926
The American Civil War: A Brief Sketch (Oxford: Clarendon Press), pp. x, 223.
'Sanderson of Oundle', *DR*, vol. xliv, pp. 59–69.

Review
Frederick Maurice, *Robert E. Lee: The Soldier*, in *DR*, vol. xliv, pp. 104–6.

1927
The English Mystics (London: Burns, Oates and Washbourne), pp. ix, 210.
'The Greek Witness to the Immortality of the Soul', *DubR*, vol. clxxxi, pp. 179–200.

Review

Arthur S. Barnes, *The Catholic Schools of England*, in *DR*, vol. XLV, pp. 87–8.

1928

'Animus and Anima', *DR*, vol. XLVI, pp. 55–66.

'The Thought and Art of Thomas Hardy', *DubR*, vol. CLXXXIII, pp. 208–18.

Review

Stephen Gaselee, *The Oxford Book of Mediaeval Latin Verse*, in *DR*, vol. XLVI, pp. 175–6.

1929

The Benedictines (The 'Many Mansions' Series; London: Sheed and Ward), pp. 112. Reprinted with intro. by J. Hugh Diman (New York: Macmillan, 1930), pp. ix, 90.

1930

'The Mappa Mundi of Gervase of Canterbury', *DR*, vol. XLVIII, pp. 237–47.

'A Greek August', *DR*, vol. XLVIII, pp. 291–314, and vol. XLIX, pp. 102–23.

Reviews

E. J. Mahoney, *The Secular Priesthood*, in *DR*, vol. XLVIII, pp. 165–6.

R. Liddesdale Palmer, *English Monasteries in the Middle Ages*, in *DR*, vol. XLVIII, pp. 327–9.

1931

Ed. with intro. and notes, Tobie Matthew, *The Life of Lady Lucy Knatchbull* (London: Sheed and Ward), pp. xxvii, 221.

'George Ambrose Burton, Bishop of Clifton (1852–1931)', *DR*, vol. XLIX, pp. 209–14.

'Essays in Monastic History 1066–1215. I. Abbatial Elections', *DR*, vol. XLIX, pp. 252–78.

'Honest Iago', *DR*, vol. XLIX, pp. 326–36.

'Essays in Monastic History 1066–1215. II. The Norman Plantation', *DR*, vol. XLIX, pp. 441–56.

Reviews

L. M. Smith, *Cluny in the Eleventh and Twelfth Centuries*, in *DR*, vol. XLIX, pp. 180–2.

E. Margaret Thompson, *The Carthusian Order in England*, in *DR*, vol. XLIX, pp. 182–4.

The Golden Epistle of Abbot William of St Thierry, trans. W. H. Shewring and ed. Justin McCann, in *DR*, vol. XLIX, pp. 187–8.

R. A. R. Hartridge, *A History of Vicarages in the Middle Ages*, in *DR*, vol. XLIX, pp. 359–60.

A. W. Clapham, *English Romanesque Architecture before the Conquest*, in *DR*, vol. XLIX, pp. 372–4.

Stephanus Hilpisch, *Geschichte des benediktinischen Mönchtums*, in *DR*, vol. XLIX, pp. 541–3.

A. Goodwin, *The Abbey of St Edmundsbury*, in *DR*, vol. XLIX, pp. 549–50.

J. P. de Caussade, *On Prayer*, in *DR*, vol. XLIX, pp. 568–9.

The Aristocratic Journey, Being the Letters of Mrs Basil Hall, ed. Una Pope-Hennessy, in *DR*, vol. XLIX, pp. 573–5.

1932

'Essays in Monastic History. III. The Norman Monasticism', *DR*, vol. L, pp. 33–48.

'Essays in Monastic History. IV. The Growth of Exemption', *DR*, vol. L, pp. 201–31, 396–436.

Reviews

A. Gardner, *Medieval Sculpture in France*, in *DR*, vol. L, pp. 145–7.

The Passion of SS. Perpetua and Felicity, ed. and trans. W. H. Shewring, in *DR*, vol. L, pp. 151–2.

Clement C. J. Webb, *John of Salisbury*, in *DR*, vol. L, pp. 513–14.

A Sister of Notre Dame de Namur, *Life of the Venerable Anne of Jesus*, in *DR*, vol. L, pp. 526–8.

1933

Intro. to J. P. de Caussade, *Self-Abandonment to Divine Providence*, trans. Algar Thorold (London: Burns, Oates and Co.), pp. xxv, 148.

'St Wulfstan of Worcester (1008–1095)', *The English Way*, ed. Maisie Ward (London and New York: Sheed and Ward), pp. 65–80.

'Essays in Monastic History. V. The Cathedral Monasteries', *DR*, vol. LI, pp. 73–96.

'Contemplative Prayer in St Theresa', *DR*, vol. LI, pp. 201–30, 406–33, 611–33.

'Essays in Monastic History 1066–1215. VI. Parish Organization', *DR*, vol. LI, pp. 501–22.

'The Monastic Horarium, 970–1120', *DR*, vol. LI, pp. 706–25.

Reviews
Monica Taylor, *Sir Bertram Windle: A Memoir*, in *DR*, vol. LI, pp. 166–8.
Nicholas Harpsfield, *The Life of Sir Thomas More*, ed. E. V. Hitchcock, in *DR*, vol. LI, pp. 173–5.
Ida Coudenhove, *The Nature of Sanctity*, in *DR*, vol. LI, pp. 187–8.
Sr. Mary of the Incarnation Byrne, *The Tradition of the Nun in Medieval England*, in *DR*, vol. LI, pp. 373–4.
Anselm Stolz, *Glaubensgnade und Glaubenslicht nach Thomas von Aquin* (Studia Anselmiana, I), in *DR*, vol. LI, pp. 728–30.
Dictionnaire de Spiritualité, fasc. I, in *DR*, vol. LI, pp. 733–5.
André Wilmart, *Auteurs spirituels et textes dévots du moyen âge latin*, in *DR*, vol. LI, pp. 748–50.

1934
'Contemplation in Saint Thomas Aquinas', *The Clergy Review*, vol. VIII, pp. 1–20, 85–103.
'The Excellence of *The Cloud*', *DR*, vol. LII, pp. 71–92.
'Essays in Monastic History 1066–1215. VII. The Diet of Black Monks', *DR*, vol. LII, pp. 275–90.
*'Abbot Cuthbert Butler, 1858–1934', *DR*, vol. LII, pp. 347–472: 'Abbot Butler: A Memoir', pp. 347–440 [above, p. 264]: 'The Works and Thought of Abbot Butler', pp. 441–65 [above, p. 341] and 'Abbot Butler: A Bibliography', pp. 466–72.
'Bec and its Great Men' [Lanfranc and Anselm], *DR*, vol. LII, pp. 567–85.
Reviews
Dictionnaire de Spiritualité, fasc. II, in *DR*, vol. LII, pp. 191–2.
David Mathew and Gervase Mathew, *The Reformation and the Contemplative Life*, in *DR*, vol. LII, pp. 332–3.
St Francis de Sales in his Letters, ed. Sisters of the Visitation, Harrow, in *DR*, vol. LII, pp. 338–40.
The Complete Works of St John of the Cross, trans. E. A. Peers, vol. I, in *DR*, vol. LII, pp. 486–90.

1935
'The Revolt of the Lay Brothers of Sempringham', *EHR*, vol. L, pp. 465–87.
Reviews
Dictionnaire de Spiritualité, fasc. III, in *DR*, vol. LIII, pp. 107–8.
The Complete Works of St John of the Cross, trans. E. A. Peers, vol. II, in *DR*, vol. LIII, pp. 246–8.

Dictionnaire de Spiritualité, fasc. IV, in *DR*, vol. LIII, pp. 394–5.
The Complete Works of St John of the Cross, trans. E. A. Peers, vol. III, in *DR*, vol. LIII, pp. 507–9.

1936

*'The Case of Saint William of York', *CHJ*, vol. V, pp. 162–77, 212–14. [Above, p. 76.]
'Rashdall's Mediaeval Universities', *DubR*, vol. CIC, pp. 300–14.
Reviews
Watkin Williams, *Saint Bernard of Clairvaux*, in *DR*, vol. LIV, pp. 275–7.
Bede: His Life, Times and Writings, ed. A. Hamilton Thompson, in *DR*, vol. LIV, pp. 278–80.

1938

'The Early Community at Christ Church, Canterbury', *Journal of Theological Studies*, vol. XXXIX, pp. 126–31.
'The Canterbury Election of 1205–6', *EHR*, vol. LIII, pp. 211–20.

1940

The Monastic Order in England (Cambridge University Press), pp. xxi, 764.
The Religious Houses of Medieval England (London: Sheed and Ward), pp. viii, 167.
'The Confessions of St Augustine', *The Tablet*, vol. CLXXV (N.S. CXLIII), pp. 456–7.
'Durham Books and English Scholars' [reviewing D. C. Douglas, *English Scholars*, and R. A. B. Mynors, *Durham Cathedral Manuscripts*], *DubR*, vol. CCVII, pp. 94–112.

1941

*'The Humanism of the Twelfth Century', *Studies*, vol. XXX, pp. 43–58. [Above, p. 16.]

1942

'Some Aspects of the Career of Archbishop Pecham, I and II', *EHR*, vol. LVII, pp. 1–18, 178–201.

1943

'The Cultural Influence of English Medieval Monasticism', *CHJ*, vol. VII, pp. 146–59.

1944

'Some Developments in English Monastic Life, 1216–1336', *TRHS*, 4th Series, vol. XXVI, pp. 37–52.

1945

'Revision to Lists of Medieval Religious Houses', *EHR*, vol. LX, pp. 380–5.

1947

Ed. with memoir, R. A. L. Smith, *Collected Papers* (London: Longmans, Green and Co.), pp. 128.

The Prospects of Medieval Studies: An Inaugural Lecture [as Professor of Medieval History] delivered on 29 October 1947 (Cambridge University Press), pp. 22.

Some Recent Advances in the History of Medieval Thought', *CHJ*, vol. IX, pp. 22–50.

'C. W. Previté-Orton, 1877–1947' [obituary notice], *PBA*, vol. XXXIII, pp. 351–60.

1948

The Religious Orders in England, vol. I (Cambridge University Press), pp. xvi, 348.

'Dom R. H. Connolly, 1873–1948' [obituary notice], *Journal of Theological Studies*, vol. XLIX, p. 129.

1949

*'Archbishop Thomas Becket: A Character Study' (the Raleigh Lecture on History, 1949), *PBA*, vol. XXXV, pp. 177–205, and, separately (London: Geoffrey Cumberlege, pp. 31). [Above, p. 98.]

'Butler, Edward Joseph Aloysius', in *The Dictionary of National Biography 1931–1940* (London: Oxford University Press), pp. 126–7.

Reviews

The Last Days of Peterborough Monastery, ed. W. T. Mellows, in *History*, N.S. vol. XXXIV, pp. 137–8.

Studies in Medieval History Presented to F. M. Powicke, in *EHR*, vol. LXIV, pp. 245–9.

S. Anselmi opera omnia, ed. F. S. Schmitt, vols. I–III, in *EHR*, vol. LXIV, pp. 363–4.

1950

*'The Last Abbot of Wigmore', *Medieval Studies Presented to Rose Graham*, ed. V. Ruffer and A. J. Taylor (Oxford: Oxford University Press), pp. 138–45. [Above, p. 171.]

Contributions on Dominicans, Franciscans, Jesuits, Monachism, etc., in *Chambers's Encyclopedia* (London: George Newnes).
Review
Studi Gregoriani, ed. G. B. Borino, vols. I–III, in *JEH*, vol. I, pp. 116–19 (vols. I–II) and 237–8 (vol. III).

1951
The Episcopal Colleagues of Archbishop Thomas Becket (the Ford Lectures, 1949; Cambridge University Press), pp. viii, 190.
The Monastic Constitutions of Lanfranc (Medieval Classics; London: Thomas Nelson and Sons), pp. xl, 149 (Latin text), 149 (Eng. trans.), 150–7.
*'The Censured Opinions of Uthred of Boldon', *PBA*, vol. XXXVII, pp. 307–42. [Above, p. 129.]

1952
With J. K. S. St Joseph, *Monastic Sites from the Air* (Cambridge Air Surveys, 1; Cambridge University Press), pp. xxviii, 283.
Ed. with M. P. Charlesworth, *The Heritage of Early Britain* (London: G. Bell and Sons), pp. 196. (With ch. by M. D. K. on 'The Heritage Completed', pp. 174–91.)
'The Case of St Albans Abbey in 1490', *JEH*, vol. III, pp. 144–58.
'Further Note on Recent Advance in the History of Medieval Thought', *CHJ*, vol. X, pp. 354–8.

1953
With R. Neville Hadcock, *Medieval Religious Houses: England and Wales* (London: Longmans, Green and Co.), pp. xxiii, 387.
*'Saint Bernard of Clairvaux: 1090–1153', *DubR*, vol. CCXXVII, pp. 104–21. [Above, p. 31.]
Reviews
J. C. Dickinson, *The Origins of the Austin Canons and their Introduction into England*, in *History*, N.S. vol. XXXVIII, pp. 169–70.
Beryl Smalley, *The Study of the Bible in the Middle Ages*, in *EHR*, vol. LXVIII, pp. 302–3.

1954
With W. F. Grimes, *Charterhouse: The Medieval Foundation in the Light of Recent Discoveries* (London: Longmans, Green and Co.), pp. xiii, 95.

Intro. to The Venerable Bede, *Ecclesiastical History of the English Nation* (Everyman's Library. History, 479; London: J. M. Dent; New York: E. P. Dutton), pp. xxiii, 382.

'English Monastic Life in the Later Middle Ages', *History*, N.S. vol. XXXIX, pp. 26–38.

'Le régime de gouvernement [des ordres religieux aux XIIIe–XIVe s.]', *La vie spirituelle*, Supplément, vol. VII, pp. 180–94.

Reviews

Der St Gallen Klosterplan, in *EHR*, vol. LXIX, pp. 139–40.

R. Foreville and J. Rousset de Pina, *Histoire de l'Eglise*, vol. IX: *Du premier Concile du Latran à l'avènement d'Innocent III*, in *EHR*, vol. LXIX, pp. 316–18.

Walther Holtzmann, *Papsturkunden in England*, vol. III, in *EHR*, vol. LXIX, pp. 433–6.

1955

The Religious Orders in England, vol. II: *The End of the Middle Ages* (Cambridge University Press), pp. xii, 407.

The Historian and Character (Inaugural Lecture [as Regius Professor of Modern History] delivered at Cambridge, 17 November 1954; Cambridge University Press), pp. 21. [Above, p. 1.]

Cistercians and Cluniacs (Friends of Dr Williams's Library, Ninth Lecture; London: Oxford University Press), pp. 32. [Above, p. 50.]

'Les Relations monastiques entre la Normandie et l'Angleterre' [text in English], in *Jumièges: Congrès scientifique du XIIIe centenaire* (Rouen: Lecerf), vol. I, pp. 261–7.

Reviews

H. Vanderhoven, F. Masai and P. B. Corbett, *Aux sources du monachisme bénédictin. I. La Règle du Maître*, in *JEH*, vol. VI, pp. 94–5.

Robert Grosseteste: Scholar and Bishop, ed. D. A. Callus, in *EHR*, vol. LXX, pp. 446–8.

1956

'Peter the Venerable', *Bulletin of the John Rylands Library*, vol. XXXIX, pp. 132–45.

'The Reforming Decrees of Peter the Venerable', in *Petrus Venerabilis*, *1156–1956*, ed. G. Constable and J. Kritzeck (Studia Anselmiana, 40; Rome: Collegio Sant'Anselmo), pp. 1–20.

'The Limits of the Law: *Lex injusta non est lex*', *Blackfriars*, vol. XXXVII, pp. 402–12.

'Lex injusta non est lex', *The Catholic Lawyer*, vol. II, pp. 237–44.

Reviews

G. R. Elton, *England under the Tudors*, in *CHJ*, vol. XII, pp. 92–4.

A. Saltman, *Theobald, Archbishop of Canterbury*, in *JEH*, vol. VII, pp. 249–51.

Cartulaire de l'abbaye cistercienne du Val-Dieu (*XIIe–XIVe siècle*), ed. J. Ruwet, in *EHR*, vol. LXXI, pp. 474–5.

1957

Cardinal Gasquet as an Historian (the Creighton Lecture in History, 1956; London: University of London: Athlone Press), pp. 26. [Above, p. 240.]

Foreword to D. E. Easson, *Medieval Religious Houses: Scotland* (London: Longmans, Green and Co.), pp. xxxvi, 204.

'Additions and Corrections to Medieval Religious Houses: England and Wales', *EHR*, vol. LXXII, pp. 60–87.

Reviews

The Victoria County History of Wiltshire, vol. III, in *EHR*, vol. LXXII, pp. 524–5.

Histoire générale des civilisations. Vol. III. *Le moyen âge*, ed. E. Perroy, in *History*, N.S. vol. XLII, pp. 140–2.

M. Grabmann, *Mittelalterliches Geistesleben*, vol. III, in *JEH*, vol. VIII, pp. 228–30.

1958

The Historical Context of the Philosophical Works of St Thomas Aquinas (The Aquinas Society of London, Aquinas Paper, 30; London: Blackfriars Publications), pp. 14.

'Great Historical Enterprises. I. The Bollandists', *TRHS*, 5th Series, vol. VIII, pp. 147–66.

'English Spiritual Writers. I. Father Augustine Baker', *The Clergy Review*, vol. XLIII, pp. 641–57.

'The Need for Catholic Historical Scholarship', *DubR*, vol. CCXXXII, pp. 120–8.

'"The Matter of Wilton" in 1528', *Bulletin of the Institute of Historical Research*, vol. XXXI, pp. 92–6.

'The Preservation of the Classics', in *The English Library before 1700*, ed. F. Wormald and C. E. Wright (London: University of London: Athlone Press), ch. VII, pp. 136–47.

'Religious Life and Organization', in *Medieval England*, ed. A. L. Poole (Oxford: Clarendon Press), vol. II, ch. XII, pp. 382–438.

BIBLIOGRAPHY

'The Portrait of St Dominic' [reviewing M.-H. Vicaire, *Histoire de Saint Dominique*], *Blackfriars*, vol. XXXIX, pp. 147–55.

Review

R. H. C. Davis, *A History of Medieval Europe*, in *History*, N.S. vol. XLIII, pp. 127–8.

1959

The Religious Orders in England, vol. III: *The Tudor Age* (Cambridge University Press), pp. xiv, 522.

Foreword to Nigel Abercrombie, *The Life and Work of Edmund Bishop* (London: Longmans, Green and Co.), pp. xv, 539.

'A Characteristic of the Mental Climate of the Fourteenth Century', in *Mélanges offerts à Etienne Gilson* (Toronto: Pontifical Institute of Mediaeval Studies and Paris: Vrin), pp. 315–25.

'Great Historical Enterprises. II. The Maurists', *TRHS*, 5th Series, vol. IX, pp. 169–87.

'Previté-Orton, Charles William', in *The Dictionary of National Biography 1941–1950* (London: Oxford University Press), p. 696.

'Brooke, Zachary Nugent', *ibid.* pp. 110–11.

'Some Enemies of Gerald of Wales', *Studia monastica*, vol. I, pp. 137–41.

'Nicholas Breakspeare in Norway', *The Month*, N.S. vol. XXI, pp. 88–94.

**'Jean Mabillon', *JEH*, vol. X, pp. 153–73. [Above, p. 213.]

'The Twelfth and Thirteenth Centuries', in *The English Church and the Continent* (London: Faith Press), ch. II, pp. 25–41.

Review

James Bulloch, *Adam of Dryburgh*, in *EHR*, vol. LXXIV, pp. 147–8.

1960

Lord Macaulay, 1800–1859 (Cambridge University Press), pp. 30.

'Great Historical Enterprises. III. The Monumenta Germaniae Historica', *TRHS*, 5th Series, vol. X, pp. 129–50.

'St Benedict', *The Month*, N.S. vol. XXIII, pp. 69–83.

Reviews

Raymonde Foreville, *Le Jubilé de Saint Thomas Becket*, in *EHR*, vol. LXXV, pp. 677–8.

The Life of Christina of Markyate, ed. C. H. Talbot, in *JEH*, vol. XI, pp. 117–18.

M. Aubert and S. Goubet, *Gothic Cathedrals of France and Their Treasures*, trans. L. and M. Kochan, in *JEH*, vol. XI, pp. 235–6.

Brian Tierney, *Medieval Poor Law*, in *Speculum*, vol. XXXV, pp. 154–6.

1961

The English Mystical Tradition (London: Burns and Oates and New York: Harper), pp. viii, 197.
'Great Historical Enterprises. IV. The Rolls Series', *TRHS*, 5th Series, vol. XI, pp. 137–59.
Article on the Papacy (in part) in *Encyclopedia Britannica* (Chicago: Encyclopedia Britannica, Inc.).
'The English Bishops, 1070–1532', in *Medieval Studies Presented to Aubrey Gwynn, S.J.*, ed. J. A. Watt, J. B. Morrall, F. X. Martin (Dublin), pp. 283–96.
Foreword to Cuthbert Butler, *Benedictine Monachism* (reprinted Cambridge: Speculum Historiale), 2 pp.

1962

Saints and Scholars (Cambridge University Press), pp. xi, 208.
The Evolution of Medieval Thought (London: Longmans, Green and Co.), pp. ix, 356.
Introduction to *The Life of St Teresa of Avila*, trans. D. Lewis (London: Burns and Oates), pp. v–xiv.
Foreword to Herbert B. Workman, *The Evolution of the Monastic Ideal* (reprinted Boston: Beacon Press), 13 pp.
'Academic History', in *History*, vol. XLVII, pp. 223–32.

Reviews

A. d'Haenens, *L'Abbaye Saint-Martin de Tournai de 1290 à 1350*, in *JEH*, vol. XIII, pp. 98–9.
A. H. Bredero, *Études sur la 'Vita Prima' de Saint Bernard*, in *EHR*, vol. LXXVII, pp. 748–9.

INDEX

The following abbreviations are used: abb. = abbess, abbey; abp. = archbishop; abt. = abbot; Aug. = Augustinian; Ben. = Benedictine; bp. = bishop; card. = cardinal; Carm. = Carmelite; Cist. = Cistercian; Cl. = Cluniac; dt. = doctrine; k. = king; pr. = prior, priory; Prem. = Premonstratensian.

Abbo of Fleury, 20
Abbot's house, 190–3; in houses of canons, 207–8; in Cist. abbs., 203–6
Abelard, 15, 16, 20–4, 27, 28, 29, 30, 41, 72, 98; and St Bernard, 44–7
Académie des Inscriptions, 236
Achery, Dom Luc d', 217–18, 219, 220, 236
Acton, J. E. E. D. (First Lord), xix, 8, 12–13, 233 n. 1, 234, 240, 250–1, 256, 257, 301, 327, 354
Acton Burnell, 244
Adam, Karl, 361
Addison, Joseph, 42
Adelaide, sister of William the Conqueror, 80 n. 2
Adrian IV, pope, 92 n. 2, 93
Aethelwulf, bp. of Carlisle, 90
Agnes, sister of Thomas Becket, 102
Ailred of Rievaulx, 21–6, 27, 30, 40, 41, 78, 83, 98, 101, 115 n. 5
Alan of Tewkesbury, 98 n. 2
Albert the Great, St, 20, 131
Alexander III, pope, 93 n. 2, 116, 120–1
Alfred, k. of Wessex, 101
Almond, Dom, 343
Almonry, monastic, 195
Ambrose, St, 43
Amelli, Dom A. M., prior of Monte Cassino, 303
Amiens, cathedral, 29
Ampleforth, Ben. abb., 284, 291
Anastasius IV, pope, 91
André de St-Nicholas, Carm. Fr, forger, 235
Annihilation, dt., 152
Anselm of Canterbury, St, 16, 20, 40, 42, 51, 55, 73, 98, 99, 100, 111, 113, 117, 120
Anselm of Laon, 23

Aquinas, Thomas, St, 20, 22, 29–30, 39, 42, 131, 139 n. 2, 146, 151, 152 n. 4, 228, 271, 284, 360
Archbold, W. A. J., 262
Aristotle, 29
Arnauld, Antoine, 224, 226, 227
Arnold, Matthew, xviii
Arnulf of Lisieux, bp., 107
Ashburnham, Lord, manuscript collector, 246
Aske, Robert, 255
Asquith, H. H., 261
Athanasian creed, 152
Athanasius, St, 31
Augustine of Canterbury, St, 269–70
Augustine of Hippo, St, 7, 22, 24–5, 29, 30, 33, 34, 39–40, 42, 43, 100, 139 n. 2, 233 n. 1, 339, 350; Maurist ed. of his works, 227–9
Augustinian (Austin) canons, 78; buildings of, 206–8
Auriole, Pierre, 146–7, 150
Avignon, 136
Aylesford, Carm. pr., 208

Bacon, Roger, 20, 251
Baines, P. A., bp. of Western District, 348
Baker, Dom Augustine (David), 268–9, 276, 280, 281, 309, 338–9, 341, 349
Baldwin de Redvers, supporter of Thomas Becket, 102 n. 4
Bale, John, 129–30
Baluze, Etienne, 220, 235
Bannister, Canon A. T., 173
Baptism, 140–4
Barber, Dom, pr. of Downside, 281 n. 2
Barking, Ben. nuns, see Mary of Barking
Barlings, Prem. abb., 198 n. 2
Basingwerk, Cist. abb., 202, 205
Baskerville, Geoffrey, 262

Dolan, Dom Gilbert, 242, 272, 278, 285, 290, 296, 299, 342, 343
Döllinger, J. J. I. von, 354
Dominic, St, 33
Dominion and Grace, dt., 135
Dore, Cist. abb., 201
Dormitory (dorter), monastic, 182, 185, 186, 187, 188, 290; in houses of canons, 207; in Cist. abbs., 200–2, 206; in houses of friars, 209
Douai, St Gregory's, Ben. abb., xiii, 276, 292
Downside, Ben. abb., xviii–xix, xxii, 241, 242–4, 253, 262, 264–320 passim; Downside Review, 285, 296, 304, 343; liturgy, 308, 309, 312, 315–16, 338; noviciate, 307–8; prs. and abts., see Barber; Butler, Dom Cuthbert; Chapman; Ford; Fowler; Gasquet; Murphy; Ramsay; school, 306–7; visitations, 281–3, 287; during World War I, 315–16; see also Knowles, Dom David
Doyle, Dom Cuthbert, 267, 268
Doyle, Fr William, S.J., 115 n. 5
Dryburgh, Prem. abb., 207
Dublin, 265
Dubois, abb. of Stanbrook, 317
Du Cange, Charles Dufresne, 220
Duchesne, Mgr. Louis, 243, 296, 343
Dugdale, William, 249, 255
Duns Scotus, Johannes, 20, 131, 146
Dunstan, St, abp. of Canterbury, 101
Durham, xxv, 129, 131, 156, 186, 187, 192, 211; bps., see Lightfoot, Westcott, William of Ste Barbe; dormitory, 210; episc. election in 1143, 77; frater, 196; library, 194 n. 3

Eadmer, 33
Ealing, Aug. canonesses, 317
Ealing, Ben. pr., xxiii, 277, 295, 312, 352, see Butler, Dom Cuthbert
Easby, Prem. abb., 207
East Bergholt, Ben. nuns, 317
Edgbaston, xviii
Education of women in twelfth century, 27
Ehrle, Franz, card., 17
Elections, episcopal, 77, see Durham, Langres, Lincoln, London, Salisbury, York
Elias Paganel, abt. of Selby, 97
Elijah, prophet, 9, 139

Eliot, T. S., 124 n. 2
Elizabeth, duchess de Guise, 226–7
Ely, Ben. cath. pr., 188, 192, 211; gateway, 195 n. 1
Emma, daughter of Stephen of Blois, 81
Enniscorthy, Ben. abb., see Mount St Benedict's
Erasmus, Desiderius, 3, 7, 8, 30
Estiennot, Dom Claude, Maurist, 221, 231, 236–7
Eudes, brother-in-law of William the Conqueror, 80 n. 2
Eugenius III, pope, 48, 49, 82 n. 2, 85, 88, 89, 90, 95, 96
Evesham, Ben. abb., 188; see Joseph, Robert
Ewenny, Ben. pr., 193

Faron, Ben. pr., 236
Fécamp, Ben. abb., 80; abt., see Henry de Sully
Fénelon, François, abp. of Cambrai, 44, 225, 299
Fideism, dt., 133
Finchale, Ben. pr., 156, 193
Fisher, H. A. L., 240, 258
Fitzherbert family, 241
Fitzralph, Richard, abp. of Armagh, 135, 136, 152
FitzUrse, Reginald, murderer of Thomas Becket, 124, 126–7
Foliot, Gilbert, bp. of London, 15, 93, 98, 99, 103, 106 n. 1, 110, 111 n. 3, 118, 120, 121
Food and meals, monastic, 190, 196; in Cist. abbs., 205; see Cluny
Ford, Dom Edmund, abt. of Downside, 242, 266 n. 2, 281, 282, 284, 285, 289, 290, 293, 297, 304, 307, 324, 329, 340 n. 1, 342, 357; pr. of Downside, 286–8, 293–4; abt. of Downside, 294–5, 305; see also Butler, Dom Cuthbert
Forde, Cist. abb., 205, 206
Fort Augustus, Ben. abb., 283, 292
Fountains, Cist. abb., 76, 78, 91, 196 n. 2, 200, 203, 206; abts., see Huby, Richard of Fountains; abt.'s house, 205; tower, 200
Fowler, Dom Clement, pr. of Downside, 272, 282 n. 2, 287–9, 293
Fox, Charles James, 5
Fox, Edward, bp. of Hereford, 172–3, 175–6

INDEX